Football and Life Lessons
With Maryland Coach Ralph Friedgen

By Keith Cavanaugh *with* Ralph Friedgen

All rights reserved under International and Pan-American Copyright Conventions.
Published by Terrapin State Publishing, Inc., P.O. Box 983, Bel Air, Md. 21014

ISBN 978-0-9788082-1-1

First edition

Printed in USA — United Book Press, Baltimore, Md.
Recycled paper, vegetable-based ink.

For additional copies, call 1-800-932-4557 or email mywaythebook@yahoo.com

Website: MyWayTheBook.com

Cover design by Dennis Tuttle. Book design by American Sports Media, Rochester, N.Y.
Back cover photo by Bill Vaughan.
Front cover photo by Tracey A. Woodward, The Washington Post.
Page 103 photo by Greg Fiume. All other inside photos and back cover photo courtesy of the
Friedgen family.

To the greatest role models a son could have, Francis and Carol Cavanaugh, and to Kelley, Jack and Madie Cavanaugh, who make every day a blessing!
— Keith

INTRODUCTION

On the eve of many seasons, Ralph Friedgen invites staff and select boosters to his Silver Spring home for a cookout and evening of relaxing before they dig in on the long season.

There's always good food and company and often a dramatic ending, which for the uninitiated can be both surprising and inspiring.

Friedgen's daughters break out the Karaoke machine and warm things up by singing for the gathering. With their theater background, Kelley, Katie and Kristina Friedgen sing and ham it up. Mom Gloria Friedgen is often in the midst of it, too.

But the most memorable parties end with Ralph Friedgen taking the microphone and crooning his favorite song, Frank Sinatra's iconic hit "My Way."

"It is a phenomenon," former Terps receivers coach James Franklin said. "He knows every word. He sings it real well. He even has some rhythm."

Gloria, who most recently heard her husband sing at his 60th birthday party in March of 2007, still gets teary-eyed. All of their years together and the memories shared, the journey and its many struggles, flood over her.

"I really believe it's his song in so many, many ways," she said.

"My Way" is Ralph Friedgen's favorite song, just as it was the man that dominated and shaped his life, his father, Ralph Edward Friedgen, a towering presence throughout.

Ralph Friedgen, the father, would sing it anywhere, be it the living room of their Harrison, N.Y., home, restaurants, even funerals and weddings.

Today his son has it on his iPod.

He sings it at special occasions and family events. He sang it with a player's mother, often at his Fourth of July party in Georgia, and his mother-in-law's funeral when the family celebrated her life into the night. Friedgen even sang it at Da Mimmo, a favorite Italian restaurant in Baltimore's Little Italy section.

For those who know Friedgen, the song is a metaphor of his life.

It tells the story of a man who after years of toiling as an assistant coach, arrived at his first head coaching job at his alma mater, the University of Maryland.

And how each step of the way he did it his way. Not always the most popular way. Not always the politically correct way. Not always the way players or bosses wanted. But his way.

It took an arduous 31 years, a period he wasn't sure would ever end, but Friedgen never changed for anyone. Never worried about image or public perception. Never worried about athletic directors or general managers. Never worried about telling it like it is in no uncertain terms, to anyone, anytime.

Just like his father. The only way he knew.

Friedgen never strayed from the task of building powerhouse offenses at every level of football, dedicated and consumed by the job at hand that career advancement often took a backseat.

When he croons the song it sums up the years, from his youth in Harrison under his demanding father, the local football coaching legend, to his dramatic rise as head coach once he got a chance after decades in the shadows.

"I think it epitomizes me. The words. You know, kinda done it my way my whole life. Maybe not always the right way, but my way," Friedgen said. "You start going through your whole life, start seeing things how they turned out, how I've done them. It's pretty apropos."

Friedgen is a bundle of contradictions. But one constant in a long and storied career, which includes a hand in a college national championship and a Super Bowl appearance, is that he stuck with the same core values and beliefs instilled, and sometimes drilled, into him by his father.

"My Way" also shows Friedgen's playful and disarming side, another of his contradictions.

That of a man who, for many on the outside, seems all business, often blustery, even cantankerous at times.

The lucky ones see the other side, though, when he sings.

One of the most poignant times he sang was at his home for staff following Maryland's victory over Tennessee in the 2002 Peach Bowl, Friedgen's breakthrough bowl win, and a victory that put the program on the national map in only his second year.

When Friedgen is on the football field he's all business. But when he unwinds and sings he is as relaxed and playful. It's a sharp dichotomy that players and staff at first took time to get a handle on.

When he sings (and no one has ever accused him of being a great singer!), it also relaxes those around him who are often on edge because of his strong personality.

"That day I saw Ralph with his family singing, carrying on, he seemed as happy as I have ever seen him," Franklin said. "He is with a group of guys he really cares about and they just had a lot of success professionally.

"I thought the song was interesting. Ralph waited a long time to become a head coach. He went through some tough times. He probably should have had some opportunities earlier. Then to see him up there singing "My Way," it was something."

Those in attendance see the verisimilitude. And Ralph Friedgen is nothing if not real, his in-your face style, his emotions, his bark. He bares all and is in full splendor when he sings. It's visceral, sometimes shrill, no pretense. It's all him.

"He is secure in his own skin. He's secure in his knowledge, his belief, and those have been forged over 30 years of seeing so many people do things, either the right way or the wrong way. And he knows that his way is the right way," said longtime booster, friend, and financial advisor Larry Grabenstein.

"It's very engaging. Very human," said Maryland athletic director Debbie Yow, his boss, of the times he has sung in her presence.

T hree years ago I sat down with Ralph Friedgen to begin the process of interviews for a book on his life story.

And did the stories ever flow.

No one had tackled the subject of Friedgen's life, especially his childhood, in detail, and few knew of the formative years and the impression, and sometimes scars, his demanding father left on him.

From his childhood in Harrison as an all-star quarterback playing for his father, to the disappointment of his college career at Maryland, to his decades in the shadows as a career assistant coach, Friedgen held nothing back in bringing to life his long and often difficult journey towards becoming head coach of his alma mater.

This book looks back at Friedgen's life, from his childhood and the figures that shaped it, to his head coaching tenure at Maryland and the teams and personalities that defined them, with never-before published material as Friedgen offered a rare look inside the program.

The only topics he asked not to discuss were game strategies and schemes.

I have selected various chapter topics – like Faith, Family, Emotion, Character – that define Friedgen and are vital in his everyday life.

It's a remarkable life and journey, one Friedgen draws on everyday for lessons for those around him, including his team and his family, which are closely intertwined.

I want to thank Ralph and Gloria Friedgen for their generous time, recollections and insights, and Gloria for her hospitality at their Georgia lake home and their Silver Spring, Md., residence where much of the interviewing took place.

And I would like to thank the many coaches, players, administrators and childhood friends that helped tell Friedgen's story.

It's been a wonderful experience getting to know Ralph Friedgen more after covering his program since 2000. And discovering more about what created the man affectionately known to most as "Fridge."

CONTENTS

1

GROWING UP

A
thletes didn't want to end up in the "green room" at Port Chester (N.Y.) High School.
There football coach Ralph Edward Friedgen meted out punishment, sometimes corporal, if his players stepped out of line. It was a storage room that held blocking dummies, and if those dummies could talk . . .

With Friedgen, Maryland head football coach Ralph Harry Friedgen's father, it was black and white. There was no in between.

"He was definitely in charge. I laugh at some of the things today that I deal with, some of the parents," said Ralph Friedgen, Maryland's football coach.

Friedgen's father commanded fear and respect for not only his towering image (he stood 6-1, 350-pounds), but as a high school football coaching giant in New York in the 1950s and '60s.

He was known mostly for two things: football and toughness.

He played fullback at college powerhouse Fordham a year after Vince Lombardi, and for coach "Sleepy" Jim Crowley. Fordham football of the famed "Seven Blocks of Granite" line. Also on his team, Peter Carlesimo, father of future NBA coach P.J. Carlesimo.

In one of his first games Friedgen broke loose for a 48-yard touchdown run in a 47-0 win over Upsala before 8,000 fans at Randalls Island Stadium. After Fordham, he played semi-pro football in the area. He was a striking figure in jersey number 49, plowing through the line. He was fit and trim, nothing like the enormous man that he would someday become, foreshadowing his son's prodigious growth.

Friedgen became one of New York's greatest high school coaches of the era, primarily at Harrison High School, where his son, Ralph, would later star as quarterback.

The father's bark was as big as his bite, and he often bit.

His players' first thoughts when they got in trouble wasn't what their parents would do, but what coach Friedgen would do. Young Ralph couldn't go out with his buddies after losses. Fortunately, there weren't many.

Friedgen was a taskmaster, a downright tyrant at times.

He'd call his players' homes Friday night before games to make sure they were in bed. If they weren't, they wouldn't play. At-risk kids he'd call twice. He had an assistant coach that moonlighted as a garbage man. If he saw a jersey hanging on a clothesline overnight he would bring it to coach Friedgen.

Once, after a loss, Friedgen called the cheerleaders and majorettes into his office and told them to lay off the football players, including his son. After losses, Friedgen would close the shades of his home and sometimes skip dinner.

"He was in control of everything," Ralph Friedgen said.

Friedgen threatened to change the locks of the doors of their home if his son wasn't home by curfew. The legend grew as "Ralphie," as he was known in his youth, lived a charmed football life with his larger-than-life father.

When Ralph, the son, years later read David Mariniss' Pulitzer Prize winning book *When Pride Still Mattered* on the life of Vince Lombardi, he said:

"All of those stories my father had told me, him beating a guy up in the locker room. It was like he was going over the same things again. The Hindenburg went over them during practice before it blew up. He would tell me all of those stories," he said of his father's mystique.

The Friedgens were well known. So when they moved to Harrison from nearby Port Chester, a local newspaper published a story and photo touting the coach and his family's imminent arrival at their "new four-bedroom colonial."

Nicknamed "Big Bear," Friedgen's father was a bit taller and more "chiseled than Ralph," said Terps assistant coach Dave Sollazzo, also a Harrison native.

Friedgen served in World War II with the U.S. Army mine planters corps after graduating from Fordham in 1940.

"He was really a big man," Sollazzo said. "Tall and physical looking. A mountain of a man.

"He was intimidating walking down the hallway. He used to walk around the hallways trying to get guys cutting class."

To know the son you must first know the father as the two are so intertwined.

It was a different time and media treatment of Ralph Friedgen, the coach, was sometimes God-like.

Headlines tracked his every game and many of his off-field moves, and filled the local papers, sometimes even the *New York Times*. His players were known to the press as "Friedgenmen."

A story in the *Daily Item* of Port Chester proclaimed as his family prepared to move closer to Port Chester High School, that "Ralph (Sr.) and his lovely missus will be moving bag, baggage, and little Friedgens into their new home next week. Their new spot is situated only a long foul away from home plate at the Port."

He left Blessed Sacrament, where he was named coach of the year in 1951, to take over at Port Chester, and columnist Arn Shein of the *Daily Item* wrote: "The wise boys predicted big things for the Rams in the not so distant future."

Once, in a rare loss to Peekskill High, Friedgen's halftime speech "put a lump in the throat and tingle up the spine of apparently everyone on hand," the *Daily Item* reported.

After knocking off heavyweight Mamaroneck, 14-12, in 1952 following six years of futility versus the school and a 28-game losing streak before he arrived "250 cars and 1,000 fans greeted the team" and Friedgen when they returned to Port Chester, the *Daily Item* reported. But Friedgen, owner of an 8-1 mark, best in 13 years at the school, wasn't part of the revelry. The paper reported his reaction to the celebration.

"Gee, we've got to go over that defense for next week!" he said.

Friedgen, like his son later as the head coach at Maryland, worked on the field and off of it for the program, be it stirring his players' emotions or even the student body.

In a preview of his 1955 team, Friedgen told the *Daily Item* that despite losing 20 of 26 lettermen his players "had tremendous spirit, while another factor a year ago was the tremendous backing by the school's student body. That same kind of support this year could do wonders for these boys," he said.

After the final game of the season Shein gushed about Friedgen following the 27-0 rout of Mamaroneck with sanguine prose: ". . . and so the handsome prince slipped the shoe on Cinderella's tiny foot and lived happily ever after! There was a fairy tale of a slightly different nature being told at Port Chester High School Saturday afternoon before the largest home crowd in recent years. But the net result was the same – the happiest ending possible – as the Rampaging Rams closed the books on the 1956 football season by handing the Mamaroneck Tigers a 27-0 thumping. The fairy tale, authored by Coach Ralph Friedgen, actually started in October of last year and Friedgen and his ghostwriting Rams may very well add a few more pages to it when the 1957 grid campaign rolls around. But Saturday's chapter, penned at the expense of the Tigers, was easily the most unbelievable of all!"

Friedgen was seemingly at every local awards banquet, association meeting, or civic event, many documented in the local press. His visage adorned the matchbook covers at Captain Starns Restaurant and Bar in Atlantic City, N.J.

Ralph Edward Friedgen was, like his son years later, progressive in many ways. In 1958 when rules changes for college football were implemented Friedgen, head of the Westchester Sports Forum, was one of the state high school coaches queried in the preseason about the new two-point conversion, which some coaches opposed.

"I think it is terrific," he boasted. "It will revolutionize the game. Think of all the work you have to do to score a touchdown. And then have the game decided because one fellow has the ability to kick. It is a burden for a coach or a small staff to develop a kicker. It is a terrific rule. It will give more strategy to the game. It will make the game more interesting. Emphasis has now been put on passing."

In 1957, after taking over the beleaguered Port Chester baseball team, Friedgen had the "Midas Touch" again, leading the Rams to their greatest season in school history with a 15-1 mark, their first championship in 32 years, and a record-setting 18-game winning streak over two seasons.

Friedgen was ahead of his time in another way.

At the end of the season news leaked out that Friedgen would give up his job as baseball coach until all of the Rams coaches began getting extra pay for their coaching duties. Port Chester did not pay its coaches beyond their school salary. The *Daily Item* reported on Oct. 9, 1957:

"There began a desperate fight on the part of many sports-minded Port Chesterites to get the Board of Education to approve the "extra work" plan. But the policy was never adopted, mainly on the basis that "It's not fair to pay some of our teachers for extra work without paying them all.""

A year later Friedgen was gone, having accepted the athletic director and head football coaching jobs at his alma mater, Harrison High School.

The move also grabbed headlines.

"Friedgen to Harrison," which was followed by a write-up in the *Daily Item* that touted a "Ralph Friedgen Night" on June 18 to fete the man who led Port Chester for seven years as football, baseball and golf coach. There was no ill will, just a lot of long faces when he left Port Chester."

The townspeople feted him with a dinner-dance attended by hundreds of friends including many of his present day and former athletes, at Playland Casino, the *Daily Item* reported. There was a committee of "25 interested persons forming the Ralph Friedgen Night Dinner Committee," which planned the event. Seating was for 700 guests but "thousands" of requests were made for the $6 roast beef dinner," the *Daily Item* reported. A contact committee was formed to notify all of his former players that lived outside of the area.

Said Bill Green, head basketball coach at Port Chester, of the outgoing Friedgen's legacy in a *Daily Item* account:

"Few persons in Port Chester are aware of Coach's Friedgen's tremendous impact upon the youth of our community. Everyone, of course, is thoroughly orientated of his great success in the victory column. But to my way of thinking, this is but a small part of Coach Friedgen's true value. Unless you have worked with a man as closely as I have for six years, it's impossible to realize how much good, how much influence, this man has had upon our youngsters."

The following day the *Daily Item* bemoaned his departure:

"The biggest, most popular and most magnetic Ram of them all strayed from the flock, shed his heavy coat of wool in favor of a lighter one and – presto! – became a Husky!"

Friedgen was a success everywhere he went, dating back to his playing days at Harrison High when as a senior in 1935 he led the county in scoring, had the highest batting average in baseball, and was unbeaten in the discus throw and shot put before moving onto Fordham, a college power at the time.

Foreshadowing what his son would accomplish turning around a struggling Maryland program years later, the *Daily Item* wrote:

"Known as a man who loves a challenge, Ralph has proven it via his won-lost records at all three county high schools at which he has manipulated his Ouija board. In each case – at Iona, Blessed Sacrament, and Port Chester – he took over when football was at it lowest ebb; seemingly unsalvageable. Almost overnight, the dynamic Friedgen transformed the three grid doormats into three grid powerhouses!"

Friedgen finished 30-15-5 at Port Chester after inheriting a program that lost 28 straight games before he arrived. He was 7-1 in his final season, 1959, and the legend grew.

But Harrison High is where the legend took off.

Popular *New York Times* writer Robert Lipsyte, in previewing the Harrison-Rye High School game on Nov. 19, 1960, which Rye entered with a 33-game win streak, said of Friedgen, who scoffed at comments that his rival couldn't be beaten:

"Harrison's massive coach who looks like a tank and speaks like a psychology professor. He said, 'Nonsense. You don't play with history. You play with boys who have good days and bad days.' "

Harrison came from behind to win, 13-7, before 12,000 fans at Harrison Athletic Field. Tailback Roger Smith led the way as did a goal-line stand. The team went on to score a county-record 197 points as Friedgen's innovative offense rolled.

T hings really took off when young Ralph took the reigns of the Harrison offense as a sophomore quarterback. He was destined for greatness if the attendant media coverage of his arrival as the coach's son with the "golden arm" was any indication.

"As a junior he was the only underclassman to crash the first-team all-county party," the *Daily Item* reported, who described him as an "awesome looking 6-foot, 200-pound senior."

Considering Friedgen today, if you haven't perused newspaper accounts and photos of the day, it's difficult to imagine the slender, fair-haired All-American of his youth.

The gangly teen grew up throwing a football through a tire that hung from a tree in his backyard. And all of those years of work soon paid off.

Said local prep scribe Shein, who helped popularize the Friedgen lore:

"Friedgen is particularly adept at firing the button-hook pass and again figures to drive the opposition crazy with his well-diversified attack."

Another scouting report in the *Daily Item* offered this description:

"Owner of an extremely accurate and strong passing arm, young Ralph completes over 60 percent of his aerials. He throws well, long or short, and his running ability keeps the opposition from ganging up against his air game. In addition, he's excellent defensively."

In the 1962 opener the precocious Friedgen completed 11-of-15 passes for 133 yards in a 19-0 victory over Horace Greeley High School. He passed and rushed for scores. His father entered the season cautioning local scribes:

"I will let him prove himself first."

But already reports in the *Daily Item* touted Friedgen as "becoming one of the deadliest passers Harrison has ever seen."

Friedgen spoke years later of the pressure growing up in his father's shadow with great expectations. His father reached out to the local media trying to downplay his son's exploits as much as possible, and it was often accommodating. But it proved a challenge.

There were accusations and whispers of favoritism, and there was jealousy when Friedgen was named the starting quarterback as a sophomore. But his father's rule was law, and there was no equivocating.

In 1962, Shein opined in the *Daily Item* in a column titled "Prejudice Is A Dirty Word!":

"The problem at Harrison High School is not whether you're white or black; not whether you're Catholic, Protestant or Jew; not even whether you are a good athlete or a bad one. The only problem at the school, the only question the young athletes seem to ask is: Who is your father?

"Roger Smith graduated from Harrison last June, leaving the door wide open for young Mr. Friedgen to face the prejudiced, envious, mouth-watering mob. We all know him as a rather shy, quiet, modest boy who, as a high school sophomore, gives promise of joining Roger Smith on that list of all-time Husky sports greats. Like Roger, Ralphie is a three-sport athlete. He's already crashed the varsity basketball team, the only soph to make it, and he's an even far better football and baseball player in this writer's book than he is a cager. But Ralph has one big drawback, His father is Ralph Friedgen, Sr., director of health, recreation and safety of the Harrison schools and also head football and baseball coach.

"Young Friedgen didn't have to wait until his junior or senior years to earn the taunts and snide remarks of his companions. His very first taste of schoolboy varsity competition this past football season was distasteful – extremely distasteful. The prejudiced goons were beginning to show again how well they operate.

"Ralph must get used to it. He's got two more years of it before he receives his sheepskin from Harrison High School. In all probability, the better the athlete he becomes (and make no mistake about it, he's going to be great!), the worse the situation will become.

"If he was 'John Doe' he would have received far more publicity for his adroit ball-handling and pro-like passing. But capital 'P' was operating at Harrison High School and the modest teenage boy is the target."

But Harrison, led by the Friedgens, kept on rolling despite any pressure young Ralph may have felt.

In 1963, as a junior, Friedgen's name was splashed throughout the media following Harrison's 3-0 start. He won the Con Edison Sports Award of the Week twice after rolling up 600 yards total offense and 11 touchdowns in the opening games. He completed 38-of-62 passes in his father's high-octane attack, which was drawing raves.

Friedgen was touted as "Westchester County's No. 1 prospect" and the *Daily Item* raved:

"He personally has made the Husky offensive attack one of the most exciting seen in the county in several years. It has become virtually impossible for rival coaches to defense the pro attack since it features power running up the middle, sweeps and roll-outs, both short and long passing as well as rollout passes by the young Friedgen."

One of the voters that week was Sam Rutigliano, the athletic director at Horace Greeley High School. Friedgen and his father appeared on WFAS Radio in White Plains, N.Y., to accept the award and discuss the team's fast start.

Harrison's first loss wasn't until the fifth game when it succumbed to Sleepy Hollow, 26-21, despite Friedgen's two touchdowns and three two-point conversion runs. The *New York Times* was on hand for the game and published a photo of Ralph running over the goal line. It ran three columns.

By now he was averaging better than five yards per carry, a dangerous pass/run threat that was fearless out of the backfield.

But after tying the next game Friedgen hurt his back and was sidelined for a 41-19 drubbing at the hands of Pelham High School.

Friedgen saved his best for last, though, leading Harrison on Nov. 16, 1963, to a 20-0 rout of arch-rival Rye High School. More than 8,000 fans saw him throw two touchdown passes as Harrison finished the season with a 5-2-1 mark. Afterwards, a compelling scene unfolded on the field, which was described by the lead of a story in the *Daily Item*. Said one depressed Rye fan afterwards as Harrison players lifted coach Friedgen onto their shoulders and gave him a celebratory ride on the field:

"How can you expect to beat a team that can lift that guy up on their shoulders and carry him all around the place?"

Years later his son's players would futilely attempt the same at College Park after Ralph Friedgen won big games.

The junior Friedgen was named all-county – the only underclassman on the team – earning the second most votes at a ceremony at Schrafft's Country Inn in Eastchester. He was also named to the all-Southern Westchester Interscholastic Athletic Conference

"Dream Team." Also on the team was future Maryland teammate and NFL standout Billy Van Heusen of nearby Mamaroneck, as well as Chuck Remmel.

In 1964, on the eve of his senior season, Friedgen experienced an emotional event with his father when season captains were announced following a team vote. It foreshadowed the emotion young Ralph would one day wear on his sleeve as head coach at College Park.

His father was clearly an intimidating presence to all that knew him. But he had a soft side, too. The *Daily Item* reported this account:

"Coach Ralph Friedgen, known as one of the toughest, most out-spoken and fearless coaches in the business, broke down and cried in the Harrison High School dressing room early last evening.

"I just couldn't hold the tears back," said the "Big Bear" after he was informed of the result of the election of the 1964 team captains by the members of the Husky squad.

"Although Ralph's own son, Ralph, Jr., all-county first-string quarterback as a junior last year, was one of those chosen, this had nothing to do with the flow of tears. It was the other choice that did it – senior center Yogi Santa Donato – who will be forced to sit out tomorrow's opener in Yonkers with a shoulder injury.

"The elder Friedgen was an extremely close friend of the late Manny Santa Donato who passed away suddenly last May. Ralph and Manny, in fact, were stars of the powerhouse Husky teams of three decades ago.

"One of Manny's last wishes," Friedgen said last night, "was that both Yogi and Ralph would be picked co-captains for their senior year. I purposefully kept this secret so as not to influence the voting by the boys. But I am thrilled that Yogi was picked. Manny got his wish."

In 1964, as a senior at Harrison, Ralph got the Huskies out of the gates with a 33-0 romp over Yonkers High School. He connected on 14-of-26 passes for 159 yards. On the eve of the season his father told the *New York World Telegram*:

"He's a wonderful passer, hard runner, and backs up the line on defense."

The routs continued, over Greeley and Eastchester, with scores of 23-6 and 40-6, respectively, as Friedgen's pass-happy offense hummed with his son under center.

Next up was Scarsdale, which fell, 33-0, as Harrison improved to 4-0. Friedgen rushed for two scores and threw for another. Washington-Irving was next and fell, 40-20, with Friedgen going 11-for-18 for 179 yards and three scores. He rushed for 63 yards.

The next game, against Pleasantville, found the opponent thinking it had discovered a way to defeat the Friedgen-led Huskies, local scribes suggested. As reported in the *Daily Item* afterwards:

"It may or may not be true that Pleasantville, as reported, has spotted a flaw in the offensive moves of Harrison quarterback Ralph Friedgen, Jr. After all, the Panthers did limit the all-county standout to a mere four completions in nine flips, good for only 69 yards, and limited his running game to 23 yards in eight carries. But when you look back at the statistics of Saturday's crucial and thrilling fracas before a standing room only gathering at Harrison High School, you discover it was Friedgen, Friedgen, Friedgen!"

Harrison won 19-14 to remain unbeaten at 6-0 with Pelham looming. Friedgen threw a touchdown pass to Tony Cassarella in the final two minutes to decide the game.

A week later it was much of the same, though many said Harrison would be "hard pressed to knock off Pelham, which routed them the year before."

A large headline proclaimed: "Unbeaten Huskies Overpower Pelham, 39-13, Behind Friedgen."

Climbing to 7-0, and 4-0 in the conference, Friedgen ran for two touchdowns and passed for two in keying the victory.

That set up the finale against rival Rye High.

A posed photo of a beaming Friedgen in the *Daily Item* ran with the cut-line, "Unusual Pose! – Opponents rarely see this smile on the face of Harrison High quarterback Ralph Friedgen, at least not while he's in his familiar grid mufti. Going into his final scholastic game against invading Rye Saturday, the son of the Harrison mentor has personally accounted for 1,416 yards, including a possible record-shattering 1,010 yards through the air, via his 64 completions. He has thrown 11 touchdown passes thus far, and has scored 10 himself, along with five conversion plunges. Friedgen, the only junior to crack the All-County squad last year, is averaging 7.7 yards for every offensive play this season, which to a large extent explains the Huskies' 7-0 record and record 236 points."

Friedgen also punted nine times for a 38-yard average to show his versatility. Local media accurately speculated that it was the first time a Westchester County passer eclipsed the 1,000-yard mark. Friedgen had thrown a touchdown pass in all but one game that season, while he had 10 rushing scores.

Wrote the *Daily Item* of his senior campaign:

"This has been a truly fantastic season for young Friedgen, who has personally gained over 200 yards per game via his magic right arm and his legs."

Harrison would go on to rout Rye, 27-0, before a record 13,000 fans as Friedgen starred again and capped the perfect, 8-0 season. He rushed for a touchdown and threw for another in a big second quarter as Harrison pulled away.

The *New York Times* attended and the newspaper wrote of the senior quarterback:

"Ralph, Jr., who says Ralph, Sr., started teaching him football 'when I was born,' was the player Rye set its defenses for and for good reason."

Friedgen rushed for 84 yards and one score and passed for 72 yards and another score.

He was named all-county and player of the year, finishing the season with 1,570 yards total offense and 23 scores through the air and on the ground.

Later, Friedgen was named MVP at the team's banquet where a special guest,

New York Giants lineman Dick Modzelewski, the former Terps All-American, was on hand to speak.

I n a fitting ending the *New York Times* ran a large, four-photo spread on the college recruitment of the "fair-haired" Friedgen. It followed him at school for several days. It was titled, "For A Schoolboy Football Hero: Praise, Friends, Offers and Problems."

There were photos of Friedgen at his locker, in the locker room with his father, playing basketball, and in a classroom. He was truly a "Big Man on Campus."

He had more than 20 college inquiries and a handful of offers. The *Times* story was the buzz of the town. It wasn't often the paper did such a large take on a prep athlete.

The story also offered insights into the experiences Ralph endured while playing for his father. Both the good and the bad.

It related a lurid account from the recruiting wars, one his current players may find intriguing. The paper revealed that "recently a representative from a Southeastern Conference football power sidestepped the normal channels of communication (National Collegiate rules specify a scout must contact a boy through the school principal or his authorized representative).

"The scout collared Ralph in the school hallway. He introduced himself, told young Friedgen what a good college he represented and then said, 'If you play with us we'll pay your board, tuition and books, find you a job and give you spending money.' "

The *Times* described young Ralph glowingly:

"He was 17-years old on April 4. He stands 6-feet, 1/2 inches, and weighs 195 pounds. He is boyish looking and gangling. He has been under more pressure than most high school athletes because his father has been his coach.

"Some of the older players were resentful when his father named him Harrison's starting quarterback as a sophomore."

Ralph told the writer:

"I could see myself at a large Eastern or Midwestern college," while his mother, Iris, said she "preferred Notre Dame for her son."

W hile the public, football side of the Friedgen's was glamorous for a young boy in a small town, at home young Ralph had to stay in line.

There was no room for mistakes, on or off the field, as star quarterback and coach's son, and he was always under the microscope.

Growing up, Friedgen said that his father hit him as punishment. And they were "punches," not taps. He knew both sides of his father's hand.

It was a different time.

"You did what you were supposed to do or you'd get your ass kicked. It was that simple," Ralph Friedgen said of his youth.

So many of the lessons of his childhood Ralph Friedgen carries to this day, though he has a softer hand.

He recalled "running home from Saturday night parties at sprinter's speed" to meet his father's 11 p.m. weekend curfew.

"I was always running. It was a different time. We didn't have any cars or anything like that. Back then you worried about your father, air raids at school, things like that," Friedgen said.

Ralph Friedgen's father was also a noted speaker and often addressed organizations and headlined banquets. There was nothing he loved more than a good debate, be it formal or informal.

At one New York football event, the annual Raleigh Football Clinic in Elmsford, coach Friedgen was one of five noted speakers. The others were Alabama coach Paul "Bear" Bryant, Maryland coach Tom Nugent, who young Ralph would play for one day, Missouri coach Dan Devine and Cleveland Browns backfield coach Blanton Collier.

Not only was his father a local coaching giant, but the family ran a summer camp, Seven Acres Day Camp in Greenwich, Conn., where his father was renowned for teaching children to swim.

Young Ralph even owned a horse, a thoroughbred, and began riding in the seventh grade. His father would not allow him to jump for fear of injury, but he still snuck some practice in. His sister also had a horse. Ralph joked years later that he first got into horses "because girls were always around them." His horse was named "Jimmy Lee," and he says today he would like to own one once he retires.

"Of course everyone says I'll need a damn Clydesdale now," he quipped.

But if young Ralph, growing up on Harrison Avenue, didn't come clean with his father he would feel his wrath.

He grew up in a historic house, which was more than 150-years old, once owned by patriot John Jay. Young Ralph always thought the nine-room Colonial on the one-acre plot was haunted. He created some of his nightmares, too.

Ralph, who admitted a hatred for studying, threw his school book against the wall one evening.

"He came in and just drilled me," he said of his father, who though his body had begun to balloon with age he still had a football player's size and strength.

One day while in the fourth grade, his father was at the table eating yogurt. He threw it at his son after he talked back. It hit a hanging light fixture and covered the walls, so Ralph bore the brunt of the punishment and the cleanup.

The Friedgens lived in a ranch house in Port Chester, with all of the rooms on one floor.

"When I screwed up the damn race was on. I tried to make it one lap around and then get under the bed. Then he'd be there with the broom trying to get my ass."

Once, young Ralph bit a boy in a fight in his backyard after he broke his sister's sandbox. The bite went through his shirt and required stitches. The police were called. Years later in high school, Ralph was in the showers and saw the boy still had the scar.

Friedgen's sister, Claranne, never felt the wrath of her father.

Ralph was the anointed one and expectations were high for him as the only son and future football star.

" 'She's going to work in a beauty salon. You're going to college,' " Ralph said of his father's plan. "It wasn't a priority back then."

But Claranne wasn't held back, either. She became a psychologist and social worker and lives in Florida. She has a master's degree from Barry (Fla.) University, where she met her husband, also a social worker. She works in the field of child abuse.

Friedgen joked that his sister was the "liberal" of the family. Nowadays, she attends some of her brother's bowl games, but she was never as active in athletics as Ralph.

Friedgen was a "B" student but said he also "liked sports and girls." Maybe some of the empathy he has for his players comes from the fact, he admits, "I had to take the SAT [test] about 40 times."

He had a chip on his shoulder from the start, scarred at an early age by someone who didn't think he would amount to much past high school.

"Before I got to college I had a high school guidance counselor tell me that I would never graduate from college. That I wasn't college material," he said.

R alph Friedgen admits his father was a taskmaster. But he was home significantly more than he is today with his wife and daughters.

Like a sponge, young Ralph absorbed everything from his dad. And the good days outnumbered the bad.

"I knew not to get on his bad side very often. He'd take guys in the 'green room.' He'd have trouble with discipline today. He'd beat the hell out of them," Friedgen said.

But there was another side.

Friedgen's father was a deeply religious man and attended church daily. He could be fair and kind, and nearly adopted two players that had hardships at home. One of the players, John Carino, attends Maryland games every year, while he takes care of Friedgen's parents' graves back home.

Young Ralph was required to take communion the night before games, and attended church the morning of games. He was a member of the Catholic Newman Club.

Harrison was not unlike many small towns with its strata of rich and poor. The wealthy parts of town were called the "Ridges," with Sunny Ridge and Sterling Ridge. These areas were heavily Jewish. Then there was Brentwood, which was predominantly Italian, and finally Franklin Park, which was a mix and where Friedgen lived. Friedgen walked through Brentwood to get to school. On the other side were the "Ridges."

"All the famous people lived up there. Johnny Carson lived up there. Joe Torre lives there now," Friedgen said.

Harrison High was mostly Jewish and Italian so Friedgen was in the minority, and defensive about not being invited to parties in the "Ridges." His family was lower-middle class. At the height of his career his father made about $65,000 between coaching and running his summer camp.

The Friedgens vacationed on Cape Cod every summer for two weeks. His father insisted on it until Ralph's junior year of high school, when he stayed home for a week to prepare for football camp. Ralph traced his family's financial means by their accommodations at the Cape and how they changed each year. At first they had a tiny cottage with one main room that was "smaller than my office at Maryland." The bathroom door was a sheet. They would wake each day, go to the beach, and come back and go to sleep. They moved into a larger house a decade later. Both of his parents worked. He has always appreciated hard work.

R alph Friedgen, in his youth, was always looking for action. He and his best buddies formed a "gang" – the "Phi Beta Caginos" – a fraternity of 15 of his closest friends, most of whom were Italian. A few attended college at Maryland with Ralph.

They had jackets made with their insignia. (Caginos is Italian for cousins.)

On Sunday nights they'd eat at a member's home and cruise town looking for fun. They did everything from put *Playboy* magazine centerfolds inside geography maps at school to turn on the gas jets in the chemistry lab.

They were in a school play (yes, Ralph Friedgen was a thespian, too), "High Button Shoes," and played the role of the Rutgers football team. Friedgen's father also had a role, as coach. Even there they couldn't help themselves, changing all the labels in the chemistry lab while changing into wardrobe.

"No one ever did an experiment right that year," Ralph quipped.

Growing up in Harrison it was one adventure after another for the gang. The group never took itself seriously. Always mischievous but seldom breaking the law, they were out for a good time not unlike many teenage boys.

In 1963, the year President John F. Kennedy was assassinated, Friedgen and his crew attended the Army-Navy football game at Municipal Stadium in Philadelphia.

A wealthy boy from Purchase, N.Y., recently transferred to Harrison from prep school, Friedgen said, and quickly rubbed the gang the wrong way. The new boy challenged the team to a scrimmage. Harrison traveled to his home, half in uniform, half in street clothes, while the preps came out in full uniform. The boy had a large home and estate with a makeshift field and even goal posts in the backyard. Friedgen, a high school junior, recalled the residents of the grand estate "feeding their dogs steaks and we thought about jumping over the fence and getting the dog food."

The bet was that if the Harrison crew won, the reward would be a trip to the big game. Eighteen of them jumped a train to Philadelphia after winning the contest. They had seats on the 40-yard line and the game ended with Army going in for the score but Navy denying them inside the 20-yard-line. All-American Roger Staubach was the Navy quarterback. Friedgen and crew stormed the field before time expired in the 21-15 Navy win. Friedgen got his hands on the game ball in the melee. Many back home in Harrison saw them on television on the field and talked about it for years.

"We had such a good time, and I laughed so much that time that I was weak," Friedgen said.

The crew was always busy be it their "Sunday dinners, playing ping-pong or just roaming the streets," Friedgen said.

Friedgen was an instigator. Cut-up. Pot-stirrer. You name it. Fun seemed to follow him and the gang, and they often tested the limits.

"But I couldn't be too bad because my old man would kill me. But I had a little wild streak, let's put it that way," he said.

Friedgen laughs when his wife Gloria opens his high school yearbook and points to classmate Herbie Streicher, who in the porn film industry was better known by his stage name, "Harry Reams" of *Deep Throat* fame.

Harrison had a little bit of everything.

R alph Friedgen learned early lessons about teamwork and bonding, on the field and off, from the gang. He said the camaraderie was one of the reasons they had a great senior season in football. The basketball team, too, had success, as it was the first in school history to advance to the sectionals.

But everywhere was his father's influence. And beneath the gruff, intimidating exterior was a man of faith, which would rub off on young Ralph.

He recalled a tight game against Rye High School. Friedgen was in the eighth grade and watched from the sidelines. It was a 13-7 Harrison victory in coach Friedgen's first season, which snapped a 33-game Rye win streak.

Rye was driving inside the Harrison 10-yard line with less than a minute to go and facing fourth-and-two. Friedgen's father called a timeout.

"We had this great linebacker. And he came to the sideline and my dad had his rosary in his hand. He said, 'Let's pray.' "

The Rye quarterback ran a bootleg but the defense stayed home and stopped him short for the victory.

Before football games the team attended 8 a.m. mass followed by a trip to their favorite diner for breakfast. They had a few hours to kill so the team would sometimes drive through the countryside.

Often they would travel to Purchase, N.Y., where there was "a lot of livestock," Friedgen said. This led to another wild time, which Friedgen was in the midst of.

"We'd be tipping over cows. Riding cows. You name it," Friedgen said.

One day they caught a pig, put it in their trunk, and took it to town to let it run free. But before they got there the animal died in the trunk. They dumped it behind a supermarket. The story made the local newspaper but fortunately, for the boys, they were never caught.

One adventure that didn't go as well came on a Saturday afternoon spent cruising.

Their cars were egged by Rye football players. Friedgen's crew bought eggs and sought revenge. A fight ensued and a woman, raking leaves in her yard, was hit by an egg in the melee. The police were on their trail, and on the bus ride to Sleepy Hollow for the game they soon had an escort.

The officers told coach Friedgen, who then began a tradition after practice: 15 100-yard sprints, which continued for some time.

" 'How you like them eggs now, boys?' he told us," Friedgen said.

The Rye players weren't done.

They took more eggs, which were stored in their glove compartment for days to spoil, and on Thursday before the game let loose a volley at the Friedgen's front door. The Rye players went to Harrison's football field where they drew a scene depicting Friedgen hanging his son in effigy.

The rivalry continued as Friedgen, then a sophomore, attended a dance with an older girl that a Rye player liked. She was a junior and Friedgen had an 11 p.m. curfew but he didn't get home until 3 a.m. His father was waiting for him at the door. Making matters worse, Harrison lost that afternoon to Rye, the only time Ralph, as a player, lost to his rival.

" 'You come in late after you got your ass waxed? You'll never date an older girl ever again,' " father told son.

Harrison, N.Y., a small town about 20 minutes outside of New York City, was a tight-knit, insulated community with no exit off the interstate. For many residents, their ambitions never strayed past the boundaries of their cloistered town.

Football was strong at Harrison High School and it dominated life for many.

Friedgen grew up adoring New York Giants quarterback Y.A. Tittle, who was starring while he was coming up at Harrison.

On the baseball diamond, Friedgen loved New York Yankees all-star Mickey Mantle, who years later had a vacation home not far from Friedgen's in Georgia. Mantle was "just a regular guy," Friedgen said, who met the man as a child and an adult. Friedgen once caddied for Mantle at Westchester Country Club in New York. He waited tables and bartended during his high school years and said he learned "a lot about human nature doing that" and the class system at elite Westchester.

Still, the most imposing figure was his father, who after playing at Fordham expected to be a lawyer. At least that's what he thought. He was a History major.

But World War II came and he went into the service, and soon married Winifred Iris Stoddard, who was English.

Ralph Friedgen's maternal grandfather was a coal miner in England and immigrated to the United States and became the groundskeeper and caretaker at the Harrison Recreation Center, where his grandparents lived on the premises.

Ralph's mother took to athletics. She was a top tennis and basketball player in high school and college.

His grandfather spent three years working and saving his money before he returned to England to collect his family.

Ralph's parents were high school sweethearts at Harrison High School. They were once named the school's male and female athletes of the year. His father played about every sport but stood out in football, basketball and baseball. His mother taught physical education for 30 years in Harrison.

On his father's side, his paternal grandparents hailed from The Bronx, New York.

Harry Friedgen, whom Ralph's middle name was derived, and Anna O'Neill married when they were 16. But his father threw him out of the house and they never spoke again.

His father was a bandmaster in New Rochelle, N.Y., but things were never the same after the hasty marriage.

Ralph Friedgen never met his paternal grandfather. As a child his parents encouraged him to play musical instruments, including the clarinet.

His father's side of the family was of German descent with some French mixed in going back to the Valois family of France on the maternal side. Friedgen joked that his father would tell him "our relative was a concubine." Friedgen said his sister, Claranne, has a statue of Marie Valois, the second daughter of John II of France, at her Florida home.

"So I got English and French and German and Irish. I got a lot of things in me," Friedgen said.

His grandparents were "kinda low-key," Ralph said, but his paternal grandmother was fiery and full of life.

"She was all Irish," Friedgen said.

Friedgen recalled going to her home after a baseball game. An older boy had taken away his glove. She found the culprit and made him give it back "but told me the next time he takes it you better get it yourself."

"She would wear you out. Throw things at you," Ralph said.

If Friedgen was walked by a pitcher in a Little League game, she would boo the hurler from her perch in the stands. Friedgen said his grandmother bet on her husband's neighborhood games back when they were dating.

Friedgen joked that he has a "little of my Irish grandmother" in him, while his wife, Gloria, says that the older he gets the more like his father he gets but "with a softer edge."

S aturday was young Ralph's favorite day as it was all about sports. He'd walk or get a ride to school some four miles away. He'd play basketball from 8 a.m. until noon before breaking for lunch only to return to the hardwood at the "Rec" to play until 4 p.m. He'd return home for dinner but be back at the basketball court until 9 p.m.

"And then I'd walk back home. I did that every Saturday of my high school career. That was it."

In 1947, the year Ralph was born, the war was over. His father missed the opportunity to go to law school with children on the way. So he took a high school head coaching job at Iona Prep in New Rochelle.

From there he went to Blessed Sacrament, also in New Rochelle, when Ralph was four. Ralph attended kindergarten with his father. They lived in Harrison and he spent two years in kindergarten after the family moved.

His father took the head coaching job at Port Chester, which hadn't won in years. After he got the program turned around he went to Harrison where he did the same. Prior to his arrival, the golf coach was moonlighting as the football coach and the program was in decline.

Friedgen introduced playbooks and a pro-style offense, producing the highest scoring offense in county history by the time his son was a senior.

Friedgen practiced his team in the courtyard of the school. When it got dark he'd turn on the classroom lights to illuminate the area. Work until the work was done, he'd say.

Harrison's rival, Rye, had a 33-game win streak years before that Harrison had snapped. Rye built another 33-game streak and coach Friedgen returned to lead another upset, 13-7, in 1960, to take the conference championship in his first year.

Young Ralph was in the seventh grade, and moving from Port Chester was a "difficult move for me" as he developed close friends.

Ralph was called by some of his pals by his middle name as well. Many referred to father and son as "Big Ralph" and "Little Ralph."

His father cast a large shadow in town and as the quarterback young Ralph had pressure to perform. He would get in fights, be it on the football field, basketball court, or the baseball diamond.

"That was a daily thing back then just to survive in my neighborhood," he said.

Friedgen was in his father's good graces most of the time because of his football prowess. Ralph learned early about schemes and formations as his father's offense was sophisticated for the day. Practices were extremely tough and the games seemingly easy, just as Ralph Friedgen would make them at Maryland years later with his regimen.

N o matter what, Ralph Friedgen, under the tutelage of his father, had an uncanny knack for pulling out games. Whatever it took, much the way he's been as Maryland's coach with many close games that could have gone either way. Somehow, many have gone his.

Friedgen was twice named all-Westchester County, was county MVP as a senior, and for many years held the county mark for passing yards in a season. He was an accurate passer with good arm strength. But best of all he was a smart play-maker.

Perry Verille, a boyhood friend who goes back nearly 50 years with Friedgen and has remained close, remembered a "6-foot-1, 190-pound cut athlete. He was sort of the prototype kid, and in those days he was pretty big for a quarterback. He woke up to football and went to bed football. I had never seen anyone as dedicated to the sport as he was."

Verille, at 5-foot-7, 150-pounds, was Friedgen's backup quarterback and also played cornerback and special teams. As the scout team quarterback he butted heads with Friedgen, who played linebacker on defense.

Verille remembered the day he traveled to College Park to see Ralph's first game as a college player with Ralph's parents. After the game he and Ralph, and their dates, saw comedian Bill Cosby perform at Cole Field House.

A handful of players from his Harrison team went on to coach including Joe Cassarella, who had a distinguished career at North Rockland (N.Y.) High School.

Friedgen was a "coach on the field," Verille said, and added that the coaches would often defer to him.

"He and his father knew what each other were thinking," Verille said. "They were always on the same wave-length."

Because of his good grades – a B average – Friedgen had college suitors ranging from Boston College, Duke, Penn and Cornell after him, while Auburn was in touch as was North Carolina and Syracuse. But his highest SAT score was 890, which held him back with some of the top academic schools. Friedgen said that he can relate to players today with lower standardized test scores because of his experience.

Friedgen had a wild tale to tell years later of his official recruiting visit to College Park.

His student host took him to a burlesque club in Baltimore and later left him at The "Vous," the popular College Park nightspot, so he could meet up with his girl-friend. His host "made $30 on me," Friedgen said, ditching him for the girl as well as the recruiting stipend.

His father wasn't interested in a long, drawn-out recruitment, and believed that if young Ralph liked a school then he should choose it. As Friedgen says today, and it sums up his thinking on the matter, "If you know what you want, go for it. Don't waste everyone's time."

Assistant coach Lee Corso was his recruiter and Friedgen liked Maryland from the start.

F ather and son took time for other endeavors during his formative years before he headed off to College Park.

On Sundays, Friedgen had some of his best times with his father.

He took his son to New York Giants and Titans football games. He had a press pass and sat in the box above while he would scalp a ticket for his son to sit below in the stands. It was a more carefree time and Ralph was independent at a young age. The trips to ballparks started when Ralph was in the sixth-grade.

"Though I'd kinda be fending for myself down there," he said while rolling his eyes.

Football was a seven-day event in the Friedgen family. Young Ralph was always learning something about the game.

They parked their car at Fordham and took the subway to the stadium. Fordham's home games were played at Yankee Stadium. At the time there were no nets behind the goal posts. Once, Friedgen ran behind the post to catch a Pat Summerall kick and "got drilled after it by the fans. Everyone was after it. I got killed."

Friedgen said he was at Yankee Stadium in the bleachers the day Giants star Frank Gifford was blindsided and, in a famous snapshot, was carried off the field uncon-cious. Friedgen said he was at the Giants-Bears game in the late 1950s when it was so cold that the Giants came out in sneakers in the second half and "ran all over the Bears. The field was so frozen the cleats wouldn't even go in."

His father was also "into the ponies," Ralph said, and insisted that his son return early from school to go to Belmont or Aqueduct racetracks.

He picked him up at the airport from college, "his excuse to get out of school and take me to the track. I'd get there and he'd ask me, 'Where's my tie?'"

Friedgen's father took him to the "Man O' War" Room at Aqueduct, so Ralph had to rent a tie and jacket at the track. He went to the betting window and placed bets for his father. If he had a big day at the track, he'd give his son "$20 or $25, which back then would go a long way," he recalled.

One afternoon his father took him to left field after a baseball game. He told him to look up. The sun was blinding and he spoke of the difficulty of catching a ball in the conditions. He was always teaching. Young Ralph would make mental notes of how Tittle played and where Gifford lined up and the formation.

"Then we'd go home and we'd always talk about what you'd think of this, and what do you think of that. We'd always watch a game and it was what would you do in this situation or that. So I was learning," Ralph said.

Friedgen recalled a time in the fifth-grade at Port Chester "designing plays and putting defenses up with checkers on the floor."

"A lot of this comes back around," he says of the old plays and his offense today.

Friedgen began calling his own plays during his junior year of high school. Even as a sophomore he overturned calls that came to the huddle. After each game, win or lose, Ralph and his father went over the game, play by play, for hours at the dining room table.

"My father always had enough confidence to let me call the plays," he said.

His father was innovative. He and Vince Lombardi were friends and the famed coach let him visit Army practices to observe.

"He was a student, that was for sure," Friedgen said of his father.

He was also something of a character and had several "hobbies."

One day Friedgen helped his grandfather clean his garage. He found his father's old college notebooks.

"All I saw in my father's notebooks. And he would kill me about my schoolwork. But in there were all his horse bets he had going or plays that he was drawing up. Here he was a college player and he was drawing all this?"

He said his father had one sentimental bet, and that was always bet on Lombardi's teams.

His father drew up plays around the house when his son was young, on napkins, newspapers and scrap paper.

"It was always, and like we do now with our offense, how many ways can you run the same plays from different formations? Different stuff and how to fit it all together.

"We were very, very multiple. In high school I ran all the pro stuff. But we also had "Single Wing," "Notre Dame Box," and I'd shift and go under center. It was amazing how we put all that together," Friedgen said.

Few in his day did all of that, while very few threw the ball as much.

Terps assistant coach Dave Sollazzo, who grew up in Harrison and played (as well as his three brothers), at Harrison High, is the closest Maryland staff member to Friedgen. He's almost a son.

Friedgen recruited Sollazzo to The Citadel and hired him in his first graduate assistant post at Maryland. Later, Friedgen stumped for Sollazzo with George O'Leary before the Georgia Tech coach hired him as an assistant coach in his first Division I-A job. Two years later Sollazzo was on his way to Maryland as a member of Friedgen's first staff.

Friedgen still calls him "David," though most call him "Dave" or "Sollaz."

"When I was a kid, Ralph Friedgen was a great quarterback at Harrison and his dad was the coach. Everyone went to all their games. You didn't go to college football games on Saturday afternoons. You went to Harrison for the games. The only talk at the dinner table was Harrison High School football."

Fordham was the biggest local college program, but around town it was all about Harrison High.

Anyone that was athletically inclined spent time at the Harrison Recreation Center, the "Rec," which Sollazzo's father ran. It had everything from courts to game rooms, and it was the place to be on Friday and Saturday nights.

Sollazzo's and Friedgen's fathers were close. Sollazzo's father ran the Midget League, which fed the freshman team at Harrison.

The "Rec" is now named the Frank P. Sollazzo, Sr. Recreation Center. Adding to the family's tie-in, Ralph Friedgen's mother's parents lived on the grounds of the recreation center, where they served as caretakers. They were traditional English so each afternoon Sollazzo's father enjoyed tea in the yard.

Sollazzo served as a bat boy for Ralph Friedgen's American Legion baseball team in 1963, a team Sollazzo's father coached.

Ralph Friedgen was known as a standout quarterback in an advanced offense. His father was an offensive pioneer, ahead of his peers, and the man that laid the groundwork for his son's innovations. Everything he did affected his son.

Ralph Friedgen's first cousin, John Stoddard, who grew up a few miles away in Elmsworth, N.Y., and attended Alexander Hamilton High School, has remained close with Friedgen and attends most of his Maryland games.

He played college football with Gary Blackney at Connecticut under Lou Holtz and Rutigliano. Stoddard said Blackney, a Plainview, N.Y., native, was "pound-for-pound" one of the toughest players he ever saw. The UConn team started with 165 players in the spring but was down to 30 by the season.

"We were called the 'Dirty 30,'" Stoddard quipped. "It was like boot camp, like Parris Island under those guys."

As a junior in high school Stoddard, two years older than Friedgen, was the county's most valuable back, an award that Friedgen won two years later. Stoddard went on to coach and serve as a high school athletic administrator for years. The two were very close, and Stoddard knows Friedgen like few others.

In fact, Stoddard "scouted" for Friedgen early in his coaching career while at The Citadel. He would check out local college teams in the east like Colgate, an opponent Stoddard visited during a spring game with a "checklist" Friedgen had given him which was "18 questions long," he said. That was a time scouting standards were less stringent.

Stoddard remembered the day Friedgen asked him to scout Florida A&M against Morgan State in the Black College Classic at Yankee Stadium.

"Florida A&M had been at his spring game and Ralph and the Citadel had no film on them. So there," Stoddard said.

Friedgen had great stature in his cousin's mind.

"Ralph was a great player and he played for a great coach, his father. Going to see his father was like going to see the priest," Stoddard said of the paternal feelings felt for coach Friedgen around Harrison.

And Friedgen's father's rule was law.

Young Ralph was a public figure and had to deal with the pros and cons of notoriety, lessons he has carried to this day with his players.

Soon after getting his driver's license, Stoddard picked up his cousin in a pouring rain in downtown Harrison. It was raining so hard that Stoddard couldn't see a red light, which he went through.

They were pulled over by police.

"Ralph just goes, 'Don't let him see me. Don't let him see me.' He's over in the corner crunching down in the seat. 'No way I can get in trouble with my father.' That was the ripple effect of his father. Thank the Lord the police did not recognize Ralph hiding there in the back seat," Stoddard said.

Friedgen was active year-round in sports.

Baseball was, admittedly, Friedgen's best sport growing up. He batted over .500 while he also pitched. He played first and third base, too. He played American Legion baseball and remembered a title game played at West Point when they "bused us up in 95 degrees. That was it for me," he said.

Friedgen once pitched a 14-inning one-hitter against Rye.

But everyone knew football would be his way out of Harrison.

"Football was the game I loved. I liked the others a lot, but football I loved. We were looking through my yearbook the other night and [his daughter] Katie said, 'You played every sport?' Kids don't do that anymore," Friedgen said.

There were times at practice when if the players didn't get a play right, the coaches lined their cars up to light the field. They practiced into the night, and until they got it right.

Friedgen was especially close to his mother, who made the drive to College Park for every home game to see him play while his father stayed home to coach Harrison.

His father watched his high school baseball games from his car in the parking lot overlooking the field at Harrison. The watchful and critical eye was always on young Ralph, critiquing all that he did.

R alph Friedgen learned many lessons in his youth that would contribute to his values and beliefs, ones he would incorporate into his coaching years later.

And sometimes he had to learn the hard way.

In a basketball game against rival Rye, fans began a chant targeted at Friedgen. Harrison was losing and Friedgen had four personal fouls. On his last foul he delivered what he admits was "a hard one." He was "chippy" with the bulls-eye on his back as a well-known athlete and coach's son.

"I knocked him about three rows into the stands," he said of the fifth and disqualifying foul.

Friedgen was a junior at the time, playing both guard positions, and averaging about 12 ppg. He helped lead the team to sectional playoffs for the first time. Once a local newspaperman from a Port Chester paper wrote a story criticizing the town and its sports for being too emphasized and, pointing a finger at, among others, the Friedgens. But his father knew when to lay down punishment, and he didn't let his son get away with much. He was always teaching and there was always a lesson involved.

"My father said, 'You quit. You don't quit. That was totally uncalled for. That's not who we are. You just wanted to get out of the game so you hit that guy.'

"That's the kind of thing he'd say," Friedgen said. "Yeah, I was frustrated. We were getting beat and they were getting on my ass. But it was one of these things. I couldn't go anywhere where no one knew who I was. No matter what I did, or when I did it, everyone knew. It was that kind of small town where everyone knew each other's business."

F ootball was his ticket and soon the small-town star was going to a big college. Friedgen was a pinpoint passer. He had solid athleticism and speed, and he had several 100-yard rushing games. But it was his mind and ability to run an intricate offense that separated him from the pack.

As a junior he was runner-up MVP to Calvin Hill, then a star at a local private school before going on to Yale and later the NFL.

"He was a natural from the start. He would game-plan and study with his dad. The same stuff he is teaching his quarterbacks now he learned from his dad back in the 1960s," Stoddard said.

Young Ralph was always challenged, be it by his father, his peers or local towns-people.

Perhaps the most traumatic event he experienced as a youth came during a high school game when his grandfather had a seizure in the stands. It was a precursor to the brain tumor that would later kill him. His grandfather "turned blue" and was rushed to the hospital.

Friedgen amassed over 200 yards in the game but Harrison lost. He went to see his grandfather the next day at the hospital. Lucid now, his grandfather, who was a mild-mannered accountant that Ralph was fond of, asked him who won. True to form he said, "I told him we lost and he said 'What the hell did you do that for?' "

His grandfather died of a brain tumor at 68, while his grandmother died six months later of an aneurism at the age of 64. He used to dote on Ralph, who struggled when his father told doctors to operate on his grandfather's brain, which changed him permanently.

Friedgen was with his grandfather when he had his seizure, and it left a lasting impression on him.

"Once he died she couldn't make it either," Ralph said of his grandmother.

Friedgen easily gets nostalgic about the old days and his family. The emotions course through him often. He uses anecdotes from his childhood frequently as teaching tools with his players and family. He bemoans the fact that times have changed from when he was a child in a simpler time.

Friedgen says that he'd never let his own children walk to school "but when I was in fourth grade I'd walk four miles to school.

"But I look back on things and you know, I really had a lot of fun," he said.

Friedgen knew that he wanted out of Harrison. Leave the small town for something bigger, though many of his friends remained.

His father stood on principle until the end, something his son never forgot.

Late in his career as Harrison's athletic director, Friedgen would not allow a wrestler to compete because he had excessively long hair. He considered it a health hazard.

The wrestler took the school to court, as far as the state Supreme Court, and won.

"My father said, 'I don't care if they grow hair down to their ass. I'm outta here,' " he recalled. " 'I'm retiring if we're going to have things like that.' "

When he stepped down and moved to Florida, a local newspaper ran the headline "Sunny Southland Beckons Friedgen Family" with a two-column photo of Ralph and wife Iris at a send-off party the town threw in their honor. It was attended by more than 200 family members and friends.

Friedgen's father died at the age of 69 in Florida of a heart attack four days before Ralph Friedgen's daughter, Kristina, was born.

"He woke up one morning and asked my mother to get him a drink of water. She went and got a drink of water and he was dead," Ralph recalled.

The passing of the man that shaped him, the persona that loomed so large in his life, was hugely significant for Ralph. He invokes his memory and lessons to this day.

Friedgen may have gained some of his wit and sarcasm from his father.

When his daughter, Kristina, was born on the eve of his father's death, Ralph told his parents the good news over the telephone.

"He said to me, 'When are you going to put a handle on one of these things?' " poking fun at the fact he had three daughters. "I am trying. I am trying," said Ralph of his father.

Friedgen's father taught Ralph's oldest daughter, Kelley, how to swim. He swam for hours in the community pool and would by morning argue politics with neighbors taking a conservative tact, and by afternoon switch to a liberal stance. He was on the debate team in high school and loved engaging everyone, as his son later would enjoy as well. The apple didn't fall far from the tree.

"He just loved to argue. He'd sit there and watch political conventions. Every speech. He loved it," Ralph said of his father.

Ralph Friedgen sees that trait in his daughter, Kelley, a lawyer, who he thinks will someday be a litigator.

The family bought a condominium in Florida a short time later. They traveled to Friedgen's games and father and son would have their "bull" sessions afterwards. His father would always ask Ralph " 'Why I did this or that' in the game," Friedgen said.

"He liked Florida because the horses were always running, the dogs were always running," Ralph said with a smile.

Of the final phone call before he passed away in 1986, Friedgen sensed something was up:

"My mom was all excited. But usually he didn't come back on the phone. He came back on and said, 'I just want to say I am proud of you.' That's the last thing he said," Ralph Friedgen said.

His mother, who passed away in 1994, lived with the Friedgens in San Diego while Ralph was coaching with the Chargers. She fell on the ice in New York and that was the final blow.

Friedgen said he would have loved for his father to see what he has accomplished as a head coach. And the father that he has become to his daughters. And the many lessons he took from him that he applies today.

"I think he would be proud of me. I think he always knew I had a gift ever since I was a sophomore when I called up my own plays. I think he knew I had a gift for it," Friedgen said.

The childhood years may have been summed up by a report young Ralph wrote as a grade-schooler.

Titled "Our Football Coach," he said of his father in a homage that offered a glimpse into some of what was to come in his coaching career:

"Our football coach has one of the toughest jobs there is. He has to compete with spectators criticizing him but worst of all, all the Monday morning quarterbacks who know everything on Monday and nothing on Saturday. The story will go on to tell all about our coach.

"It all started about 20 years ago at Blessed Sacrament, a little school in New Rochelle. Our coach had some great teams and in 1951 he had a great honor and became coach of the year.

"Then he moved to Port Chester and they had a bad team and lost 34 in a row. When the coach had his first year there, he won three, tied two and lost two. The second year he won five and lost three. Through the years the seasons became better. In 1955 we were undefeated with a 6 and 0 record. In 1957 the team had six good games under their belt. The seventh game at Mamaroneck they had 15 games in a row. Thirteen to six they were defeated. The next game was the powerful Greenwich, who was defeated by Port Chester 14 to 7. In 1958 and 1959 we had a record of 7 and 1. This year we won the first WCCC championship, which stands for Westchester Cross County Conference.

"Now you know the story of our coach who is also my father and a good coach and a wonderful father."

2
THE EARLY YEARS

W hen Ralph Friedgen arrived at College Park he was scared stiff of failing, probably based on what the guidance counselor told him.

So he worked his tail off.

"And my dad would probably kill me if I failed," he said.

Friedgen, who was recruited by Corso, now an ESPN college football analyst, got a 2.3 GPA during his first semester, which at the time was the highest among the 65 freshmen football players, he said. Friedgen followed that with a 2.8 "and then everybody here thought I was a smart guy," he quipped.

Friedgen followed with consistent 2.8 or above GPAs, even notching a 3.75 to win the George C. Cook Memorial Award for the highest GPA on the football team. He twice won the award, in 1968 and '69.

"Sure enough my father said, 'Why didn't you get a 4.0?' " Friedgen said.

Years later Friedgen used the ploy on one of his best students, place-kicker Nick Novak, the all-ACC and academic performer. During a snowstorm Novak called Friedgen at his home and asked to use the tennis bubble to practice kicking. Friedgen said he couldn't even get out of his house, let alone to the golf course where the bubble was located. Friedgen asked Novak, "Don't you have any studying to do?" Novak responded that he had three "A's" and a "B," only to hear Friedgen bark back, "What's up with that 'B'?

"That's what my father said to me. I think it was a flashback," Friedgen said.

Friedgen was recruited by the staff of head coach Tom Nugent. But a coaching carousel followed with Lou Saban, Bob Ward and finally Roy Lester serving as mentors. It would make a lasting impression on Friedgen but, for the most part, not a positive one.

When Ralph Friedgen arrived on campus the first foreboding sign for him was that "there were seven quarterbacks when I came in here," he said.

But Friedgen immediately fell in love with campus, walking in the tunnel at Cole Field House and thinking, "Wow. It blew me away. That and Madison Square Garden were the two biggest places going."

He recalled Corso taking him on the field at Byrd Stadium and asking him, " 'If you can drive the team here against Oklahoma?' "

"He was quite a salesman," Friedgen recalled.

The two men stayed in touch. Years later Corso, after a phone call from Friedgen, passed along resume information from a friend's daughter, who got a job and worked for a network for several years.

When Friedgen arrived at Maryland, freshmen could not play. Varsity players came in ahead of the freshmen to summer camp.

The second bad sign for Friedgen was hearing freshman coach Paul Massey tell one of the seven quarterbacks, Bob "Sparky" Faries, to "take the first team out."

"I thought that was a little unusual the first day knowing his name and all. So I asked one of the other players, 'How come he knows his name already?' He said, 'Well that was his quarterback in high school.' "

Friedgen ended up on second team. The Terps played George Washington to open up the season. Massey repeatedly called plays for Friedgen to "run right, run left." On a third-and-four play Friedgen checked the play and threw to an open tight end, Ron Pearson, who dropped the ball, which forced a punt.

"So I went out and he ripped my ass," Friedgen said. "So that was the last I got in that game."

The second game was against a prep school and Friedgen recalled Massey's emotional pre-game speech, "telling us about a guy playing with his leg off. Everyone got fired up."

The Terps went ahead early so Friedgen came in. But again he only got sweep right, sweep left plays. After a few of those he did it again, checking off, but this time he hit a receiver for a touchdown. He reverted to his high school days when he was a coach on the field and made decisions. But Friedgen was at another level now. He got ripped again on the sideline by Massey, but returned to throw two more touchdowns. But by Monday he had been moved to fullback.

"That was my last game at quarterback," said the former high school star. "I was upset, but back then you kinda did what the coaches told you. I played the rest of the year at fullback."

Nugent got fired after the 1965 season and Saban came in and shook things up to say the least.

Alan Pastrana, a linebacker under Nugent, was moved to starting quarterback. Pastrana's nephew, Greg Powell, would later play for Friedgen at Maryland and was a member of the 2006 Champs Sports Bowl team.

"I didn't even know Pastrana played quarterback," Friedgen noted.

Saban told Friedgen that he was going to redshirt him, "to get him bigger and stronger, and we don't know where we are going to play you."

Friedgen was the scout team quarterback and Saban liked his fiery demeanor when he got roughed up in practice. One day he fired a football at a defender's head after a cheap shot, which resulted in a fight.

"Saban liked that," Friedgen said.

But the starting fullback got hurt and in the third game of the season Friedgen was moved to second team fullback. Assistant coach Rutigliano knew his father from when he coached at Greenwich (Conn.) High School and Horace Greeley High in New York.

Friedgen got in on special teams, too, and burned his redshirt. He remembered getting his picture in a local paper for a big special teams hit against West Virginia.

Later, with his redshirt up, Friedgen was moved to linebacker. The Terps were 5-2 but several players got injured and they finished the season with a 5-6 record. Saban bolted at season's end for the Denver Broncos of the NFL. Saban never put Friedgen down for a letter, even though he had earned it, which irked him. But years later he received his letter from his boss, Maryland athletic director Debbie Yow.

Bob Ward came in as the new head coach in 1967 and all bets were off.

"When Ward came in it was like [the concentration camp] Dachau. I mean, I will go by that wrestling room [at Cole Field House] and to this day I hear the moans and screams," Friedgen said.

The period left a lasting impression on the future coach.

The team had winter workouts that consisted of four 20-minute periods. The drills began in the wrestling room, which was probably "130 degrees," Friedgen said of the poorly-ventilated Cole. There was no limit on scholarships, and Friedgen said the team began with 150 players and lost 50 within six weeks. All, he said, quit the team because of the new coach.

"We would go into the wrestling room and I remember sitting out in the hallway there by all the cages. And all we would have on is our sweats and socks. We didn't have a top. It would be like your stomach was when you played a game or before you got in a fight," he said.

Screams and yells bellowed from the room and the sound of banging on walls. The door swung open with the first group and the players poured out drenched in sweat, some with blood trailing from their noses. Ward put the players through combative drills on the mats, on all fours, seeing who could drive the other the furthest. The players were in there "fighting our ass off," Friedgen said.

Another drill was for the players to start in a pinning position, which they had to work their way out of. Another exercise was for a player to do a forward roll and two would hit him as he popped up from the floor.

But the most telling may have been "right out of [the film] *Gladiator*," Friedgen said.

"It was five little guys against three big guys in the ring. No holds-barred. There was, I mean, punching. I mean, you could have your best friend and it didn't matter. You still drilled him."

Friedgen said it got so bad that he witnessed "seven compound fractures of big toes" as players got their toes caught on the mats. There were buckets lining the walls to vomit in. The sessions were held every day and billed as "conditioning classes" to those on the outside.

"It was so bad that there were actually guys that were happy when Bob Ward died. Guys just hated him," Friedgen said.

And that was the first station.

Next, the players went on the main floor at Cole where they lifted weights for 20 minutes. The players "recuperated" on the weights compared to what was going on upstairs, Friedgen said.

The third station was an agility station run by benevolent assistant coach Dick Shiner, who was sympathetic to the players and did not push as hard. But station four, which consisted of running the stairs at Cole, was brutal. Ward would tell the players, "Gut me a lap," Friedgen painfully recalled.

The players ran to the bottom of the staircase, put a teammate on their backs, and returned up the stairs at break-neck speed.

"We would lie in the shower at the end of this hour and 20 minutes. And we lost. The next year we went 0-9. From a team that was 5-2 and had a chance to win the ACC Championship, we went 0-9. The first game we played was Oklahoma, in Norman, and they beat us 35-0," Friedgen said.

Friedgen said Ward had a practice trick that he would use on the players. He'd yell "Boomer Sooner," which gave them a chance to spear the player nearest them. Friedgen said he broke his thumb once during the "exercise." Ward knew no boundaries of how far to push his players.

But Ward liked Friedgen because he got in fights. He never knew Friedgen was a high school quarterback.

" 'You're a fighter like I was' he'd yell at me," Friedgen recalled.

Nugent wanted Friedgen light, Saban wanted him heavy, and finally Ward wanted him light again, Friedgen said.

Friedgen went from 210 pounds before Ward got to campus to 195 pounds in winter workouts, thanks to the brutal conditioning drills.

But he gutted it out.

Friedgen said Ward instructed him to block one afternoon in drills, which Friedgen had little experience doing. So Ward "punched me in the face." Ward broke his Orange Bowl watch on Friedgen's face mask, which changed his perspective of Friedgen slightly.

Ward had been at Oklahoma and Army before Maryland, and Friedgen said he thought he was "a good coach." But he couldn't relate to his players and he didn't have a great staff around him.

Still, Friedgen always introduced Ward as his college coach at awards banquets and speaking engagements over the years. Friedgen said one difference between him and Ward was that he would play the players "who loved the game more, not just based on talent alone," like Ward. That carried over to his coaching experiences and some of his personnel moves at College Park.

Friedgen hurt his knee during his senior year and could have redshirted but didn't want another year with Ward. He played guard and tackle that season, frustrated after arriving as a hot-shot quarterback. But it helped lay the groundwork for Friedgen the coach, with understanding for players in a similar predicament.

"It was a tremendous learning experience for when I had to coach. I had experienced all these things. Like what it's like to play quarterback, to play offensive line, to play fullback. You can kind of relate. It gave me a very easy ability to relate to the different positions," Friedgen said.

Friedgen took scars from those days. Literally and figuratively.

Said boyhood friend Verille:

"His college career had to be frustrating for him because you go from being on the field virtually every play to having limited playing time and four different coaches . . . And moving positions."

Friedgen was ready to become a graduate assistant under Ward, who by then had moved away from the wrestling room of horrors and used pickup basketball games (something Friedgen does today), and other means to condition his players.

Looking back to his junior year, Friedgen remembered the day he phoned home wanting to quit the football team, which resulted in the response from his father that Friedgen uses about threatening to change the locks on their home if he did.

Ward told Friedgen that he would give him a good recommendation if he decided to transfer. Friedgen was looking to transfer to Connecticut, where his cousin, Stoddard, played alongside Blackney, who would become his first defensive coordinator at College Park.

"My father told me, 'Well, come on home. But you will have trouble getting in.'

"I said, 'Why's that?' He said, 'Because there are going to be new locks on the doors. We don't have quitters that live in this house.'"

Friedgen was peeved and tore the phone off the wall.

But he sucked it up, did the best that he could, and in the end moved up the depth chart. As a 235-pound guard he played as a reserve as a senior despite the injury.

Later, he came upon the players in the lounge at Ellicott Hall dormitory. They were AWOL from winter workouts.

They told him that Ward had "clothes-lined a player going up the stairs at full speed" at Cole, and the player fell down the stairs. The next day the players boycotted the workout. They sat out a second day. Athletic Director Jim Kehoe called a meeting at the Armory with the players and Ward for the following day. Kehoe gave everyone a chance to voice their concerns about the coach. Most were intimidated to do so but after two hours, with one after another unleashing on Ward, Kehoe ended the meeting. He needed a second day to hear all their complaints. But before the next day's meeting, Ward resigned.

Things got stranger for Friedgen as Roy Lester came in as coach in 1969 but would not renew his scholarship. Friedgen had a half of a semester to go. He ended up paying his own way.

Then several players that quit under Ward came back wanting to be graduate assistants under Lester. Friedgen worked for Lester for one year with the freshman team before graduating. He enrolled at graduate school and Lester asked him to help out with the freshmen.

It was at this time Friedgen decided he wanted to coach as a career.

Despite his personal journey, going from high school star to college reserve while toiling under countless coaches with mixed messages, he loved the game and loved teaching football.

Friedgen said that if Saban had stayed "things could have been different."

"Really, I didn't care where I played. I just missed playing. It was frustrating. I was embarrassed. But mostly disappointed that I wasn't playing. I know I would have given better effort than some of the guys ahead of me if given the opportunity. Some guys were just playing to be playing," Friedgen said when summing up his college playing career.

Said his future boss, Yow, of what Friedgen told her of his playing days at Maryland:

"Obviously at the time it was a horrific situation for him as a young person trying to achieve. But in retrospect he felt that having that experience actually better prepared him to coach."

Friedgen took one of the lessons and used it after arriving as head coach at College Park in 2000.

He met with the players alone, which turned off holdover assistant coaches Mike Locksley and James Franklin, an event he still gets emotional about. His opening speech to the players was vintage Friedgen.

"I wanted to go meet the players by myself. I didn't need to have other coaches that had been here. I told them, 'Look, I have been where you are. I had three different coaches when I was here as a player. I know what you are concerned about, concerned about am I going to bring in my recruits, play my guys.'

"I said, 'You know men, I am 53-years old. I have waited a long time for this and I don't really care who recruited you. We are all Terps. The only thing I care about now is what we do now and in the future. I don't care what we have done in the past. And I want you to know that. I am just happy to have a chance to coach anybody.' "

Friedgen later met with every player one-on-one in his office.

L ooking back at Ralph Friedgen's start in coaching, Roy Lester was gone after three years and Jerry Claiborne took over in 1972. Friedgen got to know assistant Dick

Redding, the freshman coach, who helped him on board with Claiborne thanks in part to his knowledge of the freshman team, which had top players like future star Randy White.

Friedgen got a jump on landing a job off the fired staff, Claiborne picking him from the staff of the star-studded freshman team that also featured quarterback Bob Avellini. Friedgen told Claiborne that he knew the freshman team, which almost beat the varsity in a scrimmage the year before, "better than anyone."

Redding pushed for Friedgen and helped him become the final hire. The staff included Frank Beamer, Charlie Rizzo, Brett Hart, Tom Parks and Friedgen as graduate assistants.

Friedgen served as a volunteer coach and Redding liked him. Redding was "a kind man" who in later years retired to Charlottesville. Friedgen left him tickets for Maryland-Virginia games. He attended wife Gloria Friedgen's tailgate parties before passing away three years into Friedgen's head coaching tenure.

"That's the only reason I got on," Friedgen said of the former mentor.

Friedgen said he learned bits and pieces from all three of his head coaches at Maryland. He said Nugent was a great "showman," while he said he was "afraid" of Saban. He said Saban once singled out a player who missed a block on a field goal during a film session, calling him an "amoeba, the lowest form of life," Friedgen said.

But he could motivate, too, and Saban went on to a long coaching career, including in the NFL. Friedgen said Saban liked him, for whatever reason he did not know.

I n his final game as a sophomore, at Florida State, Ralph Friedgen then a fullback with a dislocated shoulder, was going through a Friday workout in Tallahassee. He went out for a swing pass but missed the catch. He couldn't get his arm up due to the harness he was wearing.

"Why didn't you catch the ball, Friedgen?" the coach screamed at him.

"I got a harness on," he responded.

"You can't play with that harness on," the coach shot back.

Friedgen was ticked. He was in Tallahassee over Thanksgiving weekend and his prospects looked slim. Rutigliano came to him that night and said, "You are going to play, but that shoulder better not come out."

On the very first play, the kickoff to the Seminoles, Friedgen got blind-sided and his shoulder popped out. He returned to the sideline and popped it back in place before the coaches were aware of the injury. He had surgery that summer and was hoping to be back by August camp.

But Ward "went nuts," Friedgen said, wanting him back sooner. In the Terps first scrimmage, against Temple, to start what would turn out to be a 0-9 season, Friedgen played poorly, not surprising since he had not practiced.

Friedgen was put on the scout team so he had to wear a green shirt, something the scout team players wore. Ward called Friedgen up before the team before the start of practice and made him switch to the green shirt. It was a huge embarrassment for the senior, one he carries today, and it affects how he handles his players.

"That was one of many low points with him," Friedgen said.

On scout team Friedgen got in several fights. One day at practice he was called off-sides. The coaches ran him, wanting to "run me till I dropped. It was a different time then."

Friedgen counted his highlights as a player coming under Saban, with most of them on special teams. When the Terps played Penn State, Saban suspended the fullback, quarterback and a few linebackers for drinking beer on the trip. He had some good friends, including Van Heusen, roommate Ed Kane and in the end, the entire all-county high school backfield from Harrison at Maryland. Back then, more players from his area came to College Park, he said.

In later years many of the players came back to support Friedgen as head coach.

"To see some of those guys now at 'Terp Alley.' I think a lot of those guys respected the effort that I gave with some of the stuff I was dealing with. Some of them still laugh their ass off at me. They bring up some of the old stories, the fights back then," Friedgen said.

R alph Friedgen, among his many duties under Jerry Claiborne, picked up practice film at 4 a.m. in downtown Washington, D.C. He said there were some real characters in the program then, including assistant coach Tommy Groom, who "would go recruiting in his Winnebago," Friedgen said.

"He'd say, 'After your day go and pick up tape in D.C. at 4 in the morning.' I said, 'My day doesn't get over until 10:30 [p.m.],' " Friedgen said.

Friedgen was a graduate assistant on an academic grant in the school of Health and Human Performance. Claiborne picked him up as his last hire for $150 a month, but with no room and board. So he and future wife, Gloria Spina, lived together while she finished her degree.

Friedgen picked up the film and met Claiborne at 5 a.m. They watched it for three hours. Most mornings, Gloria rose early and made some kind of pastry or coffee cake and Friedgen brought it for his boss to share. He could never let on to the traditional Claiborne "that I was living with a girl."

"Coach Claiborne never understood why the thing was always warm. But it was a great experience for me. I got to learn a lot sitting in there, just me and him watching tape. But he'd always ask, 'How do you get it so warm?' I remember he wrote me a letter, years later, about how he could get that coffee cake."

This was the time Friedgen first crossed paths with Bobby Ross, who Claiborne hired as a defensive assistant.

With Claiborne it was all about running the football, no "ifs, ands or buts," Friedgen said. Once, after the two watched an LSU football game on television and the Bert Jones-led Tigers lost the game, Claiborne told Friedgen:

" 'Ralph. You know why LSU got beat?' I said, 'No, why?' 'They couldn't run the football. Couldn't run the football. That's why they got beat. Passed the ball too much,' " Friedgen related.

It was a shootout game with Jones throwing for nearly 400 yards. But it was all about the run in Claiborne's book.

"It was hard-nosed football with him. But I thought he was a very, very smart guy," Friedgen said.

Claiborne had talent from the freshman team while he was also an innovator. This would help shape Ralph Friedgen the coach.

Claiborne gave every player a book about "Psycho Cybernetics," Friedgen said, which dealt with "changing their mindset with what they thought and what they could be," Friedgen explained.

Every day Claiborne drilled them on the book and its philosophy. Claiborne was stern but positive. He won in his first year (compared to the 2-9 finish the year before under Lester), finishing 5-5-1. The second year he won big, finishing 8-4. Claiborne changed the "mindset" of the players, something Friedgen would always be aware of and fostering years later in his teams.

But the public, the fans, were another thing, Friedgen said, and it was another lesson that he took from the venerable coach.

"What happened with him, and I learned from him, is you can't just win. You got to entertain. You have to win in an exciting way. You have to be able to throw the ball. Be exciting on defense. Have exciting special teams. Because you have to be able to compete for the entertainment dollar," Friedgen said, and would follow, years later with his blueprint as a head coach.

Claiborne won but he couldn't put enough people in the stands, winning "boring," Friedgen said.

Friedgen was at Murray State when Ross took over at Maryland and offered him an assistant's job. Friedgen first asked Ross if he had a quarterback, which was a lesson Ross had taught him. Ross said, "Maybe we have one in Stan Gelbaugh."

But when Friedgen arrived, much to his delight, he found three quality signal-callers: Gelbaugh, Boomer Esiason and Frank Reich. The players were hungry, and Maryland went 8-3 in 1982, their first season under Ross.

Friedgen said it may have been the most enjoyable group he's ever coached. In addition to the quarterbacks, the Terps boasted Greg Hill, Kevin Glover, Ron Solt, Tony Edwards, Alvin Blount, Tommy Neal, Lenny Lynch and Ferrell Edmunds, all of whom were players, many of whom were characters.

"We would have kicked our ass at Georgia Tech," Friedgen said of the Maryland team versus his future national championship team in Atlanta.

Friedgen credited Claiborne, despite his boring style, with bringing in top players. But it all came to an end when men's basketball star Len Bias died in 1986.

Friedgen recalled hearing sirens on campus and first thought that a dorm was on fire. He arrived early to work and soon learned that Bias had overdosed.

"It was like the inquisition. Everybody was guilty," he said.

University president John Slaughter had never come out and defended the football program much before. And after a bad experience at the Cherry Bowl, coupled with the Bias incident and the episode when Ross chased an official in the North Carolina game over a blown call, things began to unravel. UNC came from behind to beat Maryland thanks to the call and, after the game, Ross reached out and grabbed the official, all of which was caught on tape.

Clemson was the opponent the following week with Tigers coach Danny Ford himself suspended, and in the press box along with Ross, in Baltimore. They played to a 17-17 tie before 58,758 fans at Memorial Stadium.

An associate athletic director that had a previous run-in with Ross said that he was "an embarrassment to the University," which crushed Ross, Friedgen said.

Friedgen said Ross told him "he was out of there." Ross resigned at season's end and told his staff to get together and decide who would be his replacement, "but be sure to get behind one guy," Friedgen recalled.

Friedgen, George Foussekis and Joe Krivak all wanted the job and decided to meet the next day and get behind a consensus choice.

Krivak went that night, however, to express interest in the job "and jumped the gun," Friedgen said. Chuck Sturtz was the athletic director. Krivak said he would only take the job if it was a four-year deal. Friedgen said he would take it for a year. Friedgen went to Krivak and asked him if he would take it in an interim situation. Krivak said no, so Friedgen told him that the vote would be split.

Friedgen said he later lobbied for Krivak for four years once it was known that would be the scenario.

Frank Beamer split off to Virginia Tech and later offered Friedgen more money than Ross at Georgia Tech. And both offered more than what was being offered to stay at Maryland.

In the end, Friedgen went with Ross to Atlanta. Friedgen knew it was going to be a tough job at Maryland and recalled telling his wife, "This place is really going to go down right now. It's not quite the same,' " he said.

"I knew things were on the downside," he said of the program in the wake of Bias's cocaine overdose.

Friedgen said Krivak's tenure was flawed from the start when he appointed Jimmy Cavanaugh as his offensive coordinator. Why? Because Krivak, Friedgen said,

"didn't listen to Cavanaugh," who he called "a hell of a coach."
Krivak later let Cavanaugh go and he went to North Carolina and later Virginia Tech with Beamer. One of the first offers Friedgen made when he returned to Maryland as head coach in 2000 was to Cavanaugh for the post of receivers coach.

Friedgen, after Krivak got fired by Andy Geiger in 1992, called the athletic director to inquire about the job. Friedgen said Geiger told him that he was "not going to hire anyone from Ross's old staff, or anyone from the ACC."

"I told him, 'Well, the last time you all won was when Bobby Ross was coaching, and you are playing in the ACC.' That's what I told him," Friedgen said.

Going back to his coaching start, Ross interviewed for the head job at The Citadel. Before, at the football office at Maryland in the winter of 1972, Ross "interviewed" Friedgen in the men's room for a job in Charleston, S.C.

Ross asked in the middle of their conversation if Friedgen "was going to marry Gloria." That Christmas, Ralph and Gloria got engaged as they were accepting Ross' offer to come to The Citadel. Ross was a family man.

"He was in there [the coaches' bathroom] at Cole on the third floor doing his business. He said, 'Ralph, I am going to interview at The Citadel tomorrow and if I get the job are you interested in coming with me?' "

Friedgen's interest was piqued given the fact he had been turned down by just about everyone, even for a high school job, and by Corso, now a head coach. He and Gloria wrote letters to "every college coach in the country. We still have all the rejection letters. Joe Paterno. Bear Bryant. Even Corso who recruited me," Friedgen said.

Ross offered and Friedgen accepted, and said that he and Beamer went out and celebrated late into the night "because we finally got a job."

The salary was $11,000. Beamer was already married. They both headed for Charleston, where they shared an office for seven years. But before any of that happened, Ross said in the bathroom at Cole, "Ralph, you are getting married, right?"

"He was so worried about guys running around," Friedgen said.

Those were some of the best years, living in a "gorgeous six-room apartment with 10-foot ceilings. All for free and on campus. It was on the top floor, like a penthouse," Gloria Friedgen recalled.

It was also the time Gloria and Ralph began hosting players at their home for meals, a tradition they would carry into his coaching days at College Park.

Their home was situated just outside the athletic track. Sollazzo was one of Friedgen's first recruits.

"He would eat plate after plate of lasagna, or whatever it was I cooked, and he never put on any weight," Gloria said of Friedgen's current defensive line coach and recruiting coordinator.

Gloria worked as a middle and high school teacher during those years, and coached volleyball, basketball and track. She taught throughout Ralph's career at every college and pro stop as she does today at College Park. She taught as an adjunct in Education and Health and Human Performance. She currently is the coordinator for Alumni Affairs and Outreach in the new school of Public Health.

R alph Friedgen always looked to learn and absorb everything that he could. He showed an early penchant for film study. And that may be an understatement.

Back in his days with the San Diego Chargers, Friedgen saw the team's video director throwing out old tapes from the late 1970s and early '80s

"1978-82. The greatest years the Chargers ever had," Friedgen said. "Don Coryell. Joe Gibbs. What Maryland does now. All of those offenses."

Friedgen asked for the tapes and spent hours holed up in his office pouring over the film, all the while getting needled by his fellow assistants who thought he was nuts.

"In fact, Dan Fouts did our games on television and would be asking questions about plays and how do you know these plays. I said, 'I got the cut-ups.' And they were doing the same things we're doing, but doing them a lot better," Friedgen said.

Around that time Friedgen said Coryell put in three-receiver sets with talented Charlie Joiner at slot. Joiner, Friedgen said, would abuse linebackers with his quickness. That brought the nickel defense a year later, which coordinator Bill Arnsbarger implemented.

Friedgen saw another trend the following year with the Chargers. When faced with "man" defense he'd run pick patterns, "killing defenses that didn't switch," he said. The following year he saw defenses evolve into zone, witnessing the evolution before his eyes with talents like Kellen Winslow, the athletic tight end with receivers' speed, wide-out John Jefferson and, of course, the prolific Fouts throwing them the ball. Years later, Friedgen had star Vernon Davis run similar routes during his All-America junior season at Maryland in 2005.

"To me," Friedgen said, "tapes are like books. But I learn more from tapes than reading a book. See things. See how people are playing. Learn techniques, match-ups. I just spent hours and hours watching tape. I can watch the same tape 40 times and learn 40 different things from the same tape."

Friedgen still has the tapes in his basement. At Georgia Tech he had a room in his office full of shelves to hold the approximate 5,000 cases. Some of it was 16-mm film from 1974 that he cut himself. He cut it, hung it on the wall using Scotch tape, and named each play. Then he spliced it together. Later he converted all of his San Diego Chargers film to video.

"I remember coaches, during the transition from 16-mm to VHS, there were coaches who didn't like VHS because it didn't make the noise of a 16-mm camera. Coaches are slow to change," he said.

Of the evolving offenses, the always-evolving Friedgen said:

"It doesn't change that much and sometimes it all comes around."

Friedgen would go back and watch the same play again and again, spotting differences in "two or three yards" as the difference between plays timing up correctly or not. He put his quarterbacks' plays from successive seasons together on reels as learning tools for them.

"I have always been gifted, I think, as far as being able to pick things up and whether the line blocked or whether it's reads or routes. It just comes very easy to me." Friedgen said that plays and formations run through his mind constantly.

They come to him in church, while he's sleeping, while he's driving. And that he can remember them without having to write them down.

With Bobby Ross at The Citadel they had success running the two-back "veer" offense. Later they switched to the "veer" out of the "I" formation, which Friedgen loved.

Friedgen left for other jobs and later returned to Maryland with Ross. Ross was first an NFL special teams coach and later a running backs coach before coming to Maryland as the head coach. So he had an idea of what he wanted to do offensively.

Friedgen said it was similar, in ways, to what his father did at Harrison with the same plays but from multiple formations. Ross, Friedgen, Krivak and Cavanaugh put together the offense. It was the genesis of his offense today.

"So coach Ross said, 'I want four three-step drop routes.' And we all had a board. I put up my 4-5 [plays] and so did the others. Then we did the same thing for the five-step, seven, play-action, and how we were going to run the ball and so on. So it actually was a conglomeration of putting an offense together but we were mostly two-back," Friedgen said.

Later at Georgia Tech they added two tight end/one-back looks, and later three "wides" with one back. But it was mostly a two-back offense.

When they arrived at San Diego they had a rookie quarterback, John Friesz, who was finishing his first year. The Chargers fired Dan Henning, who was running Coryell's offense, but general manager Bobby Beathard wanted the new staff to run it as well. Beathard didn't want to train a new quarterback. So the coaches learned the old offense. The Chargers went from three wins to 11 in a year after dropping their first four games.

Of what became the offense that he runs today, Friedgen said:

"What happened was it was a natural blend of how to put two backs and one back together in a cohesive package that people could learn. I came up with a system that people think is complicated, but what's complicated is we have plays that are named because they just worked when I got them and I just kept them in. As far as the formations and the motions and all of that, that fits together very well. That and learning how to get certain match-ups is the biggest thing I took from pro football."

It was fitting that Friedgen once taught "The History of Football" at Maryland when he was a graduate assistant.

R alph Friedgen picks up new things all the time.
One year he went against Delaware and its "Wing-T" offense, which he loved for

the way it outflanked defenses. He also liked elements of the "Run-and-Shoot," and said: "If I had the right personnel, I would go back and run the "Single-Wing" like I did in high school. It will all come back."

His father preached to him about the evolution of offense, from the "Single Wing" to the "Split-T" to the "Notre Dame Box" and how they all progressed.

"I guess I have always been a student of the game and a visionary," Friedgen said.

Friedgen has long fought for the underdog, giving kids second and third chances, sometimes to his detriment. That may date to his roller-coaster ride as a college player. He never thought he would get into coaching, but coming from a family of teachers, not to mention his love for athletics, it helped shape his course.

But as a student-teacher Friedgen, at first, wasn't fond of the job. He recalled teaching at nearby High Point High School just up the road from College Park.

"I think it would have just been a matter of time before I killed somebody," he quipped.

But after serving as a graduate assistant for the Terps, Friedgen was hooked. Head coach Buddy Beardmore, who was the lacrosse coach first and foremost, "didn't even know if a football was pumped up," Friedgen joked.

The good news was that he put Friedgen in charge of the defense. And the young coach stayed up late drawing formations, how each gap should be stopped, and so on. He loved teaching the freshmen, using practices as a "laboratory" away from the pressure of the varsity.

"We didn't even run the same stuff as the varsity was. And we were going undefeated and everything else," Friedgen said.

For the first six years that was all he taught, defense. But it gave him perspective on both sides of the ball.

Friedgen had "Fifty bucks in the bank back then," he said. "But it's one of those things you know. That this is what you are meant to do."

3

ARRIVING

R alph Friedgen considered Maryland an underachiever for as long as he can remember.
He had been at College Park twice in between stints at The Citadel, William & Mary, Murray State and Georgia Tech. But Maryland, by far, had the most potential the way he saw things.

Not everyone shared his view, though.

"Bobby Ross used to tell me, 'If you asked me which school had more potential, it's not even close between Maryland and Georgia Tech,' " Friedgen recalled. "And I wouldn't agree with him. We [Maryland] had so much potential that we never realized."

For starters, Friedgen pointed to the fact Georgia Tech did a better job of fund-raising and its booster group was incorporated. And that "they are their own entity," he said. "They don't share their money with anybody," Friedgen added.

Friedgen long believed Maryland was a "sleeping giant" waiting to be awakened.

He rattled off other factors, like the university's location between two major metropolitan areas, in the nation's fourth largest media market, and around an "educational mecca," with many internship and career opportunities nearby.

Ross left in the late 1980s over the lack of support for the football program, making Friedgen's turnaround job, based on his prior knowledge of the school, more compelling. Friedgen had the blueprint and knew what worked and what didn't. And what needed a shot in the arm.

"In a lot of ways he took what we learned in the 1980s, when we went downhill so quickly because they wouldn't make the commitment, and said that will not happen," said longtime strength and conditioning coach Dwight Galt, whose career has spanned five head coaches at College Park.

"Northern Virginia is becoming Silicon Valley East. There's not a major I can't get my kid an internship in around here," Friedgen said. "And we are the state's only

Division I football program."

With more than 150,000 living alumni within a one-hour radius, compared to Georgia Tech's 58,000, Friedgen said he saw the potential as staggering.

But what Maryland hadn't done was attract a lot of Terrapin Club members, and donations, for its scholarship fund.

Friedgen said in men's basketball, where the Terps reseated the fans when the Comcast Center was built (which in turn drove Terrapin Club membership), that when football undergoes the same process "that's when things will really start cooking."

"At Georgia, for instance, it takes $400 per ticket to qualify to buy tickets within the 40s [yard line]," Friedgen said Georgia coach Mark Richt told him at a coaches' retreat.

"Richt told me he asked his [athletic director] if he could raise some money to improve some facilities. In two weeks he raised $8 million. They have 92,000 season tickets holders. You do the math," Friedgen said.

Friedgen said men's basketball coach Gary Williams deserves a lot of credit for getting the Terps program to that level.

Friedgen admits that reseating Byrd based on donations will be a "delicate time" for long-standing football season ticket holders, and as Yow points out, longevity should be taken into account for 20, 30 and 40-year ticket holders, much like Virginia Tech did with its stadium expansion.

Friedgen points to the job his friend Beamer did at Tech building the program. And how at Virginia it never happened until coach George Welsh took the program to the next level.

Friedgen knows it comes down to on-field performance as well. The Terps have numerous pro teams to compete with, stuck between the Baltimore Ravens to the north and the Washington Redskins to the south, so they must win to win the fans' entertainment dollar.

"We have already shown that we can do that [compete with the pro teams]. And you not only have to win, you have to win in an exciting way. You have to have an offense that is exciting. You have to play aggressive defense. You got to have great special teams. You got to want people to enjoy themselves seeing your teams play. Coach Claiborne won but it was boring and attendance fell off. We're competing for the entertainment dollar," Friedgen said.

"But the college experience I really think is so different than the pros. People come and they enjoy themselves and they have a good time and it's affordable. I think we can compete, I really do."

Verille, Friedgen's boyhood friend and former high school teammate, at the time of Friedgen's hire headed land acquisitions for Toll Brothers builders in Cary, N.C. Verrille is someone Friedgen has long respected for his business acumen.

Verille told Friedgen in 2000 that he needed to run the Maryland football program "like a business because it's really a $4 million-$5 million business. It's one-fourth of this entire athletic program, and there are more than 25 teams here," he said.

Years ago, Verille and Friedgen were best buddies and double-dated. Verille married his high school sweetheart, Joyce. The Verilles attend most Terps games, home and away, and remain close with Ralph and Gloria. Verille was a member of the boyhood gang the "Phi Beta Caginos." One of Verille's former companies, Brentwood Homes, a high-end development company, he named after his old neighborhood.

Verille had an offer from Friedgen to be his first operations director at Maryland but Friedgen "couldn't afford him," he joked.

Verille, before he got into the home building business, spent 20 years in marketing research for Fortune 500 companies. So the two sat down and developed a five-year plan for Friedgen, who was a neophyte with most business matters.

Verille wanted Friedgen to have the plan to communicate with the AD and everyone on campus to be sure they were all pulling in the right direction. And their goals clear.

They drew up a plan, 36 pages, and sent a copy to both President C.D. Mote and athletic director Yow to "always be on the same map, and where we are going to go, so they understand where we are going to go," Verille said.

The two high school chums spent a long weekend in 2001 at Friedgen's lake house hammering it out. It was about wins and losses, graduation rates, facilities, season ticket sales, etc., and proved prophetic in many ways.

Verille drafted the plan and Friedgen was "blown away" and wanted to take a copy to Yow immediately.

Yow liked it and wanted to talk to Verille more. The two spoke for more than an hour and Yow wanted to hear more. So Verille flew to town and spent a day going over the plan while Yow provided information like the Terps marketing budgets.

Yow approved it.

The plan was exhaustive in not only outlining what Friedgen expected to do at College Park, from wins and losses, budgets, facilities, recruiting and even handling the media, but also the histrionics of why Maryland hadn't won before. That included an apathetic fan base, poor talent levels and low expectations. It also analyzed the rest of the ACC and where Maryland fell among conference schools. It included threats to possible success.

The two men sugar-coated nothing.

Titled "University of Maryland Football Program Five Year Strategic Plan, September 1, 2001 to August 31, 2006," Friedgen and Verille covered it all.

Wrote Friedgen in his introduction:

"As background, the University of Maryland Football Program began a new era on Nov. 29, 2000 when I was named Head Football Coach. While I thoroughly enjoyed my tenure as Offensive Coordinator at Georgia Tech, this opportunity not only provides me with my first chance to be a head coach, it enables me to return to my alma mater where I hope to lead in returning the football program to national prominence in partnership with the University.

"While many have been kind enough to credit me for much of the offensive success the various teams I have been associated with during my 32-year coaching career have enjoyed, I personally credit the long hours of intensive game preparation as the most important reason for this success. Given my belief that game planning and adequate preparation are important ingredients in a successful football program, I strongly felt that a well-conceived, well-written strategic plan to guide the operation of the Maryland Football Program over the next five years was an absolute necessity in order for the program to improve significantly."

The "Mission Statement" was just as ambitious:

"The University of Maryland Football Program strives to be considered as one of the top football programs in the country. This will be achieved through the success of its players on the field, in the classroom and in our society after graduation."

The plan included 10 sections from Current Assessment of Maryland Football Program, Strengths and Weaknesses; Threats To Success; Action Plans; Five-Year Goals and Objectives; and Current Environment in The ACC.

Friedgen touched on salient points starting with recruiting and he wrote:

''We will especially concentrate on those successful high school programs in Maryland and D.C. which regularly produce Division I talent, many of which, until now, joined major college programs outside the state."

Friedgen targeted a "4-5 hour drive to our campus" as the primary recruiting area with "Maryland, the District of Columbia, Delaware, Pennsylvania, New Jersey, New York, Connecticut, Virginia, West Virginia, Ohio and North Carolina" as primary states, while "we will do supplemental recruiting in other areas for high school football such as Florida, Georgia, South Carolina and Texas.

"As the leading Division I football program in Maryland and D.C., a special goal of the program will be to secure all of the top recruits from this area. Simply stated, the best high school football players in Maryland and D.C. should play for the University of Maryland."

Of the student body, which was not supporting football at the time, he wrote:

"It is our belief that an important aspect of our ability to succeed as a football program, namely the intense involvement at home games of a significant percentage of our student body, has been missing at Maryland for quite some time now."

Of the alumni base, which he also viewed as apathetic, he wrote:

"Similarly, we believe that the football program has not received an acceptable level of support from university alumni for many years. With over 150,000 Maryland Alumni living within an hour's drive of the campus, our home games should always be sold out."

Of the program's boosters he wrote:

"At the present time, it is believed that Maryland ranks seventh out of the nine members in the ACC in terms of scholarship fund raising. We believe that one of our ACC opponents, Clemson, has 52,000 members in its booster organization. By comparison, the Terrapin Club has only 5,200 members. This level of support is simply not acceptable if we are to achieve the goals and objectives of this strategic plan."

On the media, which he has always been open and accommodating with, he wrote:

"We understand that a high percentage of the impressions that the public and our target markets receive concerning our program are a direct result of the media coverage that our program receives. We will work hard to develop an excellent relationship with media representatives so that the message that they convey to their readers, listeners, and viewers presents the football program in a fair and balanced way."

On the Current Environment In The ACC, Friedgen put it bluntly as well, highlighting Maryland's 35 percent overall winning percentage, and lowly 28 percent in the league, with only Duke and Wake Forest, historic cellar-dwellers, as teams the Terps finished above in conference standings more than once.

"The Atlantic Coast Conference assumed its present membership and size in 1992 when Florida State became the ninth member of the conference. For analytical purposes, using the 1992 season as a starting point, the performance of the University of Maryland football program since the conference assumed its present configuration can be termed mediocre at best."

Friedgen, based on the last few years, was slightly off on one assessment when he wrote: "Given the information that is known at this time, there is no reason to believe that Florida State will relinquish its stronghold on the conference in the near term. Further, it is believed unlikely that Wake Forest or Duke will significantly improve their conference standing in the near future. Thus, it would appear that Maryland will be competing with Virginia, North Carolina, Clemson, Georgia Tech and North Carolina State over the next several years to determine which two teams will join Florida State at the top echelon in the conference."

Florida State, which was 70-2 in conference play since 1992, had shown no signs of buckling at the time. Friedgen was candid when he said that the Seminoles were at an advantage by "the simple fact that its academic requirements to admit a gifted student athlete tend to be somewhat less stringent than many of the other universities in the conference. Thus, we would not expect FSU to, in effect, come back to the rest of the field. Rather, other members of the ACC face the challenge of improving their programs to a point where they can be competitive with Florida State."

Friedgen said that only in the instance coach Bobby Bowden retired "could other conference members have a small window of visibility to gain ground on FSU, but this will probably not last for an extended period."

In the Current Assessment Of The Maryland Football Program section, Friedgen pointed out as "strengths" the great support he had already received from Mote and

Yow, and said, "The support received thus far is definitely considered to be one of the strengths of the program."

He also praised "a number of prominent Maryland boosters and friends, who have risen to the occasion to support Coach Friedgen and their efforts through such organizations as the Terrapin Club and the Maryland Gridiron Network," but he reminded everyone that they still had a long way to go.

Other positives included the staff Friedgen was able to assemble; the work ethic the players showed in winter workouts; early media interest; and good student support "evidenced by the standing ovation the student body gave Coach Friedgen when he was first introduced at a men's basketball game in Cole Field House; a definite strength of the new program is the relationship which has begun to develop with the student body."

The strategic plan also pointed to a new marketing campaign for the upcoming season, and soon the Terps would have "Fridge Fever – It's Red Hot," as a slogan the department named after the new coach.

In terms of threats to the program, Friedgen and Verille pointed to several, led by a "losing attitude that has been associated with the program since 1985. Unfortunately, losing begets losing and this attitude must change before the program can begin to recover. Losing, to some degree, has been accepted in the recent past. This weakness cannot and will not be tolerated any longer."

Friedgen pointed to how the losing cycle brought recruiting down, which he said "is not considered a strength at the present time."

As far as the current "talent level," Friedgen wrote:

"Given Maryland's won-loss record since 1992, it is fair to say that our talent level has not been on par with the upper echelon ACC teams. While we are pleased that the new recruiting class is believed to have improved the overall talent level of our team, realistically it will take several successful recruiting classes to bring our roster up to a highly competitive level within the conference."

Friedgen cited poor attendance (an average of 34,129 in six home games in 2000, which was 71 percent of capacity), while more disappointing was the final three game average of 26,552, just 55 percent of capacity at 48,055 seat Byrd Stadium. Friedgen pointed to the fateful last home game versus Georgia Tech, for whom he was serving as offensive coordinator at the time, as rock bottom:

"Particularly discouraging was the final home game of the season against Georgia Tech, when a winning season and possible bowl invitation was at stake, and a season low of 24,701 people attended the game. Playing before a half-empty stadium is certainly a de-motivator for players. In addition, the lost revenue due to poor attendance has a substantial negative impact on the athletic program in general and football in particular."

They were just as honest about the state of facilities at Maryland.

"While it is recognized that the University has invested approximately $25 million since 1993 in Byrd Stadium, the Gossett Football Team House and other facilities for the football program, an honest assessment of these facilities is that they are no longer state-of-the-art, nor competitive with those offered by the majority of other ACC universities."

Friedgen pointed out that even league bottom-dwellers Wake Forest and Duke, in addition to N.C. State, completed or started expansion projects. He rated Maryland's football facilities third-to-last in the ACC, leading only Wake Forest and Duke (before its planned construction project). Friedgen added North Carolina likely had the "best football complex in the conference," and that "it has been estimated that state-of-the-art facilities could mean successfully recruiting a minimum of 3-4 top athletes per recruiting class for a university. Given this, Maryland is currently at a disadvantage in the ACC."

Friedgen called for expansion and modernization of the team house to include a dining room and larger meeting rooms, more outdoor practice fields, an indoor practice facility and other items, nearly all of which he later achieved.

"These improvements will do much for our recruiting efforts and ability to reach our goals and objectives. Perhaps just as important, it will be tangible evidence of the fact that Maryland Football is back. Without these improvements, the Maryland Football Program will continue to have difficulty recruiting quality athletes away from other ACC universities which have far better facilities to offer."

Friedgen asked for other items for his players, be it continued provisions for priority class registration, early afternoon class times, striking the maximum number of players that could be in a same classroom (15 at a time), to on-campus housing for academic exemptions, players who previously had to live off-campus. All were things Yow was already doing.

In addition to other items (including suggesting a non-conference match-up with Penn State), Friedgen said the Terps must make steady improvement from year-to-year as they ascend the ACC:

"Maryland's task over the next five years seems to be clear. We must first move from the lower third of the conference, hopefully in the first year of this plan. During the middle years of the plan we need to do well in the second tier of the conference. This will hopefully put us in a position to join the first tier by the end of this five-year plan. Steady improvement year-to-year is a reasonable goal to expect to achieve."

Finally, and perhaps of most interest when looking back, were the wins and losses that Friedgen projected for his first five years. Friedgen cited Overall Record, ACC Record, ACC Standings, National Ranking, Bowl Game Appearances and Graduation Rate as his six most important categories.

The season records he projected were:

2001 – 6-5, 4-4 (ACC); 5th place finish ACC; not ranked; No. 5 ACC Bowl; 53% graduation rate

2002 – 7-6, 4-4 (ACC); 5th place finish; not ranked; ACC No. 5 Bowl; 60% graduation rate

2003 – 7-4, 5-3 (ACC); 4th place finish; Top 25; ACC No. 4 Bowl; 65% graduation rate
2004 – 8-3, 6-2 (ACC); 3rd place finish; Top 20; ACC No. 3 Bowl; 72% graduation rate
2005 – 8-3 6-2 (ACC) 3rd place finish; Top 20; ACC No. 3 Bowl; 75% graduation rate

Friedgen also went into great detail about statistical goals, covering everything from points to sacks to turnover margin to punting average.

He drew up a 25-person employee chart reflecting the organization's hierarchy starting with Mote down to his secretarial staff.

He also projected, in terms of finances, the Terps to improve from a 2001 football budget expense of $7.4 million to $8.1 million by 2005-06; revenues from $7.1 million to $12.1 million; expense-to-revenue-ratio from 1 to 0.96 to 1 to 1.50; average paid attendance from 22,000 to 40,000; and the average ticket price (blended) from $18.00 to $29.75.

Some of the other goals are still a work in progress.

Friedgen left little to chance and, in closing, said:

"In developing this five-year strategic plan to guide the Maryland Football Program, we have attempted to honestly assess the state of the current program and outline what we believe to be fair, reasonable and attainable goals over the next five years. We believe that if the program receives the support it needs as outlined in this document, we will have an excellent chance of producing the desired results."

Respectfully submitted,
Ralph H. Friedgen
Head Football Coach
University of Maryland
September 1, 2001

Friedgen blew it early, his five-year plan out the window in his first year. Instead of going 6-5, the Terps streaked to the BCS Orange Bowl with a 10-2 record. He always had confidence but few, even him, could anticipate the magical run the Terps enjoyed during his rookie campaign, which included national Coach of the Year honors for the former career assistant.

As a backdrop, there were several ACC coaching changes that year including Al Groh arriving at Virginia and John Bunting at UNC, the program many thought had the most talent heading into the 2001 campaign. But Friedgen assembled his staff the fastest, another factor some point towards for his early success. He got his coaches settled in apartments or homes and, by mid-December when the staff came off the road from recruiting, it worked long days on the new playbook and was ready for spring camp.

The Terps beat North Carolina in the opener, a team that later went on to upset FSU that season. Friedgen was there, front and center, leading the upheaval.

His master plan involved everything from season ticket sales, Terrapin Club contributions, attendance, graduation rates, expansion at Byrd Stadium, salary structure, wins and losses, and where he hoped to be in five years. He had 32 years pent up inside of him, and was ready to burst getting it up and going.

At the time, Friedgen did not share with the players his five-year plan or the stated goal of 6-5. The players' goal was to qualify for a bowl. Any bowl.

That was seemingly Friedgen's private goal as well. The players wrote their goal on a piece of paper and gave it to him before the season started.

Verille had more faith in his longtime friend and predicted, to himself and later to Friedgen, a 7-4 record.

The season ticket sales total was just 10,000 the year before Friedgen arrived, and he penciled in a goal of 15,000 in his plan while Yow said they would get 13,000. Yow nailed it, the Terps improving to 13,000 then 21,000 followed by 28,000, 30,000 and 32,000 in the first five years.

Verille suggested they go back and revise the five-year plan not only because of what was accomplished in the first year, but because of the rush of stadium expansion across the ACC that soon got underway.

Friedgen, ever on point, later complained of season ticket sales:

"I thought alone I would sell 5,000 myself. I didn't realize how apathetic we were."

But in the areas that they were on schedule after five years, such as selling out the season, which they did in 2005 despite coming off a losing mark, and graduating 79 percent of the players by his fifth year, a tremendous figure above the normal male student population on campus, he was ahead of schedule.

But it may never have happened had Friedgen not had some early advocates. Never one to push the envelope for jobs or circulate his resume, one colleague that made sure Friedgen someday got a head job was George O'Leary, his former recruiting adversary, colleague, good friend and later boss at Georgia Tech, who helped propel Friedgen into the Maryland job.

Friedgen never stumped much to be a head coach. He didn't have a great image, real or perceived, and wasn't seen as a warm personality. At least not in the public eye, which didn't know much about him in the first place.

And, for the most part, he was content, according to many close to him, running things as a respected coordinator and "co-coach" in Atlanta alongside O'Leary. He didn't get the break his pal Beamer did, who slowly built a powerhouse at Blacksburg over the decades.

But Friedgen had great football intellect. He was an excellent teacher, a hard worker, he could communicate with his direct approach, and buried beneath the tough veneer, he had strong "people skills." He would just show them in different ways, sometimes more "traditional ways," going back to his roots.

With the exception of an occasional plug from ESPN, his name was not circulating in head coaching circles.

But Friedgen wowed members of the search committee at Georgia Tech with his presentation when the school went looking for a head coach. But they had Bill Lewis already penciled in before things started.

Going back to when Ross left Maryland in 1986, the staff got together and backed Friedgen for the head job, he said. But Penn State Coach Joe Paterno knew Krivak, interviewing him once for a job, and gave him a strong recommendation for the Maryland job.

Krivak, the Terps' quarterback coach, was hired. That was Friedgen's first miss at the head job, though he did not make a huge push for it.

O'Leary always involved Friedgen "in the problems of a head coach, unlike Ross, who was more secretive about internal and sensitive team issues," Friedgen said.

Friedgen moved to Georgia Tech where they won a National Championship in 1990 thanks, in part, to his prolific offense, and he later went the pro route to the San Diego Chargers. Friedgen coached quarterback Joe Hamilton to a runner-up finish in the Heisman Trophy race and later George Godsey, on paper not much of a talent, to all-ACC honors.

Still, Friedgen didn't get a call and didn't venture out much looking for a head job.

When Ross left for San Diego, O'Leary, Friedgen and East Carolina's Bill Lewis were finalists for the Georgia Tech head job. But Tech had already decided on Lewis, who was supposed to be on the rise in the profession. Friedgen put together a strong presentation, covering everything from fund raising to staff, but it was seemingly moot.

Gloria Friedgen recalled getting a phone call from a friend on the athletics board who told her that Georgia Tech athletic director Homer Rice had already decided on Lewis despite the fact Friedgen impressed the committee. This put Friedgen at an interesting crossroads.

The friend on the council was a successful businessman and alumnus who was so impressed with Friedgen that he offered him a job, on the spot, with his metals company that was opening a new office in Kentucky. He wanted Friedgen to run it.

For a month Friedgen was in limbo about whether he would go into private business or continue coaching.

Gloria said this was the first time she felt her husband did not get a job "because of image issues."

Friedgen believed he was ready as being a coordinator he was a "mini head coach," he said. While he had experienced just about everything a coach would, from organization to teaching to motivating to recruiting. Some say concerns for his health held some people back from attempting to hire him.

"Lewis was the 'coach du-jour.' He looked good on TV. And we had the 'John Madden look,'" Gloria said. "And I do believe, and no one is going to come out and say it, but it was appearance. That perception denied him opportunity."

The Friedgens took inventory one night at their Marietta, Ga., home. How blessed they were with their children, their life at Georgia Tech, and how financially stable they were, including their new lake home, which was on the way.

"As rich as we were in many ways it's the one thing that we couldn't accomplish. It cut like a knife," Gloria said.

When Maryland hired Mark Duffner in 1992, Friedgen never got a call.

The next time around, in 1997, when Ron Vanderlinden was hired, Friedgen was contacted and sent a FedEx package of information.

But before that happened, Northwestern defensive coordinator Vanderlinden, one of the hottest head coach prospects in the country, got the nod. Friedgen was left in the cold again at his alma mater. Friedgen had also been mentioned for the South Carolina job, a job Lou Holtz got.

Finally, when Vanderlinden was let go in 2000, Friedgen got a call from the athletic director at Maryland. This time around, though, he had his doubts.

O'Leary, all the while, was trying to prop his friend up for jobs. He'd send Friedgen to Heisman Trophy and other award banquets to get his name and face out to the media and among head coaches. O'Leary called Yow and others that he knew on the selection committee at Maryland and spoke highly of his colleague.

O'Leary said that Friedgen, over the years, may have been caught in the "appearance or perception game, not his football substance as it should have been."

"When the Maryland job opened up I went out of my way to make sure . . . he was a natural. He was an alumnus of the school and we were successful at Georgia Tech," O'Leary said. "That was a natural hire."

Friedgen got the call from Yow over Thanksgiving weekend as he prepared for the annual Georgia Tech-Georgia game. His cousin was in the room at the time.

"The first call and she says, 'I would like to talk to you about the head coaching position at Maryland.' And he says, 'I gotta play Georgia on Saturday. I don't want to talk to anybody until after the Georgia game. If you want to talk let's do it after the game,' " Stoddard recalled.

The game was at Georgia and Stoddard rode the team bus as he often did. By the time they got home, Yow had called and left a message, on Saturday night, to meet at the Atlanta airport on Sunday morning.

Yow also wanted the Friedgens – including Gloria – to come to town to meet the search committee, Friedgen said. The Friedgens didn't want to call a babysitter for fear of causing alarm, or news, so Stoddard and his wife babysat their daughters for three days.

"And Tuesday night he walked in with a good contract," Stoddard said. "We sat there from about 10 [p.m.] until 4 a.m. reading the contract. He was like a kid at Christmas."

Stoddard played the role of "devil's advocate," he said, pointing out that the first two times Maryland did not interview him. And asking his cousin, "do you really want to go work for a woman?"

"I was firing shot, shooting shots," Stoddard said.

Friedgen said what impressed him most was that Yow seemed absolutely determined to have a good football program, and that she would provide for the best staff possible.

Stoddard said Friedgen told him:

"This is the perfect time. They have been down twice. Down for a while. This would be the perfect time to go."

"And he was right," Stoddard said.

Later, showing his loyalty, Friedgen offered Stoddard a quality control job on his staff. Stoddard, who had recently retired to McCormick, S.C., with his wife, Ray, called it a "dream job" but respectfully declined.

Later he joked:

"I told my wife I made a prediction. The funny part about it is this is the job I have always wanted, where I always wanted, and I know Ralph is going to be a winner. I know it is going to be fun to be part of it. However, on the negative side of it, I have seen him be very upset with people that work for him and I didn't want to be in that situation."

Initially, Friedgen had reservations, based on past experiences, about the Maryland job.

Gloria remembered receiving a telephone call from the late Mark Asher of the *Washington Post*. He asked if she was aware O'Leary gave Maryland permission to talk to her husband about the job, and that there were "eight or nine candidates for the job."

"I told him, 'Ralph leaves at 5 a.m. in the morning and by the time he gets home I am sound asleep," Gloria said. "So how would I know anything?"

When she and her husband finally spoke they agreed that they were not interested. That was on Monday. Friedgen had consulted his agent, Jack Reale, as well as headhunter Bill Carr, who was also working for Yow.

But a persistent Yow called Friedgen and said, "We're very interested in you."

Friedgen said he told her, "See me after the Georgia game."

They spoke on the phone for over an hour.

Friedgen was armed with a lifetime of coaching knowledge. He had an "A," "B" and "C" list of potential staff hires all based on what kind of budget Yow could afford. Later in their negotiations she slid him a piece of paper with a dollar figure that suggested the "A" group.

Friedgen was getting excited now.

There were many subplots to the Friedgen hire, including Ross, who called with a recommendation at the time the Terps hired Vanderlinden. But some thought he was calling Maryland for the job himself, which news of leaked out.

Before, in the previous hire, Ross called Friedgen to tell him that his conversation went well with Yow and that "he believed Friedgen had a very good shot at it."

The Chargers had lost the day before, on Sunday night to New England, and Friedgen had to pull an all-nighter preparing for Monday's phone interview. But he got a call that night from an insider who said forget about it, Yow had decided to hire Vanderlinden. So that was in the back of his mind when he approached the job again in 2000. "I was really upset. We had just come off the Super Bowl and I felt that I was more than ready for the job. And it was my alma mater," Friedgen said.

Friedgen didn't see himself in pro football for the long-term, disliking "the phoniness" at the pro level, he said. He considered the Terps job a perfect fit. He helped win a National Championship at Georgia Tech, and as a first-time coordinator in the NFL he helped take an underdog in the preseason to a Super Bowl.

O'Leary called Friedgen and told him, "Tell us what you want to come back [to Georgia Tech]."

Friedgen accepted but he was peeved about how the Maryland deal went down. He told O'Leary, "Sure, but with one caveat."

"One of the ones is I get to name the score against Maryland," Friedgen told his new boss.

O'Leary and Friedgen jockeyed back and forth when Georgia Tech and Maryland met the following year and Friedgen tried to run up the score. O'Leary tried to block him from doing so. It was the game Vanderlinden came out and went over his two-deep on the field before a stunned Friedgen, obviously knowing something was up.

"Maryland was the furthest thing from my mind. I used to get pumped up to play Maryland. I loved to beat their ass," Friedgen said.

Bunk Carter was the groundskeeper when Friedgen played at Maryland and he was there when he returned for the game in 2000.

"I remember getting off the bus and Bunk said, 'Take it easy on us today, Ralph.' I said to Bunk, 'Not today. I am going to beat up on them.' "

Tech hung 30 points on Maryland by halftime before O'Leary insisted Friedgen call off the dogs in the 35-22 rout. There were about 10,000 fans in the stands by game's end. Then the surreal happened.

"I was walking off the field singing the fight song. The Maryland fight song. That's my alma mater. I just kicked their butt," Friedgen recalled.

Friedgen admits that he was never a "guy looking for the next job," which he said "you probably have to have to get a head job." He said he was intent on doing the best job he could at his present post, wherever that was, and "that everything would take care of itself."

Friedgen says now, when looking back, that he believes Ross "could have done more" to help him with a job when he left Maryland in 1986, and later at Georgia Tech. Friedgen admits he was "very upset over that."

In the end, Friedgen knows that if he was working the phone lines, going out in public and meeting people, politicking more, he may have advanced himself faster.

Friedgen said that when the North Carolina job opened the same year as he was hired, the job John Bunting got was the one he coveted the most at the time. But Friedgen never got a call. Homer Rice called John Swofford, then athletics director at UNC, but to no avail. Friedgen even called Swofford, who went on to become commissioner of the ACC:

"I think that woman up there hates me. She must have something on me. She had a chance to hire me and she didn't," Friedgen theorized.

Swofford told Friedgen that the league "needed a winner at Maryland" for television and the northern markets. That year Swofford asked him if he had interest in the Wake Forest or Virginia jobs. None were open at the time but soon they would be, with Al Groh and Jim Grobe coming on board. Still, Friedgen coveted the UNC job but Swofford discouraged that. All four opened up and Friedgen said, "Swofford knew something then."

Friedgen thought UNC was the best situation, yet he had a soft spot for his alma mater. N.C. State was another job the year before, but athletic director Les Robinson, he said, told him that he was concerned with how Friedgen would "handle the press," one of the reasons that may have held him back. Years later Friedgen said he learned that was not the reason. Chuck Amato got the job because he helped win a national championship at Florida State and he was an alumnus, Friedgen said.

Friedgen had no problem with that, but still he hurt over not getting the job. Friedgen knew Robinson from their Citadel days, while many believed Friedgen was more qualified on paper than Amato, who was more of a recruiter and a position coach.

Amato was let go after the 2006 season, and after Friedgen dominated him in the Terps-Wolfpack series.

Some close to Friedgen didn't think he would go after a head job after the N.C. State miss.

All told, Friedgen formally interviewed for three jobs: Georgia Tech, N.C. State and Maryland.

O ne of the more compelling stories that came out of Ralph Friedgen's interview with Debbie Yow, when he got an interview that meant something, came just after she offered him the job. He turned the tables, asking her: "I want to know why you haven't been winning here for 18 years. Really, since I left?" he said.

Yow saw Friedgen's face light up when she passed him the piece of paper indicating that the money would be there to get his top staff.

"I had determined if we were going to make the change, we were going to do it right," Yow said. "When he looked at the numbers that were written on the piece of paper he said, 'I guess we are going to be hiring the 'A' group.' And when he said that I knew we had a real possibility that this might work out because it seemed encouraging to him that Maryland was willing to make that level of commitment for his staff."

Friedgen's coordinators, for instance, hit the ground running at what then was a high salary, close to $250,000.

Yow went on for 45 minutes explaining about debt, budgets and support for football. Friedgen said his second question to her was "What does this football program mean to you?"

She told him, "Well, if you can fill Byrd Stadium we'll net $4 million right off the top. We can pay the debt off. The next hire I have is the most important hire for me as an AD."

The two discussed Friedgen's philosophy, how he believed in the true 'student-athlete,' and how football should be fun and a part of their education.

"All the things I believe in," he said.

Yow asked Friedgen who he would hire. He responded that he had a three-deep.

Yow showed Friedgen his proposed salary and, given he now knew something about budgets, was impressed with how much money Yow was dedicated to spending on his staff.

Yow threw everything she could at Friedgen, including different scenarios and how he would react and handle each if he was the coach, and all before he got to the points he wanted to make. Friedgen had a presentation ready but before he got into his spiel "she put her hand on my knee, tapping it, and said, 'You belong at Maryland. We now have what we need to be successful.' "

When Yow first called Friedgen to express interest he recalled telling her, "I am interested but don't jack me around. I'm tired of that.

"I mean, I don't know the lady. If this is just something you are doing to appease the alumni I'm not interested. I can't do this anymore. She said, 'We are very interested. I want to interview you as soon as possible,' " Friedgen said.

Yow targeted Friedgen as her top candidate, and this time around she had more resources to add a top shelf staff.

Yow had followed Friedgen at Georgia Tech, especially his development of quarterbacks, listened to some of his television interviews over the years and loved his candor, which came across clearly. And the fact he had great family support was a plus in her book, too.

Yow also had a greater comfort level, having been on campus for another five years, seeing the department's financial picture turn around on her watch.

Yow personally took over the process from the headhunter, setting up a Sunday meeting at the Atlanta airport Marriott where they met in a suite. Bill Carr called Friedgen that morning and asked if there was anything he could help him with for the interview. The interview went for four hours and before he knew it Friedgen, with Yow running up against her flight, was driving her to the airport. She loved his vision for the program he detailed in their meeting.

"I didn't know her. Had never met the lady before. Didn't know if I would like or dislike her. But we hit it off pretty good. It went better than I thought it would. When I went back home to see Gloria I was pretty pumped," Friedgen said.

Yow insisted that Friedgen travel to College Park the next morning with his wife. But on the way Friedgen still had reservations. On the flight he weighed the pros of where he was, making $280,000 as coordinator at Georgia Tech and building a dream house outside of Atlanta, where he would someday retire.

"If I don't think we are going to win, I'm not going to take it. You know how I am when I lose," he told Gloria.

After the two talked salary and agreed on his base of $700,000 plus bonus money, things moved along despite the fact Friedgen left his notes at home. A rare miscue for a remarkably organized man.

Associate AD Michael Lipitz picked Friedgen up at the airport and gave him a tour of the football team house, which Friedgen wasn't overly impressed with. They ate at the Inn & Conference Center on campus and Friedgen went to his room, which was strategically full of Terps gear. Nice touch, he thought.

The next morning "was like an interrogation," he said.

Friedgen met with Mote. Friedgen always believed that the Terps had an inferiority complex, but he never did. Not once, he said.

"It pissed me off before and even now when we go to places like Virginia. It pisses me off. Well, Mote begins his spiel about wanting to be the best in academics. Athletics. The arts. I'm thinking here's a son-of-a-gun that thinks like me. I can work with this guy."

Friedgen said he expected the president to be all about academics. But he was soon energized by Mote's philosophy. They hit it off immediately, another good sign for Yow. In all, six candidates were contacted but the process moved swiftly because Friedgen was her top target from the start.

Then Friedgen met with the football support staff, strength and conditioning coach Dwight Galt, and a panel of players, "who told me they weren't getting enough to eat. It turned into a bitch and moan session," Friedgen said.

Friedgen showed some of what was to come when he met with Galt, who was asked by Lipitz to meet with Friedgen for, what he thought, was on behalf of the search committee. Instead, Friedgen, who had already been offered and accepted the job, turned the tables and began interviewing Galt.

The eight-year head strength and conditioning coach had been an intern on the staff when Friedgen was an assistant coach at Maryland under Bobby Ross.

"But I don't think he knew I existed," said Galt.

The two met for almost two hours at the Inn & Conference Center.

"He started asking me my philosophy. I was thinking after the first 15 minutes maybe I should be asking him stuff," Galt said. "He never really came out and told me he had accepted the job, he just came out and said, 'Well, I'll tell you what. I am going to give you six months to see what you can do. If you get the job done, I keep you. If you don't you are out.' "

Galt, a Maryland graduate who has worked on campus for 22 years and is one of the few remaining links to the past, said he appreciated the candid meeting. He got a full dose of Friedgen from the start.

"I really respected his honesty and bluntness, and I felt like he told it like it was. I knew where he was coming from. And I knew I was going to keep my job, at least for six months. It ended a lot weirder than I expected it to, though."

Team stalwarts Dennard Wilson, E.J. Henderson, Todd Wike and Aaron Thompson were on the players' panel to meet the incoming coach.

"It was cocky confidence," Wilson recalled, who was a freshman yet was emerging as a team leader. "It wasn't too arrogant. I mean, he said, 'I'm gonna come in here and we're gonna win. We aren't just going to be 5-6 or something like that.' It was point-blank. He was one of those guys, the way he came off, this guy knows business. We took him seriously right from the start, especially us older guys who had never won."

Friedgen heard the kinds of things he wanted from the linebacker Thompson. The Baltimore native and resident team "tough guy" asked, "So what are you going to do to make us win?"

"Of the whole day, that was probably the toughest question to answer," Friedgen said. Then came a classic Friedgen response:

"And I said to him, 'When we play our first game you are going to be bigger, stronger and faster than you have ever been in your life because you are going to work. The second thing is I am going to teach you how not to lose. I'm gonna teach you how not to beat your-self, turn the ball over, and then what's gonna happen is you are going to gain confidence. You are going to beat a few of the people because they beat themselves. And then you are gonna start thinking you are pretty good and then we are going to be on our way.'"

Friedgen couldn't have scripted it better than he did in the first meeting, predict-ing exactly what would happen. Thompson would go on to be a favorite of Friedgen's for speaking up, not to mention his play in helping lead the Terps to the Orange Bowl in his first season. Even Friedgen called it a "Cinderella season."

Friedgen's knowledge of the game, his speed in implementing his plan, and his way of motivating the players took off from the start.

"I took it all in because he was a breath of fresh air and he was the man. And to me, someone who wanted to someday be a coach? Wow!" Wilson said.

But Friedgen still had to get through the search committee, a panel he knew a few members of including Dr. Jerry Wrenn, one of his teachers while he was a student at College Park.

One committee member asked Friedgen if he was an "offensive genius," as his reputation preceded him. Friedgen kept it light by joking, "Well, I got Dr. Wrenn here. He could tell you I am no genius."

The meeting was light but it went over well. Next up was Dr. Linda Clements, from admissions, who Friedgen also knew from before.

Friedgen was seemingly the perfect come-back from the telegenic but unsuccessful

Vanderlinden, who didn't like confrontation and had a hard time reaching his players.

But Friedgen first told Yow, "First of all, there are some things you need to know about me."

He said that if she hired him that he would run the show, including everyone he hires and fires. He said he would consult her but that all decisions were his.

The next thing Friedgen said he told Yow was, "Don't ever lie to me. You lie to me I'm gone,' " he said.

"Gloria was like, 'You're messing it up again,' " Friedgen said.

Friedgen left the meeting feeling good about things, with Liptiz taking him and his wife to the airport.

Friedgen's loyalty came through at the next step. Maryland wanted to release the news locally but Friedgen insisted he first return to Atlanta to tell his players at Georgia Tech. Yow conceded the point. Friedgen stayed up much of the night with his cousin Stoddard, and his wife, and Yow called at 6 a.m. to see if he would accept.

At about 4 a.m., Friedgen decided that he would. He was up all night but still had to catch a 1 p.m. flight back to Maryland to accept publicly at a news conference at the student union.

Friedgen got to tell his quarterback, Godsey, the news first.

At his Maryland presser, Friedgen promised to be successful and said he would "not let anyone down. I waited too long and hard for this. I knew I was prepared. I knew I was ready. I just wanted a chance, you know."

"Then when we won 10 games in the first year I was fulfilled," he said.

Georgia Tech was headed to the Peach Bowl. Friedgen was having dinner with his good friend, Harold Reynolds, of Reynolds Plantation in Georgia. At the restaurant, ESPN analysts were also eating.

ESPN approached Friedgen and asked him to come on its telecast. He declined. But Gloria convinced him that ESPN had been good to him over the years, especially Dr. Jerry Punch talking him up as a coach-in-waiting. Friedgen did a pre-game interview in a friend's box at the Georgia Dome, and television cameras caught him between the action.

Friedgen wanted to be there for his players because of loyalty, but O'Leary wasn't too pleased, saying it was unfair to new offensive coordinator Billy O'Brien, who Friedgen would later hire at Maryland.

Afterwards, he went to the team hotel to tell the players.

"It was hard. I get attached to the players. I really do," he said.

A year later, after Friedgen's breakout year and BCS bowl berth, Georgia Tech came calling, dangling its head job. But Friedgen said he stayed at Maryland because of his loyalty to his alma mater, and his trust in Yow.

There were compelling reasons to go back to Tech, including his new lake home, his daughters in school in Atlanta, a greater salary, and less headaches building a power, he said.

"That would have been a lot easier for me. They would have paid more and it would have been a lot easier. But I trusted her more than the guy down there [AD Dave Braine]. She has never lied to me to this day," Friedgen said.

Said Verille, who Friedgen consulted on every job search:

"He called me and he told me, 'I'm loyal. They gave me my shot and I just don't feel like I can just leave after a year.' Tampa Bay and Georgia Tech offered him a job."

Friedgen, warned by some that Yow was a demanding boss, said five years later: "She is the best athletic director I have ever worked for. She doesn't play golf. She's in the office in the morning when I am in. She's in at night when I am in. She actually works. All she does is work. You are the first athletic director that actually pulls a whole 'eight,' " Friedgen said. "She expects a lot of herself and others."

Yow learned to handle Friedgen's immediate demands. She responded when he wanted everything done "now."

"You're going light-years, light-speed," she said.

They have a strong rapport and he would reply:

"I only got just so many years left and I want to win a National Championship. Everything we do is designed towards that. You know what we got to do to get there."

There was a sense of urgency as Ralph Friedgen started, maybe making up for lost time, maybe realizing all the work that needed to be done at College Park.

His first defensive coordinator, Gary Blackney, could empathize as he waited 21 years as an assistant coach before getting his first head job at the age of 45. He tried for Dartmouth, among others, before landing the Bowling Green job.

"There was a sense of urgency, a sense of now because you don't know what's going to happen tomorrow. You better do it now, today, kind of a carpe diem type of thing. It might have been, 'This is my chance and I'm not going to screw it up,' " Blackney said.

Blackney said everyone fell in line quickly because Friedgen asked more of himself than his staff, which was a lot. As something of a co-coach and confidant, Friedgen gave Blackney autonomy to run the Maryland defense, a role he loved.

Yow went out of her way to accommodate everything Friedgen asked for including new practice fields, which the Board of Regents at first rejected. She borrowed money for the project as it was one of her promises to him.

Friedgen calls Yow "a very good friend and confidant," and said he relies on her advice for big decisions, especially when "dealing with the bureaucracy here," he said.

Yow re-negotiated his contract twice, the second time following the Gator Bowl win in 2003, which extended him through the 2012 season with an annual salary of about $1.8 million.

"We're an odd couple. She told me one time that we were joined at the hip and I told her that was not a pretty picture. She thinks I'm half nuts. But maybe I am good for her, too. She knows there is no pretense. I'm not here giving you a song and dance. Not playing mind games. What you see is what you get," Friedgen said.

The two keep each other on their toes.

At the Peach Bowl in 2002, in the exchange of gifts ceremony before the game between the Terps and the Tennessee Volunteers, the schools came together. Yow represented Maryland while a vice president from Tennessee was on hand for the Vols. He came to the podium with sheet music of the school fight song, "Rocky Top," and told Yow that they play it after every touchdown (the gifts can also be gags, which this was).

Yow responded by saying they "won't be needing it because if they play it after every touchdown, and since they weren't going to be scoring very often, I won't need to hear it," she said.

The crowd roared.

Everyone got a chuckle but afterwards, when Yow and Friedgen were celebrating with fans and boosters following the win, Friedgen told her, "You put a lot of pressure on me there. That could have turned out differently."

Yow responded:

"I had faith in you and the team. We only heard that 'Rocky Top' song one time. That was it. And that was only for a field goal."

The two consult each other on big decisions and even small ones. Yow had hired the NCAA Division I Coach of the Year in men's basketball, Charlie Spoonhour, at her previous post, Saint Louis. But Yow and Friedgen connect better. Yow said she is "more candid" with Friedgen.

"I think we have shared values," Yow said. "Our foundation is built on those shared work values. There's a tremendous degree of trust and we are able to speak candidly about many things, whether it is student-athletes and their academics or the social aspects of their lives or their family issues."

Yow got involved with football matters, and addresses the team on school, athletic and 'life' issues, usually a few times a year. She is on hand for most official visit weekends with recruits, at Friedgen's request, meeting top prospects and their parents. She even had "the sex talk" with the players as well as "the drugs talk."

The two are a solid one-two punch for the program, and the players know Yow holds no punches.

"I reinforce things. They need to understand they're not going to get sympathy from me. If you think he's tough on you and you are going to come to my office and I'm going to fold under the pressure, that's not going to happen," Yow tells the players.

It's obvious both she and Friedgen care about the players, but they both expect them to do the right thing.

Friedgen has an insatiable appetite and wants things done now, if not yesterday. And he can be head-strong, maybe part of his German descent. The two have candid conversations "about wants and needs," Yow said, but she has always come through, often putting other items on hold for football. By then, the Comcast Center had been completed for basketball and football got most of her attention.

R alph Friedgen said he will never forget his final game at Georgia Tech, which came against Maryland, when Ron Vanderlinden approached him during stretching and proceeded to go over his personnel.

Vanderlinden covered everything from the fact that he had "a talented running back, Bruce Perry, redshirting," to "quarterback problems," to the fact he had some "good, young linemen," Friedgen said.

Friedgen said what stood out to him was the team's linebackers, led by Henderson, Leon Joe, Leroy Ambush, Aaron Thompson and Mike Whaley.

Friedgen said he liked Vanderlinden, and that before their strange meeting he wrote Friedgen notes or letters about how highly Maryland people thought of him.

"He seemed like a very, very nice guy," Friedgen said. "But I didn't really know what the hell he was doing. He started telling me all about each player. Everybody laughed because all the other coaches were looking at us. He must have spoken to me about 10-15 minutes and I don't talk to many people before games.

"I really didn't realize he was under that much heat. I thought 5-6, and he'd been close. And she had hired him. I never thought she was interested in me or what. Even when she called I thought it was just to satisfy the alumni. But he must have known something."

Yow had seen that Vanderlinden had been a terrific recruiter, but that it was time for a change in the football staff.

Friedgen shook things up immediately after he was announced as Maryland's new coach. He commanded and got respect from the start, and the hungry players rallied around him. He may not have fit the "image," but he knew what he wanted and went about getting it at an alarming pace.

There was no time for grousing about the demanding new coach. The staff and players were just too busy. And he was super-charged.

"I remember when I got hired and [radio talk show host] John Thompson said 'Hallelujah, brother. They couldn't hire a black guy and then they hired a fat guy.' And I said, 'Right on.' I can laugh at myself and can go through that. I don't remember taking it that serious. I think more people worry about that than is necessary. But I do think people are discriminated against because of it," Friedgen said.

Said Verille, who makes it to most of Friedgen's games:

"I think everybody that knew him, and knew how hard he worked and how good he was with people, knew that if just somebody would give him a chance that he could do it.

"Football coaching is not a beauty contest. They looked at him and said, 'Well, he's not the image we want.' They never tell him that . . . but you can get some pretty handsome coaches that don't get you anywhere. He is sort of rough around the edges, but I think he is a regular guy and people really appreciate that."

Friedgen assembled a strong staff led by defensive coordinator Blackney, offensive coordinator Charlie Taaffe, one of the best teaching offensive line coaches (Tom Brattan) and two rising coaching stars and recruiters in Mike Locksley and James Franklin.

Blackney, who grew tired of the non-coaching responsibilities a head coach faced, hadn't been retired two weeks from Bowling Green when Friedgen reached out with a telephone call. He wanted to get back to teaching, not fund-raising and other non-football duties.

"The only plan I had at the time was to go to Cancun, clear my mind, and get a fresh start somewhere, sometime. I was not thinking about Maryland," Blackney said. "Lo and behold I got tapped for duty sooner than I thought."

Blackney said he knew Friedgen was a "great football coach" and that he had tremendous confidence in himself. He said he was confident enough to hire former head coaches like himself and Taaffe with no insecurities.

Blackney said Friedgen told him he "would lean on me, bounce things off me as a former head coach," Blackney said he never came to Friedgen with suggestions, only gave them if asked. That was a key in his first few years when Friedgen had to learn to be CEO, coach and "head bottle washer" for the program, always on the front lines fund-raising, promoting and everything else as he went about rebuilding the struggling program.

"The thing I told him is you can't be everything to everybody," Blackney said, though Friedgen certainly tried.

The two holdovers from the former staff, Locksley and Franklin, spent three weeks driving Friedgen around on local recruiting calls before he made the call on whether they would stay on the new staff. There were some tense moments, as Franklin recalled, so much so that he worried about making a wrong turn as they drove around the D.C. area. Friedgen barely said two words the whole time, Franklin said.

"I think he liked to see how you were going to handle stress," Franklin said. "I remember waiting and waiting for days to actually sit down with him and have a conversation. But that never happened."

Friedgen shook things up, even during the in-home visits with some 15 recruits that were on the bubble after committing to the former staff. When some of the recruits asked whether Franklin, their recruiter, would be retained. Friedgen told them, true to form, "I don't know yet."

It was Friedgen constantly testing those around him, and he was never scared to speak his mind. That kept everyone on their toes in the early stages. Both Franklin and Locksley were nervous about whether they would make the cut, and Locksley said it was "eerie" how quiet Friedgen was.

Finally, one afternoon at Boston Market over lunch, Friedgen, in a round-about way, told Locksley he would have a job at Maryland on the new staff. He quickly accepted.

Friedgen's first stop on the local recruiting trail, on his first day, was at local power Wilde Lake High School, just up the road in Columbia. There he saw star running back Mario Merrills, one of his first recruits. Coach Doug Duvall served as a graduate assistant with Friedgen at College Park years before.

Next up was Howard High School, also in Howard County, where Friedgen visited standout athlete and track star Gerrick McPhearson. The next day he was in Baltimore and saw emerging cornerback Domonique Foxworth of Western Tech, one of the building-block players who would become a Friedgen favorite.

Later, Friedgen stopped at DeMatha and took a commitment from offensive lineman Tim Donovan, who some on the staff had mixed feelings about. But Friedgen saw the importance of more offensive linemen and, just as important, more Stags. Assistant coach Buck Offutt was a longtime friend.

Maybe one of the biggest building-block recruits was Westlake High School's Randy Starks, the star defensive tackle and prized recruit that had narrowed his choices to Maryland and Penn State. The Terps had an uphill battle, not only having to woo one of the nation's most sought-after tackles, but having to battle PSU recruiter Larry Johnson, who was known in the area as the first black high school head coach in the county. Maryland had to battle pro-Penn State feelings in the high school.

But in the end Friedgen won Starks's mother over. She liked his disciplinarian, tough love ways, as she was constantly pushing her son, too.

Franklin and Locksley had a unique perspective as they coached many of the players Friedgen inherited. They told him they only had "solid" talent, but that they had "great kids on the team hungry to win," Franklin said. "And then here comes a guy with unbelievable vision, and not just in coaching, but for the entire program."

Friedgen credited Vanderlinden and his top recruiter, Locksley, for bringing in "character kids" and "tough kids," like Wilson, Madieu Williams, Latrez Harrison, Thompson and Marlon Moye-Moore, to name a few.

"Myself, I had good scholarships, but I still wasn't ranked in the top whatever. I felt like I could play with anybody," said Wilson, who may have summed up the personality of the first team.

The team had many players that wanted to play in a big college program, and many that wanted to win. But most didn't know how hard the work was going to be to get there. Only a few players, Rovell Hamilton and Kevin Bishop, both from

Florida, left in the first few months of the Friedgen era.

"I remember one of those kids saying, 'You're a 1960s coach and we're being brutalized.' I don't even think we got to know them yet," Friedgen said. "But we coach hard, there's no doubt about it. Either you were in or you were out. That's where the saying came from. I would tell the guys you can't have it both ways. You want to be a good football team, then . . . "

Friedgen had been at Maryland as a student and coach before, and he had been in the NFL and at another ACC school. So he had the experience and foresight to map everything out. Even down to the team's identity, making sure that 'Terps' in script, was on the helmets because "We are the only Terps. An 'M' could be Michigan, Maine, whatever. There is only one 'Terps,' " he said of his pride, not to mention his attention to detail.

"His vision for the university was what amazed me so much," Franklin said. "Ralph comes in and almost pushed everybody to the breaking point. That season was a very, very difficult year on the coaches, players, everybody. But they wanted to be successful so bad that those kids would run through a wall if they thought it was going to help them win. When we went out and had some success on the field, well it was just a brush fire and fed off everyone."

Some say it could have gone either way had the Terps not experienced the success they did because Friedgen was so tough and demanding. He could rip your head off in an instant, as both coaches and players experienced, and he set a harsh tone early. It was his way or no way.

But it paid off. After he won 31 games in the first three years, much of the chip was off his shoulder of "I told you so's," knowing all those years that he could pull it off despite some of the nay-sayers.

"My first impression was, 'Wow, this guy really wants to win and really has the formula for doing it,' " said offensive lineman Todd Wike, one of the pillars of Friedgen's early teams at College Park.

The players said Friedgen told them, especially the seniors, what they had been doing wrong and how that was going to change. And how they would go about doing it.

S tarting in the weight room, at the most base level, Ralph Friedgen was in-your-face from day one. He "amped" up the workouts in the bowels of the Gossett Football Team House. Literally.

At the time he arrived the players worked in groups of 20 with Galt in the off-season conditioning and lifting program. The staff focused mostly on individual work to be sure the players worked the right way. There was a lot of coach-player interaction.

"But he came in and said, 'You know what? You are doing a good job here but I want this place on fire. I want the music blaring. I want these kids screaming and yelling, getting after it. I want it a very, very intense situation here,' " Galt recalled.

Galt went from four smaller groups of 20 to two larger groups of 40. He put more volume and intensity in the program from a physiological standpoint, as well as got the music cranking. He got more aggressive with the players and "became more of a yeller and screamer from a positive standpoint in here. I mean, we got after it," Galt said.

Assistant coaches. Friedgen. Everyone was coming through the weight room to challenge and push the players. Peer pressure kicked in as expectations quickly grew. Galt, at first, thought it would be too much on the players physically and emotionally, and the program that he used through the 1990s was already pushing the limits. At least he thought.

"I was really hesitant. But he was the boss and that's what he wanted to do. And darned if the kids didn't get stronger than ever. They thrived on it. He was right. I was wrong," Galt said.

Later, Galt realized that Friedgen wanted it more like the mid-1980s when he served under Ross and the weight room was "wild," Galt said of a time the team was full of colorful personalities.

Friedgen pointed to a lack of discipline and accountability in the program and told the players they "need to start pulling their weight because before we had a lot of gray areas in the program," said guard Lamar Bryant.

Ralph Friedgen brought in technology to back it up, immediately upgrading the Terps' video system with a new Avid system to help bring the program out of the "dark ages," he said.

He told the players that he was a perfectionist, whether he was running the offense or making sure they were going to class or breakfast. Even how they watched film.

He told the team, specifically for the first game against North Carolina, that they would "out-tough and out-physical them" and that they would have to "really kill themselves during the summer to get ready," Wike recalled.

"That's how we are going to beat them," Wike said of Friedgen's pre-season speech. "We're gonna run the 'iso' [running] play. I don't care if we run it 10 times in a row, we're going to keep running it down their throats and wear them down."

"He broke it all down for us and showed us we are not too far away from it," Wike said. "He laid it all out."

The players were stunned when they came out in the opener and did just that in a lopsided win. Things snowballed from there. Every little thing Friedgen predicted came true. The players were willing to follow him no matter what the sacrifice.

Said safety Wilson:

"He was a brain. It was the level of coaching we started getting. He brought in that perfection as far as coaching."

"At that point, we were willing to do anything he told us to do," Wike added.

Said running back Bruce Perry of his new mentor:

"It was simple. We didn't want to lose anymore and we had someone with the formula."

Friedgen brought new discipline to the program (no drinking indefinitely, for example), and raised the bar of expectations. The players said his preparedness, toughness and no-nonsense approach, not to mention his motivational ploys and emotion, were some of the differences between him and their former coach.

Friedgen also laid out a new graduation plan for Yow so his players would excel off the field as well. She loved his focus on graduating football players.

Many of the top players that played for Vanderlinden, and before him Mark Duffner, "got 'NFL-itis' " and didn't go to class in their final year. They didn't graduate because their mind "was on the league."

Many left without a degree. That would not happen under Friedgen, who soon boasted a stellar graduation rate as one of his recruiting tools.

Friedgen's new plan required the players take 12 hours in the fall and spring and six in the summer, totaling 30 a year, so four years to graduate. Most would have only three hours in the summer so they could work out with the team. Friedgen insisted on both. His players would be done before they hit their final spring semester, thus avoiding the problem of the NFL.

Friedgen went to bat for his players, lobbying the state on five occasions to get $1 million for a new academic support unit at the team house, which he eventually got when the department chipped in funds.

Friedgen quickly put his mark on all aspects of the program, including his players' lives.

"He gave us that responsibility, and once we started winning games it seemed to snowball," Bryant said. "We weren't a terrifically talented team. We just had a lot of guys who were willing to work harder than the other teams."

Friedgen and Yow saw eye-to-eye on most things starting with academics. The football program has been an example for other programs on campus starting with its graduation rate.

Their shared vision included Byrd Stadium expansion, which is scheduled to begin after the 2007 season. On that topic, Friedgen said Yow was more optimistic than he, though there were stipulations in his contract about expansion.

The two have been in lockstep about building the program and neither could have done it without the other. It's clear that she has been a catalyst from the start.

"You talk about a person that perseveres? She's a bulldog. She doesn't back down. She's a pretty extraordinary person," Friedgen said. "Do I get along with her all the time? No. Do I agree with her all the time? No. I tell her, 'The big things you are unbelievable at.' She never flinches. She is right there. She's got a plan. I know she wants this to happen."

Friedgen laughs about it, and some of the red tape he experiences at College Park. "She told me once that you're a football coach. And if you want to go from 'A' to 'B,' sometimes you need to go to 'C' or 'D.' I said Debbie gets to 'B' as fast as possible."

Yow has been there when Friedgen has made all his big moves at Maryland. That includes stadium expansion, which will add 64 luxury boxes at Byrd and hopefully jettison the program to the next level by providing funds over time for other projects.

D ebbie Yow helped Ralph Friedgen in a variety of other ways, too. Friedgen, who was known as "Cyber Coach" in the NFL because of his heavy use of computers in the early 1990s, has long been a technology fan.

He set up a database in the early years, one which had all of his pass patterns, loaded against coverages – man, zone, and pressure – with tendencies and success rates. Friedgen's daughter, Kelley, who was 14-years old, helped him learn about computers in 1992 starting with basic data programs. He tested his players on the information, which he put in by hand.

"I can remember sitting in there trying to figure out Kansas City's man coverage. So we were racking our brain. I'd pull up the database and say give me a route versus 'man' coverage formation, third down, or red zone. Out of the program would come 10 routes to help you fit those parameters," Friedgen said.

Friedgen still lives up to his moniker, always getting the latest technological goodies. That is where Yow, as well as the MGN, have come in handy.

"I have kinda scanned the whole gamut. Some of these young guys don't realize what the old guys had to do," Friedgen said.

The first big ticket item Friedgen took care of when he arrived was the Terps' antiquated video system. Maryland was way behind, and an upgrade to the Avid system was something he insisted on before he agreed to come on board.

The Terps had one machine in the video control room and everything they did was off cut-ups. The coaches walked around with tapes in their hands, but before long each had a system at their desk and it became automated.

Friedgen went to Avid's offices to learn to operate the system, as did his coaches, as he believed they gained a day-and-a-half each week having the system instead of tape. "That time is huge," he told them.

Friedgen had an Avid system at Georgia Tech, and soon some of his ideas were part of the system. He knew it as well as some of its creators.

Friedgen was adept enough that he didn't need video technicians to make his tapes. He did it all himself.

Before his coaches got to the office, between meetings and practices, he'd spend hours at his desk putting them together. If he has a hobby, it's film work.

The assistant coaches used the first spring to learn the new video system. Friedgen told his staff that without it "they would be lost."

Friedgen insisted on at least five coaches' stations at the start.

But Yow told him she would get it all, perhaps not knowing a complete system cost about $1.5 million at the time. But Friedgen, because of his work with the company, got the system for $700,000 if he agreed to endorse the firm. Of the $700,000, former quarterback Boomer Esiason contributed $70,000 to help his former coach.

The program required $50,000 annually for maintenance alone. Friedgen kept the staff's laptop computers free of e-mail and other programs to avoid viruses.

"We could never have that crash," he said.

Friedgen knew what he wanted, and at Georgia Tech used the system to improve his quarterbacks' vision. Tech was one of the schools that used it in the early years.

Friedgen made cards with formations and coverage, and on the back listed the routes they ran out of the formation. He'd flash them for players like Joe Hamilton to help him speed read. Later, Friedgen put it on a PowerPoint presentation and at Tech every student had a computer. That's when he started sending his players offensive plays via e-mail, something he used to have on flash cards.

In 2005, he got the Football Simulator from Gridiron Technologies with virtual reality tools, taking the next step in the technology world.

"They have the ability now to take video and turn the video into the robotic creatures you see on 'Madden.' So you can take your video and turn it into those guys and once you do that you're in their world. You can click on the quarterback and see what he sees from that viewpoint. You can click on the offensive guard and see what he sees. So it's a pretty good teaching tool, and for all players," he said.

Friedgen has seen the system even help with recruiting. Some high schools have it and can produce and send out highlight films, which makes Friedgen's job easier when reviewing prospect film.

Blackney remembered the old days of cutting and splicing.

"We never had anything like that at Bowling Green," said the former defensive coordinator who retired after the 2005 season. "Once I learned it, it made me a lot more time-efficient because I could get the information I needed, collect it, and look at it and really isolate it, whether it was a third down pass or a second down pass. Whatever. I had never had that advantage before. It made me a better teacher and a better strategist. Ralph was always ahead of the curve on all that."

It was part of Friedgen's vision. And implementing it at warp speed was a key.

Friedgen brought in an Avid rep each year to update the staff on the latest innovations. He doesn't look at games anymore. Just opponent defenses and formations, fronts, coverages and frequencies. That's how he game-plans.

Friedgen is up to over 30 stations, which puts Maryland in the top five percent nationally, he said.

"The bottom line is that I can break down an opponent. As far as breaking down the actual film, what used to take me 5-6 hours I can do it in six minutes," Friedgen said.

Like Joe Paterno, who at a time was a leading-edge coach, one of the first with an indoor facility and player apartments, Friedgen leads the pack in technological advancements.

"What he has learned is to stay ahead of the 'Joneses,'" special teams coach Ray Rychleski said. "To me he is a new-age coach as far as anybody in the country. And the tools are all good. But you have to know how to use them and he does. That's where he is really good. He uses it to the maximum and makes his coaches do the same. He's way ahead of everybody in my opinion."

Ralph Friedgen had ambitious plans once he got started at Maryland. Very ambitious.

Friedgen wanted the Terps to become "America's Team" and went about marketing it that way. He wanted to be a step ahead of the competition in every way.

"Fridge TV" was one of those innovations, a free web site offering an inside, compelling video look at the program. It was created by former Terps and Washington Redskins kicker and local television personality Jess Atkinson.

Fans, recruits, anyone can access game highlights, player and team profiles, locker room pre-game speeches, even a reality coaches' show. Beamer had something similar at Virginia Tech but his was a web page at the start. Friedgen's site added the video element first, and he proved a pioneer by opening up the program in a way that would probably make old coaches like Claiborne cringe.

Recruits can watch morning conditioning workouts, players in classes, or hear their personal stories, all of which Atkinson has a good eye for. Atkinson's best work may have been the *Gladiator* highlight film on the eve of the win over Virginia in 2003, which was shown to the team as a motivational tool.

"One of the first things I do when I go into a home [of a recruit] is I pull it up on the computer and bookmark it for them," Friedgen said of how he uses "Fridge TV" as a recruiting tool.

Like his father in the 1950s and 1960s, Friedgen knew the importance of the media and allowed it great access to his program, more than most. And he showed a bit of his "showman" side, reaching out in an entertaining way few had done before.

Friedgen said he text-messages recruits when new features come on the site. Friedgen lets Atkinson be as creative as he wants, but he gets a look at the final product and has a chance to edit. There are Signing Day specials and off-season features like coverage of pro days, in addition to spring and fall practice coverage. The only thing Friedgen has edited, he said, are a few expletives in practice.

"All that stuff is a way to expose yourself that people wouldn't see. It's another way of taking our program to the people. It's another thing that had never been done here, and that's why more and more people are interested in our program because we are reaching out to them," Friedgen said.

Friedgen knows the power of the Internet, the media and marketing. And "Fridge TV" combines it all.

"Someday, and that may be real soon, this will be the way to market most things," he said in 2004.

Friedgen lurks but does not post on the site's message boards, as he does other sites like *TerrapinTimes.com*, that cover the program.

Friedgen also used his connections with former linebacker and Under Armour founder Kevin Plank to put Maryland in the lead with the trendy Baltimore company with an exclusive uniform and apparel deal. Not only did it put the Terps in snappy Under Armour uniforms, and later shoes, it showcased the program in its national television advertising spots including spots with former players and current coaches including Friedgen, Sollazzo and Franklin.

Former players Eric Ogbogu, Vernon Davis and Jamie Bragg, among others, served as actors in the commercials, many filmed at College Park.

"One of our recruits, Zach Marshall, committed after seeing the Under Armour commercial. Said he got fired up," Friedgen said.

Friedgen said area high school teams played the advertisement the night before games to fire them up. The jingle "We Must Protect This House" was known nationwide with the Terps at the center of the popular campaign.

Maryland, as well as Georgia Tech, was among the first schools to use Under Armour apparel, and now it has spread to SEC powers like Auburn, which has a sponsorship deal.

Working with a limited budget Friedgen also got his players custom-made, $1,000 a pair knee braces, spending $30,000 in year three to protect his linemen.

He also added a Swim-Ex workout pool at the team house at a cost of $100,000, with funds raised from the MGN, private donations and his golf tournament.

None of it could have happened until he stoked the fan base and the MGN, the program's booster group, something he swears is vital to the program's success.

When he arrived at Maryland there were a few hundred MGN members and the group raised about $40,000 a year. Five years later, he had just under 1,000 members with close to $500,000 raised each year. That included about 175 "Gold" members who gave $1,200 annually.

Friedgen would like to see the group grow to 5,000 or 6,000 members. The revenue pays for everything from team house expansion to private jet time during recruiting to new black game jerseys the players wore in 2005.

Membership gains fans extra access to the team, be it at private practices or pre-season "chalk-talks" with Friedgen, to the organization's annual golf tournament, away game bus trips and the spring gala. Friedgen also hosts events like cocktail parties at his home.

It was all part of his plan and vision, and methodically he went about accomplishing most every goal.

After Byrd Stadium expansion, the last big ticket item on his list is an indoor practice facility.

A s a testimony to his preparedness as he embarked on his first head coaching job, Ralph Friedgen, as the players came out of the tunnel for the Friday walk-thru before the 2001 opener, greeted each one personally.

His cousin, John Stoddard, stood near him on the field.

Friedgen took the best and worst of all the coaches he served and played under, including his father, and molded it into his own coaching dynamic, which Maryland would experience with full force.

Said Stoddard, who stood by him and listened as his cousin prepared for his first game just months after taking the job:

"Every single kid, every single kid with a brand-new coach and in many ways a brand-new team . . . every single kid he knew their name and had a remark for them.

"One kid comes out and he says to one of the seniors, 'Hey Bobby,' and just for kicks we'll use that name . . . 'I got to apologize to you. I checked on that deal with the class and they made a mistake and you were in that class like you said you were. I am sorry I got upset about you, I apologize.' "

"Then E.J. Henderson comes out. He says, 'Coach.' And Ralph says, 'E.J.' I said what in the hell is up with that? And Ralph says, 'Nothing. He can just play.' "

Friedgen was a galvanizing force on campus from the start, knowing how to reach players, administrators and fans. And he was never bashful about expressing himself to anyone.

And soon he enjoyed a transformation. He took all of what was bottled up in him as a career assistant and became an extrovert with the public, something few anticipated, showing his personality in spontaneous ways.

In 2001, when asked to address the band during two-a-days, a band member bet Friedgen that he didn't know the fight song. Friedgen said, "Sure, play it and I will sing it." He did, and afterwards told members, "When we beat North Carolina the first game I'm gonna come over and we're going to sing it again," something he has done after every win.

The tide had turned for Maryland football and the program was back, led by a man who thought he could do it and then got his chance.

Galt had seen Maryland coaches come and go but it was different after 2000. Finally something took hold.

"I don't see anybody doing what Ralph did. You know . . . I thought, I felt, that we were doing pretty good in the weight room and preparing the kids (under past coaches). But he took it all to the next level as his demands were so much higher. We had the same talent that was winning 4-5 games. Those kids were so hungry, so prepared, so motivated and believed. Coach Friedgen just wanted more."

"Ralph brought an attitude, developed a culture for winning. It may have come under Vanderlinden. Nobody would ever know. But it did happen because of the way Ralph pushed and poked and the way he prepared that team," Locksley said. "We could have won that year under Vanderlinden, but we never would have been 10-2 or in the BCS."

Yow, who met with the team the day after Vanderlinden was released but before Friedgen's name leaked as the top choice, said she heard in the meeting a player say, "How about that guy that's the offensive coordinator at Georgia Tech?"

He must have read her mind.

"It always helps that you are a graduate of an institution, although it is not necessary. But when he came in I think that his aura of confidence is what won the players over," she said.

"They had already seen Ralph at work as offensive coordinator. They had to play against his offense defensively, so he already had a certain level of respect here. So he comes in as head coach, his first head coaching job, but I don't think in their eyes it seemed to him at all that he was a first-time coach.

"But what he did was rally and galvanize the team at that level, so soon, and that was what surprised me. I knew we had some talent but they had such a history of being mediocre that I felt it would take time to build their psyche. I think the results surprised me."

Yow was as surprised as any with the BCS run in year one. But she took a preventive measure just in case.

In a shrewd move before the season, one showing foresight, Yow took out an insurance policy in case the Terps won the ACC title. The staff bonuses for a title were over $500,000, but the Terps found an insurance company that would write a policy for $13,000 as a safeguard just in case the staff hit a home run.

"They looked at our history and determined, based on our history, that there's no way that could be done," Yow said. "I told our Chief Financial Officer, 'Close the deal today.' We ended up winning the ACC, paid out a half million dollars, and it cost the athletic department $13,000."

The Terps haven't been able to get such a deal since.

"We got on the bus after the N.C. State game [in Raleigh when the Terps won the league outright on the final day of the season] and Dr. Mote and his wife Patsy, who rarely travels with us because his schedule is too full. Well, he got on the bus and Dr. Mote said to me, which is a logical question, 'Do we owe the coaches anything additionally for bonuses for winning the ACC?' He said, 'Ballpark, how much is it going to cost us?' I said, '$13,000.' He said, 'How could it only be $13,000?' I told him we insured it for $13,000. And he just said, 'Brilliant.' "

Friedgen often references his first team when others come up for comparison sake. He has had some great teams at Maryland, including his Gator Bowl champion team that he called the "Gladiator team" because it was such an emotional year. The Peach Bowl team, the year before, because of the walk-ons that stepped up to help dominate Tennessee. That season the Terps played like "We belonged. That we were the better team. That we were out to pulverize people," Friedgen said.

But nothing compares to his first at Maryland.

"That team will always be special to me because it was Maryland, my alma mater. It was special we went to a BCS game. And we won the conference. That team will always be special to me because not only it was my first, but because they could have been just happy to tie. They could have settled for that. But they won it outright [at N.C. State]. That's why I am so proud of them."

Friedgen has been consistent throughout, hard and tough and always sticking to his vision. He didn't show much fallibility until year four when the Terps, with quarterback woes, stumbled to a 5-6 mark, his first losing season. Friedgen put it on himself. "What did I do wrong? I can't let down," he told himself.

Friedgen went through a lot of introspection at season's end, re-dedicating himself and demanding more of his staff. He cancelled spring break, sent his staff on the road to get fresh ideas from college and pro teams, and immersed himself more in the offense. By year six he took over as offensive coordinator. Friedgen went back and broke down every game and play in self-evaluation.

Many asked the question: could anyone have pulled off what Friedgen did at Maryland between his work, vision and bringing a school and fan base together so quickly?

His first eight months on campus were so dramatic that it knocked the players and coaches back on their heels. And he hasn't changed much, still aggressive, no compromises, no cutting corners, in your-face with his players, bosses, boosters, telling them not always what they want to hear, but what he believes is the truth. No matter how gruff it may seem at times.

"There was a belief, a fear," Galt said, "from the start. But everyone accepted it and conformed."

Friedgen hasn't lost many players because they could not take his style. Getting his players to respond has not been much of a problem because he has a proven formula and he has won.

Blackney said it well:

"I have often asked myself could anyone else have done it but Ralph Friedgen? The reason I say that is because if I stand up here as a graduate of Connecticut, not the University of Maryland, and I tell them they should be embarrassed by how much they're contributing to the university, to the program in general, I am going to get a lot of hisses and boos. But Ralph is one of their own and he's a guy that lays it on the line. Tells it like it is. And they accept that. When I look around to all he has done and how he's done it, I have often asked myself is there anyone else who could have done that. I don't know. It would have been very difficult. He's blunt, he's direct and he's not afraid to ask. Everywhere he goes he asks people to open up their checkbook. It has been amazing. That's what was needed around here."

Said Wilson, who came back in 2007 to serve as a graduate assistant:

"He's a pyschology major. Head coaches do certain things to get certain things out of you. Like I'm gonna challenge him, I'm gonna play mind games. I believe coach Friedgen was good at that. He knew his players and what certain buttons to push with them. We needed that authoritative figure."

Friedgen quickly got the campus behind him in his folksy way, and gave fans hope that Maryland football could be big-time again. Friedgen continued to evolve, singing the fight song after games and stepping out of character, all to fit the moment, something he likely never imagined himself doing.

Verille said he had never seen Friedgen as content than when he walked off the field after defeating North Carolina in his first game.

"When he came off the field I could tell a sigh of relief like, 'Yeah, I can do this.' It validated all of those years when he waited for that opportunity. And when he had that he won it.'

"To me he's kind of a [Rick] Majerus. Everybody can relate to him. He's the common man," added Verille. "And you know basically he is a good person."

Said Yow:

"Focus and fire. Attitude and action. And he knows what he wants.

"We want to hire people at Maryland who aspire to be the best. This is a terminal destination. This is not a pass-through place as it used to be. We want the best, people who are dedicated to seeing their vision completed, and Ralph is that."

4

FAITH

aith plays a significant role in everyday life for Ralph Friedgen and his football program.

From pre and post-game prayers in the locker room, to Friday night devotionals with speakers that Friedgen hand-picks, to the rosary he rubs during games, there are examples everywhere.

It builds on a sense of family and faith that Friedgen instilled at the start, one that began for him as a child. Friedgen holds to many traditions and links to the past, this being one of the greatest.

Friedgen's religion is personal and private to him. But it creeps into the program in many ways.

Friedgen doesn't push faith or religion on his players. And among the significant differences between his staff and others that preceded him, Sunday morning isn't for work.

The staff typically gets to the office at 1 p.m. Friedgen is considerate of Sunday mornings. He attends mass early before arriving to the office for film study, to check his injured players and hold to his teleconference with reporters.

A highlight of the week for many in the program is the Friday night devotional. A favorite speaker for the players is "Father Bill" of the campus Catholic Student Center. William Byrne also mentors some of the players. He is a dynamic speaker with a different message each week.

Assistant coaches and sometimes players' parents have given devotionals. In 2006 sophomore guard Jaimie Thomas's father, a minister, addressed the team about perseverance before an emotional win at Clemson's Death Valley.

Ralph Friedgen often uses real-life examples from his father, be it from home or the athletic fields.

His father dedicated Ralph's high school senior season to the memory of teammate Yogi Santa Donato's father, a dear friend and neighbor.

Ralph's father and Yogi's father were high school teammates in the 1930s. Santa Donato had been with the boys since their youth league days but died suddenly before the season, at the age of 44, of a heart attack.

Friedgen's father was devastated.

The friends had a ceremonial bottle of expensive wine they promised to drink only if they beat rival Rye High School. It was an emotional, inspirational season, spurred by his memory. At season's end they sipped the wine in a solemn ceremony.

A t Maryland, it starts early on game day for Ralph Friedgen. Friedgen sits, sometimes kneels, in his hotel room and says four full rosaries before each game. He's done it throughout his college and pro football days. It takes about an hour-and-a-half, and it dates back to his father who he attended church with before every high school game.

Religion was everywhere in the family.

His father was Catholic and his mother Episcopalian. But the priest at their Harrison church would not marry them. They never returned, instead going to a church in nearby Larchmont, N.Y. Ralph's wife, Gloria, later helped Friedgen's mother convert to Catholicism in 1980.

Some of Friedgen's favorite rosaries deal with miracles. And he's seemingly had a few on the football field, he'll tell you.

Friedgen meditates on them and tries to apply them in everyday life. Gloria Friedgen never knew of her husband's game day ritual until she traveled to the 1994 AFC Championship Game in Pittsburgh, Pa., and saw it first-hand.

Ralph told her of the ritual and she asked to pray with him.

Later that afternoon, he said, he may have got some "intervention" on the football field.

"We were losing most of the way," Friedgen recalled. "There was a third-and-17 with about four or five minutes to go in the game. They were playing a zone blitz and Dom Capers was the defensive coordinator. Marvin Lewis was one of the coaches on the staff. I told Bobby [Ross], 'You know, sometimes you just got to say the hell with it. They've been squatting on us all day.'

"So I called a '989,' which is a 'go' route and they blitzed. And their corner squatted and we ran right by him for a 55-yard touchdown to Tony Martin. And Tony told [quarterback] Stan Humphries in the huddle, 'Look, he's playing outside of me so I'm gonna go inside.' Stan never even saw it. He got hit when he threw it. But it was perfect."

Friedgen pointed to the time the Chargers played the Steelers just two weeks prior in the regular season, and they were on to them running the counter trey.

"Pittsburgh was reading it so well that even the safety and corners were making plays in support," Friedgen said. "So let's run that, and run a great fake in, and release the receiver. So we put the play in and Humphries said, 'Who the hell put this play in? We're not going to call this play in the game, are we?' I said, 'Yeah, we might.'

"I called it in the game and the receiver was so alone that Humphries told me after the game that he was so open I didn't want to miss him. He caught it. That was a 45-yard touchdown and we won the game, 14-7. Neil O'Donnell was their quarterback. They had the ball on the five-yard line and took four shots at it and didn't score, [Chargers] linebacker Dennis Gibson swatting one of the final attempts. That meant we were going to the Super Bowl. And the Pittsburgh people were so upset."

Said Gloria of the last play to stop the drive:

"It was like the hand of God coming down. It was unbelievable. That compared to the Pittsburgh people, who just wanted to kill us."

Ralph Friedgen also points to the Terps-N.C. State series since he's been head coach at Maryland, and shakes his head over some of the outcomes.

"Eight minutes to go and we're down 20 points. How do you win that game?," he said of the 2001 game, and the game-changing hit linebacker Leroy Ambush laid on T.A. McLendon in 2003. "So many of these things come up.

"You know, I see so many things happen in football. Whether it's luck or someone above looking out for you, I just have tremendous faith in that."

Friedgen rubs a rosary that he keeps in his pocket during games. One time he forgot it so ran to his office at halftime to get it.

"Against Tennessee [in the 2002 Peach Bowl] when Randy Starks went down [with an early groin injury] and I'm playing with two walk-ons and they average 400 yards a game rushing. How we win that game? Divine intervention or what? That just doesn't happen," he said of the Terps' lopsided win.

One of the contests he said he had to "scratch my head about" came in the final game of the 20th century, during the 1999 season, when he was at Georgia Tech as offensive coordinator.

The Yellow Jackets played Georgia two years before Friedgen returned to College Park as head coach. Tech was up big, driving, and about to put the nail in the coffin.

"But quarterback Joe Hamilton threw an interception. Kerry Washington gets in a fight and tossed from the game while Kelly Campbell gets hurt. Meanwhile, Georgia comes back to tie 48-48 with about 30 seconds left and one timeout on the Tech two-yard line. I am ticked because we had like 600 yards total offense," Friedgen said.

All Georgia had to do was kick a field goal to win. But Bulldogs' head coach Jim Donnan wanted a touchdown.

"They run the ball but fumble at the goal line. The replay shows later that the runner was on the ground when he fumbled. We recovered in the end zone and attempted to run the ball out but got tackled. Georgia called a timeout and the game goes into overtime," Friedgen said.

Friedgen said Hamilton approached Bulldogs' quarterback Quincy Carter, who had never beaten Tech during his career, and said to him, 'Hey 'Q.' Let's just get it on and have some fun out here.'

"And Carter was just totally psyched out," Friedgen said.

Georgia won the toss and ran a "jailbreak" screen for about seven yards on first down. Then Carter had a receiver open but floated the pass, which Tech picked off. Friedgen said O'Leary told him to run two plays to get to the left hash and kick a field goal on third down. But the ball ended up on the right hash.

The kick was blocked, but quarterback Godsey, the holder, an average athlete, somehow out-jumped two Georgia players and snatched the ball. Tech got the ball on the left hash and kicked the game-winner.

"Now that was pretty bizarre," Friedgen said.

Friedgen remembered another instance, this one at Virginia, when the Cavaliers were ranked No. 1 in 1994 with Shawn Moore and Herman Moore starring on offense. Friedgen said he saw broadcaster and Maryland alumnus Tim Brant before the game who asked, "How could you possibly beat them?"

"They're still Virginia," Friedgen replied. "We're going to kick their butt."

Virginia went up early before Tech rallied to get within 38-35 in the fourth quarter with Tech driving on the final possession. Suddenly, the head phones went out on the sideline.

"I am just cursing like crazy [in the coaches' booth]. The radio team is right next to me and I hear them say, 'Obviously, Ralph Friedgen is quite upset today,'" Friedgen said.

Friedgen preached and preached to his quarterback, Shawn Jones, once he got in the "red zone" to protect the ball, whatever it took, throwing it into the ground or out of bounds. Jones, on third down, threw the ball out of bounds. The headsets began working and Jones told Friedgen, once he got to the sideline, that he was sorry about throwing the ball away.

"I told him, 'That's okay. That's what you should have done. We're going to kick a field goal, the game is going to be tied, and we're going to go down the field and score and win the game. That's what I have been trying to get you to do for years.'"

Friedgen had a play in mind but at the last moment changed to one he hadn't run all year. Running back William Bell caught the ball and advanced it more than 20 yards but he got hit and fumbled. But Bell was ruled down.

"Why I called that play to this day I cannot tell you. It just came into my mind," Friedgen said.

Tech completed two more passes, got into field goal range, and narrowly won, the same year they won a national championship.

"I told Gloria after the game, 'I feel like I am at the craps table and I'm rolling "sevens." And I am not going to play another game this year conservatively. I am going to go out and play aggressive as I can play. Because I think we have a chance to go undefeated.' She looked at me like I was nuts," Friedgen said.

Later that season Tech met Nebraska in the Citrus Bowl while Notre Dame played

Colorado in the Orange Bowl. It was New Year's Day and "75 percent of that stadium was in gold," Friedgen said.

Friedgen told Ross beforehand that he would "leave no bullets in his gun," that day.

On the first play, Jones scrambled nearly 70 yards to set up Tech's first touchdown. Before long they were up big.

Friedgen had picked something up while scouting Nebraska on film. One of its top defensive linemen was deaf. Nebraska played many of its games on turf, and when the Cornhuskers made defensive adjustments they pounded the turf. It was more difficult to do on grass, so the Yellow Jackets threw numerous motions and shifts at them. Heading into the fourth quarter, with Tech up 45-21, Friedgen was throwing the ball at every chance.

Ross got on the headset and asked him what in the world he was doing. Friedgen told him that if he scored 50 points against Nebraska, "then there would be no way we could be denied national champions."

"He said," Friedgen said of Ross' animated reaction, " 'Ralph, run the damn football.' I didn't throw a pass after that. We just ran the football."

Ross's mother was ill, so after the game he immediately flew to be with her. Friedgen and O'Leary were left to stump for a national title. Friedgen "swears to this day that if Bobby had stayed there we would not have won a national championship. Bobby wouldn't have politicked for it," he said.

Friedgen said he never knew as competitive a person as Ross, but added that stumping for something "was not in his nature."

Tech was 11-0-1, Colorado 11-1-1, but the Buffs had the controversial five-down series against Missouri early in the season.

Fans carried the goal posts out of the stadium. Late in the Notre Dame game, Rocket Ismail broke a punt return for what could have been the game-winner. Friedgen recalled the hotel, where the team was staying, "literally shaking" on the play. But it was called back on a penalty.

The next day O'Leary and Friedgen were at a news conference lobbying for the title. Later that night, back in Atlanta, Friedgen was driving to a television station to make an appearance when he heard over the radio that Tech had won the *UPI* Poll, for a share of the title, by a narrow margin.

"I went nuts. I started screaming in the car and went off the road. We just won the national championship. I don't care if it was one vote or not. You just never know who you might have influenced," he said.

"The euphoria of that game . . . you got to remember we came off a 3-8 season before that. Nothing in pro football, even the Super Bowl, could compare to that. I have just been in so many unbelievable games."

Another example came the season before, this time against Clemson.

Georgia Tech receiver Campbell had nearly 20 receptions in the game and the

Yellow Jackets had thrown almost 60 times. But still they trailed.

During a two-minute drill, with Tech trailing by six points, they faced third down on the 16-yard line with less than 20 seconds to go. Campbell couldn't play because he was so tired. Friedgen wanted to run a "sting" route, a fake on a corner route turned into a post. Friedgen knew that the closest he could run it was from 18-yards out.

The clock stopped and Friedgen told receiver Watkins to get ready for the route. Then he told Godsey that he will have to throw it quickly. Two years before it was déjà vu as Tech was in the same spot against N.C. State in overtime.

Fast-forward to Clemson, and Watkins ran the route but was pushed to the ground by a defender, which Friedgen said should have been a penalty. Watkins was down but didn't stay down for long, bouncing up to run the rest of the route and make a one-handed grab for the score and the win.

"Now, if that guy doesn't push him down I don't know if we have enough room. That bought some time to go ahead and make the play. An unbelievable play. At Georgia Tech they call it 'The Catch,'" Friedgen said.

Friedgen said Watkins had been through a lot of adversity during his career and that "he could have stayed down." But he made a play that will "last forever in the annals of Georgia Tech football," Friedgen said,

R alph Friedgen often attends mass at 7:30 a.m. on weekdays as well as mass on holy days and, of course, on Sundays.

He attends nearby St. Mark's during the season and St. Peter's in Olney during the off-season. In Georgia, at their lake house, the Friedgens attend church where they donated a stained glass window, which cost $50,000.

"Yeah, she told me about that later," Friedgen quipped of wife Gloria's largesse.

Friedgen has never pushed religion on his players, former safety Wilson said, "but it was there if you wanted it," he said. "And you could tell he was a strong believer."

Wilson said Friedgen did a great job of "freeing your mind of football to put everything else in perspective."

Friedgen is always at the team devotional and around after breakfast for prayers on game day at the hotel. Turnout is always solid, with some 50-60 players attending voluntarily.

R alph Friedgen's faith was called into play following his second season at College Park when he went in for hip replacement surgery in the spring. After a painful operation he developed blood clots in his leg, a potentially dangerous situation.

His blood pressure dropped to 60/40 and he couldn't hold anything down. He had to wear a stocking for months to help prevent more issues with the clots.

Friedgen, for many years, had back problems. The wear and tear on his body added up, not to mention his weight. But what put him over the edge was a Nike coaches' trip to Hawaii. He could barely get off the plane and later struggled to move around on the golf course.

When he returned he wasted no time going in for treatment.

"I was really in a lot of pain," he said.

Friedgen tried acupuncture at first.

"You should have seen me. I had about 100 needles sticking in my ass. And I had a hat [a medical device] on that was smoking. It was supposed to go through to my brain."

Nothing worked and soon the pain was shooting through his groin. He had trouble getting on planes during recruiting.

An MRI revealed the problem was his hip and bulging disks in the fourth and fifth lumbar. Doctors told him the hip was "shot. Bone on bone. There is no cartilage," Friedgen said.

Because of his back trouble he was walking awkwardly trying to compensate. His hip was the casualty.

At first Friedgen got epidural shots, a total of three, and the second was the worst pain he said he ever felt. It was designed to shrink the disk and relieve pressure on the nerve. The relief was short-lived as he attended the MGN Gala and after a night spent on his feet told his wife, "Get me in a car and get me to the damn hospital. I was running to the hospital," Friedgen said.

One drawback to the operation is that he can no longer run, while he can't move his leg in full range of motion either.

"And my golf game. I lost about 30 yards on my shot," he said.

Friedgen has to watch himself on the sidelines. A player running into his porcelain hip could be disastrous. In the first two games that season Friedgen coached from the press tower. But after two losses he quickly returned to the sidelines. Later, his doctor admonished him for running the risk of a cerebral hemorrhage if he was hit while on the blood thinner Coumadin.

After Friedgen returned to work he was told not to sit for extended periods. He developed blood clots in his leg because it was difficult with film study and long meetings.

"I sat for like two hours. When I looked down at my leg it looked like I had elephantitus," he said.

Friedgen returned to John Hopkins where doctors discovered he had blood clots both above and below his knee. He was also hit by an intestinal virus, and "stuff was running out of me the whole time," he said.

He spent a week at the hospital followed by a week on the couch at home in his basement, which flooded during the time he was laid up.

He had physical therapy that spring and summer and continued with a battery of shots. He was told to use a cane for the rest of the summer, but after two weeks he ditched it only to get floored again by pain. He returned to golf three months later, at least his "short game," he joked.

Friedgen kept his humor throughout the ordeal despite the excruciating pain of his hip being dislocated and punched through a small incision as part of the operation. His intern, who was helping manage the clot by administrating Coumadin, was a "Dr. Christmas." He had some fun with that.

"About 32-years old. Really pretty. Everybody spoke with such reverence for her," he said with a smile.

His doctor had gone through Friedgen's buttocks, not his hip, to perform the replacement, which was a new technique. So Dr. Christmas inquired about the procedure.

"So she said, 'Would you mind if I look at your incision?' Gloria was there and I said, 'No problem.' So I rolled over and pulled my drawers down. And she looked at my ass and said, 'Magnificent.' I said, 'Dr. Christmas, do you know how long it's been since someone has told me that?' Gloria said, 'You are unbelievable.' After that everyone called me the 'Magnificent.' It was such great timing."

He joked with his occupational therapist, who was a Florida football fan. But he was in a lot of pain and on top of that he had to go recruiting. He had a table placed in his office so his chiropractor could visit him.

On a sad note, Friedgen's doctor, Dr. James Wenz, one of the best in his field, months later died in an automobile accident that also took his wife. His children survived the wreck.

It happened as the Terps were preparing for the Peach Bowl and Friedgen was shaken.

"It was very sad. I remember before that I was dancing again in the locker room after the N.C. State game that year. His father saw that on TV and Dr. Wenz said to him, 'Yeah, I did a good job. He's dancing already.' And then he was gone."

After hip surgery, Friedgen's health woes weren't over.

He had trouble sleeping and was evaluated for sleep apnea. Friedgen twice fell asleep while stopped at red lights while driving home from work. He said the stress of his first losing season led to restless nights while a deviated septum from his childhood resulted in him breathing through his mouth, including while he slept.

He first tried a mask that blew air down his throat but he became claustrophobic.

What kept Friedgen up most at night, he said, was when he felt his players were underachieving or he wasn't reaching them.

Stress added to his back woes and he began seeing a massage therapist once a week. She visited him at home and at work. He had face, head and foot massages.

Friedgen also developed vertigo, which manifested itself when he would awaken and "the room was spinning 5,000 miles an hour," he said.

Friedgen thought at first that he was having a heart attack, and he couldn't get to the phone. It happened first when he was on the road recruiting. He saw a few specialists and a crystallized growth and infection was discovered in his ear, which threw off his equilib-rium.

It was disconcerting when Friedgen was on the road recruiting, up sometimes from 5 a.m. until midnight, jetting between cities to visit prospects' homes. It led to increased private jet time for him during the January recruiting period.

But he always kept his wit.

Good friend Beamer called to wish him well when he was laid up after surgery, but he also asked if there was anything Friedgen could do to help the Hokies get into the league during the time before ACC expansion.

"Gloria had him on the phone and I told her, 'Tell Frank I got other problems right now,' " Friedgen said.

Friedgen was happy but still in a lot of pain when he was named Man of the Year by the Archdiocese of Washington that spring and made his acceptance speech though still on crutches.

F ormer quarterback Sam Hollenbach recalled a pre-game speech that Ralph Friedgen gave before the 2006 Florida State game at Byrd Stadium.

He strayed from football talk and stuck to "loftier" themes and how "we are a team of destiny," Hollenbach said.

Friedgen expanded on what the preacher said to the team the night before in chapel, and how he was up for hours on the eve of games at the hotel praying for his players.

"He was choked up and it was hard for him to say. But he said every night I am up for two hours praying for you guys. I want you to do well so bad," Hollenbach said.

Hollenbach said the image of Friedgen as a "tough guy" was dashed at times like this.

"That he would spend his time doing that, it kinda opened my eyes to him being spiritual and having another side to him beyond game personality."

Hollenbach said he frequently passed Friedgen going to church or encountered him at the Catholic Student Center on campus.

The team's Bible Study group, which has been around for years, took off in 2006 under senior leaders Hollenbach, the most devout Terp, and Josh Wilson, among others.

Hollenbach was so devoted to the cause that he organized a summer road trip for teammates to a Promise Keepers gathering in Baltimore the year before.

The Bible Study group met on Mondays at the team house, with usually some 20 players, to share a passage or life experience with the group.

The players took cues from Friedgen, who thanked God after every game, win or lose, for their health and their growth from their experiences on the field that day.

Josh Wilson recalled a high school teacher at DeMatha who attended church with

Friedgen and how he joked, "I'm gonna tell coach Friedgen at church" if Wilson was cutting up.

"The main thing from the group was that we were men, not just football players, and we acted like a team and men coming together spiritually," Wilson said. "We didn't just go on the field and then leave and not have anything to do with each other. That's a connection and bond we had last year [in 2006] that kept us hanging in there during some tough times."

Wilson said there was no better example of Friedgen's faith than at halftime of the Virginia game in 2006.

The season hung in the balance, and had the Terps lost (they trailed 20-0 at intermission), they were possibly looking at a 3-9 season, given the fragile nature of the team.

As a backdrop to the comeback, Friedgen had never won at Charlottesville since returning to his alma mater, and most were lopsided losses. The Terps hadn't won in Charlottesville in more than 15 years.

On offense, defense and special teams they were horrid in the first half. Their prospects looked dim.

Wilson walked off the field at intermission sheepishly. He'd been burned on a long touchdown pass. Wilson walked alongside Friedgen but soon couldn't believe what he heard.

"I'm standing right next to him in the locker room. I'm like, 'This game is over. We're down 20 points. We might as well go home right now. We lose another one to Virginia.' "

Wilson later saw Friedgen from the corner of his eye, smiling despite the sorry state of affairs. They had an exchange, Wilson said.

"I said, 'What is this guy so happy about?' He says, 'We're in it. We're in it. We're in it. We're right there.' I'm saying to myself no we're not. We're down 20 points and can't do anything. And he's like, 'We're right on the edge. We're about to get them. I can feel it. I can feel it,' " Wilson said.

"I think, and I can really say it now, I thought he had gone crazy. Something is wrong with him," Wilson recalled.

Wilson said the Terps came out of the locker room for the second half, stayed positive, and everything that Friedgen told them would happen did happen. They came back to claim a narrow victory, 28-26, to jump-start the season at the midway mark. It started with a fumble recovery early in the second half on a punt in Virginia territory, with senior walk-on Greg Powell, a Friedgen favorite because he suffered from ADD, forcing it and the Terps recovering.

"He had our backs. He saw it coming. He said things would start popping for us. It was like, 'Wow, I was ready to give up on us.'

"That was another point we got on a roll. He knew we could do it but we just had to figure out that we could do it. He just saw something," Wilson said.

I n the locker room after games, following the singing of the Maryland fight song, the seniors stand and count off the number of victories. Then Friedgen gives a quick speech and the players recite the Lord's Prayer.

Friedgen stands in the middle of the team as they begin.

"In a very gruff, staccato . . . it's not like a nun saying it," said booster Larry Grabenstein, who had the opportunity to observe the ritual once after a win. "This was 120 percent testosterone in the voices as the Lord's Prayer was being said. But it was a very strong presence in that locker room and that struck me."

R alph Friedgen's insatiable desire to win, though, has sometimes trumped the man upstairs.

At the Champs Sports Bowl in 2006, the Fellowship of Christian Athletes breakfast the day before the game was something players like Hollenbach looked forward to with appreciation.

But Friedgen was on such a tight schedule and under such self-imposed pressure to game-plan for Purdue, that he opted not to attend. He said he contacted Boilermakers coach Joe Tiller to see if he was attending so it would not look awkward if he was not there.

Hollenbach attended, along with a handful of Terps early that morning, and the senior quarterback gave a moving testimonial about his career ups and downs and how his faith helped carry him through.

Some would have preferred had Friedgen been at the event, and it was the first time he missed one at a bowl as Maryland's head coach.

Football and faith. For Ralph Friedgen, there's a fine line between the two.

R alph Friedgen's unwavering faith in his players is seen when he takes on the role of "Father Flanagan" for players needing a lift or a wayward son needing structure or direction.

He's always trying to save kids, if they can be saved, and gives them every chance.

"He will listen to any kid's tale of woe," said cousin Stoddard. "He will give a guy a chance."

Former center Wike, coming off the breakthrough Orange Bowl season, was considering quitting the team. He was depressed about not being able to play in the game and "feeling like I had let people down," he said.

"I was down in the dumps about everything."

Wike said he spoke with Friedgen for an hour and the coach cited personal experiences of faith and perseverance in his life and how he could empathize with Wike. He had gone through much of the same.

Friedgen told him how special his senior year would be. Wike left the office feeling renewed and went on to finish his career as a captain, all-ACC performer, and with another bowl win on his resume.

"He was right about everything. I would really have regretted it if I hadn't," said Wike, who arrived at Maryland as a tight end but played guard and finally center as a senior.

Friedgen's faith in his fellow man is seen through the many second-chance kids for whom he's served as a last safety net.

From troubled kids like Randy Earle, pampered ones like Sam Maldonado, or walk-ons off the football scrap heap such as Henry Scott, Scott McBrien or Justin Duffie, Friedgen sticks with them.

There are many scattered through his Maryland tenure, and their stories trace back to his youth, to the times he needed a boost.

"I'd like kids to have a chance to be successful. The time where I wanted to quit my father wouldn't let me. He was the main difference in my life. And I don't quit many things. So maybe that has something to do with it," Friedgen said.

Friedgen would like to see parents do a better job of raising their children. As well as get tougher. Countless times he has welcomed players into the program only to see how lost they are because of a troubled upbringing.

"Too many times they are too worried about whether they like them or not," he said of parents. "That's why so many of them are screwed up because the parents aren't doing the right thing. It's not a popularity contest."

Friedgen tried to save the New York standout linebacker Earle, who signed with Maryland in 2002 but barely made it through a year at College Park.

Earle, like former Terps All-American basketball player Juan Dixon, lost both parents to drug-related AIDs. Friedgen took Earle's commitment and it came on the heels of the Dixon-led national championship in Atlanta. Friedgen did all that he could to downplay the parallels members of the media were attempting to draw.

Earle had done little in football, Dixon so much, so he said comparisons were premature. Earle needed to prove himself first. And Friedgen was very matter-of-fact about it.

Friedgen and Sollazzo, Earle's recruiter, knew his high school coach so decided to give him a shot.

Said Friedgen:

"I told him one time that I thought he got way too much publicity for having lost his mom and dad to HIV/AIDS. I told him one time, 'You know Randy, this is only a good story if you are successful. If not it's another statistic.'

"And he is [a statistic]. He never did anything."

Earle repeatedly violated team rules and was gone before he stepped on the field to play, the "4-star" national recruit squandering a chance to raise his prospects in life. Friedgen helped Earle transfer and get a scholarship to Hofstra, but that blew up in his face, too.

"Now that coach [at Hofstra] is pissed at me," Friedgen said. "So I guess I gave him a second chance but he still couldn't handle it."

Said Franklin, the Terps' recruiting coordinator at the time:

"When you say he was an uphill battle, well it was more like a mountain. Ralph did everything he possibly could to help this kid and it just didn't work out. That's really frustrating and sad because that's why Ralph's in the business."

Friedgen is known to give kids "eight or nine chances," Franklin said, "and only if in the end he knew there wasn't any hope or chance" would he cut them loose.

Maldonado was one that worked out for the most part.

A former prep All-American and all-time leading rusher from New York, from none other than Harrison High, Friedgen had a soft spot for him.

His father (also Ralph) was a Puerto Rican immigrant at the age of 14. He built a successful parking garage business in New York City. He began by parking and washing cars.

Ralph Maldonado, who stands about 5-foot-5 and has a high voice, once drove his Bentley from New York to College Park for a spring practice. Once he treated assistant coach Sollazzo to a night in his box at Yankee Stadium, with the chance to meet his childhood hero, Yogi Berra.

Maldonado signed with Ohio State out of Harrison, but academic shortcomings and other issues had him packing his bags after a year and a half in Columbus.

Friedgen accepted him as a transfer but with a caveat: Maldonado would have to come as a walk-on and prove himself in the summer with an ungodly course load and, 38 credit hours, in his first year. Friedgen put him to the challenge right away.

"When I met the parents the first time I said I don't think he's tough enough. But if he comes in and does things right in summer school, I'll give him a shot at a scholarship. But the first time he screws up I'm washing my hands of it," Friedgen said.

Maldonado would go on to be a bruising back for two seasons at College Park before a knee injury, and his inability to be a consistent blocker, slowed him.

But when he once slipped up, skipping class, Friedgen sent his friends back in Harrison, the Maldonados, a scholarship bill for $8,000, which startled them to put it mildly.

Friedgen dislikes nothing more than truancy in his players, so it set him off.

"So Nelly [Sam's mother] calls me up and says, 'Coach, we just got a bill for $8,000. Sammy's on scholarship.' I said, 'No, let me tell you about this "scholar" part. Sammy didn't do crap last year. All he did was hang out with his girlfriend and drive that Lexus around. I'm not paying for it. Someone needs to pay for it.'"

Friedgen got Maldonado to turn things around and he graduated in 2007.

He remembered calling him to his office while he was struggling and laying into him. He told him, "Why don't you transfer to Massachusetts because you ain't doing anything here. You ain't getting it done. You can play right away up there. Get out of my hair."

Maldonado was pampered growing up, lavished with the comforts his father never had, Friedgen said. But he got it together thanks to some old-fashioned "encouragement" from his coach.

"He's not dumb. He's a smart kid. He was just lazy and he thought he was better than he is. And I told him that. But what kid doesn't?" Friedgen said.

"Get your degree. Why would I lie to you? I want you to be successful. I don't want you to have to work for your father but if you did, with a college degree, you'll get paid more than your other two brothers. But if you don't get your degree you're never going to be what you can be. You're going to be disappointed," Friedgen explained.

Friedgen asked Maldonado's father why he wanted "to spoil Sammy so much?"

"I can remember his father telling me I want him to have the things I didn't have coming up," Friedgen said. "I said 'Make the son-of-a-gun work. I am the only guy that has made him buckle down and do anything he was supposed to do. He came to us from with Ohio State with barely any credits. I love the kid. I think he is very personable and bright. But if you don't get your degree here you're not in my top-10."

Friedgen has been known to well-up when speaking of the players he has taken a chance on, high-risk kids that overcame adversity and made it. Often times not the biggest stars, but the ones that touch him the most.

Walk-on defensive tackle Henry Scott, who worked two part-time jobs to carry his tuition bill and three times was cut at walk-on tryouts before making the team, was one such player.

Scott, a little-known high school player from Baltimore, had a brother in jail for attempted second-degree murder.

Friedgen approached longtime booster Grabenstein about getting Scott a summer job in 2004 at his investment firm. Each summer, one hand-picked Terp worked for him.

"I didn't know who Henry was. I was kinda hoping it would be a name-brand ball player as opposed to a walk-on because it might be more fun following him," Grabenstein admitted.

Scott turned out to be Grabenstein's best worker. He assisted in client investment reports.

"He could have just as easily, given the vulnerabilities of his old neighborhood, you know 'there but for fortune go any of us,' " Grabenstein said.

Scott worked part-time at Bentley's in College Park, a popular restaurant and night spot, and also had a fledging car stereo business while in school.

"Ralph often times has identification with the underdog," Grabenstein said. "Really scrap for a position or scrap to make the team. Or scrap to be on the travel squad. For the kind of person for whom everything hasn't all lined up.

"From his heart of heart that's where he gets his most satisfaction. When you sit

Ralph Harry Friedgen was born in 1947 to proud parents Ralph and Iris Friedgen. He was the first of two children.

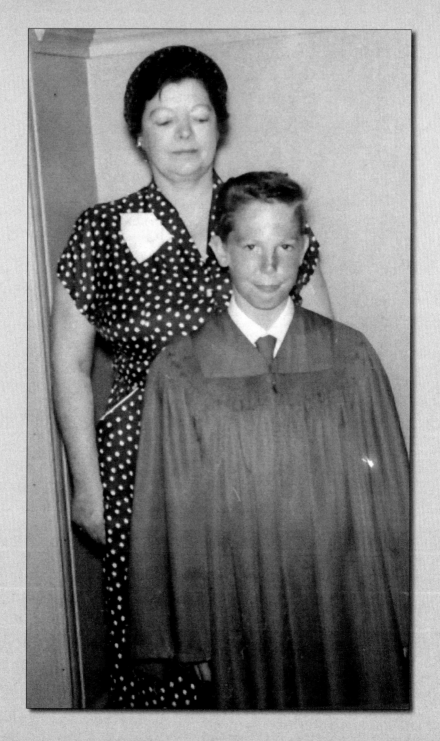

Ralph Friedgen, here with his grandmother, Annie O'Neill, had a strict Catholic upbringing, one that included mass before every football game.

Young Ralph grew up in the immense shadow of his father, who was one of the greatest high school football coaches of his era in New York.

Ralph Edward Friedgen played fullback for Fordham — a college power at the time — before becoming a high school football coach.

Young Ralph and sister Claranne grew up around sports, including swimming, which his father taught at their day camp in Greenwich, Conn.

Ralph Friedgen lines up over center at Harrison (N.Y.) High School, where he was feted by the local press and even the *New York Times*.

Ralph Friedgen as a player at Maryland. He arrived as a quarterback, but after three coaching changes finished his career as an offensive guard.

Ralph Friedgen accepts the 2001 National Coach of the Year award alongside past recipient Larry Coker of Miami.

Ralph Friedgen and quarterback Sam Hollenbach have one of their many sideline chats in 2006.

Ralph and Gloria Friedgen at the White House with President George W. Bush in 2001.

down and say, 'What does it all matter?' And, 'Who cares if I was on this earth?' Or, 'Where did I really make a difference in someone's life other than letting them smile on a Saturday afternoon?' I think you look at a kid like Henry Scott where he did make a difference and he was a champion for that kid."

Few players that had success under Friedgen but came from so little compare to quarterback Scott McBrien, another player Friedgen had tremendous faith in.

McBrien was quickly discarded by new West Virginia Coach Rich Rodriguez when he took over at Morgantown.

While at a spring golf outing with players and coaches, Rodriguez, McBrien said, told him that he couldn't believe the former staff wasted a scholarship on him. Later in camp Rodriguez kicked a ball that hit McBrien between the legs in a sensitive area. Writhing in pain, he questioned his toughness. That was the end of things in Morgantown. West Virginia hasn't signed a DeMatha player since.

McBrien, who was lightly recruited by the Terps out of high school as a walk-on punter, came to College Park as a walk-on quarterback in 2001. He had to sit out a year under NCAA transfer rules, but in practices there was no denying his whip of an arm, accuracy and athleticism, which was quickly apparent to the staff.

Just 6-1, 175-pounds, the lefty could "bring it" as everyone saw.

But like many quarterbacks at Maryland, it took McBrien time to master Friedgen's complex offense. He also had confidence issues, which on a few occasions led him to nearly quit the team.

"He struggled to get things, and a lot of times once he got it he had a confidence problem," Friedgen said. "The Florida State game he was just afraid to challenge those guys, to throw the ball on time."

McBrien had a meltdown after the 35 10 loss at Tallahassee after throwing an interception. He had to be convinced not to quit a day later by quarterbacks coach Taaffe.

Friedgen said he brought McBrien into his office time after time to talk to him and build his confidence. Physically, McBrien had all the tools. But mentally he could crumble at times. And in a hurry.

"So one time I sat him down and showed him the weekly ACC stats and then the career ACC stats in passing," Friedgen said.

"I showed him Shawn Jones, Joe Hamilton, George Godsey, Boomer Esiason and Frank Reich. Five guys, all-time most yards total offense. And I said you are as good if not better than all of these guys. You need to learn to go out and relax. Let it happen. Just go out and play."

Friedgen brought McBrien into his office again. He was on a list as the 11th most efficient quarterback in ACC history.

"I said, 'This is for all-time. The last 50 some years.' I said, 'I'm telling you. What do I got to do? What do you think, that I'm bulling you? You got a gun for an arm. A quick release. You are very evasive and have good vision. Just go play.' "

Finally, things started to click against Virginia that season as McBrien got on one of his famous rolls, leading the Terps to the Peach Bowl with 11 wins and a 30-3 decision over the Volunteers in Atlanta, running and passing for scores in the game. And letting it all hang out, as Friedgen urged him to do so many times, smiling all night on his way to MVP honors. His coach always had faith that he could do it.

Ralph Friedgen's faith is intertwined with many aspects of his life on and off the field.

He keeps the departed in mind. He gets emotional when talk moves to Rodney Culver and David Griggs of the San Diego Chargers, both of whom died in tragic accidents while he was coaching with the NFL team.

Culver died, along with his wife, in the 1996 ValuJet crash in the Everglades returning on Mother's Day from The Bahamas. Culver was the first black captain at Notre Dame. He was a reserve back who never complained. He died a year after the Super Bowl. Griggs died in an automobile accident in 1995.

"[Culver] was one of those guys, 'I'll always be here when you need me, coach,' " Friedgen said. "We were up in New York playing the Giants. It had just snowed and they were throwing ice balls at us. Our starting tailback got hurt, Stan Humphries got hurt, and we had to win this game to get to the playoffs and Rodney came in and rushed for 100-some yards and broke one late in the game. He had a broken thumb and still played."

When Ralph Friedgen and his cousin, John Stoddard, relax on the balcony of his Georgia lake home, Stoddard says Friedgen sometimes reflects on the past.

"We sat there one time. Looked out on the lake. On the boat. His dad liked boats. My dad liked boats. My dad liked to fish. He liked to fish. My dad died in '88. His dad died in '86. I looked at him and said, 'You know, they would have liked this.' And Ralph would say, 'They do like this.' "

"Physically, his father is not there. Spiritually, he is still there with him," Stoddard said.

5
FAMILY

Those that know Ralph Friedgen say they have heard him remark on many occasions, "I have three daughters and 120 sons."

"I think truly he thinks that way," Sam Hollenbach said.

Said former assistant coach Mike Locksley, the offensive coordinator at Illinois: "He definitely treats the kids like the sons he never had."

Former slot receiver Rich Parson, who had a tough childhood, once stood outside of Friedgen's office door and remarked, "I'm waiting for daddy."

"You know, we kid about that but I do treat the players like I would my children," Ralph Friedgen said. "If I had my sons or my daughters here, I'd want that from the coach that is here. I feel like the parents trust their kids to me and they want me to treat them like they would their children."

Friedgen often tells the stories of the "tough love" he got from his father, "but that's how you are going to grow to be a man. That's what it means. A strong man. A man of character," said Hollenbach, who heard many over the years as the two built a strong, personal relationship.

Early on Friedgen instilled accountability in his players like that of a family. If one player slipped up, they all did. That fostered a familial bond in the program with each relying on the other, not easy with more than 100 players.

Friedgen has long kept his finger on the pulse of his teams. And he has many ways of cultivating unity like that of a family.

In a group setting Friedgen can be heavy-handed and blustery in his coach-player relationships. But one-on-one with his players he is much like a parent, often nurturing, a side the public rarely sees.

"Ralph is your tough dad," said wife Gloria. "I know his players, as much as they might be mad at him or angry at certain points, that they know his intentions. His sense of fairness with them, which is very straight-forward. It's not like he's going to sidestep issues. He just seems like, and looks like, a daddy."

Friedgen was overheard telling All-American tight end Vernon Davis' grandmother, who raised him through tough times in Washington, D.C., "these are my sons and I am going to do what's best for them," when the subject of Davis leaving early for the NFL came up.

Friedgen wants to prepare his players for life after football, and he won't cut corners in the process.

"There is no doubt he is a tough-love guy," said Galt. "He's a love and discipline guy, which is fine. A lot of times he doesn't back down too much, sometimes he does."

Galt recalled times when Friedgen asked him to back off the players in the weight room when he thought he was pushing them too hard.

Friedgen knows his players intimately, unlike recent coaches at College Park. He involves himself in not only their football and academic lives, but their personal lives as well. He has one-on-one meetings with the players a few times a year, in addition to countless informal sessions thanks to his open-door policy.

Some say the team becomes his family because he has so little time to give his own family away from the team house, where he spends most of his waking hours.

"He has incredible work ethic, works incredibly long hours. He cares a great deal," said one assistant. "He probably has a real problem with winning, and the more you get to know him there simply is not a lot of time to spend with the family. But without a shadow of a doubt, the time he does spend is amazingly quality time and I think he is a good father. His kids and his wife are totally devoted to him. There's no doubt in my mind that some of the personality, the strength he shows with the team and the coaching staff, the aggressiveness that he shows, he also does with his family. It's a real testimony that he loves them to death."

Blackney said that like a strong father Friedgen is a "disciplinarian but understands the imperfection in kids. Maybe to the group and the outside world he kinda portrays the kind of taskmaster, the disciplinarian who is going to make you toe the line. But when you get in there with him one-on-one, you see the soft side. He's got a big heart."

Blackney had his own family issues. His wife, Loretta, suffered a stroke at the age of 39 while he was an assistant coach at Ohio State. She required 24-hour care and was confined to a wheelchair. They have four children. Loretta attended most home games at Byrd Stadium and Blackney took her to dinner on many Thursday nights during the season. Blackney wasn't asked to do a lot of road recruiting, and none in his final season at Maryland in 2005. Friedgen was accommodating.

Winning is clearly tops on Ralph Friedgen's list, but a close second is his players graduating. And conducting themselves as good citizens around the program and on campus, much like a father expects from his sons.

Friedgen gets irate if they slip up in either area. Friedgen takes it personally, even venturing to the College Park strip late at night to check the popular night spots for his players. If an incident occurs, he's often the one heading downtown in the wee hours to sort it out.

If a player doesn't graduate "he feels like he has failed them," Blackney said. Friedgen promises parents on their recruiting visit that he's not only going to coach their sons, but also see them graduate. He stays after his players long after their time is up at College Park to return and finish their degree.

That's why he has one of the highest graduation rates on campus, which peaked at 79 percent in 2006.

Friedgen's paternal side gets the greatest satisfaction from the wayward son that makes it against the odds, kids that persevere as he had to as a college player.

And return years later, with their children, to thank their coach

"It's very rewarding when they graduate and get a nice job," Friedgen said. "And come back and joke about this or that I said years ago but it sunk in later."

Lamar Bryant remembered when Friedgen recruited him at Georgia Tech. Bryant was torn between Maryland, North Carolina and Tech. He knew that he was going to play in the ACC, but after three weeks of wrestling with the decision he finally decided, on a Sunday afternoon, that whichever coach called him next would get his pledge.

Former head coach Ron Vanderlinden called and after a 20-minute conversation Bryant committed to the Terps.

"Coach Friedgen called me next and said he wasn't mad because he went to Maryland. He told me if you ever change your mind we have a spot for you down here at Georgia Tech," Bryant said.

Bryant played for two years under Vanderlinden before Friedgen took over. Bryant sang the National Anthem at the Peach Bowl banquet and later at a lacrosse game at Byrd Stadium. Bryant said Friedgen is a loving father but knows when to put his fist down.

"The biggest difference was coach Vandy was too nice. Coach Friedgen would put the hammer down like a father sometimes has to do," Bryant said.

Friedgen showed his paternal side with Bryant when an academic issue arose. Bryant, a bright kid who didn't always apply himself in the classroom, was accused of cheating during his sophomore year on a group project and was dismissed from school. He received a letter indicating that he would not graduate.

Friedgen went to work, calling Bryant at 11 p.m. with a plan. Bryant had a 2.2 grade point average but needed a 2.7 during the semester to stay in school. Friedgen laid it out for him.

Bryant earned a 2.75 and was later reinstated through a school process. After that he recorded 3.0 and 3.2 GPAs in the next two semesters and graduated in four years.

"I didn't do it," Bryant said of the accusation. "And no one could ever tell me how can you possibly cheat on a group project. But he held me accountable and said, 'I got you back in school. I got your back. But now you got to do your part. I am not going to take it easy on you. If you have to be in study hall till you graduate, if that's what it takes, that's what you are going to do.'

"It happened for a reason and I am glad it did. If I hadn't gone through that I probably wouldn't have graduated, anyway."

Bryant said that after he failed a physical with the Atlanta Falcons, Friedgen told him that he would always be welcome at Maryland, be it to work-out or even work. Bryant worked on the grounds crew for two years in between playing Arena League football and volunteering as a coach at his high school, nearby Crossland.

"After I graduated he said, 'Job well done. You made it through and you helped raise the program up to a higher level,'" Bryant said. "That was nice."

R alph Friedgen is very giving and often sentimental. Especially with his family, though the public doesn't get to see that side often. His family is led by wife Gloria, who may very well have broke the mold of coach's wife.

It's difficult to find a football couple that works in tandem as well as Ralph and Gloria Friedgen. They are a true team, and it's easy to see where the sense of family begins.

Gloria's mother lived with the Friedgens at their Silver Spring home during her final years before passing away in 2004. Ralph's mother the same in San Diego before she passed away. Family and loyalty. Always.

Gloria never attended her husband's post-game news conferences at Maryland until 2002, thinking it may be an intrusion. But she won't miss one now.

She lives and breathes Maryland football with seemingly Ralph's every breath, especially on game day.

"Because I kind of live and die with him on these things. And I just want to be there," she said.

While stretched thin serving as coach and mentor to his players, Friedgen's time with his own family is limited, almost nil during the season, which runs for all but a month or so each year. The football season, winter recruiting, spring camp, spring and summer recruiting and finally summer schoolboy camp before two-a-days in August all don't allow for much quality time.

But Friedgen's family is remarkably committed and supportive, and there is no jealousy over his time. It has always been that way, and Ralph has Gloria to thank for it. The family dynamic of strong, supportive wife and daughters has lent itself well to his football family as they work in tandem.

"He has three daughters, he always tells me, and maybe it was God's way of having me take care of all these guys that I've got," says cousin Stoddard. "There is nothing he will not do for one of his players or his family."

Gloria is everywhere around the program, living the football experience with her husband. No coach's wife at Maryland has ever been as involved or immersed in the program. She is ubiquitous, from her renowned tailgate parties to the media room after games, sometimes with comments and applause from the back row. Then there's Ralph's golf tournaments and even team practices, where she arrives with birthday cakes and cookies. She lives it all.

Ralph is the dominant force in a family full of women but Gloria, a former coach and longtime teacher, is the one holding it together.

With Gloria in the lead the Friedgens' home has always had an open-door policy.

With her Italian background and love of family, friends and cooking, the dinner table always has room for extra guests.

There are feasts and gatherings of all sorts in the Friedgen household, from star players to walk-ons, boosters and bosses, fans, and even people they have just met. Though on the go with her own busy schedule, Gloria keeps the family enterprise humming and she rarely has a bad day.

Even when sick she's been known to come to the football offices to stuff envelopes, help with the MGN, visit a player.

"Gloria is the glue that keeps it all together. She is an amazing person," said Stoddard, the best man in Ralph and Gloria's wedding. "She doesn't do what any other head coach's wives do. They are all prissy and sit up in the press box."

Said Locksley:

"She is the first lady of Maryland football definitely. She is heavily involved, kinda like the First Lady is with the President. The players all know her and love her."

There are Ralph Friedgen stories. And then there are Ralph Friedgen "stories." None may be as amusing (and sentimental after all the years), as how Ralph and Gloria met and became engaged.

Friedgen, who joked about being a "lady's man" back in the day, was engaged to his hometown girlfriend while at Maryland. He bought her a ring.

But along came Gloria Spina, who was all Italian and fire and spunk. Three-fourths Neopolitan and one quarter Sicilian. Friedgen quickly met his match.

Gloria grew up in Brooklyn a third generation Italian. At the age of three her family moved to Westbury, on Long Island, followed by Bethpage at the age of 11. She lived with her parents while her paternal grandparents lived in their home. Family was important for Gloria as well.

She hailed from an athletic background, too. She played competitive field hockey, volleyball, basketball and softball. She showed spunk early, running track on the boy's team as a sprinter and long-jumper. Bethpage High School didn't have a girl's team at the time.

Her father, Ernest, was a service manager at the local Cadillac dealership while her mother, Anna, was a homemaker.

She had three brothers, Ernie, Fred and Sal, and she played sports with them including football. Two brothers captained the football team at Bethpage.

Gloria attended SUNY-Cortland near Ithaca, N.Y., to study to become a physical education teacher. She double majored in biology and physical education. As a senior, her advisor, Bill Tomik, a PhD from Maryland, suggested she continue her studies. She had been offered a job at $8,000 a year in Suffolk County as a elementary physical education teacher, but he recommended that she pursue graduate work while teaching.

She applied to Maryland and Illinois in 1971, and Tomik wrote recommendations to both schools. She had never been to Maryland before.

She recalled the day she went to Cole Field House looking for a roommate. Not long after, Gloria and Ralph (who was a year ahead of her in the same masters program), met at orientation.

While busy taking notes she remembered "two guys with cut-off jeans just kinda waltzed in. I am thinking, 'Who are these two losers?' " Gloria said.

The next day, in badminton class, the students partnered up. Friedgen's roommate, Roger Rees, asked Gloria to be his partner. Ralph, meanwhile, was on the other side of the net with a classmate, Joyce, his partner. Gloria wasn't exactly on her game that day, she said, and kept apologizing for missing shots and having to bend down to get the shuttlecock.

"Ralph said, 'Don't worry honey. It's not a problem,' " she quipped when she looked back at their first meeting.

Gloria thought Joyce, who she knew was engaged, was engaged to Ralph. A roommate of Ralph's who was friendly with Gloria's roommate helped move her to a new apartment. So Gloria cooked a meal, as a thank you gesture, to be served at the boys' apartment. She knew Ralph would not be there, busy with football. Ralph was in between the staffs of Roy Lester and Jerry Claiborne and hoping to get a job as a graduate assistant.

While cleaning up afterwards Ralph returned and Gloria warmed food for him. They talked into the night and as the hours dragged she recalled him saying, in his blunt way, "Are you spending the night?"

"I was pretty naïve and said 'No' and nearly jumped out of my skin. I went out to my car. We were still talking and he kissed me through the window."

A few days later, while studying at Cole Field House, Ralph asked Gloria out for coffee, then three weeks later to Homecoming.

One of the funniest moments of their courtship came early in the process.

After being stranded at a party and getting a ride home from another young man that Gloria invited in afterwards to be courteous, Ralph arrived. She didn't know what to do. Ralph soon lightened the mood, as he's been known to do.

"I told him there's somebody else here." He said, 'Well, is there any dessert?' He comes in, sits down, asks the guy for the sports section and then says, 'Isn't your time up?' The guy got up and left. Ralph never left after that."

Gloria remembered calling her mother on the telephone smitten over Ralph, "unlike the other three boys she had dated," she said.

Ralph was exciting, funny, and they had a lot in common. On Sundays they attended mass followed by breakfast at a favorite little French restaurant

"It was just the nicest time," she said.

Ralph and his family were hooked on Gloria right away. The first time he brought her home to meet his parents in Harrison, just after Thanksgiving in 1971, they went to dinner at the Cherry Lodge, a local restaurant. Not long into the evening Gloria began playing the piano and the bartender sang along.

"My father looks at me and says, 'Where'd you find this one?' " Friedgen said.

Fittingly, their wedding song was "Make It With You" by the band Bread.

Joked Ralph Friedgen years later:

"My father said, 'What the hell does that song mean?' "

Said Gloria, while bantering with her husband over "their song," recently:

"Make it through life, Ralph. That's what it means. It's a lovely song."

Ralph's mother, who became close with Gloria, knitted her clothing including the dress Gloria wore on their honeymoon, which she still has today and it still fits.

The couple gets a kick out of new visitors' reaction to their wedding picture, which hangs at their Silver Spring home, with a much slimmer Ralph.

"One of Ralph's players said, 'Oh, I didn't know you were married before,' " Gloria said with a laugh.

The year they met Ralph was collecting data for his graduate school thesis about athlete's stress levels measured by the palmar sweat index. He tested wrestlers pre-and-post practice and at meets to register open sweat glands, and how they varied under the stress of competition.

It was titled "The Emotions of Varsity College Wrestlers Prior to and After Both Competition and Practice as Measured by the Palmar Sweat Index."

"I'm in the bathroom and these guys are puking pre-competition. You know how that is with wrestlers. And he's got these slides collecting samples on," Gloria said of how she assisted Ralph in the collection of "data."

Gloria typed it up, an unenviable task, she said, as computers and "white-out" didn't exist. But Ralph dedicated the thesis to her:

"My deepest gratitude to Gloria Spina for the dedicated manner in which she typed and assisted in the preparation of this thesis."

Said Gloria: "I remember his professor saying to him after his oral, 'What if you don't marry this girl?' "

Before they were engaged, though, came another memorable story in Ralph-Gloria "lore."

Between his junior and senior years Friedgen was engaged to his high school girl-friend, a girl a year older that attended Hunter College.

His grandfather, the accountant, had given each grandchild $1,000. His mother was all for Ralph getting engaged. His girlfriend, Patty, even lived with Ralph's parents while in college and traveled to College Park for a spring formal. Her brother also attended Maryland and played football with Ralph at Harrison High.

Ralph took his grandfather's gift to buy the engagement ring. But the two broke up not long after. She was living with Ralph's parents but dating other boys, he said, and Friedgen summoned her and told her, "Either the ring or your finger."

But it gets better.

Ralph went to a pawn shop years later when he needed money. Later, on the Friday before Christmas and on the eve of Ralph and Gloria becoming engaged in Florida, Ralph and Stoddard went to New York City to get a new ring. They were delayed and the safe where the ring was in hock was on a timed lock which would not be open again until Monday, well past the time Ralph was due in Florida.

So Stoddard cashed his football coaching check and paid for the ring. Ralph had a ring, made it to Florida to his parents' home on Singer Island, and on Christmas night asked Gloria to take a walk on the beach. They made a fire, spread out a blanket and Ralph was "very romantic," in asking her hand in marriage.

"Tears came to my eyes," said Gloria, who was 22 at the time. "But on the blanket he said, 'Here's what you got to do when you go back to New York because I am leaving for The Citadel. You are going to have to go to . . .' "

Stoddard ended up taking care of the exchange, getting Ralph's original ring and going to "trade up" for a nicer ring for Gloria.

"I earned that ring," she said with a laugh.

Ralph and Gloria came from close-knit families. Evenings weren't so much spent at restaurants or out on the town, but around the dining room table over meals with family, friends, neighbors "and even people we didn't know," Gloria said.

Conversations and debates raged into the night. The exposure, she says, was tremendous, something she continues today with her children. When Gloria coached years later she marveled at the "education" her students — disadvantaged youth from rural parts of South Carolina — received over the dinner table. At a Steak & Ale Restaurant during a state track meet, Gloria said she would never forget the time her students ordered crab legs and didn't know what to do with them.

"It's all part of this. I think I have always been an advocate as a teacher, in my profession, and of course, I have always loved sports," Gloria said.

In later years, when Ralph came back to Maryland under Ross, the Friedgens began inviting the offensive line, including Kevin Glover, to their Bowie home for dinners. After spring games and other important events the players saw a more human side of their demanding coach.

"And boy she can still cook," Glover says today. "The amazing thing is I was out at a golf event recently and she was out there playing. And I said that's just amazing. Back in 1982-85 when I was here, Gloria was perky, energetic, always on the go, always giving out hugs. Always seeing how everyone is doing. And watching her today, nothing has changed."

Gloria is always on point despite the hectic pace that she keeps. She remembers names, dates, thank you cards, once even sent a reporter a gift on the arrival of a daughter. She bakes items, which she brings to practice for players and coaches. She is in constant motion but takes pride in every little thing that she does.

"Ralph has always said to me, 'If you can't do something first class then don't do it,' " she said. "I have lived with that feeling."

Things changed once Ralph became a head coach and they didn't have the same interplay with his position unit. Now it's the entire team, which changed her role slightly.

Gloria knows most every player's business from how they are performing on the field and in the classroom to their personal relationships with girlfriends. With life issues she is ready to spring to action and help. It continues after the players graduate and move on as she keeps in touch with many.

At Thanksgiving in 2006, newly arrived quarterback transfer Josh Portis and his mother, Patricia, shared a holiday meal at the Friedgen's home, while in Easter of 2007, quarterback Jordan Steffy stopped by to dine at the Friedgen's table.

Yow and her husband, Dr. William Bowden, have shared Thanksgiving and Christmas dinners at the Friedgens' home and have visited their Georgia lake home as well. That's not common among coaches and their bosses.

A paradox of Friedgen's is both the fear and love his players have for him at the same time.

"Like, how he can yell and scream at you Thanksgiving morning at practice," Rychleski said, "but opens up his house and dinner table to the kids four hours later. Kids are resilient, but still it's an unusual thing."

It is a fine line between his bluster and his warmth, and many have felt it.

After the players graduated, Madieu Williams and Latrez Harrison visited the Friedgens for their annual Fourth of July party at their Georgia lake home. They are two of several that have seen him casually, or socially, in the off-season.

Rychleski has been with Friedgen from the start, hired as his first special teams coach after he was impressed coaching against him at Wake Forest.

Rychleski has seen a lot in his day and doesn't mince words. He served as the closest thing to an associate head coach Friedgen has had at Maryland when, in 2006, after Friedgen took over the offensive coordinator duties he delegated more responsibility, like game management, to Rychleski. He is a good judge of character.

"In my opinion, Gloria is a special person. I have been around here long enough to know. I got a good sense on all that stuff. She is, to me, a very, very good person."

G loria Friedgen has always been there for her man. She responded in kind when Ralph came to College Park as head coach.

She took over many of the day-to-day operations of the MGN, the program's booster group, in the winter of 2006. The MGN is a group that Friedgen relies heavily on for key needs in the program, not to mention it operates as a social connection between fans and the program.

Gloria's open, game-day tailgate at the team house, famous for Italian delicacies that she prepares, became the MGN's tailgate.

She spends days preparing dishes, all headlined by the seven gifts of the Holy Spirit. She grew up in a household where Christmas Eve was meatless and fish was the main course. She prepares it for Christmas Eve dinners at home, too, which often involve boosters, neighbors and players, sometimes as many as 25 guests, some who can't make it home for the holidays.

Her tailgate interpretation of the meal is a variety of pasta dishes, sausages, peppers and sweet and sour meatballs. All prepared in volume. One of her closest friends, Debbie Bebee, spends a day with her shopping and preparing the meal. They met at a middle school bus stop when she dropped daughter Katie off on her first day after the Friedgens arrived in town. The weekly tailgate feast can run close to $1,000 a game, all out of Gloria's pocket.

Gloria's tailgate had a twist, though, in recent years.

She wanted to include players and their families, even recruits if they stopped by, but was not permitted under NCAA rules as it was deemed an extra benefit. So she turned it into a positive. The Terps required that those in attendance be paid members of the MGN. That helped drive membership in recent years.

Gloria, who sits on the Executive Board of the MGN, also helped revamp the organization's website, which wasn't very user-friendly before she got involved and enlisted the free help of a web designer, John Edwards, whose son Danny is a walkon on the football team.

Gloria also puts together the MGN newsletter, which comes out several times a year, while she is a fund-raiser for Friedgen's annual spring invitational golf tournament, selling corporate sponsorships in excess of $120,000 in 2006.

Gloria has always been involved in the MGN's showcase event, the Spring Gala, the group's black tie dinner dance and auction. From stuffing and mailing letters to auctioning items such as a "Cooking with Gloria" dinner at her home, she in is perpetual motion.

She assists in group correspondence by answering e-mails from the MGN's web site while maintaining its e-mail list-serve of some 6,000 names. She sends e-mail reminders to members about "Terp Alley" and other football events. Gloria's often at the front of the line with her daughters welcoming the team at "Terp Alley" on game days.

It's truly a family football enterprise.

"Gloria is thoroughly engaged in the process," Yow said, "and proud of the role of being the head coach's wife. And smart and articulate. Ralph sees her as part of the fabric of the program and she always has his back."

She also hosts "Breakfast With Mrs. Fridge" once a month at the newly established School of Public Health (formerly the College of Health and Human Performance) where she works. It's an event some football players attend as several are students in the college. Approximately 100 people attend each breakfast, and from all walks of campus life from students to faculty to athletes. She is no football snob and opens her door to all. Gloria provides the food and drink, also at her expense. She has been hosting something similar since the early days of her husband's career.

Sollazzo, who was a lineman under Friedgen at The Citadel, remembered the day, after dislocating his hip in a game, that Gloria was immediately at the hospital with a dish of lasagna. For years she hosted the line at her home for Italian feasts, with lasagna her signature dish.

Gloria also stands by her man on the front lines, taking on the role of publicist, shield, and sometimes mediator. She screens and answers his university e-mail, which can range from inquiries from recruits to irate fans expressing their displeasure with the coach or program. And she can dish it, too. She's never been known to back down.

"I did answer one [nasty] e-mail earlier this season, which said that it's a shame to be a Maryland grad. And that my husband was stupid. The guy actually wrote twice, after the West Virginia game and later after one of the close wins we had early in the season. I read it and responded, 'Thank you. You are entitled to your opinion, but I read it and respond to Ralph's e-mail.' Then he wrote to my Gloria e-mail and now I put it as 'spam.'

"But before I did that I called the development people, because he put a name to it, and I asked is this man a season ticket holder, does he donate? And it was neither. But to be really honest, in the years we have been doing this he has gotten a lot more good than he has bad."

Gloria knows her history, too, and how there can be a fine line to walk as a head coach's wife.

"I can remember at one point in time Bill Battle was coaching at Tennessee. I was a youngster then. It was the '70s. And the Tennessee fans put a moving van in front of his house. So things could be worse," she said with a laugh.

"I look at it with Gary Williams this year [2006-07], and they judge every single

game. But you got to sit back and look at the whole thing and that's why it's so difficult. And if you live on every single game like that and be so critical, then you have
too much free time."

G loria Friedgen has long been an ambassador for the program. She ties up many of
the loose ends that her husband doesn't have time for. Her background in education makes it a smoother transition as she comes in and out of so many worlds between
football, academics and campus life.

"She understands the entire team concept from the players to the game day to doing
whatever it takes for Ralph. She will do anything in the world in support of him," said
longtime booster Barry Gossett, who the football team house is named after.

"It is truly a unique situation. To me it's inspirational, it really is, that you can really have it all," said Franklin, currently the offensive coordinator at Kansas State. "To
have such a strong family unit."

Hollenbach remembered the time Gloria approached him and congratulated him
on a specific play after a game. The woman knew the specific play?

"I think you know it is a football family when the wife is talking to you about what
you know coach Friedgen said to her. She would say stuff like, 'You know, you read that
one well.' Or, 'It's a good thing you saw the safety there.' It's funny but she's just great."

Gloria seems the perfect complement to her husband, often a buffer when he's full
of bluster, be it around his football family or his family.

"Some will say it's that 'good cop, bad cop,' " she jokes. "Like he loves his children so much but he goads them."

Gloria visits the football office a few times a week. She and Ralph do a lot together when he has free time and, harkening back to his childhood, Ralph took her horse-
back riding on the beach in San Diego when he was with the Chargers. He taught her
how to ride.

"She's always the opposite. Well, not the opposite, but if he's being critical about
something she will be, 'I know he said this to you. You're doing a good job. You need to
keep going and you will be okay.' She kinda completes him in that way," Hollenbach said.

Said Sollazzo:

"She's not your typical football coach's wife. She's really just one of the gang."

Gloria works countless hours on campus at her job while also serving as a tutor to
some of her husband's players.

One of the players she helped was quarterback Jordan Steffy.

She made flash cards for Steffy and worked with him once a week. She also
helped tutor running back Bruce Perry, attending every one of his Plant Biology labs
for a semester.

"I know because Jordan and I were roommates," Hollenbach said, "Jordan would say if it wasn't for coach Friedgen's wife I wouldn't be passing this class. She really provided the best way for him to learn.

"On the one hand, you got coach Friedgen trying to teach the best football methods to quarterbacks. And on the other hand you have Mrs. Friedgen trying to teach the best academic methods to the student in the football player."

She would serve as a buffer between Friedgen and his players, as Perry related.

"I could talk to her about personal issues. She was a real friend and she understood where we were coming from dealing with coach Friedgen," he said.

After Josh Allen suffered a major knee injury in 2004 two weeks before finals and fell dangerously behind in the classroom, Gloria took over. She, along with Allen's girlfriend, got him to review sessions or attended sessions when he couldn't get around. She made note cards. For three straight days they drilled the information into him. He got an 83 grade to pull out of the hole.

Gloria also worked with place-kicker Nick Novak among others, and said Novak was "Bar-none, the best student I had come across.'

"And when he finished that class he e-mailed me that 'we' got an 'A.' I was so excited. It's all part of it. I love teaching," she said.

Ralph Friedgen joked that the best thing about his wife is that "she remembers names," which in his busy life is important.

"That's just her," he said of his wife's role in the program. "I have never asked her to do any of that. I just think she is really a true partner. She just wants to be involved in anything she can do to help. She is really a great ambassador for the school."

Said Gloria:

"I accept it. Not to sound derogatory, but I am a low-maintenance woman. I love the attention I get from him when I get it but I do have another life. I work. I get a lot of appreciation for what I do on the outside. But I am very involved with the football program and that's a good thing. It has been a long time that I have known what it is all about."

A running joke between Ralph and Gloria during their seven-year stay at The Citadel was that he promised her they would move a lot in the profession. They then moved three times in three years "and I never spoke again," she said.

There's no question Gloria did much of the heavy lifting raising their three daughters, who have turned out exceptionally well given their father was rarely around.

"I am very involved with my daughters. I never felt like I missed anything. I am very strong and assertive in my public life, but as his wife I can be a little bit deferential. Maybe that's bad but it works well," Gloria said.

Some think she may push the envelope, at times, of decorum for a coach's wife.

Once, after a loss at Georgia Tech, she was heard in the back of the interview room commenting, "that's enough" as far as questions from the media for her husband.

But her intentions are altruistic and few could argue, with much merit, that they are anything but to protect her husband in what can be a harsh profession, given the demands of fans, boosters, bosses and the scrutiny of the media,

"She is an energetic lady," Rychleski said. "She might stick her nose in sometimes where she shouldn't some might say, but she always means well every time she does it. She really cares about people and it is important to her."

One incident came in the spring of 2007. The coaches were in film session with Ralph between spring practices. Unannounced, Gloria popped in the meeting room. It was just after the Virginia Tech campus shooting and she gave out ribbons for the coaches to wear in support. Ralph at first grumbled and then greeted her with, "Well, good morning Gloria. We're happy to have you."

"She wanted to do something that was appropriate to do, and I wore that thing the whole weekend," Rychleski said. "It felt good that she thought about us. She does a lot like that people don't even know about. And she puts up with Ralph [laugh]. Everything is important to her. When you are a very good person then it really doesn't matter."

She completes the softer side of Ralph, a side some of the players get to see though the public does not. Players like Hollenbach said Ralph Friedgen "goes the extra mile to help someone out. He does the behind-the-scenes work that a father would do."

Be it talking to a professor, parent, or girlfriend, neither of the Friedgens are bashful about approaching someone in a player's inner-circle.

Hollenbach was in Friedgen's office on many occasions when he overheard his coach dealing with players' family members or girlfriends. One was roommate and close friend Danny Melendez, a wide receiver out of Lancaster, Pa., who had a tough childhood and wrestled with some issues, as well as injuries, throughout his career.

Between the summer of his junior and senior year, Melendez went AWOL from the program and could not be reached. The word was Melendez, whose girlfriend recently had a child, was considering quitting because he missed a morning conditioning run and incurred Friedgen's wrath. He didn't respond well and bolted. Friedgen told Melendez to either make up the run the following morning or "you're off the team."

Melendez did not return phone calls, including Friedgen's, so the coach dialed up Hollenbach to mediate.

"He told me, 'Look, I can't get ahold of him. He's not answering my calls but he'll listen to you. So you need to tell him that I am going to be behind him if he wants to get out of here, if he wants to transfer that's his decision. But he needs to know that we want him here. We want him on this team. You need to express that to him.' "

Melendez returned and went out on top as the team's best receiver as a senior in 2005, hooking up with his roommate on several key plays including maybe the most dramatic of the season, an 80-yard touchdown catch and run at North Carolina in the Terps' 33-30 come-from-behind win.

"To give Danny a second chance . . . the perception was coach Friedgen didn't really care about him and didn't want him on the team, and maybe that's just his tough guy personality. But talking to him about it really kinda surprised me."

It's not often players have the home phone number of a coach. Especially the head coach. But that's the case with Friedgen. In fact, the Friedgens' home phone number is listed.

Cornerback Josh Wilson recalled coming back to campus after Thanksgiving weekend in 2006, after watching Miami beat Boston College to keep Maryland's ACC title hopes alive heading into the finale against Wake Forest. The players were glued to their television sets at their homes that weekend, but none had been in touch with their coach yet.

Wilson called Friedgen's home and Gloria answered. She warned Wilson that no one had spoken to him since the game ended. And that he was very animated. Wilson wanted to bask in the Miami upset with his coach.

"He started going crazy at the other end. He said, 'If you're not on the boat you're getting out of here. I'm not having anybody on this team that's not trying to win this game.' I wanted to go play right then. I said man, this guy is high. He was ready to go, as intense as I ever heard him," Wilson recalled.

Wilson said Friedgen told him to call his home anytime, for whatever reason. Besides some late-night crank calls, it has worked out well for the Friedgens as he is always just a phone call away. Many players have called him or Gloria in times of distress, sometimes in the middle of the night.

"It's very rare that I call coach Friedgen and he doesn't answer," said Wilson, who also has his cell phone number. Wilson said he even called him once about a matter concerning the dorms.

Friedgen has welcomed freshmen to his home for a cook-out before camp. He is in his element and more relaxed, joking with the players, shooting pool, always holding court.

The sense of family pervades the program, which many see as an extension of the Friedgen family.

"You are going to do whatever you can for your family. And when you consider this football team your family, he is going to do everything you can for his family and give them every opportunity. You don't want to see your family not succeed. He takes pride in seeing that every kid has a chance," Rychleski said.

Players and coaches alike point to a poignant time when Friedgen was in full splendor as proud papa of his team. It came at the Champs Sports Bowl team Christmas dinner in Orlando in December of 2006.

During the weeks of practice in College Park leading up to the game, Friedgen joked, after informing the team that it would spend the holiday in Florida, that he may don a Santa Claus outfit for "a little Christmas surprise."

Little did they know that the staff was hustling around town trying to find a red suit large enough to fit. Five shops and three days later, the Terps found one his size and shipped it to Florida.

The season had its share of ups and downs, from personnel issues in the pre-season to the slow start and letdown on Thursday night in Morgantown. And there were a number of times when Friedgen could have lost the team. The blown opportunity to win another ACC championship crushed Friedgen after consecutive losses to Boston College and Wake Forest at the end of the season, winnable games the Terps helped give away.

But no one could have scripted a better "feel good," or improbable, ending in Orlando before the Terps' first dominant win of the season, the 24-7 rout of Purdue, a win that restored faith in the program and its coach.

Four nights before the game Friedgen gave the team something it would never forget. He sat on the stage in the banquet room in a Santa Claus suit, with the young children of the coaches' on his lap, giving out wrapped presents. Even Yow, the model of decorum, sat on his knee.

Santa Claus, er, Friedgen, asked her if "she had been a good girl this year," and "what she wanted for Christmas?" Yow responded, "A big win over Purdue!" which brought the house down.

"No one saw that coming," Josh Wilson said. "Coach Friedgen is a serious guy. When you see him coming in there as Santa Claus talking about 'Ho, ho, ho' and handing out presents . . . this guy was crazy right now. This is our head coach. I know a lot of grown men wouldn't do this and this is a Division 1 head coach."

Friedgen nailed the Santa Claus role, waistline and all, and he was in rare form. He had done it for years when his daughters were young, and once owned a Santa suit. He did it at a few bowl games in the 1980s while an assistant coach. Among the sights to behold that night were the players and coaches scurrying for their cell phones to take pictures of Friedgen as Santa Claus.

"He was laughing. He was doing his 'Ho-ho-ho' thing. I remember going up to him and just shaking his hand and giving him a hug and saying, 'Thanks for doing this, coach.' And he looked at me funny and said, 'Coach? I'm Santa.' I was like, 'Oh my God, he's really into this,' " Hollenbach said.

Said Yow: "He has his tender moments but that may have been the best I had seen."

Hollenbach admitted it was a long season and Friedgen wore on the players at times, especially him. But his role as Santa Claus struck a chord that some said helped the players relax and play their best game of the season.

It's all part of his strong personality, but at the same time his playful, disarming side that shines through at times. Many in the program would like to see it more.

"Coach has such a powerful effect on our team. I mean, his mood is going to determine our mood and his attitude is going to determine our attitude. There are times when guys on the team may be questioning if he is working us too hard or what not, but there's no doubt about it that he is a leader and he is the guy everybody is going to look to for his attitude and his determination, and we definitely draw off that," Hollenbach added.

Rychleski summed the night up for the team:

"That amazed me. That is one thing that I will never forget. And like [quality control assistant] Dan Hickson said, everyone will remember that we won that bowl game, but they'll remember that Ralph Friedgen played Santa Claus for them.

"That was a perfect example of him lightening the mood. The same kids he was yelling at practice the day before, and here these same kids are all jumping up and down taking a picture and laughing their butts off. That was definitely a highlight of the trip, and it may have been a big reason why we did so well to be very honest about it."

Wilson said that during the season when the Terps went on a five-game winning streak and won several close games beginning at Clemson, Friedgen told the players to "have fun," while he also let up on the practice field a bit.

"He knew when and how to do little things to get us excited, laughing, getting us enjoying our time down there. That was a change in him."

The family bond connects all things in the program, the players say, with Friedgen playing the role of doting papa.

Said Hollenbach:

"I'm moving on now but what I will miss the most is the father-like role of coach Friedgen. And his caring ways. He cares about what's going on more off the field, like how you are doing, what you are doing, how things are going at home. That mentally you are alright before you step on the field because if you have other things on your mind, you are not going to pick up the football stuff. He is like that caring parent."

Friedgen protects his players in a fatherly way by always having their back and never rushing to judgment. He knows that some have to be treated differently than others, and he knows when someone is trying to "snow" him.

But he is fiercely loyal all of the time.

In 2006 at the President's Cup luncheon to honor the athletic department's top student-athletes, Hollenbach was seated at a lead table with Mote and Yow when Friedgen started lobbying for his team.

"It was kinda cool. I just sat back and listened. He was bragging about our team and sticking up for us. There were a lot of teams there. It's kinda cool to have someone who is going to go out there for you. He wasn't bashful at all. He took the lead role at the table talking like that to his boss, the higher-ups at the university, just putting us out there," Hollenbach said.

The loyalty runs deep and back to his family.

It's rare to see Ralph without Gloria or their three daughters on game day. Wives of past head coaches were rarely seen or heard. If they were seen, it was above in a box at Byrd Stadium. Gloria is emotional on game day, be it in the stands, even on the field afterwards. Same for her daughters, who have been known to take the field after big wins and seek out their father for a hug.

"I come from an Italian family. We hug and kiss people. We don't shake hands,

we don't get sick that much. You know what I am saying," Gloria said.
    If Ralph is the father of the program, Gloria is clearly the mother hen.

A fter Ralph Friedgen took the Maryland job, Gloria arrived the following spring
    before the family moved. She attended her first practice.
    She suffered a coughing bout so went to the team house to get a drink. She walked past the training room and met kicker Nick Novak, who got his new coach's wife a throat lozenge. Later she bumped into Novak's parents at practice and formed a lasting relationship with the family that extended past graduation. He became one of her favorite players.
    In 2002, when senior receiver Jafar Williams was in the dumps over playing time, academics and his girlfriend, he had something of a meltdown and wandered off campus. He wasn't found for 24 hours.
    "He said, 'I got nothing going,' " Friedgen recalled Williams telling him.
    Later, Gloria found him hunched over a computer in the academic support center on Friday afternoon as the team prepared to go to the hotel. She sprung into action, telling him, "You're going with me."
    Williams arrived at Maryland, along with high school teammates Bruce Perry and Scott Smith, from Philadelphia's George Washington High School. But despite being a great-looking athlete and former track standout, he had confidence issues. He butted heads with both Franklin, the receivers coach, and later Friedgen, while mysterious injuries seemed to hold him back.
    Gloria needed permission to drive Williams anywhere and feed him at her home, what is called an "occasional meal" by the NCAA.
    ACC Live!, the television show, was expected with a film crew at the Friedgen home that night to film Gloria preparing her tailgate meal. So she briefed the crew on the situation and said she was going to feed Williams first and they would have to wait. Williams sat in Ralph's easy chair in the basement and de-compressed while watching television, and soon he snapped out of his funk.
    Gloria spoke to Williams that night about "having to be ready to play," using the Frank Reich-for-Stan Gelbaugh story from the "Miracle of Miami" game that Ralph was involved in in the early 1980s. And "how that's going to happen for you," she said.
    Later, she would act as a mediator between Williams and his girlfriend.
    Williams would go out on a high note with a dramatic touchdown reception in the Gator Bowl in Jacksonville. A year later, after he got his degree and first football coaching job at Moravian (Pa.), Williams called Gloria and left her a message on Mother's Day, wishing her a wonderful day. He also called Ralph Friedgen wishing him well after hip surgery and thanked him. The two had a tempestuous relationship at times during his playing career but that all seemed to wash away. In 2007, he

climbed the coaching ladder to Division I.

Gloria had close relationships with several Maryland receivers, and when Derrick Fenner had his appendix removed, she visited him in the hospital and brought home-made brownies.

"I don't think Ralph makes it in coaching like this, with his kind of level of commitment, without the support of Gloria. It is truly a partnership," Blackney said.

Said Terps All-American rush end Shawne Merriman of the one-two punch of Ralph and Gloria:

"Family, football and winning. That's life for Ralph Friedgen in order. Period."

G loria Friedgen has had her moments, too.

While at Georgia Tech, head coach George O'Leary, a longtime friend, colleague and later boss of Ralph Friedgen's, had to move her seats twice at Bobby Dodd Stadium because "of her arguing with fans around her," O'Leary said.

"But I think that is fine. That's the competitiveness in people. That's how strongly she believes in what was going on. She's not afraid to voice her opinion, and obviously when things aren't going right some games the guys that get the heat are the head coaches or the coordinators."

Ralph Friedgen, whose father after he retired attended his son's games, sat in the stands and sometimes his ears would shudder.

"I remember after the games he'd joke, 'Have you ever heard her at the games? It's unbelievable,' " Ralph said.

Gloria insists on sitting in the stands among the fans, not in a private box away from all the action.

"They had faculty and staff seats on the 15-yard line," Gloria said of her experience at Georgia Tech. "But those faculty and staff people sometimes gave tickets to the other team. So I would get into it with the people that would be there for the other team, and they would do taunting cheering in your face. I'm really not [a problem]. But they moved me to the 40-yard line and I sat with 'Yellow Jacket' people, people in the Jacket Club, like the Terrapin Club, who were very happy that we were there."

Gloria has had other issues with fans while defending her husband and the Terps in places most football wives don't venture.

She was struck by water bottles at N.C. State in 2001. She also had a scary moment when daughter Katie got knocked to the ground after the breakthrough win over Clemson at Byrd Stadium in 2001 when fans stormed the field. At N.C. State that season, Gloria asked security to remove a fan that was taunting her, waving his shirt close to her face.

"She's low protocol. But I mean that as a compliment," said Grabenstein, who is close with the entire Friedgen family. "It's not, 'You can't talk to me, I'm the coach's wife. We're all one big family here. My phone number is in the phone book. We're not unlisted phone number type people.' "

Gloria never forgets a player, either.

The Friedgens plan to hold a graduation party in South Carolina for former Georgia Tech quarterback and Ralph Friedgen disciple Joe Hamilton, who returned to school to get his degree after years of chasing the pro dream. Next to Hamilton, George Godsey, Shaun Hill and, most recently Hollenbach, were the quarterbacks that Friedgen was the closest with. Godsey works on O'Leary's staff at Central Florida while Hamilton did color commentary for the Georgia Tech radio network in 2006.

Hamilton immediately called Friedgen when he got engaged and invited his former coach and wife to his wedding.

Hamilton may have been the quarterback that tested Friedgen the most. He needed constant babysitting during his early years at Tech, be it class attendance or enjoying too much nightlife, Friedgen said, but later matured into a leader and an all-ACC standout.

Hamilton visited Friedgen and the Terps during a spring practice in 2007. Afterwards he addressed the players about getting their degree. He was in town for Friedgen's 60th birthday party, which Gloria organized and more than 100 family and friends attended, including Hamilton and his wife.

"She has obviously done so much in furtherance of everything he is after as she looks upon it as her win-loss record as well as his," Grabenstein said. "She has also observed a whole lot of other coaches' wives in the process. In the many years she has seen which ones have been supportive like that and which ones haven't."

Gloria finally got her husband to ratchet things down as far as his schedule. At least based on his first five seasons at Maryland. Finally he is "enjoying the moment" a bit more, she said.

The family would typically spend a week or so summer's vacation at one of their homes in Georgia or South Carolina.

Rarely would Friedgen give the staff a weekend off after recruiting, which he did over President's Day Weekend in 2007. Friedgen also let them have time with their families immediately following the Champs Sports Bowl, another rarity. There have been years, like 2006, when the staff did not get a spring break.

Gloria approached her husband before President's Day Weekend and spoke of the staff members' children having Monday off from school, and that they should get a "long weekend." Borrowing from Gloria, he went to the office and told his staff: "I have been thinking about this . . . that we are going to do these days."

"So at least I am glad he heard me," she said.

Gloria is used to her husband getting up at 4:30 each morning and leaving the house by 5:30 for work. During the 2006 season he typically didn't get home until midnight.

But he is sleeping better these days after adding a device for breathing during the 2005 season.

Gloria also got her husband to finally renovate their South Carolina beach house after years of talking about it but never getting around to it.

"I wanted him to get away and relax," she said. "All work and play makes Ralph a dull boy."

Gloria has tried to lead the charge for her husband to eat better and exercise more frequently. She knows when to push and when not to as it remains a sensitive subject. Friedgen is not a big eater, which is part of the irony. She believes the fact that he is under constant stress, coupled with his sedentary lifestyle, attached to his desk for much of the day, has added to his weight.

"We'd go to all-you-can-eat places and he wouldn't have it," said Locksley, who recruited on the road with Friedgen many times. "And I'd have three plates."

Friedgen, who as a freshman at Maryland weighed 190 pounds and was slim and athletic-looking growing up, saw his weight balloon to upwards of 380 pounds in recent years. He tries to eat light and slower these days, but heredity has taken over, he said, and he's followed in his father's footsteps. Also, during the season he rushes his meals as he allows himself little time to eat.

Friedgen has tried to stick with exercise plans but they tend to fall off when the season starts. In 2002, he dropped nearly 40 pounds after being put to the challenge by boosters including Gossett, who offered him a reward of $100 per lost pound in the form of a donation to the program. Once a week Friedgen got on the scale as Comcast television crews filmed him.

"Hereditary. Hereditary. Look at my father, my uncle, my kids. I can starve myself and still won't lose a whole lot," Friedgen said.

After hip surgery he gained even more weight.

Now he tries to walk on the treadmill or ride an exercise bike.

"Every day my wife thinks about it. It annoys the hell out of me. But I am going to enjoy my life. If I die tomorrow I have had a great life. I can try to do it but I am not going to not enjoy my life to lose the weight. I have all these people worry about me and I appreciate that."

Some have recommended gastric bypass surgery, something Friedgen has no interest in pursuing.

"I am sure as soon as I do something like that it will only screw something else up. Then I am really going to get pissed," he said.

Said Stoddard:

"I am sure he is in touch [with his mortality], but I think he is too busy to think about it."

Gloria, who tried but has resigned herself not to dwell on it, said:

"I don't know. It's not important what he looks like. When I look into his eyes he's still 25-years old."

N othing is more sacred to Ralph Friedgen than his daughters, Kelley, Katie and Kristina, who crave his limited time.

All have carved their own niche and enjoyed successes in the shadow of their father.

Kelley, 30, is an attorney at Arnold & Porter in Washington, D.C., specializing in pharmaceutical and medical device law. And she is the "intellectual" of the three, her father says.

She was the only Friedgen daughter that grew up on both pro and college football. She has a law degree from Emory, which she attended as an undergraduate as well. She was on full scholarship, had a 4.0 GPA, and edited the law review.

"Ralph always called her a 'blue-chip,' " Gloria joked.

Ralph took rare time off to take Kelley on a spring tour of colleges, visiting North Carolina, William & Mary and others. He also attended many of her volleyball games in high school while coaching with the San Diego Chargers.

Kelley attended LaJolla Country Day School, where Gloria taught, and she played four sports. She was recognized with a Brian Piccolo Award for the top scholar-athlete of Italian descent in San Diego County.

Kristina is a senior at Maryland majoring in Theatre and is "intellectual but more artsy" and quieter than her sisters. She is a College Park Scholar and had a high school GPA of 3.87 and played volleyball.

Katie is a sophomore in Studio Art at Maryland and is also into the arts and made a 4.0 her freshman year. But she is more like her father in terms of being "more conservative and not as liberal as the others," he said.

Ralph Friedgen said that both he and his father would have been lawyers had they not been coaches as "we love to argue."

"I just can't see her not being a litigator," Friedgen said of Kelley. "She likes to argue just like me."

Kelley, who is fluent in German, prepared a study on HIV/AIDS in German. Friedgen marveled at the $25,000 signing bonus she got to work for Arnold & Porter. In high school, he said, Kelley would raise her play when he attended her games. She was around football the most as the oldest daughter.

"She is a football brat," said Stoddard. "And she knows more about football than a lot of men. The guy she brings home to marry better be a football guy. That's going to be an interesting phenomenon."

Both Kelley and Kristina studied abroad at the university's campus in Genoa, Italy.

The two youngest have a flair for the dramatic, likely from their mother and a bit from their father. In 2006 Kristina served as drama director at nearby Elizabeth Seton and co-directed at her high school, Sherwood, while she also worked at Arena Stage as a theatre coach for children's plays.

She acted and directed through high school and college in plays including *Jane Eyre*, *Bye, Bye Birdie*, *Mame*, *42nd Street* and *Gypsy*.

Gloria got them started early by taking them to plays and getting them involved in the arts.

Youngest daughter Katie's passion is art and photography. She was asked to be a teacher's assistant in the university's photo department. She also works in the art gallery at the student union. She shot the Maryland-Wake Forest football game from the sidelines in 2003. She is more effusive than Kristina and perhaps has the most charisma of the three, her parents say. She played volleyball at Sherwood where she carried nearly a 4.0 GPA.

"We are very, very proud of our daughters. And handling the pressure of moving around a lot. They're tough kids," Gloria said.

One of the few interruptions Ralph Friedgen allows during the work day is when his daughters stop by, which was more often in recent years with the two on campus. Often it is the only time they have dinner together. Friedgen is rarely home for family dinners much of the year.

The early joke in the neighborhood, where the family moved three days before Ralph's first game, was whether "the lady of the house was married," Gloria said. Gloria has always taken things in perspective, noting that if she was "high maintenance we'd be in trouble in this profession."

"The neighbors didn't see me until after the season," Ralph Friedgen said. "That's just the way it is."

One night when Friedgen could not break away from a staff meeting to see his daughter Kristina in a play at Sherwood, a special dress rehearsal was staged. There were only two people in the crowd, Ralph and Gloria Friedgen.

Recently, the Friedgens got together for a family portrait in their backyard, one Ralph gets emotional about.

"I look at pictures now and I say where the hell did those times go? There's definitely a trade-off," he said.

Gloria has always been involved, as both a teacher and coach for her daughters, dating back to their days living in California. Gloria taught biology and was an assistant volleyball coach.

"I think because we have girls it works. If I had had a son it might have been different, might have been more difficult," Gloria said. "People will often say, 'Don't you wish you had a son?' And I say, 'I don't. I really don't.'"

Gloria takes pride in the sense of identity of each of her three daughters, and said Kelley will "always be Kelley Friedgen even after she gets married. She is a professional woman."

When the family is on vacation is the time Ralph Friedgen's focus turns to his daughters.

"The times that I have seen him the happiest is when his three daughters are all in the room," Grabenstein said. "It can be sitting downstairs watching a football game in the family room or whatever, but he just radiates whenever he's got all three of his daughters around because it is such a rare occurrence. He doesn't get it all that often."

There's little doubt that the Friedgens having girls was a blessing.

As Gloria explained:

"It's a very nurturing environment. Now, he'll say it's too estrogen filled and there's too much chatter at the table and everyone talks too much. But it really is a very nurturing environment.

"If we had had a son, or seven, you know a boy child," she said, "I think there would be a lot of pressure on that child. And maybe some need for Ralph . . . he could be totally concentrating on his 'other' sons. So we think we are very lucky we have great girls and he's enjoying them.

"We always tease him, like you know our son would have been a ballet dancer. Not that that would have been bad," Gloria added. "When we were pregnant with Katie, our third, he kept saying during the sonogram, 'Are you sure, are you sure it's a girl?' He wasn't convinced until she was actually born."

Said Ralph:

"Obviously I would have loved to have had a son. But I learned a long time ago that God knows what he is doing. My daughters always joke that because of how wild I was [growing up] that's why I have daughters. Gloria jokes because I am around men all the time some hormones kick in [laugh]. But I can't change that. I can't worry about things I can't control.

"Maybe that's why I enjoy coaching. A lot of guys don't like dealing with all of the problems. Sometimes some of my favorite guys are the guys that have the most problems."

One thing is constant, and that is the respect and love he gets around the house. He lords over dinners at the family's table and keeps everyone on their toes with his verbal jousts.

"He is treated like a king," Yow said. "He wouldn't say that but I will. The wife and three daughters are just crazy about him and would do anything for them."

Friedgen interrogates his daughters before a date. He'll joke that he'll tell the boys gossip about his girls. Maybe even joke about threatening the boys if they don't stay in line.

R alph Friedgen always has time and energy left for his "other" family, and he gives them equal doses.

Friedgen has a handful of players that he took under his wing and formed special bonds. And most because of their problems.

The list included Jafar Williams as well as receiver JoJo Walker, the moody Texan "who would speak his mind, which I liked about him," Friedgen said.

Walker wrestled with attitude problems and was something of a team cancer during his junior year. But Friedgen beamed when he was voted to the Terrapin Council as a senior and finished his career strong.

Friedgen wanted to see character come out in Walker, and it finally did, though after some struggles.

Williams did much of the same, bouncing back after Friedgen gave him some tough love. Friedgen told him he would have a lot tougher things to deal with in life than what he was experiencing now and that "You can't quit. You got to learn how to deal with it. You are going to have to sometimes reach that point to determine if you are going to make it."

Friedgen showed the toughness again when he suspended Williams for walking out on the team for a week but told him: "Before the end of the year is out you will come back and make big plays and help us win big football games. We'll find a way around all this."

Friedgen showed his other side by getting in touch with Williams's girlfriend, who walked out on him over other issues. Gloria and Ralph got them back "for coffee that week,' " he said, and got them talking again.

Williams came back to have a big game against Virginia, catching a bobbling one-hander to set up a touchdown, followed by another big game versus Wake Forest and then the Gator Bowl, collecting five touchdowns in his final three games. Williams got a free agent look with the Washington Redskins and called the Friedgens after every scrimmage.

Williams had issues with his body cramping up, which limited his ceiling, but he had a solid college career.

"Now he got to the point where he thought he could be really good," Ralph Friedgen said. "Those confidence issues went away."

The connection to the players and their families is strong.

Friedgen became close with fullback James Lynch's mother, Brenda. She was legendary for her Sunday night dinners for the players at her Washington, D.C., home just off Florida Avenue.

Many of the stalwarts of the early teams visited for her home cooking led by Lynch, Curome Cox and Ricardo Dickerson.

James, nicknamed "Greasy" for the way he sweated profusely, was one of the more popular players on the team and a bull of a fullback. He was a "quiet tough guy" and everyone feared and loved him at the same time.

Lynch's mother worked numerous jobs trying to keep the family afloat, including as a cook at a downtown hotel. But Lynch's mother got gravely ill and passed away during his junior year, so Lynch went pro early.

Friedgen visited her at the hospital four days before her death, spending several hours with her as she slipped into a coma, and prayed for her. Locksley stayed the night with James in the hospital. Brenda Lynch was huge in James' life, also raising James' infant son.

Friedgen was there when it was decided she would be taken off of life support. James nearly dropped out of school, devastated by the loss, and went pro to help his family, which included two siblings.

Friedgen attended her funeral as he did the mother of another extremely popular player, Madieu Williams, when she passed two years later. Some 40 players and coaches attended the funeral including assistant coaches Blackney and Rychleski.

Former safety Dennard Wilson said Friedgen's personal relationships that he builds are best for the players from out of state who don't have a local family support system, or high school coaches around in time of need.

"Coaches are vital in your life," said Wilson, who was at both funerals. "They put a stamp on your life. I didn't need a father figure. I have a great dad. But they are vital because this is a time you are becoming a man. Coach Friedgen is one of those guys who's going to leave an imprint on you."

Wilson said he felt comfortable going into Friedgen's office at any time. And he often did, airing out team issues or other problems.

I n a twist – and a sideline to how the first team came together – Dennard Wilson said he felt "disrespected" by Maryland at first because the Terps did not offer him an early scholarship during the Ron Vanderlinden era. Ralph Friedgen may have missed on one of his favorite players if things hadn't changed.

Wilson said that not until Alabama, West Virginia, Northwestern and others offered did Maryland tender him one. Wilson hadn't camped at Maryland and the Terps wanted him to visit campus first. He considered Alabama strongly and they had the inside track with former Stags fullback Marvin Brown there. Wilson said it was "a dream to go to Alabama."

Wilson visited unofficially and told the 'Bama coaches that he was coming. Before he left for his trip his Maryland recruiter, Locksley, told him, "We really want you, and we know you are not going to come here. But you are going down there and they are going to tell you all the right things."

Wilson loved the tradition at DeMatha and saw the Tide program as the DeMatha program on a larger scale. But after returning the homebody Wilson, who had never been away from his family, decided it was too far. Wilson consulted his parents, who wanted him to stay local, and later he decided on the hometown team.

"I called 'Locks' up and told him, 'I got news for you.' He said, 'Go ahead and tell me the bad news.' I said, 'Locks, I'm coming to Maryland.' He was like, 'What?' "

Over the years, players have come back when their playing days are over in need and Friedgen has helped them out. Be it helping with a one-time rent loan, giving job references or making a call to someone in the profession, Friedgen has always been there as a safety net.

"When he's away from football he's a heck of a guy in terms of just talking and listening. We can talk about anything. On the field it's business, 'My way or the highway.' And he tells everyone that and they know it," Dennard Wilson said.

Another player that Friedgen inherited, a secondary player that he preferred not name, was involved in an alleged assault during the early years. The player was often getting involved in scrapes, "usually the second guy," Friedgen said. And then he got his girlfriend pregnant.

The player came to Friedgen and asked if he could live with his girlfriend.

Friedgen, frank as always, told him, 'You know, I don't know what kind of message I'm sending you. Knock a girl up and you get to live off campus.' I asked him what did his dad say about this, and his dad was a military guy, a big guy."

The father agreed to the plan but only if Friedgen gave his blessing. Friedgen made a deal that as long as he maintained a 2.5 GPA he could live with his girlfriend. The player never got lower than a 3.0 the next two years, while he became a better player. And he didn't get in trouble again.

"It was because of his girl. She was such a positive influence in his life. If I had been a hard-ass maybe he wouldn't have been as productive as he was. As long as I am not being taken advantage of I really try to help kids as much as I possibly can as long as they don't abuse me. And sometimes I let them abuse me a couple times before I get hard on them."

Friedgen has become softer each year, he said.

He let Jermaine Lemons and Patrick Powell quit the team during fall camp in 2005 only to welcome them back a week later. Lemons was at the airport on his way home to Florida. The staff didn't want either player back. Neither player came to say goodbye to Friedgen.

But he let them return in good standing.

Lemons is still with the team while Powell transferred to Massachusetts after knee injuries slowed his Terps career.

Always lessons being learned on Friedgen's watch.

"I told Jermaine when he came back, 'Okay, now you've got an opportunity. What are you going to do with it?' It's like me being a coach, an assistant coach for 32 years, before I got an opportunity to be a head coach. Well, the day I took the job here I made the promise we weren't going to bail."

Friedgen said that he's had players come to him and complain, "You don't know what my life is like. I live in the 'hood.' I deal with this and I deal with that. You can't understand what it's like."

"I said, 'Well, that may be true. But I do know one thing: you've got an opportunity and you got a decision you got to make. Are you going to take advantage of the opportunity or are you going to be back in the 'hood' like all those other guys on the corner saying 'woulda, coulda, shoulda,' telling everybody what a great player you were going to be for the next 30 years of your life?

"You got an opportunity and that's all you can ask. If you don't do anything with it, don't be bitching and moaning. I am willing to give that to you.' "

Gloria recalled her husband only getting cross with their daughters once, and it was many years ago. Maybe, in part, because Gloria was always the one around to mete out punishment, which was rare to begin with. Either way, it has worked out well for them.

G loria Friedgen said her husband has mellowed more each year, getting further away from his father's tough side. And that his teaching side shines through more and more.

"It's funny," she said. "Remember that if your child does something bad do you say to your child 'just leave this home and don't ever come back?' Think about it.

"And that's really what it is like. If your child makes a mistake what you will try to do to is correct that mistake, let them see that it was a mistake, and hopefully change the child to see the right way of doing things. Now, we're under constraints. We can't give them 100 chances, but we certainly can give them opportunities."

Ralph Friedgen said that he is amazed how well his daughters have developed "without their family always being around."

He said he's had no problem with them drinking or suffering through other embarrassing situations.

Friedgen attributed much of it to his wife, who read incessantly to their daughters when they were young.

"Always read to your kids. Read to your kids," he said.

"They didn't have any of the computer games, only learning ones," Ralph added. "I brought home the 'Madden 2000' [the popular football video game] and Gloria didn't even want me to buy that. She said only for me, not for them."

I n 2005 Ralph Friedgen returned to Harrison, N.Y., for the first time in years. The trip was planned for him to visit his parents' graves.

His childhood home was no longer there, instead a few new homes on the lot. He has few relatives left in the area.

He combined the weekend with a play on Broadway followed by dinner with Sam

Maldonado's father at a neighborhood Italian restaurant in Harrison. Friedgen struggled with his emotion while discussing the nostalgic trip.

Friedgen is connected to the past and never forgets it, with a foot in it as he plugs
forward into the future.

Ralph Friedgen was named "Father of the Year" by the Father's Day Council, ben-
efiting the American Diabetes Association, and honored in June of 2007 at the
Ritz Carlton in Washington, D.C.

"He comes back to tell me about the award. And he said, 'I'm father of the year
because I am never around my kids. I haven't been able to screw them up,' " Gloria
joked of her husband's reaction.

Said Stoddard of his cousin the family man, the football man, and how he combines the two:

"I think they are very, very supportive of their dad. If they had their druthers they
would like to have him around more. But they know that is not going to happen. They
have learned to live with that. He has worked 18 hours a day for as long as I have
known him."

There's nothing better in the Friedgen household when there is downtime, which
is rare, then to pop in a movie or watch a football game.

They don't get out to the movie theatre as often as they once did, but Friedgen
loves action flicks, like those starring Arnold Schwarzenegger, and Mel Gibson films,
while he showed his soft side as he laughed throughout the drama *Something's Gotta
Give* with Jack Nicholson and Diane Keaton in recent years.

Gloria also bought him a "tough guy" collection, he said, *The Essential Steve
McQueen* for Father's Day in 2006, while he was moved by Gibson's *The Passion of
the Christ*.

"We'll get a DVD and watch it with the girls," Ralph said. "But there's not much
else I do because I don't got the time."

Friedgen enjoys an occasional drink, relaxing with a Dewars and water, a glass of
red wine over dinner, sometimes Sambuca afterwards. He plays golf and fishes with
his daughters. He'll even ride waves with them at the beach in the summertime, or
hang out in the community pool at the lake. He plays cards but prefers chess.

They even had a "Friedgen Family Olympics" when they were living in San Diego.

Friedgen's mother, in town for a visit, got involved, shooting at a tiny-tot basketball hoop during the basketball portion of the games. There was swimming, diving,
and other activities. Gloria still has it on video in the family collection.

There's always competition.

Gloria said her husband learned to treat his players fairly because of the disappointment he experienced as a college player.

"It's why he's able to reach people and communicate and be straight with them," she said. "It had a deep impact to the point where it made him a better coach in terms of all facets of coaching. Not just the X's and O's, but the compassion and caring for the kids.

"He can relate. He'd get beat up. He'd talk about how his shoulder would come out and he'd put it back in and he'd go back in. He has been there before so he knows what his players are going through."

Fittingly, the Friedgens were invited to a small reception at the Hay Adams in Washington, D.C., to celebrate the news of the "Father of the Year" award. But Friedgen could not attend. He was at the Annapolis Touchdown Club "with his son, Sam Hollenbach, who was getting an award," Gloria said.

Still, it's always been a team and nothing has disrupted the Friedgen family football enterprise.

"That's the story of our life," Gloria said.

Ralph Friedgen recalled the day his boss, Debbie Yow, first met Gloria:

"I remember the first thing she said was 'We got a 'two-fer' here,' " he said with a hearty laugh.

6

CHARACTER

R alph Friedgen learned much about character from his father at an early age. Once in a Little League baseball game came a situation which he would draw on years later in his Character Education program at Maryland.

The scenario was if the official made the wrong call, would you say anything?

Friedgen's father sat in his car at Ralph's baseball games. He watched his son play from the front seat.

One day Ralph was playing third base and missed the tag on the runner. The umpire called him out but Friedgen told the ump that he missed him. The ump reversed the call.

"People were booing me," Friedgen recalled. "Even my own teammates were pissed off. Later I came back and I remember my dad telling me, 'I have never been so proud of you.'"

Ralph Friedgen doesn't wear his 1990 National Championship ring, the one he won at Georgia Tech as offensive coordinator. Nor the AFC Championship ring earned as offensive coordinator with the San Diego Chargers in 1994.

Instead, the one he brandishes most is the 2001 ACC Championship ring earned at College Park. Not because he won it in his first year as head coach of his alma mater, but because of how his players won it.

The Terps clinched at least a share of a title in the second-to-last week of the season with a dramatic win over Clemson at Byrd Stadium. After the game students stormed the field and carried off the goal posts.

It was the first "big-time" atmosphere at Byrd Stadium, Friedgen said, the kind that he envisioned all along at Maryland.

Friedgen came into the locker room moments before kickoff and told the players that Florida State had just lost, "and if you want a ring all you got to do is take care of your part out here."

Assistants Locksley and Taaffe sat in the press box stunned after the game. They watched the field "erupting with fans swallowing it all up," Locksley recalled.

"That was unbelievable. It was what I dreamed the atmosphere would be at Maryland," Friedgen said.

Bryant said Clemson jumped off sides on the first series to intimidate the Terps. But it was the best offensive line Friedgen had at College Park with C.J. Brooks, Bryant, Melvin Fowler, Wike and Matt Crawford, all-ACC talents from left to right.

Defensive back Domonique Foxworth, a true freshman, had to step in for starter Tony Okanlawon and responded against the Tigers' red-hot quarterback Woody Dantzler.

"It was something you only see on TV," Bryant said. "I had never seen a crowd with that much energy. The place was full when we came out for warm-ups."

Bryant, after he fought through the crowd and into the locker room, said that by the time he got back his helmet had been "stripped of its decals as the fans were so out of control." He also got hit in the head with an orange as they prematurely celebrated an Orange Bowl bid.

It was not that night but a week later in Raleigh, N.C., against The Wolfpack, when Friedgen saw the seminal moment.

Nothing was going right and the Terps were on life support late in the game, a game that was fast becoming a letdown after the euphoria of the Clemson win the week before.

Slot receiver Parson fumbled the ball on the State one-yard line after a long catch and run. The Terps also fumbled in the end zone. They could have packed it in and settled for a share of the title. Instead, they came back to win a shocker, 23-19, to take the league outright and advance to the BCS Orange Bowl.

"I was very proud of that team not only to come back and win that game, but when they weren't at their best," Friedgen said. "It would have been very easy to say, 'Hey, we had a great year.' Or, 'It wasn't our night.' But they didn't do that. I think it took tremendous perseverance."

At the game, Friedgen had his famous chair throwing incident at halftime in the locker room to get the players' attention. It got so bad inside, the players experiencing the wrath of the volcanic Friedgen for the first time, that Sollazzo draped a towel over a camera ESPN mounted on the wall for a piece it was preparing on the new coach.

Friedgen was livid that his team was going through the motions on a day when it could capture the ACC title outright.

Typically, he addresses the team (when he is upset) for about 30 seconds at halftime. This time he lambasted them for almost four minutes. Halftime, which Friedgen runs like he did in the pros, is about adjustments, not speeches.

The players had a blank stare on their faces and didn't move despite chairs hurling through the air. But they responded, overcame the emotional letdown of the Clemson crescendo, and prevailed, manhandling the Philip Rivers-led Wolfpack.

Friedgen kept the players in it until the end, cheering and encouraging them on the sideline. Friedgen didn't want them to settle for a tie, he wanted it outright to prove to them it could be done. During the halftime salvo he had so much emotion running through him that tears flowed down his cheeks.

It was a physical game with brutal hitting. Throw in his halftime tirade and the emotional way that they won it, and it created a polar opposite afterwards. The players saw a giddy Friedgen dance in the locker room after the win, letting loose emotions and joy they hadn't seen before from their taskmaster coach.

It was the game that affirmed for many that Friedgen's formula worked if the players bought into it.

Many around the program saw it as the seminal moment of the Friedgen era. The Terps were up against the sophomore standout Rivers on his home field and were taking punches but never countered. At least until the second half, after their coach connected with them in a visceral way.

Said Galt, who was in the locker room:

"That was a dramatic point in the program's development where he was not just going to accept anything. If we were going to go down, we were going to go down with 100 percent effort, not lack of willingness to win. That was the first time that we saw that."

"That was a sign of him saying what I do works," safety Dennard Wilson said. "Don't turn the ball over. Play physical. Get turnovers.

"And it all solidified things afterwards. It was like in his mind he was saying, 'I should have had this job 30 years ago.' It was a beautiful thing."

The game had several twists and turns but the Terps kept getting opportunities. They hung around as Friedgen had preached to them.

"He kept telling us when we went over to the sideline, 'It's not over. We are going to get the ball back and we are going to score,' " Wike said. "Then we saw how tired their defense was and Shaun [Hill] kept going and kept pushing us. Looking back, and how amazing that last pass to [receiver] Guilian [Gary], that's one of the memories I will never forget."

It was about strength of character for Friedgen, something his father instilled in him early, be it in practices, games, even at home. Be prepared. Persevere. Never wilt in the face of adversity.

Said Locksley:

"Everything with him is, 'You got to finish. Finish. Finish. Finish.' Games. Practices. Everything. And that's what that game was all about as they could have just rolled over."

Friedgen also pointed to the 31-31 tie the Terps had heading into the final quarter in Tallahassee, Fla., in Friedgen's first trip to Doak Campbell Stadium.

It was another defining moment that, despite the loss, the team showed great inner-strength, and that it would follow him into war.

It started during pre-game stretching.

"I can remember that game. We got in an altercation in warm-ups and I was all upset over that," Friedgen said. "But [assistant coaches] Franklin and Locksley came in [to the locker room before kickoff], and they were so happy the guys were fighting back."

Ralph Friedgen's first season was a magical one.
Quarterback Shaun Hill, tight end Jeff Dugan, center Melvin Fowler, safety Dennard Wilson, center Todd Wike, linebacker E.J. Henderson and corner Curome Cox stood out, among others.

They were some of his favorites: low maintenance/high yield types. And leaders all.

"We had that special thing, that chemistry. We had that the first 2-3 years, and very strong. Nobody cared who got credit for what. We were all on the same page," Blackney said.

Dugan, who has enjoyed a successful career in the NFL, was the 'E.F. Hutton' of the team. He rarely spoke but when he did everyone listened. No one messed with him. Friedgen gets emotional when he speaks of his former tight end from Pittsburgh.

"Out of all the players, I think I missed Jeff the most," Friedgen said of the first team and some of its personalities. "He wasn't a guy that spoke a whole lot, but when he said something he meant it. And he didn't care who he said it to. He could say it to me or E.J. [Henderson] or whoever. He was a hell of a kid."

Friedgen points to the first team as the model. It was a "starless" group, but a group hungry to win after years of being down, so that individual success didn't matter. It was about the team, and counting off the "W's" each week, as the players frequently did.

And the breaks went Maryland's way. Sometimes inexplicably. It was part of the good "karma" they experienced all season.

The players, Friedgen said, didn't mind the discipline. He said that he had to be a disciplinarian to change things, and the "kids liked it" eventually.

"The only thing they have to understand is why you are doing it. If kids know that you care for them they don't have a problem. You discipline your children but it doesn't mean you don't like your children. But in the long run they appreciate it. Because they grow up with the right ideals or they have the inner strength to be successful. And I think it's the same way with the players," he said.

Friedgen knew that he had to strike a balance between the two. He said one of his college coaches, Bob Ward, couldn't achieve that balance.

"Bob Ward was unwavering all the time. No one could relate to him," Friedgen said. "You got to hug them [players] when they do well. And you got to tell them how proud you are of them. No one's ever told them they are proud of him."

In 2005 he used wide receiver Drew Weatherly as an example. He came from a tough background with a single mother and modest means. Weatherly called Friedgen on the telephone and beamed about getting a 3.0 GPA.

"They are crying out for it. They have not had it in their lives, for a male figure to say to them, 'Hey, you are doing a hell of a job,' " Friedgen said.

E very game that first season it seemed like different players stepped up. All season long it happened. Everyone played a part.

The running game carried the Terps early and by the Troy State game quarterback Hill started to click through the air. Receiver Gary was a play-maker, Lynch a quiet leader at fullback. But most of all, Hill moved the team, didn't make mistakes "and reserved the right for the Terps to punt the ball," Locksley said when looking back at the keys of the season.

The player that may have been the heart and soul of the team was Dennard Wilson, the safety from DeMatha, who was sick of losing.

Though not blessed with track speed or great athleticism, Wilson was a warrior and laid it on the field each time out. He also spoke his mind, telling Friedgen right away, "I want your job" as his dream was to someday be a coach. (Five years later, after a stint with the Washington Redskins and assistant coaching at DeMatha, Wilson joined Friedgen's staff as a graduate assistant in the spring of 2007).

Wilson summed up the hunger of the team after many down seasons. He was never shy about speaking his mind and he had an independent streak. The character of the team helped form around him and Friedgen loved him.

"They prepared us like others couldn't," he said. "We memorized our plays and we knew the tendencies of the other teams over and over. But I always believed when game time comes you don't play for coaches. You play for yourself. You play for each other. You go out and execute what they taught you earlier in the week. I knew we were prepared and in shape but it came down to how we were going to play together. It's Xs and Os,' but it all came down to unity, the great chemistry that we had, and all the years we played we had that."

Wilson said Friedgen inspired the players "because right when he got here he said he wanted it all. Wins. New stadium. You name it. He didn't hold back."

And, he said, Friedgen was consistent with team issues, from the top player down to the last one on the roster.

"He was the same all the time. Once you know him, you know him," Wilson said.

Hill, the yeoman JUCO quarterback who bounced around before sticking at College Park, summed up the ideal for Friedgen.

Recruited out of high school as a tight end, not a quarterback, Hill, a Kansan, reminded Friedgen of former Minnesota Vikings quarterback Joe Kapp.

Hill quickly absorbed Friedgen's offense and got it to hum despite his physical limitations. Hill had average arm strength and little foot-speed to speak of. But he was tough, physically and mentally, something Friedgen hoped for in a signal-caller "to deal with the system, and to deal with me," he said.

Hill earned respect from his teammates for his leadership ability, as well as the fact he would take a hit and not run out of bounds. He was a "gamer," always coming up with big plays in clutch times.

"Shaun was a competitor. And the more he learned about quarterback, the better he got," Friedgen said. "I can remember Shaun at the Orange Bowl. I can remember him competing till the end even though we were down by 20 something points. He never gave up. I would have loved to have had him for more than one year because I think he could have been something special."

Said Bryant:

"Shaun was just a play-maker. He wasn't really smooth-footed or anything like that. But he knew how to get the job done. And he had that swagger successful quarterbacks need to have."

"He was the kind of guy Ralph wants as a quarterback. Be a leader. Lead the team. Move the chains. Be smart with the football. And he did all of that," Locksley said. "He had that innate ability. Not the prettiest, but able to win."

Friedgen said that he watched the Terps under Vanderlinden the year before on television, including the Clemson and North Carolina games, and remembered telling O'Leary about Hill.

Otherwise, the first team was a mixed bag as far as talent. Heading in, Friedgen said of some of that talent:

"I thought our wide-outs were kinda average, had no juice. Guilian Gary, he never ran a route the same way twice [laugh]. Jafar [Williams] had a lot of ability but at that time didn't really believe in himself. And then we had [Jeff] Dugan, who early on didn't really believe a lot."

But he had kids that had played a lot, and hunger was their primary emotion.

"That made our job easier to coach them. They were very attentive, even when they didn't have a great practice. I remember the first time in two-a-days I threw them off the field and they started to go but realized that wasn't a good idea. They came back and had a good practice. But they had some good leaders," Friedgen said.

The season, and the Friedgen era, got off with a bang in the victory over North Carolina at Byrd Stadium in his debut game.

It was an example of the team hanging around and overcoming turnovers and adversity, notably Willie Parker's long touchdown run on the first play from scrimmage.

Blackney recalled staying up the night before racking his brain about whether to blitz or drop a safety in the box and play an eight-man front against the Tar Heels. After Parker's run to start, Blackney told Sollazzo, "I'm glad I didn't unpack all those boxes."

But Friedgen kept the faith. He told the players to buckle down and their turn would come.

An unlikely hero was walk-on punter Brooks Barnard, who arrived late to the pre-game meal at the hotel. So Friedgen locked him out.

Barnard helped win the game through the field position battle thanks to his booming punts, seven of which landed inside the 20-yard line.

"I remember [special teams coach Ray] Rychleski comes running up to me and says, 'Are you suspending him?' And I said, 'No, I'm not suspending him because he's not going to eat a pre-game meal. I'm not stupid,' " Friedgen said.

Barnard, a bit of a free spirit who first attended Oklahoma as a walk-on with hopes of becoming a weatherman, was named for Baltimore Orioles legendary third baseman Brooks Robinson.

And Barnard was the last player you wanted to starve before games. The punter hid sandwiches in the kicking nets on the sidelines during games, sneaking bites because he had a nervous stomach. This time, sent on the field with no pre-game meal, he had his cousin shuttle him hot dogs from the stands during the game. Barnard said he ate four during the game, while Foxworth snuck him fruit, unbeknownst to Friedgen, beforehand from the breakfast bar.

"I actually walked in one minute before breakfast was to start. But that wasn't the time on Friedgen's watch, I guess," Barnard recalled of Friedgen laying down the law early in his tenure.

The Terps prevailed against a talented UNC team led by All-American Julius Peppers. And it gave them a huge shot of confidence.

"We kinda won the game going away, you know, where they scored seven points on the first play but we kind of shut them down from there," Friedgen said of the 23-7 win.

Fans at Byrd Stadium probably thought that after Parker's run it would be a case of "Here we go again." That nothing had changed in the Maryland football program.

While past teams may have fallen back to old ways and tossed it in, not this group.

Said Bryant:

"Coach Friedgen had already instilled in us that things are not always gonna go your way, exactly the way you want them to. We have to keep fighting through games. That first touchdown, mentally and physically we just got stronger and those things didn't even happen."

Dennard Wilson said the team believed it could play all day long. They could thank Friedgen's winter and summer conditioning program despite the balmy day.

"I remember it like yesterday. It was hot, maybe 100 degrees outside, and they broke that run but we settled down. It was a new era, a lot of pressure. But we showed each other collectively that we could play together and we had the heart and determination and grit. Everything turned magical that year."

Said Friedgen:

"I told them we wouldn't beat ourselves and the other guys would be tired before they were."

Another high-water mark was the game that may have signaled the Terps were for real. It was the Thursday night overtime shocker against Georgia Tech in Friedgen's return to Atlanta.

It came, in part, thanks to Henderson's defensive heroics and Novak's field goals, including the game-winner in overtime.

Friedgen remembered going to the players before the game and using a little "psychology" by telling them, "there's only one person that knows both teams and that's me."

"And I went player by player, the match-ups. And I told them we're better here. We're close here. It's gonna be who's going to play the best. I made it so we were better. We were the better team because I felt like I had to give them something for their confidence. I thought we got after them pretty good at the beginning, and at the end of the game they were really getting after us."

Before his big fumble recovery, which he returned for a score, Friedgen remembered telling Henderson, "Right now they are taking it to us. If you want to win this game you got to bow up. You gotta stop them."

"The next play we sacked them and they were off schedule. Then [running back] Joe [Burns] went out of bounds. He did that because he's a competitor. I know George [O'Leary] told him to stay in-bounds. We got the ball, drove the ball down, and kicked the field goal to tie it up and go into overtime. It was a hell of a football game."

The Terps entered the nationally televised game confident but unsure of themselves as a national player.

"That kind of solidified us and all the hard work we put in. We always fell short in that instance before. And that game it was the defense that had to carry us. It was that never-say-die attitude we had all season," Bryant said.

Friedgen said it was the "strangest game of my career" because of his mixed emotions, something he said he never experienced before.

So many emotions coursed through him that night and in the practice week leading up to the game, that "he had a glow in his eye all the time," Dennard Wilson said.

The game was back and forth. Things didn't go Maryland's way for long stretches. But in the end the ball bounced their way, something that would define the season with the breaks they both made and somehow got. It was their year.

Friedgen ran place kicker Novak through extra pressure situations that week in practices just in case it came down to a final kick, which it did.

"When he hit that kick, man we all went off. That and winning at N.C. State were the two greatest games I had at Maryland. And coach Friedgen came and hugged all of us just to show how proud they were of us. I will never forget that game," Dennard Wilson said.

Another important game in 2001 came against Virginia at Byrd Stadium when the

Terps "physically crushed them," Locksley said.

"I remember [Virginia coach] Al Groh had a quote in the paper afterwards. That that Maryland team was the most physical team that we've played, and we got to get to playing like that. That's a game Ralph really, really wanted. That was a climactic one as well," Locksley said.

There were numerous subplots that season with young stars emerging like freshman corner Foxworth when starter Okanlawon went down with an illness. Then there was the group of academic deans that dyed their hair red, making good on a bet with Friedgen if he won the ACC Title.

The Terps went on to play the Florida Gators in the Orange Bowl, a sobering game against a "world-class group of athletes," Friedgen said.

They came at Maryland in waves.

Friedgen said it was one of the best teams he ever played against at the college level, while it was a hungry team after coming up short in a quest for a National Championship that season.

The Gators, led by quarterback Rex Grossman, blew the game open early and it was never much of a contest after the opening quarter. Friedgen said he made a few key mistakes, like being too aggressive with his play-calling.

With four minutes to go in the first half and down 21-7, Friedgen went to the two-minute drill. But the Terps were unsuccessful on three plays, giving the Gators the ball again before halftime. They quickly scored and the game was out of reach before intermission.

"Knowing I was up against a better team . . . run some clock. Let's get out of there. We'll come back the second half," Friedgen said of what he should have done.

The other mistake came in practicing the team too hard, he said, while trying to get his young players ready for the following season. He even practiced heavy during exams. He was still learning and balancing things as a first-year coach, and has scaled back bowl prep ever since.

The Terps also went into the game with Wike sidelined with a leg injury and Perry a wrist injury. Perry was limited while Wike didn't play.

The Terps may have arrived, at least as a program, too early to the game. Riding a wave of emotion, exceptional coaching and overachieving players, they simply didn't have enough talent.

Friedgen knew recruiting would have to catch up, especially team speed, if the Terps were going to contend on a national level.

Blackney came to Friedgen at halftime and told him "nothing's working. He looked at me like I understand. It was one of those nights," Blackney said.

"I think it was a great experience," Friedgen said when looking back. "It was the first time I had been in a BCS bowl. And it was very, very exciting to come out of that chute and see a sea of red in the stadium. It was unbelievable.

"I don't think there had been many Maryland teams that had experienced something like that. Our kids played hard. We were just over-matched. They were vastly better than we were."

Florida had too many weapons and so much depth. But the Terps realized they had reached the top and knew what was needed to take the next step.

They used it as motivation for the following year, when they beat up on Tennessee in the Peach Bowl. Friedgen learned much that first year, and soon carried it over as he laid the groundwork for future success.

"Shoot, when we played Tennessee I don't think any team in the country could have beat us that night," Dennard Wilson said. "We learned so much, learned how to play on a national stage and everything that came with it. And Coach learned from practice what we had to do."

In 2003, coming off the Peach Bowl and beginning in winter workouts and through the summer, the players broke every huddle chanting, "National Champs."

It was a long way from the first goal of the players, who listed six wins, or Friedgen's goal of simply getting into a bowl game.

"We quickly went from winning six games to eight or nine to win 'em all. Beat everybody on the schedule," Dennard Wilson said. "We felt we could have it all."

Friedgen helped shape several players on that first team, some into coaches. It may never have happened had the program not turned around and the players tasted victory and loved the game after many disappointing seasons.

Gary, Williams and Wike, among some of the stars, worked as coaches while Hill, after his NFL run, hopes to get into coaching.

Friedgen got Wike, a strong student in philosophy who wanted to pursue a law degree, a summer job with Montgomery County judge Durke Thompson, who wrote Friedgen letters about his exemplary work. But Wike soon jumped into coaching after working Friedgen's summer camp. He got his start on the staff at Georgetown.

Character is what stood out to the first-year coach.

"It seemed like it was so easy to talk to that team," Friedgen said. "I remember Guilian [Gary] coming to me the last game of the year saying he was going to miss my Friday night talks. It seemed like every game was a cause, and they were ready. They were so close for so long but they just didn't know how to do it."

Whatever it was – chemistry, breaks, fresh schemes the opposition hadn't seen, or their turnover margin (which led the nation at times that season) – it all came together in one of Friedgen's most rewarding seasons.

Said Locksley:

"It was like an out-of-body experience. That year was surreal, almost. The way it happened and just built up game by game. You saw the momentum coming. But with each win he demanded more from the kids and they stepped up."

Four years later, when discussing a young 2006 team in the pre-season, Friedgen held up the example of the 2001 team and hoped his current team would follow suit. A never-say-die attitude summed it up best, and it came straight from Friedgen.

"He instilled in kids never give up. There was always a way, a chance, if you keep fighting, fighting, fighting. Look at Rich Parson dropping that ball at N.C. State," Blackney said.

"There was not a situation in practice our kids had not been in before and faced. They learned and grew from it, like the two-minute drills under Ralph, which made it as game-like as possible. Every little situation Ralph made a big, big deal of. They had been simulated and practiced from Day One."

Fortune was clearly on Maryland's side on many occasions, but so was a strong will.

"I believe some of it is luck, but I don't believe all of it is," Friedgen said.

Said Wike:

"I remember the Clemson game the Orange Bowl year was my favorite moment. To come out to that kind of crowd. We had never seen that before. I remember looking at the scoreboard in the fourth quarter and coach [Tom] Brattan pointed towards it and said, 'This is what it's all about, guys.' "

A ccountability is huge with Ralph Friedgen. Much of his character-building is tied to it.

Friedgen's two losing seasons at Maryland, he said, could be attributed in part to "special situations" he had. Occasions when maybe 'I' crept into 'team' and derailed things, distracted the players, affected their focus.

There are many defining players and personalities scattered throughout the Friedgen era at Maryland.

But few are like Shawne Merriman.

In 2004 the standout rush end/outside linebacker, one of the most celebrated Terps, wasn't a "negative guy," Friedgen said. But with his obvious NFL size and talent, not to mention a big personality, his days were numbered as he entered his junior campaign. And most around the program knew it.

Merriman came to Friedgen and asked the coach if he could skip certain practice drills to protect himself from injury.

Friedgen told Merriman that he always protected his players, especially those with pro potential and on the cusp of being drafted. Just as he did in practices with linebacker D'Qwell Jackson a year later, following wrist surgery and before he was drafted.

But Merriman had outside people whispering in his ear about positioning himself for the pros, which didn't help matters.

Merriman was excitable and quick-tempered. He'd get in weekly fights in practice with tight end Vernon Davis and offensive tackle Stephon Heyer, players he'd line up against. Sometimes Merriman would arrive on the practice field talking trash to

Davis before drills had even begun. Merriman also fought offensive lineman Ryan Flynn and defensive tackle Conrad Bolston, among others.

But it was part of his aggressive, in-your-face style, a style he had no qualms frequently displaying. Merriman would turn out to be one of Friedgen's biggest personal projects, a kid he helped innumerable times but one that tried his patience just as well.

"But I am not going to hold him out on 7-on-7 drills. He gets a couple reps and he gets out of there. I got to get him ready to play, too," Friedgen said of the predicament.

It wasn't just Merriman that season. Other factions arose. Maybe it was because of all the success and glory the first three teams experienced that the new crop had a false sense of entitlement. But it was soon something Friedgen was all over at the team house.

"When you got a good team you don't have special situations. Everyone's pulling together," Friedgen said. "It doesn't matter whether you've got talent or not. If you got the 'I' syndrome . . . why is it me? That team (in 2004) was so concerned with how any rules affected them. 'Why do I have to go to breakfast, coach? I got a 3.0 [GPA]?'"

He drew on his first team when comparing why one group of perhaps lesser talent won and another didn't.

"The reason we won the first year was because all those guys that were sitting on the fence, 'Are you in or you out?' Well, we got rid of that. Everyone was in. Everyone was doing what they had to do to win whether they were in our PAT, field goal protection, whatever. And we were strong because we did that. We took joy in our victory because we did it together. It wasn't, 'We didn't run the ball enough,' or, 'I should be playing more.' A lot of these guys hadn't even played. They hadn't worked. They hadn't got their ass beat. A lot of times these were the guys complaining."

Friedgen recalled the time that players returned from winter break and expressed frustration about sitting home for the holidays for the first time, and not on the road at a bowl game.

"They came back over break and they didn't like watching all these teams playing in the bowl games. I said, 'That's up to you. I've been to all the bowl games. You want to go to bowl games, you gotta work. Stop bitching and moaning about it all the time,' " Friedgen said.

Friedgen saw Merriman "trying to grow up too fast" and shutting out his coaches. Listening to outside influences about how to handle his career and his position, when he could have got that advice at the team house.

Merriman, who was incredibly likeable, was mature and "street smart" in ways. But he was immature in others, like how he handled situations.

Coach and player would have long talks, sometimes Merriman "looking for fatherly advice and in other words trying to feel out where I was on things," Friedgen said.

Merriman was recruited by Vanderlinden as a sophomore and later offered as a junior by Friedgen.

Merriman said Friedgen was a "great salesman when he came to recruit me as the top player in the state of Maryland. He told me he expects me to get on the field early, and everything he told me happened. That was music to my ears," Merriman said.

Merriman never visited other schools.

Friedgen brought him into his office when he was a high school senior and told him, "Let's shake on it, man-to-man," Merriman said. "And I was a Terp just like that," he said.

Friedgen told Merriman that he would be a "hybrid" player, both a linebacker and a defensive end, which would benefit him later as a versatile talent that could move positions.

Merriman, who blossomed almost overnight, going from 215 pounds as a high school senior to 270 pounds as a college junior, was a physical specimen at 6-foot-4 with a 4.6 40 time.

Merriman's mother, who gave birth to him when she was 17-years old, had health issues. She had an immunity problem that started in her colon and led to other complications, Merriman said. Twice "she was on her deathbed at local hospitals and doctors told me they weren't sure she would pull through," he said.

With his mother ill and the family having little money to speak of, Merriman's decision to go pro following his junior year was inevitable. Plus, he had two younger sisters to help care for.

Merriman was the man of the house. His father was in jail in Georgia and Shawne never knew him. Merriman came to Maryland not only to remain close to his mother, but to set an example as a "local guy makes good" coming from a disadvantaged background, he said.

Friedgen tried to step in as a father to Merriman on numerous occasions, to provide structure and, frequently, counseling.

Friedgen spent hours with Merriman and did what he could to get him Pell Grant money to help the family. The money would go towards food. Merriman lived on the fringes when he was away from campus.

Once, at a Friday night team devotional before a game, the minister asked, "Where's that 'Lights Out' guy? I understand he needs prayers."

Friedgen would make concessions for Merriman, but he would also say no to him. Sometimes Merriman would miss workouts to deal with family issues that suddenly arose. Initially, Merriman didn't want Friedgen to come to his home on a recruit visit in the rough Forest Creek neighborhood for fear of him getting a bad first impression.

Merriman said he hit it off immediately with his coach as they had great respect for one another. Both had odds to overcome growing up, though Merriman's were decidedly different.

Merriman's home burned down when he was a sophomore in high school. His mother lit candles after their power was shut off for lack of payment. He lived with friends, and later coaches, while his mother got situated.

"I sprinted a mile that day straight home when I heard it happened. The whole right side of the house was gone," he said.

Merriman lived with a coach, his sister, and finally his grandmother while his mother lived in a shelter after the fire. He said the low point came during rides home from practice with his coaches when he knew there was no food or light awaiting him.

There were times Merriman, his sister and his mother would stand outside of their church and ask for charity.

His outlet was the football field, where at times he was seemingly full of rage.

"There was a lot to process at a young age," Merriman recalled. "Football was everything. I never thought of it there [on the football field], but right after practice when I changed clothes I started having to think about it."

He was a rags-to-riches story and Friedgen respected him for his perseverance.

Merriman started working when he was 12-years old as a landscaper in Bethesda. Nine hours a day in the summertime, to earn money for his family, which included younger sister Sade, who he took under his wing.

He also worked at PetSmart during the summers and during school breaks in Bowie. His high school assistant coach, J.C. Pinkney, served as a father figure.

When things got most desperate at home, Merriman went to work for 84 Lumber in Upper Marlboro by day, World Gym by night, his boundless energy keeping him on the go. He moved lumber all day for $8 an hour.

Merriman had since moved from Forestville to Upper Marlboro. His mother was a teacher, but her struggles with illness prevented her from steady work.

"My job [at 84 Lumber] . . . well, they called me 'yard boy,'" Merriman said. "That was my job description. They had this big field in the back where it was just open, full of all kinds of wood and lumber. I was too young to operate any kind of equipment yet so I would have to haul it to the front on my shoulders. Sun beaming down. Sweat coming down off me. It was the worst, the worst. But I had to do it for my family. It paid pretty good and it provided long hours."

Merriman put away a few thousand dollars each summer. He'd shovel snow and cut grass seasonally. He was flamboyant from the start, natural for the budding star with a great smile and an infectious "can-do" attitude. He had another nickname, "Hollywood," and admitted he loved the "spotlight." Merriman later modeled and began a men's clothing line.

"Being a star athlete, I couldn't be driving around in the worst car. So I was able to save up and buy a decent car for myself," he said.

He had a 1996 Oldsmobile.

There were situations, like when he approached Friedgen late one night and asked if he could be showcased more than the "Leo" position offered.

Merriman wanted to play the "Mike" inside linebacker position or defensive end. Once he even asked Friedgen to play tight end. Merriman played receiver in high school and said he wanted to "be challenged. Challenge my body to the maximum."

Merriman thought there was a better chance he would be named all-ACC at defensive end than linebacker because there were so many good linebackers in the league that year. There was even talk of possibly transferring to Florida, where the Gators reportedly promised to showcase him more. Former assistant Locksley was at Florida at the time, and was his recruiter in high school. Merriman approached Friedgen about a possible transfer and Friedgen almost became apoplectic, Merriman said.

Friedgen couldn't believe what he was hearing, but wasn't shocked as Merriman surprised him with requests like these.

"I said, 'Shawne, look, you are being showcased. There's only so many people that can play this position.'" Friedgen said. "I said where else are you going to go where you are going to have to play against a tight end, an offensive tackle, and be able to drop in and cover running backs and wide receivers? I said I don't think anyone can showcase you anywhere else better than here.

"And that drove his stock up. Here's a big guy that can play in a 3-4 or bulk up and go in a 4-3. And all these 3-4 teams are the guys that want him because they can't find that position. Now all of a sudden he's going around proud he's at that position. That's just all those people in his ear. That's the problem."

It got so bad that Blackney recalled a fan approached him at booster event. He heard a rumor that the Terps were switching to a 4-3 defense to accommodate Merriman.

Friedgen teased Merriman "if he wanted a pillow," or, "when would I feel good enough to practice," needling his star. Blackney called Merriman only by the first half of his nickname ("Lights"), until he lived up to his potential.

"Counseling him . . . now he's not a bad kid. At the time he was a little selfish, but when he got drafted in the first round I said, 'How do you feel about the 'Leo' position now?'" Blackney said. "And he just laughed. But I said to him, 'You know something? You were a royal pain in the ass.'"

Looking back, Merriman has to laugh as well.

He said he wouldn't have wanted to ruin the local boy made good ideal by leaving Maryland for another school.

Merriman had even tangled with the coaches as early as his freshman year over playing time. The Terps had the more experienced Mike Whaley and Jamahl Cochrane starting ahead of him in his first two seasons, neither of whom was as physically talented, but both were more consistent.

Merriman worked out on his own after team workouts, using a local high school track coach to enhance his speed. On the eve of his junior year he came out a sculpted 6-4, 255-pounds, and exploded as an all-ACC performer and later first round NFL pick. Memorable were the images of Merriman tossing a lineman with one hand and tackling a ball-carrier with the other. Or keeping up with backs and receivers with his speed and his 38-inch vertical leap.

At 275-pounds at the NFL Combine, his body fat was measured at six percent. It was as low as 4.5 percent early in his college career. He benched 435 pounds, squatted 565, and power-cleaned 335.

"My thought was 'Leo' was not a classifiable position," Merriman said. "It was a tough position. It was very demanding. I was always tied up with the tackle."

Friedgen knew best in the end, as Merriman's versatility to play two spots only vaulted him higher as far as his NFL value.

"But it put me in the position I am in, to be honest. The position really defined me and gave me a second option to play in the linebacker corps as well. It turned out what they told me was right," Merriman said.

Nicknamed "Lights Out" and "Pepco" because he could knock players out (as well as the fact the power companies often cut the family's utilities), Merriman cut quite a figure.

In addition to playing football and being a student at Maryland, he worked to help support his family. The community took him under its wing, too, including Washington Redskins linebacker LaVar Arrington. Merriman was friendly with Arrington's younger brother, who he played sports with in high school.

Arrington attended some of Merriman's football and basketball games, and took a liking to him early. He gave him advice and helped steer him. Merriman regularly called Arrington with football and life questions.

Merriman had rage issues, which led to another predicament at Maryland that Friedgen had to deal with.

During his junior year he got in a tussle with teammate Sam Maldonado when the running back egged him on after what first started as good-natured ribbing soon took a turn.

Maldonado called him a name and Merriman lashed out, picking him up and slamming him head-first into the dorm room floor.

Maldonado was momentarily knocked unconscious, and was rushed to the hospital. He lost feeling in his neck for a brief amount of time.

The two often needled each other in the past, but this time Merriman snapped. Merriman walked out and later was kicked out of campus housing. Maldonado emerged with a sprained neck and a bit dazed.

Merriman and wide receiver Derrick Fenner once got in an off-the-field scrape over a girlfriend. Merriman had a temper, but it was mostly seen on game day as he was one of the most electrifying defensive players in decades at College Park.

He was there when the ambulance arrived to take Maldonado away, and he was apologetic.

"I was very concerned. And we made up and talked and it was basically a team thing that happens. But both of our careers could have been in jeopardy," Merriman said. "It was something that happened and you wished it never did. If it had happened on the field, where I got in many fights, it wouldn't have mattered."

In all of the 32 NFL team meetings Merriman had prior to the draft, each team asked him about the fight.

But he was resilient, that's for sure.

During two of his summers at Maryland the budding star lived at a local Ramada Inn where he worked as a security guard to help cover room. He gave much of his earnings to his family.

After his junior year Merriman finally spoke to his father, Darrin, for the first time in 12 years. Merriman initiated the dialogue by contacting his uncle to help locate his father. His father left the family when he was an infant.

"I had a long talk with him," Merriman said of his father. "I can tell you right now it wasn't pleasant. I never raised my voice too much. I just came at the situation, 'you made a mistake and you are paying for it now.' And he agreed."

His father said he followed his career on the Internet.

"But I told him it's a little too late. I basically took care of myself and my family," Merriman said.

Merriman may have had some excesses and erratic behavior. But in the end Friedgen believed he reached him and he helped him.

"That's another thing coach Friedgen . . . we talked about a whole lot. He had a lot of respect for me because of that. For me being able to take care of my family and for reaching out to my father.

"It's been very personal to me also, things with his dad that he can relate about tough love at the time you may not believe in it. But in the long-term really looking out for you and your best interests. We talked about everything under the sun."

Merriman credits Bill Johnson at Frederick Douglass, Pinkney and Ronald Tubb of the Forestville Boys and Girls Club as male figures that looked out for him and kept him straight. He said Johnson and Friedgen are similar in ways with their "tough love," but that each had a "softer side."

"When I look back on things, every step my coach was always really my father," Merriman said. "From Boys Club to high school to coach Friedgen at Maryland, they were the dad I never had. Coach Friedgen just added on to that. He showed me that tough love that we talked about."

Merriman bought his mother a condominium in Suitland after he signed his first pro contract. His sister, a student, lives with him on and off and wants to join the Coast Guard. He bought a condo in the area for himself because he said he has a "phobia" of big homes.

Friedgen appreciates what Merriman has done since moving on from College Park. He hasn't forgotten his roots.

From the start Merriman was interested in helping the disadvantaged. In high school he began what would later turn into a publicized coat drive for the poor that he holds annually on campus. He returns each winter to the Comcast Center to host the drive, collecting coats for local charities and shelters.

"It is a beautiful thing. Seeing folks with things that I should have gotten coming up. Things you need," Merriman said.

Merriman's first drive at Maryland collected 3,000 coats. His second more than 5,000. Returning to help were former teammates Williams, Novak, Kyle Schmitt, Ed Tyler, Heyer and others. Merriman holds one each year and attends despite the demands of the NFL season.

Now he has millions of dollars, was NFL Defensive Rookie of the Year, and was an all-star and MVP candidate in just two seasons.

He can remember a night sleeping in his closet after hearing gun shots outside of his Forestville home. He credits Friedgen and Maryland with giving him a nurturing environment.

"It's incredible. Sometimes I have to remind myself of where I came from. Anyone had to be put in a situation like that probably would have crashed, be it selling drugs or just giving up. I can't do it. Too much on my plate. Just fall into that crowd. But I knew football and my coaches were always there keeping my faith, and keeping my faith in the man upstairs."

Merriman visits the team house and the coaches a few times a year. He said he will likely give back to the program in a monetary way soon. Friedgen joked on Draft Day, after Merriman was picked in the first round, that he hoped to have "Shawne Merriman Indoor Facility" at College Park, hinting at a big donation.

Friedgen always told Merriman he had character, but it needed to come out more. Merriman choked up when Friedgen, who once Merriman decided to leave early for the draft and was tapped as the No. 12 pick, told him he was "one of the greatest players he had ever coached."

Friedgen told Merriman that if he was going to be drafted high, that he should go and gave him his blessing.

In 2006, Merriman gave his high school $10,000 for new uniforms and equipment and had plans to open a local restaurant, perhaps something with the nickname "Lights Out" in the name. He also helps run youth camps in the area.

Merriman laughed when he recalled the way Friedgen ended each conversation with him. And they had many.

"He would tell me, 'Look Shawne. I'm El Supremo. Always.' The buck stopped with him. I used to think that was so funny," Merriman said.

"But his tough love, through that he really prepped me for life in the NFL. Life in general. It's a hard world out here."

"No matter how well I was doing, if I didn't practice well he'd tell me, 'You don't practice, you don't play.' He would never let up."

Ralph Friedgen often puts his players in competitive situations, be it in practice or off-season conditioning drills to foster competition, camaraderie, and character.

He holds basketball pickup games and dunk contests during winter conditioning sessions instead of football drills, to keep them fresh and interested.

He has a "12 perfect plays" drill that he runs at the end of practice. The players must execute it perfectly or run sprints. Everything is a challenge, a battle to build character and a winning attitude. He loves pitting the players against each other to see how they respond. That can come on or off the field as there are daily tests with Friedgen.

One thing he always has is his players' backs. That's been demonstrated at times when Friedgen has taught about character from the top down.

Cornerback Josh Wilson, who helped guide Maryland to a 9-4 season and a Champs Sports Bowl victory in 2006, recalled a Sunday evening phone call he got from his coach when he was a sophomore. Friedgen summoned Wilson to his office immediately.

"I lived in the farthest dorm away from the football complex and the whole way over there I'm walking and thinking, 'Man, what did I do?' I am trying to think of everything," Wilson said. "I had this for that and that for this. No matter what he hit me with I had an answer."

When Wilson walked into Friedgen's office his coach confronted him with alleged comments he made about another player, a player that was competing for his spot. Friedgen said the player's parents called him and said that Wilson threatened to transfer if he was not named the starter.

Wilson vehemently denied it. So Friedgen rung the parents on the telephone and put them on speaker phone. And, as it turned out, on the spot.

"Coach Friedgen said, 'Okay, Josh is right here and he said he never said it.' Then all of a sudden the parents' voices changed and said, 'Oh, we didn't want to get him involved in this problem.' Coach Friedgen then said, 'Well, you got him involved in this when you said his name.'

"So the whole story fell apart," Wilson said. "Friedgen got off the phone and looked at me and said that's the way I do business with my players. And I really appreciated that. That he didn't just assume what this person said."

Many in the program point towards the 2002 Peach Bowl as the Terps biggest bowl triumph, thumping an SEC power – Tennessee – in Atlanta. It was another instance in which Friedgen used a character-building lesson.

Tennessee came into the game boasting that Maryland couldn't keep up with its speed and run game. The Georgia Dome was packed with what seemed to be a 3-1 ratio of orange to red fans, many humming "Rocky Top" during warm-ups.

Friedgen used his theme of "finishing" after the rout at the hands of Florida in the

Orange Bowl the year before. He told the players that they wouldn't want to be known as a team that couldn't "finish the deal" after consecutive 10-win regular seasons but no bowl victory to show for it. All week long he screamed "finish," and personally challenged his players in practices and meetings.

Maryland came out flying, hungry not to repeat the Orange Bowl performance, and hit Tennessee in the chin. The Vols never responded. Friedgen pushed the right buttons again, and the result was a windfall for the Terps.

The Terps didn't tire while Tennessee appeared listless and uninspired after Maryland delivered the initial blow. It was just like their coach told them, like he did before the North Carolina game to start his head coaching tenure at Maryland.

R alph Friedgen has gone to great extremes to help his players develop as people. He's stepped in and filled a void for many that have come through his program without male figures in their lives.

He has no problem stepping in and rolling up his sleeves with their life issues.

"I think it is an admirable quality," said Yow, a coach and athletic administrator for 31 years. "He knows there is a need there. They are away from home. I think he also sees it as helping in terms of building trust between him and players. It is important for them to see him outside of the practice field where things can be pretty tough."

But not all of them work out.

Talented offensive tackle Brandon Nixon, a "4-star" signee out of Pottstown, Pa., came to College Park with fanfare as a 6-foot-6 athletic lineman.

After he was shipped home early in freshman camp because of a NCAA Clearinghouse matter with his transcript, which was later resolved, Nixon violated a team rule in the spring of 2006 and was ruled ineligible for the season. But he could still practice with the team.

Nixon, who had two siblings in jail and a tough road to hoe, was given a final chance by Friedgen, who kept him on scholarship, in the dorm, and on the meal plan.

He practiced through the season, and Friedgen was hopeful he would pay his dues and finish his career strong.

Nixon, who as a senior in 2007 was expected to vie for a starting job, flamed out after all that work. He flunked out following the fall semester of 2006 with just one semester to go. Nixon was sent home mid-year and had to clear his things from the dorm before the team traveled to Orlando for the bowl game.

Nixon went through the exercise of practices and team meetings only to fail out despite Friedgen propping him up at every turn. As his father picked him up for the final time, he saw Gloria Friedgen outside the team house and thanked her and her husband for everything they tried to do for his son.

Nixon, because his pass protection skills had fallen off as a junior, was moved to guard. Nixon's father, at the time, asked Friedgen about it, complaining, "Brandon didn't like playing guard as much."

Friedgen reacted in true Friedgen form.

"I told him this isn't about playing guard or him playing tackle. Quite honestly, your son underperformed last year. I don't care if he ever really plays football again. I am giving him a chance for the rest of his life. This is not a football decision."

Nixon blew the opportunity. He was a talent with pro size, and possible potential, if he ever got his act together.

"It was more or less me being a nice guy, which in the end screwed me," Friedgen said when looking back at the incident.

"If it was me, I would have pulled the scholarship and brought in another guy and given it to someone else who could play from the start," Josh Wilson said. "But that's coach Friedgen."

Friedgen loves to see his players fight through adversity and tough times. It's almost as satisfying as a conference win.

An example was Lamar Bryant in the N.C. State game in Raleigh, N.C., in 2001 with ACC title hopes on the line.

Bryant fractured his left wrist and sprained his left ankle in the first half. In the second half he sprained his right ankle. But he played on.

"Ralph knew it but he knew I was going to play through. I had to play through it. I told him that. We had come too far. That would have been messed up," Bryant said.

Ralph Friedgen, trying to instill character in a player in 2006, came close to meeting his match.

California "4-star" quarterback prospect Josh Portis, who Maryland recruited out of high school, chose Florida with Maryland a close second in 2005.

A tremendous pass-run threat with great measureables (6-4, 205-pounds, 4.5 40-yard dash, 38-inch vertical jump), Portis came as a package. The other half was his mother, Patricia Portis, who was very involved in her son's life.

Friedgen has been around a lot of involved parents, but of Patricia Portis he quipped: "There's some like her, but none quite like her. She's the queen of the mother's club that I have."

Portis played as a true freshman at Florida and showed promise. But he was stuck behind hot-shot Chris Leak, a sophomore, and incoming recruit Tim Tebow, so he sought a transfer.

A handful of schools were contacted, but Maryland shot quickly to the top of the list. The Terps connected well with Portis and his mother on their official campus visit the year before, while a distant cousin, Clinton Portis, was a star running back for the Washington Redskins.

It is only Josh and his mother as his father is not involved. And she runs the show.

She moved to Gainesville when her son signed with Florida, and drives a black Mercedes Benz sedan with vanity tags to and from Maryland for games, spring practices, even the team banquet.

Her reputation preceded her, and from the start she asked that her son have a private room and jersey No. 7, Friedgen said.

Neither was an option, Friedgen said. Both had to be earned.

Friedgen called a meeting with the Portis' and quickly outlined his ground rules.

"I said, 'Look. I think you and Josh should go to Oregon or somewhere else. They said, 'What are you talking about?'

"I said, 'Well, you are not going to tell me how to run my program. So I don't think this is going to be a good marriage. I think you all ought to go somewhere else.' "

Both were incredulous. But Friedgen said he couldn't operate a program with parents listing their demands.

A native Alabaman and former basketball player, Patricia Portis is an imposing woman at 6-1. And she is headstrong and has a gift for gab. She works as a telemarketer. She insisted things be a certain way.

Said Friedgen, who will gladly pass on lessons to players and parents alike:

"I explained to Josh why we don't do that stuff. I said you are going to come in here and want to be a leader of the team and you are going to have to earn it. If I start giving you special privileges then everything breaks down. I have a policy on what jersey you get and I think it will come available to you if you have a grade point average and do a good job with the team. You'll probably get that if you want to. As far as a room goes, that goes on seniority and also grade point average. If I violate that, there is going to be a lot of pissed off people at me and at you, and once I lose my credibility I am done. I ain't going to get that back. I ain't doing that for you or anybody else."

Josh Portis told Friedgen that he respected his decision and had no problem with it. Friedgen responded, "Good. Now tell your mom that."

Patricia Portis told Friedgen that he should sympathize with her plight. That she was a single mother and her son had it tough growing up.

Friedgen praised her for raising him on her own and then gave some fatherly advice.

"I said, 'Patricia, you have done a hell of a job. The kid's a great kid. I got no problem with your kid. Why don't you let me help you raise this kid, teach him to be a man, teach him how to grow up. But things are not going to come just because you want them to come. You got to earn them.

"I got other parents, too. I have to treat everybody the same way. I can't treat one guy over another guy. If you can't deal with that, then take him somewhere else.' "

The family returned to California for Christmas. Soon Friedgen got a call from Patricia while at his lake house in Georgia. She brought up the room issue again, and this time Friedgen blew up. Gloria Friedgen was shocked at how her husband handled her on the phone.

Patricia Portis even suggested Friedgen run her son more in shot-gun formation. "I told her this is a marathon, not a sprint. Josh is not going to get this overnight. He's progressing and probably at a faster pace than most. The last time I looked, everybody in the NFL doesn't run the 'gun.' That's where you want him to end up, right? That's what this is all about, right? Let him learn both," Friedgen said.

The two learned to work with each other, though there were some ups and downs. During Thanksgiving of 2006, Josh and his mother enjoyed the holiday dinner at Friedgen's home.

C onversations with Ralph Friedgen often lead to mentions of his favorite "character kids." A few of his favorites he's even dreamed about, he admits. He's consumed with his team and his players, and it comes out in various forms.

"I had a dream the other night. I was telling Gloria about it. I called [Denver Broncos head coach] Mike Shanahan and told him what two great character kids he's got of ours, Curome Cox and Domonique Foxworth. She said why don't you do that, and I did."

Cox made the Broncos as a free agent and has been a special teams performer and a nickel and a dime back, while Foxworth was drafted by the Broncos and has been a steady performer ever since. Foxworth's parents have a motivational speaking business, and their highly-motivated son rates as one of Friedgen's all-time favorites, he said.

"A guy like Domonique. We are a better program for having him in it. Such a class kid and class family. The kid is going to be so successful in life, in life skills."

Foxworth wrote a book after his rookie season that detailed his first year in the NFL. It contained motivational messages and passages throughout geared towards young adults.

Ralph Friedgen couldn't have been prouder when Foxworth returned to campus for the Terps Pro Day in the spring following his rookie season and told him of the book.

7

LEADERSHIP

A fter years spent working for top coaches like Jerry Claiborne and Bobby Ross, Ralph Friedgen said one of the most important things he learned was that communication was crucial between coaches and players.

And a big part of that, he said, was listening.

Friedgen has always had a good ear for his teams and his players, something seen on many occasions.

"If you listen to what their concerns were, you were going to stay closer in touch with them," Friedgen said.

Friedgen believed that the most important thing – if he wanted to lead when he first arrived at Maryland as head coach – was to establish his vision for everyone to see. Both inside the program and out.

Part of that, he said, was going to the public in a way none of his predecessors had tried.

"No one ever went to the fans here," he said.

Be it through "Breakfast With The Fridge," "Terp Alley," "Fridge TV" or the slick Under Armour marketing campaign, all were efforts to reach out to the public and make the program more accessible.

With each year Friedgen said he has been rewarded by more fans and supporters that share his vision, "many of whom when I first came here thought I was nuts," he said.

Fans fell in line. And many above and beyond the call, inspired by his message of getting Maryland football back to a level of prominence.

In 2001 booster Bruce Killian began the "Stock the Fridge" grass-roots fund-raising campaign on the TerrapinTimes.com message boards, raising more than $40,000 to donate to Friedgen for how he saw fit to use in his fledgling program.

Six years later Killian started a similar campaign on the website, this time to raise money for the Byrd Stadium expansion project, which was set to begin in 2007. He raised $17,000 in the first month, all from ordinary fans wanting to pitch in.

The endearing Friedgen, who has a group of rabid fan followers called "Friedgen's Legion" which tailgates and travels to away games, inspired the kind of reaction from fans, administrators and politicians.

People from all walks of life made a connection with their "everyman" coach with the big belly, receded hairline, and "never-say-never" attitude.

Friedgen said he heard the skeptics when he predicted another upper deck at Byrd. Or fill the stadium. Or win an ACC championship. Or beat Florida State.

"They were all like, 'Yeah, right,' " he said.

But as he accomplished each goal over the years more skeptics fell in line with his ambitious vision for the program.

Establishing his vision for fans and players alike was the start. Instilling a stronger sense of leadership in the players wasn't far behind.

R alph Friedgen's Terrapin Council, a group of player leaders voted on by their peers and representing all classes, is a committee Friedgen uses as a go-between for coaches and players as well as a means to build leadership. It centers on his theme of listening and communicating, and ultimately, knowing your team.

The Council created a sense of ownership for the players, who could make suggestions to the head man. It became more powerful each year, with the players allowed to voice their opinions on significant issues.

Leadership was lacking in the program before Friedgen arrived, said longtime strength and conditioning coach Dwight Galt, who admitted the Terps had too few leaders, "as they were too afraid of not being popular. They didn't want to offend their teammates by putting their foot down, which you need to have to be successful."

No staff member saw it on the front lines or in the trenches like Galt, a Maryland alumnus who works with the players year-round with lifting, off-season conditioning and also by the fact his twin sons, Tommy and Deege, signed with Maryland in 2006. No staffer has his finger on the pulse of the team beyond Friedgen like Galt.

Friedgen leads by example with his work-ethic, something that has never been challenged and likely never will, in addition to his strong words and his other devices to promote leadership.

"It's real. It's not put on. He can get furious," Galt said. "He's very off-the-cuff, and it can be very effective in leading the kids and the coaches in his own way."

Friedgen wanted the players to lead themselves, too, and the vote for the Council also told him something about who they believed to be the leaders as well.

The committee has long been a fixture in the program. Friedgen has the power of veto if he thinks an unsuitable choice has been selected to the Council, something he has yet to do.

He admitted twice that he added players that were close in voting. He did it to inspire the players, both seniors, to become leaders. He declined to name the players, but one was a senior who the players listened to, the other was on the bubble in terms of attitude but turned the corner in the end. Maybe the confidence gained on the Council helped.

Friedgen arrives at weekly Council meetings with passages and quotes from leadership books that he likes. The players keep notes.

Friedgen encouraged players to come to him, whether it was popular or not, with issues or concerns, even if it meant relaying unfavorable information about a teammate. It opened the lines of communication between players and coaches, while Friedgen could take the temperature of the team on important issues. Better to have the players get it off their chests than have it fester in the locker room.

On more than one occasion Council members have come to him on behalf of the team to tell him a variety of things, including when he needs to ease up on them in practice.

"The only thing you have to watch for is it doesn't turn out to be a bitch-fest, which it has not," Friedgen said.

Voting has nearly always represented the best "team" guys from each class. Four seniors, three juniors, two sophomores and one redshirt freshman comprise the Council. The players set examples in everything they do, be it making breakfast to reporting team rules violators. There is pressure.

"You are on the Council and with that comes responsibility I tell them," Friedgen said.

Friedgen meets with the Council once a week during the season, sometimes over dinner in the cafeteria.

There have been examples, including during Virginia week in 2002, when the Council acted at critical times. And sometimes to Friedgen's chagrin.

He had burned the team out in the run-up to the game, and the players' legs were shot. The result was a bitter loss at Charlottesville.

Another example was in 2004 when Friedgen made a new schedule for the players in the spring, for Tuesdays and Thursdays, with lifting in the morning and running in the afternoon. It was a means to be sure they were at the team house for dinner. But the Council told him that there was no way, with that schedule, they could make study hall at night. So Friedgen took the Council's advice and planned study hall before dinner.

"They were happier. They got their work done in the morning and they got to rest a little more in the afternoon. So that type of input, instead of them having to keep that in and bitch and moan," he said.

"Plus, the other thing it does is it tells the other players there is credibility in the Council. So if you have a problem, go the Council. I don't always agree with them but I listen to them."

Another issue that crops up is bowl gifts, which Friedgen lets the Council pick by

a player vote as well. Bowl gifts are big among the players, and are greatly anticipated. A designated amount of money is allocated for each player for a variety of gifts
and bowl gear to choose from.

It became an issue at the Peach Bowl in 2002 when one of the gifts was a ring.
But Friedgen believes in rings only if a conference championship is won, not for every
bowl game appearance.

Foxworth, a Council member, lobbied hard for a ring, pointing to its symbolism.
The team delayed gifts until after the game, Friedgen telling the players that they
would get a ring only if they won, which they did in the rout of Tennessee.

Another twist came when the deadly tornado hit campus in Friedgen's first year.
The Council urged Friedgen not to take them out to practice and into the elements.
Friedgen rarely calls practice.

"It's one of the few times. I said we better have a good practice tomorrow,"
Friedgen recalled.

Josh Wilson recalled approaching Friedgen in 2006, following the Florida
International game, a week before the ACC opener at Georgia Tech. On behalf of the
team he said that despite it being a bye week, Friedgen was working them too hard.
Their legs were dragging and their performance was suffering.

Wilson said he encountered a beat-down Friedgen in his office as the early season
disappointments, despite a 3-1 mark, had taken their toll. The humiliating loss on
national television at West Virginia blew the team's chance to prove that it was better
than that, and Friedgen was at a tipping point. Even an engine blew on one of the team
buses on the way up the mountains to Morgantown.

Wilson, never at a loss for words, said Friedgen "was waiting for someone to just
come up and talk to him."

"He was just talking on and on about everything, just so intense that he was all
over the place. I just told him if you just lighten up, everyone will come out to play."

The Terps played their most inspired game of the season to that point despite losing to the
ranked Yellow Jackets in Atlanta. Wilson provided some fireworks with a 100-yard kickoff return.

The empowerment of the Council, Wilson said, enabled him to have the forum to approach
his coach, which isn't always the easiest thing to do with the intimidating Friedgen. Members
of the 2006 team said that the turning point of the season was the Georgia Tech game.

"He's the head man, and sometimes being on top nobody talks to the guy on top
because you are scared to talk to the guy on top. I feel like nobody went in there and
talked to him. He wasn't able to speak his mind, get things off his chest."

Thanks to the Council, future all-ACC end Kevin Eli remained a Terp.

The defensive end was ready to quit the team before his senior year following an
injury-plagued career and moving positions. Dennard Wilson, who was on the
Council, got wind of it and brought it to the coaches' attention. They convinced Eli not
to bolt. Eli had not planned to tell the coaches of his departure.

There have been bumps in the road with the Council, too. In 2004 it lost a little credibility. Members skipped breakfast and soon it led to other problems.

Friedgen allowed his players with a 3.0 GPA or better to skip three breakfasts a semester. The Council, which had a few flawed players that season, came to Friedgen and asked for a sliding scale with the higher the GPA, the more breakfasts you could miss. Up to as many as 10 misses.

Friedgen gave in but later realized it had become a "caste system, backfiring and developing divisions on the team," he said.

"It became a problem so we went back to the old way," he said.

In 2001 there was a split over former quarterback Calvin McCall, who quit the team to walk-on the basketball team but later wanted to return to football. The players debated it and it got heated, the most emotional Council members have become over an issue.

Friedgen, who was flush with quarterbacks, compromised by telling McCall that he could come back but it would be to play in the defensive secondary. In the end, McCall stuck with basketball. That may have been a good call. McCall, along with his father, had wrestled ferociously with Vanderlinden over playing time, and what they perceived to be favoritism at the quarterback position.

Ralph Friedgen said attitude, and most importantly discipline, permeates through the program with every little thing.

He said some of his best Council leaders were Jeff Dugan and Dennard Wilson as "neither would take bull from anyone. Dugan stood up one time, his vote on something at the time maybe wasn't the most popular one with some of the guys, and he challenged every one of them. He didn't take any crap."

The Council fostered communication, accountability, and leadership, and gave the players a stake in the program.

It is a huge honor to get voted on the Council by teammates. Sometimes players are not voted back on the Council, which can be devastating.

But it has been very effective, Friedgen said.

"Any level, from pro to midget football, you got to have a team that's together," he said.

Friedgen admitted there have been a few oddball requests when perhaps a few council members have gotten ahead of themselves.

Like at the Peach Bowl when they came to Friedgen and asked him to lift their curfew when they saw that their opponent, Tennessee, had none.

"Yeah. But when we're kicking their butt they changed their tune," Friedgen said.

One day the players didn't want to practice because it was graduation day, though it was an abbreviated workout. Friedgen was peeved. Dugan approached Friedgen and told him, "I think you are over-reacting."

Friedgen loved hearing from his tight end, one of his best leaders.

"You know, I miss him because he wasn't afraid to come up and tell me. He didn't say a lot, he didn't show a lot of emotion. He had that kind of dry way about him," Friedgen said of his former tight end.

Dugan, who Friedgen called his best blocking tight end, took it a step further on another occasion.

When Friedgen didn't make him run after missing a class because he had a 3.3 GPA, another player with a lesser GPA had to run, There was a rift on the team over the issue, but Dugan stood up in a heated team meeting and said he would run anyhow.

"He's another guy who will be a tremendous success in whatever he does. A solid, solid guy," Friedgen said.

Friedgen is versatile in his player management style, drawing on his youth and his father for old lessons but always open to new ideas to lead the players. Even gimmicky ones at times when he's proven cerebral.

Friedgen credits his predecessor, Vanderlinden, for recruiting many "character kids," which helped him hit the ground running when he arrived in 2000.

That year, Bryant saw the confidence his new coach had in his players. Against N.C. State, Bryant and line mate Eric Dumas, while the Terps were in a two-minute passing situation, told Friedgen on the sideline that "we can run the ball and even have more success right now. Get big yards doing it."

Friedgen said, "Fine. Go ahead and do this. We're going to do this unilaterally."

The Council once turned the tables on Friedgen when they questioned his leadership with the famous "Are You In Or Are You Out" ultimatum.

Dennard Wilson, a headstrong leader of Friedgen's first team, said the players had that slogan before Maryland made it a marketing pitch on billboards and commercials a year later.

"Man. I saw this billboard over on Greenbelt Road saying, 'Are You In Or Are You Out.' I said, 'Hold up, man. Is he getting credit for this?' I need some money from this, you know."

Wilson said it came to him the year before when Friedgen challenged his dedication and he came back at him.

"He said that when he got here. That you are going to be in with us for the cause or are you going to be out?' That's because we had problems when he first came with academics and stuff like that. I remember he'd smack us in the face with that slogan," Wilson said.

But after the magical Orange Bowl season, Friedgen's name was linked to the vacant Tampa Bay Buccaneers' head coaching job. Friedgen had been on the banquet tour and was "worn out," he said, after collecting several coach of the year awards. He was driving home from the airport from his last trip, to collect the Bobby Dodd award in New Haven, Conn., when his agent, Jack Reale, called him on his cell phone.

"He told me, 'Ralph, I think I got something you might be interested in. Tampa Bay just called me and they want to talk to you about being a head coach there.' I said,

'I am really not that interested.' He said 'You should be.' I said, 'Why?' He said 'I think they are offering $5 million a year. In two years you are going to make as much as you'll ever make at Maryland.' "

Said Friedgen of the incident:

"Here is where I made my mistake. I said call them back and see if they are offering me $5 million a year. Well they did. He said they were. So how do you say now, 'I'm not interested?' I never thought anybody would be interested in me at $5 million. A year ago nobody even wanted to hire me."

The Glazers, the team owners, wanted to meet Friedgen at a Ritz Carlton in Virginia, but Friedgen said that would be too public. He told them to come to his house where it would be quiet.

His star was bright. He was a former pro coordinator and his offensive pedigree shined in year one at Maryland. The NFL was calling and would more than triple his salary. It was all very exciting for someone who worked in the shadows for more than three decades.

Friedgen told his boss, Yow, of the Glazers' interest and the coming interview.

"She said, 'You won't like working for those people,' " he said. "I said, 'Well, some people said I wouldn't like working for you and I do. So how would I know if I won't?' "

Friedgen did the interview in his living room. It lasted from about 6-10 p.m. He called Reale and told him how it went. Then he went to bed to get ready for morning workouts the next day.

"All of a sudden my phone's ringing off the hook. It's on SportsNite. What the hell. I ain't going down there. Anybody that leaks things out that fast. I think I was more upset than anything," Friedgen said.

Friedgen had little idea what would face him in the morning at conditioning drills at the Armory, where the team congregated at 5:30 a.m. The night before the players were shocked to hear reports on ESPN that Friedgen had met about the opening.

The players were up late watching sports highlights and playing video games, Dennard Wilson said.

"All of a sudden I hear 'Ralph Friedgen.' I see a plane. And I hear 'Tampa Bay.' And I say, 'Oh no, this ain't gonna happen. We are a family and we are going to do this together.' All the things he had been preaching to us. He was going to turn this program around and he was going to leave? I was offended. I got real offended."

So Wilson woke his teammates, stirring them out of bed well after midnight. And this was with a 5 a.m. wake-up call looming. Wilson started with Dugan, telling his fellow Council member, "We're not practicing until we hear from him."

"My phone was ringing off the hook the night before," Bryant said. "We all said we're not doing anything until coach Friedgen has something positive to say about him not going."

They gathered the next morning at the Armory for drills, jackets still on, and sat on the wall just inside the building. The assistant coaches hadn't heard the news. And, as one, the players marched at Friedgen as he entered through the door.

Friedgen had come to mean so much to them, and their chances for success, that it was a body blow.

"It was like a mob," Friedgen said.

Dennard Wilson did most of the talking. He instructed the players to keep their jackets on. He said to Friedgen: "We're getting ready to go to bed last night and were watching SportsCenter. We hear that they are talking to you about the head coaching job."

"I said, 'That's right,'" Friedgen said.

Wilson responded: "Well, we got one question for you: 'Are you in or are you out?'"

Wilson said it "smacked Friedgen in the face."

Friedgen paused for a few seconds before answering.

"I think he actually made his decision that day. I'm not positive, but I think so," Wilson said.

Others chimed in about the show of faith.

"I don't know if betrayed was the right word. Maybe, more disappointment," Wike said. "We couldn't believe that it was happening. It was kinda we felt we really worked together and he was a big part of it, what he did and what we did combined, is what made it happen. It's like now we are losing it. We got to where we want to be, got the ball rolling, and now you are walking out on us?

"At that point we realized how important it was, how much we wanted him there."

The players said the event moved their coach.

After a brief period of silence Friedgen barked, "I'm not going anywhere. So get back to work."

The players said Friedgen later applauded their initiative. Friedgen took a moment to compose himself over the display from his players and later spoke with Wilson, now a graduate assistant, about it at length.

Said running back Perry:

"We were going to turn around and go back to our rooms because we felt like you started something when you got here and we had one year of success and now you are ready to leave. We didn't think that was real commitment. That's when Dennard hit him with, 'Are you in or are you out?' He showed us it wasn't just the money."

Said Friedgen, who laughed about it later:

"I said to them, 'What if I had said I'm out?' 'We're going back to bed' is what they said. Dennard's always been one of my favorites. Football is so important to Dennard. A great character kid."

Another part of Ralph Friedgen's character building is the Character Education Program, which he hired former Terps great and all-pro center Kevin Glover to help start at Maryland.

Glover, who played for Friedgen when he coached the offensive line at Maryland in the 1980s, had discussed with Friedgen coming on board in some capacity two years prior, before it became official in 2003.

As a backdrop, Glover, who as a freshman at Maryland in 1981 was a defensive lineman, moved to the offensive side of the ball during the last practice of the season. It peeved him. Friedgen coached him for three years at left tackle and center, and Glover learned to love the offensive line and went on to a decorated college and pro career. Glover said everything he learned about the trade came thanks to Friedgen.

"I had all the trust in the world in him," said Glover, who was a high school tight end at Largo High School and didn't want any part of defense at first.

Glover marveled at the coach and teacher in those early days.

"The way he coached us as an offensive line unit, we all knew and believed and trusted that we could control any game," Glover said. "By the way we played, the tempo of every game, every practice."

Glover recalled going into games with the offensive linemen saying they would generate 300 yards rushing offense. And go out and do it every time.

"I mean, we had games where we had three backs over 100 yards. It all goes back to what he taught us and what he instilled in us," Glover said.

Glover joked that he still has flash-backs when he hears Friedgen yelling "tempo, tempo, tempo" at practice, just as he did when he was an assistant under Ross. And he can predict, with great accuracy, when Friedgen is about to start a practice period over if he sees that the players are dragging.

Glover, selfless as a player, was charged with character education for not only the football team, but all varsity teams in the face of the many issues student-athletes encounter.

Said Merriman, who used Glover to help guide him through the NFL draft process:

"You can't not listen to a person like Kevin Glover, who has been in the league, has been around, and whose name is so great around the league."

Glover was the perfect fit, having been a player at all levels and respected as the man Barry Sanders asked stand for him at his Hall of Fame induction. He also once worked as a player agent in the D.C. area so he had been on both sides of the fence. Glover, even during his playing days at Maryland, thought about returning to his alma mater in some working capacity down the road.

Their bond was tight. When Friedgen was in San Diego and at a crossroads in his career, trying to decide whether he wanted to follow Ross to Detroit to coach the Lions or branch off to Georgia Tech, he reached out to his former player.

Friedgen, Glover said, decided that if he wanted to be a head coach he needed to break off. He called Glover and asked him whether he thought the Lions could win a championship with the talent they had coming back. The two spoke for more than two hours. Friedgen asked him, most importantly, if the team had a quarterback that could lead a championship-caliber team. Glover was honest, telling him no, they did not.

Looking at the Character Education program at Maryland years later, some of the early discussions between Friedgen and Glover stemmed from the problems the Terps had with agents trying to get close to the program. From there it spread to other areas of concern for student-athletes.

"I had already been here. Had gone through what they were going through, what the student athlete had gone through, and been where most of them want to go," Glover said. "I could tell, and just help them know, it's not as easy as they think it is to get there. That it's important to get your degree, also."

Glover is known as a giving person and he wanted to give back, mostly helping educate players and their families about agents and the process, all the while being realistic about it. He has business experience as well, and along with his wife, who is a lawyer, owns a local boutique.

Character Education programs were starting to crop up across the country, with Georgia and Arizona State a few schools before Maryland that had programs. Friedgen, along with Yow, was ahead of the curve again, starting the program with Glover as an ideal choice to lead. He was experienced enough to know how things happened, while he was young enough that many players remembered him.

His office is in the football team house, though he works with all student-athletes on campus.

Glover had some compelling figures come to campus in the first few years to address student-athletes, including Dexter Manley, the former NFL star, who spoke of the dangers of substance abuse. In later years, Manley admitted to being illiterate in college as well.

A former Mafia boss spoke about the dangers of gambling. He gave examples of how he approached athletes on college campuses and worked his way into their lives and influenced them. The football program, as well as the men's and women's basketball teams, took particular interest in a session they had with the former mobster. He arrived with security.

"He told one story about flying over the Statue of Liberty in a private helicopter full of money," Glover said. "He had trash bags full of money. One of the guys joked about all those tourists down there, and they sure would like to have some of this money. And they turned around and dumped out like a million dollars in cash and laughed about it."

Glover's guest speakers have covered many subjects ranging from agents to drugs to date rape to HIV/AIDS. He's had former prostitutes come to campus to talk about sexually transmitted diseases.

Glover said the thing about Friedgen is that he has known head coaches in the past that want to win, but in reality are "just there to collect a check." He said everyone knows that Friedgen, once you are around him on the field or off, there's no questioning his dedication and passion for both the game and his players. None take it as personally as Friedgen.

R alph Friedgen will toe the line, set an example, no matter who the player or the consequences.

In 2006, when post-season hopes hung in the balance heading into the final two regular season games, a situation arose with one of his top players. It cropped up weeks later as well at the Champs Sports Bowl, a game Friedgen wanted badly to help atone for two losing seasons in the program.

Despite the pressure, he would make do without his best physical talent on the offensive line.

Jared Gaither, a man-mountain of an offensive tackle at 6-9, 325-pounds with a 4.95 40-yard dash, turned down a basketball scholarship as a junior in high school to the University of South Carolina to pursue his football dream at College Park.

Perhaps the most gifted big athlete to ever come through the program, Gaither was that "freaky" kind of athlete on the line, what former Terrapin Vernon Davis brought to the tight end position. He revolutionized the position at Maryland, and perhaps beyond, with his immense physical skill.

But Gaither turned what looked like a meteoric start to a college career as a freshman into a serious sophomore slump.

The behemoth from White Plains, Md., was suspended for the first two weeks of August camp for team rules violations, only to follow that by a one-game suspension for another rule violation.

Gaither seemed to want to set his own schedule, which his line mates weren't too excited about.

But that was only the start.

Late in the season, before the Terps traveled to Boston College, he spoke back to a coach during practice and junior guard Andrew Crummey took offense. It resulted in a melee with the two having to be separated and Gaither leaving practice.

Order was restored, but Gaither lost his starting position to the blue-collar but less talented sophomore Dane Randolph, who filled in admirably, though there was a talent dip.

Then Gaither had a neck injury and barely played in the game at Boston College. The Terps lost both of their final regular season games, but Friedgen stuck with his guns and played Gaither sparingly, though he said he was healthy again as the Terps prepared for the Champs Sports Bowl. As Friedgen has been known to say, "You don't practice, you don't play."

Gaither spent the final month of the season as a reserve with Randolph getting the starting nod in Orlando at the bowl and Gaither, who many projected as a NFL first-rounder, getting three series in the game.

"It's about the program, even if it is a star. Jared is a hell of a football player and that took a lot of guts. That took a lot of character and what he is about," Josh Wilson said of Friedgen's decision. "You always want your best players on the field. That is human nature. Jared can do physical things on the field people his size should not be able to do. Dane could get things done, but Jared can get it done amazingly. We, as a team, we're hoping Dane could step up and he was able to and the offensive line rose up that day. That took a lot of character, and showed what kind of person and coach he is."

Gaither was ruled academically ineligible at the end of the spring semester in 2007 after being sidelined during spring camp to focus on his class work. Friedgen called him the best "big athlete" he had ever seen, college or pro. Gaither got frustrated easily and Friedgen, at every turn, tried to help him on the field and off. It was one of the biggest time investments he made in a player next to Merriman. Gaither declared for the NFL Supplemental Draft in June of 2007 and Friedgen held a Pro Day for him on campus in early July. The Baltimore Ravens later took Gaither in the fifth round.

"That hurts us. I am sick over it because I look at it as if I failed him. But he won't go to class . . . you don't want to work, they just want to hang out," Friedgen said.

Said Hollenbach:

"Morally, he felt that was the right thing to do. It may not have been a popular decision among the team or the fans or what-not, but that's what happened."

Ralph Friedgen and defensive coordinator Chris Cosh, who came on board in 2006 for a second stint at Maryland, had a character lesson even for the savvy senior Josh Wilson.

Wilson, known for his mouth and willingness to use it on teammates or opponents, was approached by Cosh in the spring. He asked Wilson to lighten up on the young and inexperienced quarterbacks, who he had a tendency to verbally bait and ride at practices.

"They told me if I said anything it had to be positive. The rap sheet on Josh was he would say anything, and a lot of time it wouldn't be positive. The quarterbacks would be struggling and I said something and coach Friedgen wouldn't want me to be saying something. Talk about one of the hardest things I have ever had to do. But in the end it showed good character, and I was willing to do anything to help the team."

Friedgen is a master of pushing players' buttons to inspire them for their own good or the team.

An example came at the end of Hollenbach's junior season, and with Friedgen depending mightily on his quarterback to lead the Terps into the following season. It would be crucial for a young team looking for leadership, and a team capable of going either way.

Friedgen called Hollenbach into his office and laid out print-outs of Hollenbach's junior passing statistics. Hollenbach was a player still looking for confidence after a junior season plagued by 15 interceptions against 13 touchdowns.

"We spent about two hours in there and he threw out all these numbers. He is such a numbers-based guy," Hollenbach said. "Everything is percentages or tendencies. So he brings out these numbers about me being second in the conference in efficiency, passing yardage . . . and he said you are beyond these stages. You should not feel like you don't know if you can do this because you can. Look at these numbers. You are competing with the best, the top of the conference in terms of numbers.

"The question in your mind should not be can you do it, but are you going to get better? Can you be the best? Because right now you are definitely doing it, it's just a matter of how good you are going to get. You can get so much better.

"It was just really an encouraging meeting, especially at the end of the year and the way things had been going. It was good to hear him say that, and it kinda set the off-season for me as far as my mental, my mind-set, and my willingness to get back on the field and prove that we could be good with me as the quarterback."

Hollenbach said Friedgen is never too proud to admit mistakes, which the quarterback said proves he is a leader.

Hollenbach said Friedgen put the Georgia Tech loss in 2006 in Atlanta "on his shoulders for his play-calling down the stretch." Hollenbach was sacked repeatedly on the final series inside the Tech red zone, and took a beating as the Terps fell short in their upset attempt.

After the 2006 season, Ralph Friedgen wanted to build leadership and tighten a few things in the program. So he instituted a new off-season program, one that quickly bore fruit.

Based on a points system that a handful of schools like Florida, Georgia and TCU used to build teamwork and leadership in the off-season, Friedgen met with Galt and came up with the Maryland Football Points System.

Friedgen got some of the ideas from the staff at TCU while speaking with head coach Gary Patterson at the coaches' convention in Texas in the winter.

He put it in place after the 2006 season when he saw accountability and leadership in the program needing a boost.

"It's a great way to get the guys to try to develop leadership and accountability and teamwork and camaraderie. And guys helping other guys with discipline issues and also to motivate to perform well," Galt said.

The Terps put it in place in January for the spring semester. The players, walk-ons included, were divided into 10 teams with 10 players per team. Each team had a senior or two serve as captains, a few a top junior, all of whom Galt appointed.

At the start the players had a "draft," selecting players they saw as the most responsible and reliable.

"I wanted to make it where they were accountable to each other. A guy like [junior center] Edwin Williams really took the bull by the horn. He actually started calling kids up, getting them up for breakfast," Friedgen said.

Points were assessed for infractions ranging from missed classes to not being prepared for study hall to missed lifts, a messy locker area, and so on. The more points the worse, and there were penalties and rewards.

One overzealous player took the lead in preparing a teammate for study hall so he would not accrue points. He asked [academic support head] Heather Arianna "how to prepare for study hall. I just want to know what he needs to do," Friedgen said.

There was peer pressure for the players to keep up.

Some football programs do it as a rewards system, others for rules enforcement and accountability, the category the Terps fall under.

In the Terps' system, points can be deducted for exemplary performance, be it in the classroom or in the weight room.

Each day Galt keeps a large spread sheet updated with the scoring. Staffers report to him about who made it to breakfast, study hall, and so forth. The results were so anticipated that players huddled around the bulletin board, or the electronic ticker in the locker room, when the team scores were posted.

"Usually, we start lifting at about 2:15 p.m. each day. And at about 1:50 p.m. or so I will take an updated, huge master spreadsheet with all the players, the teams, infractions, and staple it to the bulletin board in the locker room. When I walk in there with it in my hand, everybody gets up and before I get it stapled there are 20 guys looking over my shoulder. That's when I realized that it was important to them and they were buying into it," Galt said.

The peer pressure to perform, and not make their teammates deal with morning punishment runs, inspired seniors and freshmen alike to be more accountable than ever.

One junior had a walk-on player assigned to him by his team to be sure he was getting up for class. Another shadowed a team member to class to be sure he was attending.

"'Deege' [Dwight Galt] ranked them 1-98. Where do you fall on this line?" Friedgen said he asked the players.

Friedgen had exit meetings with the players at the end of the spring, and asked each where they thought they stood in the rankings.

"Out of 98 kids I would say number 90 is at eight points and the highest is 11.5 [points]. Everybody else is under that. So eight guys out of 98 guys are problems. A lot of those are also about ready to flunk out of school. It's the same guys. The kids will say it's the same guys and I say now you know what I know. You talk to them and it goes in one ear and out the other. I tell them, 'We'll, you got the same success that I had.' "

But Friedgen saw some of the "problem children" rise up, gradually getting better after starting with a flurry of points.

The other trend he noticed was that the good kids, the leaders on the team, had "minus" points for good behavior. There were some 30 players in that category, without a point, a third of the team. Senior tackle Dre Moore, a problem guy in the past, was one of them, turning the corner in an impressive way, Friedgen said.

At first, most of the players had to run in the mornings as just 10 points per team resulted in penalties. And most of the players needed the first week to get used to the new program.

The most a team had to run was five mornings. As far as individuals, four players had to run five mornings. Two were true freshmen, one a redshirt freshman, one a junior, and one a senior.

The rewards were a key as well.

Players could earn the right to be excused from mandatory breakfast, conditioning workouts, or even enjoy dinner at Friedgen's home in June, with a menu of their choice, which was one of the top prizes.

The leaders of the top two teams, by the time the spring game arrived, Dre Moore and Chris Roberts, were named game captains. Lance Ball and Edwin Williams led the second-place teams and also served as captains.

The winning team also got exempted from the pre-season conditioning test in August, which may have been the biggest carrot at the end of the stick.

Galt admitted he was skeptical at first "but I didn't have the vision that coach Friedgen did. I didn't see the reward being worth all the work. But he obviously had the vision for this and it worked out very well."

"A lot of programs tell their players to be leaders, but I think we are one program that we don't tell them to do it. We teach them how to be a leader. I think this is a great mechanism that really does that," Galt said.

At first there was resistance from some players, often the ones with habitual problems. But soon they all bought in.

And trends emerged for Friedgen and Galt.

Like the freshmen, with their lack of experience and youth, who were frequent violators at the start. Freshman receiver LaQuan Williams was a poster child for accumulating points early, but he rallied in the end and finished strong.

Just one upperclassman accumulated points throughout, not a great sign for the junior heading into the 2007 season. Several upperclassmen stepped up, including walk-on Colin Nelson, who made sure one player woke up each day for class, while senior defensive tackle Carlos Feliciano made a point to see freshman quarterback Jeremy Ricker was getting out of bed.

The first year, Galt said, was used to install the program, while year two should reveal more about the team in a broader sense.

In the exit meetings Friedgen joked with one player, telling him, "You rank 97," when the player was dumbfounded over where he stood.

"Yeah, and there's only one slacker worse than you," Friedgen quipped.

Linebacker Dave Philistin was one of the best turnaround stories, especially his work in the classroom.

Friedgen laughed when he related the story of how linebacker Chris Clinton, a red-shirt freshman, picked up five points on the first day but got only four the rest of the way.

"He had like 10 hate-mail letters on his locker. 'We're going to get your ass in gear, or we're going to beat your ass,' " he joked of what teammates told him.

"If that was me I might have hit a kid over the head with a two-by-four. In the old days they'd give him a 'blanket party.' There would be all kinds of stuff he had to deal with," Friedgen said with a chuckle.

Friedgen said the new program boosted many of his players' grades above honor roll, which is 3.0 or better. He said he may have his most honor roll players yet as he awaited final grades in the spring of 2007.

R alph Friedgen is cerebral as a leader in business circles as well, and he has attracted many top boosters and donors to his inner-circle.

He has gone to great lengths to raise money for the program and facility expansion projects, be it auctioning off dances at the Maryland Gridiron Network's spring gala to making a wager with boosters for a public weight-loss contest.

No football booster is as big as local businessman Barry Gossett, 66, a football enthusiast who traces his Terps days to 1951, when he was a Boy Scout working games at Byrd Stadium as an usher.

Jack Scarbath, Bernie Faloney and Frank Tamborella were his boyhood heroes. In 1969 he began work with A.V. Williams, a former Maryland football player, who went on to build a local building giant, Williams Construction, for whom buildings on campus are named in his honor.

Later, for Gossett, there was Williams Mobile Offices, which became Williams Scotsman. Gossett was a major shareholder in the modular office company when it sold.

A longtime supporter who has served on the MGN, the Terrapin Club and the Maryland Educational Foundation (the predecessor of the Terrapin Club) and now serves on the Board of Regents, Gossett has put his wallet where his heart is, donating close to $5 million to the athletic department and for football facilities.

In 1998, the football team house was named in his honor. He gives for other causes on campus as well.

The College Park-born Gossett, a modest but no-nonsense businessman, said Friedgen's passion and candor attracted him first. At the MGN Gala, Gossett often buys some of the priciest gifts, dropping thousands of dollars that are channeled back into the program. Gossett is at every home game and has only missed two road games in the last decade. He often travels on the team charter along with his wife, Mary.

"The one thing I really love about the guy is what you see is what you get," Gossett said. "It comes from his heart as well as the discipline he learned as a kid. I remember some of the stories he told me, that he relates to his family as well as his players, where he was having a tough time down in College Park and he was going to quit. He told his father he was going to quit but he said, 'That's fine, but you come home the locks will all be changed. You'll have to find your own bed.' "

Gossett said the story resonated with him and, while away for a weekend with the Friedgens at their lake home in Georgia, he witnessed it first-hand. How everyone would get "fatherly" leadership from Friedgen. He has a hard time turning it off away from the field.

"On his boat trying to get the girls [his daughters] water skiing. If they couldn't get up on the first time, man he was all over them. So, he treats his family almost the same way he treats his players. You look at him and you think the king and his court no matter where it is," Gossett said.

Gossett said Friedgen gets the "big picture" more than any coach he has seen at Maryland. Gossett said that at first Friedgen had little patience waiting for new facilities, a bigger budget, or a private jet for recruiting. Gossett has proven just a phone call away when Friedgen needs something. He was one of the first to reserve a box at soon-to-be expanded Byrd Stadium.

"To me, and I have been around so many coaches at the school and even if you go back to Bud Millikan and other football coaches, non-revenue coaches. They are there to be the coach of the team and not always part of the system. Ralph believes in the school as much as anything else and I think he is able to say, 'Okay, my job is I'm the head football coach. I put the product on the field and I win but it's for the school as much as anything else.'

"He talks with all the deans. With [University President] Dr. Mote. He has a great relationship with Debbie Yow. He's part of the institution and what he does contributes to the institution as much as anything else.

"It's not his ego. If it's possible it's controlled, so to speak, for what he wants for the football team, and what he wants from a National Championship. I think it is more for a school than for Ralph. That's why he is such a genuine guy and people like him and believe in him to lead and will do anything for him because it's not for him. It's for what we all believe in."

Gossett said he can project Friedgen in any context in the business world. Currently, he is working with Friedgen on his vision for the next phases of expansion at Byrd Stadium.

Gossett said that Friedgen is both "big picture but also a master of detail."

Gossett has been around some of the business world's best, including 'The Donald,' who he shared boardrooms with in the 1990s.

"[Donald] Trump is 'Mr. Ego,' there's no doubt about it. But he is a smart guy. He can visualize and see a lot of things. But honestly, Ralph probably . . . his intellect and ability to see is as good as Donald Trump.

"Ralph is pretty unique in the people that I have met and I have worked with."

Ralph Friedgen has seen many players return and surprise him years later as high school or college coaches, always a compliment to most coaches. Many he never thought would turn out to be coaches.

Two approached him in 2006 at the coaches' convention in Texas: receivers Guilian Gary and Jafar Williams, both small college assistants who bumped into their former coach and thanked him.

Not everyone loves Friedgen when they play for him. But they appreciate him later as the great ones often experience.

"It's fear. It's tough love. But it's fair," said Dennard Wilson. "He pushes your buttons because he wants to know how you respond to adversity and certain environments. He wants to see if you are going to fold or rise to the situation."

In 2002 when the Terps were involved in a shootout with N.C. State at Byrd Stadium, the Wolfpack was running up and down the field on Maryland late. The score was tied.

Friedgen brought the defense to the sideline, threw his headset to the ground, and started blasting away, losing his composure for a moment. He turned and stared at Wilson and said, "What are you going to do?"

Wilson snapped back at him:

"I said, 'Calm down. We got this.' "

The longtime Council member was one of the few players that could pull it off. The defense held, the Terps scored, "and game over," Wilson said.

Maybe the Council experience paid off.

"He came to me . . . and remember he's not a guy with a lot of accolades for you. But he just smiled and gave me a wink as we walked off the field," Wilson said.

Said Friedgen's cousin Stoddard, who has been with him around his players at every coaching stop:

"I don't see fear, though he has that if he wants to use it. I see it as kids being well coached and wanting to play. Talented athletes who want to showcase themselves and want to be led."

8
EMOTION

There's no greater contrast with Ralph Friedgen than his legendary bluster and rage compared to the times, well, he turns to emotional mush. He gets choked up and overcome, sometimes over the slightest thing, that it's common for him to well up and mumble his words.

And it doesn't take much.

Friedgen can be discussing something as innocuous as his depth chart with reporters, or telling boosters at a breakfast about a player overcoming the odds, when it hits him.

Friedgen is mostly private with his emotions. But at times he has difficulty keeping them in check.

He can blow across the emotional spectrum after big wins, bad losses or particularly galling to him, lack of effort. That's when it comes through at its rawest.

His anger, which pours from him instantly, stunned players and coaches at first.

More legendary, though, is the joyful emotion and spontaneity that spills out of him after big wins, times Friedgen will do anything from dance to cry.

Those close to him say his most emotional period was after the North Carolina, N.C. State and Clemson wins in 2001 as a rookie head coach. The incredible crescendo of the first season built with each win and took him along in its wake.

Friedgen fought back tears as he got through pre and post-game speeches in the locker room. After the North Carolina win in his first game he bellowed, his voice cracking, "Get used to winning because this is what it's going to be like around here."

The emotion runs in his family, the softer side tracing back to his mother, the mercurial side to his father.

"He is a very passionate man. Everything is important to him," says wife Gloria.

His family background and his college playing days, when he developed the empathy he displays for his players, helped forge his emotional strain.

Friedgen is compassionate, though his bark and bluster often mask it. He wears his emotions and isn't afraid to show them in the most public of places.

Most of all, Friedgen is remarkably human, warts and all, perhaps the thing that attracts many to him, and what allows his emotion to be so outward at times

"That goes back to your core values," said Blackney. "And his are pretty clear going back to his family and upbringing. You know what makes him up genetically."

T he 2006 team banquet, after the bowl season, was one of Friedgen's emotional times.

When it came time to honor senior running back Josh Allen — who lost his mother to cancer at an early age, bounced from friends, players and coaches' homes during high school, and overcame a major knee injury to sign as a free agent with the Chicago Bears in 2007 — Friedgen had great difficulty. Here was a young man that persevered, perhaps Friedgen's favorite character trait.

The coach fought off tears as he told the audience that if he had a son, he would want him to be like Allen, who was the consummate representative of the team despite his hardships.

Allen came to Friedgen as a senior in 2006 distraught over his diminished role. But he stuck it out and left with another bowl victory.

As a college player, Friedgen bounced from quarterback to linebacker to fullback to guard during a disappointing career. Friedgen has compassion for the players he may never have had had it not been for his own experience. And he shows it often when his emotions get the most of him, mostly around his players or talking about his players, with whom he feels a deep connection. His presence has a significant impact on his players, whatever the setting.

"It's drop a stone here in the water and a hurricane on the other end," Gloria Friedgen said. "He is so giving, but he is also so demanding because he values things so much. It flows right out of him."

Friedgen's emotion has manifested itself in many ways over the years.

Friday night is when he is at his highest emotional pitch beyond after big wins.

Once, in one of Maryland's greatest games, his emotions took on physical form.

That season he had shingles, and on account of the stress, Friedgen got so worked up that he aggravated the condition. He broke out across his back. Every time he got nervous, a band of red dots appeared which he said felt like "needles were being stuck in my back."

It happened when he was an assistant coach and the Terps traveled to Miami in 1984 and trailed the defending national champions 31-0 at the half in what would become the "Miracle of Miami" game.

"I was getting stuck all over the place," he said of the pain.

Miami had a team full of first-round draft picks led by quarterback Bernie Kosar. But

Friedgen thought the Terps had a solid game plan nonetheless. Down big to start, things started to slowly change when the Miami players started trash talking, "which got our guys upset and they were saying we're going to kick their ass and all and Bobby [Ross] got upset. He said, 'Just everybody be quiet. If you don't play better the second half when we get back, don't be getting in your cars with your girlfriends. Go right into the team house because we are going to scrimmage if we don't play better,' " Friedgen said.

Friedgen said Ross came to him and asked, "Okay, what do we got?" I said, 'Coach, they're not doing anything we're not anticipating them doing. Our game plan is still there. We just got to do a better job of executing.'

"He said, 'Alright. Frank [Reich] you are in for Stan [Gelbaugh].' I think Kevin [Glover] and a couple guys were saying something to him and he said, I don't want to hear another word. Just start thinking about what you are going to do when you get back out there.' "

"We didn't make a correction at halftime. Not one. That was the extent of it," Friedgen recalled.

Friedgen said the coaches didn't talk to the players. They just sat there.

Left tackle Tony Edwards hurt his knee so the Terps moved J.D. Maarleveld to the left side. Edwards stayed in to shower but got locked in at halftime. The Terps took the first drive and scored and then got a turnover and scored again. Friedgen started doing the math and said to himself, "We can get back in this thing."

The rest is history as the Terps won and Friedgen's shingles finally abated. He still jokes about how Edwards "missed the greatest comeback in college football history." Friedgen's emotions settled down, at least until the victory celebration.

"He is what he is," said Stoddard. "He wears it all on his sleeve. He is kind of like a big bull, not real complex. He doesn't hide a lot of things, especially his emotion."

Those that work for him say Friedgen works remarkably hard and takes nothing for granted. He appreciates everything. Some point to the strong connection with his father, who was an emotional man, and how he is not that much different.

"When Ralph talks to the team or the coaches he speaks from the heart. It's an emotional thing. He's not BS'ing people. He's an emotional, passionate man. He doesn't always break down all the way and cry, but you can always tell there is a lot of emotion in what he is saying," Stoddard said.

When he won both ACC and national coach of the year honors in 2001, a wave of emotion flooded over him at the coaches' convention when he saw the names of the winners that preceded him.

"All these things. After 30 years of planning and coaching and working towards this, to have it pay off . . . his vision, all coming together, it's a powerful experience for him to go through," Franklin said. "And he's not afraid to show it."

Hollenbach recalled a pre-season team meeting when Friedgen went over scheduling and other matters. Friedgen moved along and covered the basics before he began to choke with emotion. Friedgen told the team that he saw a student on campus wear-ing a Southern California NCAA Championship tee-shirt after the Trojans captured the college football title the year before.

That was all it took.

"He said, 'You know men, this is my dream for this program,' " Hollenbach said. "He said, 'This is where we are going to get.' It was really the first time that I had real-ly seen him get that emotional about something so . . . I mean, we were kinda just going over the schedule and the next thing he is welling up in front of us. We all looked at each other and said, 'How did this happen?' "

"To me, it was just he is so committed to doing this. It's something that just drives him and eats him up."

Dennard Wilson, one of the players on the first team that Friedgen was the clos-est with, remembered Friedgen's pre-game speech before the Virginia game during his second season. No opponent gets Friedgen as primed as Virginia, a school he's never hid his dislike for.

During the practice week his nerves are typically frayed, he stays later, he's more aggressive with the players. He considers Virginia "a different breed," Wilson said. "They are up on their high horse. We're more blue-collar. We put on our work shirts and go to work each day."

Friedgen and Al Groh butted heads in the college and pro ranks. The border rivals have engaged in many recruiting battles. Maryland considered Virginia something of a rival but Virginia wanted no part of it, looking down on the Terps.

"He would make it known that that was his game," Wilson said. "It was more than just a game."

"Coach Friedgen began pounding on things in the locker room and told us 'We're going to be on them like swarming bees,' " Wilson said. "It just all came to a head and he started crying. He told us, 'I love you guys no matter what happens.' "

Said Rychleski:

"With Ralph, you put so much time into it that it's almost a relief that you let it all out after the game because of all the work you did and your accomplishment came through. That overflows with him."

Glover remembered his senior season when the Terps began the season as the fifth-ranked team in the polls but lost to Vanderbilt and Syracuse in the first two games. Friedgen called Glover into his office, told him to close the door, and blasted away. There was no holding back.

"He got emotional and aired some things out," Glover said. "I got emotional and aired some things out. As the captain of the offense, he knows that I could have an effect on the players and get things turned around. It was from the heart.

"We got it turned around, finished 9-3, including one of the great games in Maryland history, the Miami game. It's life for him."

All-America end Merriman recalled the Clemson game during his junior season when Friedgen was so fired up "he jumped 7-8 inches off the ground" at midfield.

"And he's not a very mobile guy, as you know. I'm like, 'Man, this is what you come here for.' "

Merriman said he had never been so pumped for a game.

"And I'm a pretty amped up person anyhow. It was very emotional for me. I am already fired up. I talk trash. I do anything I can to get someone into it. But that day that was never expected. I will never forget that. He probably doesn't even know I saw that and feel that way."

Merriman said what's unique about Friedgen is that "you never know what can come out his mouth. He would tell us he would rather die before he would lose. And that's the kind of player I am. That's when I found out the kind of person he is."

Players say the darkest moment for Friedgen came following the 55-6 thrashing at Virginia Tech, coached by his good friend and former colleague Beamer. The game, during the 2004 season, came on national television on Thursday night for the nation to see.

Quarterback Joel Statham coughed up the ball repeatedly to start the game, while backup Ryan Mitch was left home due to academic suspension. Third-string Jordan Steffy got knocked out of the game after suffering a concussion trying to make a tackle on an interception return. Finally, fourth-stringer Hollenbach was pressed into duty. The cart fell off the wheels early for the Terps, and the onslaught ended in a steady rain at Blacksburg. It would spell the first of two 5-6 seasons for Friedgen at College Park, his low point as head coach.

Adding insult was losing in such fashion in his first game against his friend Beamer.

"That was as embarrassing as it gets. And losing that way to your best friend doesn't make it any easier," Dennard Wilson said. "He came into the locker room and you could see it in his face. He was really upset. I remember he told us, 'If you guys don't want to play for me I'm out of here. I'll leave. What is it? I don't know what it is. I think you guys don't want to play football for me. I don't feel like you are behind us. I think it may just be better that I move on from here.' We were like, 'Is this guy quitting on us?' That was one of his more dark moments."

The next morning, Wilson said, Friedgen apologized to the team.

"I think it's just a reflection of how personal all of this is for him," his boss, Yow, said.

Other incidents have taken on legend at College Park as well.

The day he head-butted safety Chris Kelley during warm-ups before a Virginia game stands out.

Kelley, a beat up athlete by his senior year after three knee surgeries, played on emotion and was the nerve center of the team. He made up for some of his physical limitations with his reckless play. He was always willing to start a fight, be it with opponents or teammates.

Friedgen was so excited before the game that he jacked up some of the players in the locker room, and later on the field with head-butts, slamming his head against their face masks.

"I remember there was just so much energy flying around. The next thing you know coach head-butted him above the face mask," Bryant said. "There was so much testosterone flying around that I don't even think he felt it. That was the most hyped I think I saw coach Friedgen."

Another dust-up occurred during the Virginia pre-game the year before. Franklin got things going with a verbal exchange at midfield with Groh. Before long, players from both sides were going at it and Maryland was flagged for unsportsmanlike conduct before kickoff.

The Terps carried the emotion through a cold and windy night before an ESPN national television audience, routing the Cavaliers, 27-17, thanks to 257 yards rushing from sophomore running back Allen. The game wasn't as close as the final score.

Hollenbach recalled a time at the team hotel on Friday night before the 2006 Clemson game at Death Valley, when the Terps were 6-2 at the midpoint of the season. A worked up Friedgen stood before the players and asked them, " 'What do you want to be? 10-4 or 6-8?'

"He had all the numbers messed up he was yelling at us so much. He had us for 14 games when it was only a 12-game season. Everyone knew what he meant, but it kinda just broke his rhythm. It was funny," Hollenbach said.

Friedgen would get so caught up in game-planning that he'd forget to tell the players and coaches key things, like one day what time practice was.

"We all showed up at the wrong time because he never told us," Josh Wilson said. "He was so deep into what he was doing."

Friedgen loves to get emotion from his players as well. Perhaps none as much as his quarterbacks.

In 2006 he pushed the senior quarterback Hollenbach to the brink. But it revealed a new side of the signal caller.

Hollenbach described a time at practice when the Terps, heading into the Virginia game, had Friedgen in their faces and yelling throughout the practice week.

"Even the ball boys were getting yelled at," Hollenbach said. "It was one of those weeks."

Hollenbach threw an incomplete pass behind tight end Joey Haynos. So Friedgen jumped him. He barked:

" 'You got to make that kind of throw if we are going to win. How are we going to win if you are not playing well? What are you doing today? Where are you today?' Those kinds of things," Hollenbach said of his coach's words. "And I just turned around and started screaming at him. He was in the huddle and was right in my face while I was getting the signal for the next play. He walked with me to the huddle and was still yelling at me. I just yelled at him, 'Get out of this huddle right now. Get out of here. We don't need you in here. You are making it worse.'

"I watched him walk back. I made sure he was out of there. We ran the play and I remember some of the guys coming up to me and saying that was pretty sweet. But I did not know how he was going to be. I wasn't sure if that was going to change our relationship. That was a Thursday practice and the next day in meetings, in Friday night meetings at the hotel, he announced to the whole offense, 'I can tell you guys are really into this, your emotions are high.' And he turned and looked right at me and said, 'You know, I love when I get you fired up like that.' So that brought me back to, 'Okay everything is fine.' I guess that's what he really wanted.

"Later we talked about it on a one-to-one basis and he said, 'I love when I can get under your skin like that because that means I am getting to you. You are listening to me,' " Hollenbach added.

Former colleague and friend O'Leary said Friedgen's "bark is worse than the bite." And it goes back to his roots, ones similar to O'Leary's, he said.

"He's a New Yorker. New Yorker's are going to pretty much tell you what they think. You may not like the way they do it, or how they approach it, but I think he's just trying to be genuine and honest about things in football and life."

He gets emotionally invested in his players and knows how to reach them at that level.

Many in the program point to the time former kicker Jess Atkinson prepared a highlight film to motivate the team on the eve of its game with Virginia. The film was set to the music of the popular film *Gladiator*, and it blew both the players and coaches away, including, most of all, Friedgen.

The assistant coaches said it was one of Friedgen's most emotional times.

"It really broke him up. He was crying," Sollazzo said. "It was from the heart about how important the players were to him, how important everything about the football program was and how badly he wanted everyone to win and to have that success."

Friedgen lets his emotion and spontaneity get the best of him, sometimes in funny ways.

Perhaps none like when he first danced before players after the comeback win at N.C. State in 2001. It was captured by television crews and shocked viewers.

The team came into the game lacking emotion in the first half after the Clemson win the week before. So Friedgen provided a lift with his halftime tirade.

That set the stage for a big emotional reversal by game's end.

"That was out of his comfort zone. He really let go," said Dennard Wilson. "It was a sight to see and they got it on film because it wasn't just this coach, this head of this unit, but a little kid came out. And it was honest. It was a genuine. I enjoyed that."

Friedgen's emotion has put him in a tough spot on campus a few times.

He blew up at men's soccer coach Sasho Cirovski and field hockey coach Missy Meharg when they had their teams on the turf practice field. He had some choice words before he probably thought about what he was saying.

Later, he had to deal with Yow about the matter. She pointed out to him, "We have 27 sports, but we are all one team."

Galt, Class of 1981, has worked under five head coaches at Maryland and said he has "never had a coach, any coach, with his strength of personality. He is very blunt, honest, not afraid at all to rip your ass," said Galt.

"He really didn't appear to have any concern about your feelings if he went to criticize you. That first 4-5 months of that spring in the weight room, in spring ball, in winter workouts, he pretty much screamed at me and his coaches. It affected the guys tremendously who had never worked with him and obviously, at the start, the players were scared to death of him.

"But I think it had a great deal to do with how successful we were that year. There is no doubt about that."

Some close to him say he has a bit of "Lombardi philosophy" in him, where he will knock you if you slip up but it feels good when he compliments you, however obscure the compliment. Friedgen doesn't come right out and say it, but in his own way, often indirectly.

Galt agreed:

"A lot of time he doesn't come right out and say, 'You did a great job.' But he'll say 'Hey, our guys were stronger than theirs.' He's done that with me many times, in his way, and it makes you feel good. It makes you want to work for the guy."

It's all part of Friedgen's many contradictions. He's old-school in ways, new in others, while often disarming along the way with his emotions.

"You gotta read between the lines. If you have been around him long enough, you tend to grab those moments. It keeps you motivated because you know we all want to please him," Galt said.

No example of how raw Friedgen's emotion can get was like an incident on the eve of the 2006 football season.

At a "Top Terp" kickoff event Friedgen bared all. He entered the season with more pressure after taking on the role of offensive coordinator coming off two 5-6 seasons. Some said he looked like "death warmed over" that winter after recruiting as he was also busy game-planning for the spring.

At the podium while addressing the crowd he said, "When I lose I want to die."

That prompted concern among the boosters and administrators on hand. The crowd fell uncomfortably quiet.

"He is just a very emotional man," Gloria said. "And it kills him to lose. We hadn't lost in a long time, and we had that losing streak and it was an awful, awful time. But I am concerned. He's a very intense, very passionate man in all aspects of his life."

One of his contradictions is that despite his bluster and my-way-or-the-highway attitude, one-on-one with the players Friedgen can be, well, a puppy dog.

And some have tried to take advantage of it.

When a player slips up they want to come see him first. But sometimes their motivation isn't pure. He invested a lot of time in Merriman and Gaither, one for the better, one that didn't make it through.

"It's funny," Galt said. "He'll get so angry in practice or group team settings. And then the players don't understand how he can care so much one time, yet be so tough at others."

But with all of the success has come incredible admiration for the man that made it possible.

"They are appreciative of the opportunity, players and coaches," Rychleski said. "Maryland had not had much recent success before Ralph got here. It was struggling in football for 15 years. To have the great success of the last six years is very rewarding, and realizing that a lot of it has to do with how Ralph has set the standards for the program."

Coaches and players alike know that rarely will they not be prepared for an opponent. And they know the Terps have out-coached better competition at times, which has made up for a talent gap.

The Terps worked all week on their "red zone" offense against certain Purdue pass coverages they scouted heading into the Champs Bowl in 2006. And their first score came thanks to the advance work.

Haynos was the second read and was wide open in the end zone for an easy Hollenbach toss. It was the 2006 game that Maryland dominated the most in the coaches' booth, and it wasn't close after the first quarter. Friedgen was at an emotional high after the game following the long grind of the season, and it showed among coaches and players in the victory celebration. Even former defensive coordinator Blackney, retired and living in Florida, found his way to the Terps' locker room after the game.

"When you do all those things you have nothing but respect. After the game Joey said, 'It's just like we practiced.' When you have that thing that's how you win the close games. That's the sense of accomplishment everyone feels good about," Rychleski said.

In locker room celebrations after wins is when Friedgen bares most.

He can dance, sing, or jump up and down. Some assistant coaches get concerned that he may injure himself or damage his artificial hip. Such joy and energy that sometimes Friedgen can't speak the words on his lips.

"He's a dancer. He's a hugger. It's wild in there," Galt said. "This man is obsessed with winning, and winning is a very, very powerful emotion in his life. A big victory, an important ACC victory, is as good as it gets for coach Friedgen."

After the long grind of his first season, when he was very much the taskmaster, there was nothing as stark a contrast than the New Year's Eve party in the hospitality suite at the team hotel in South Beach.

Players and coaches were shocked to see Friedgen dancing, having cocktails, kids hopping up in his lap, carrying on like they had never seen.

After the Terps lost a heartbreaker to Clemson in 2005, a game in which they were up big only to fall in the final quarter, Grabenstein brought his elderly parents to town from Cumberland, and to the team house after the game.

Both were on walkers and his father would pass away later that year.

Grabenstein, who endowed Friedgen's office where a plaque hangs with his family name, took his parents to see it for the first time. Grabenstein didn't know if he would have another opportunity.

"We were sitting by his door when he came in and he was in one of those real, real rages. You know the kind of rage he was in after that kind of loss when they had it in the win category. I saw him come in and he couldn't give a hoot about anything or anybody. He was just that mad." Grabenstein said.

"But he saw my parents there and all of a sudden he became very quiet and respectful and didn't let this emotion show and said, 'Hello.' That I know is hard for him to do in that kind of situation."

Later that year Grabenstein brought his parents to a men's basketball game to sit in his courtside seats. During a timeout, "Ralph bolted out of his chair and went over to say hello to them. I was very, very touched by that," Grabenstein said.

Grabenstein jokes about the range of his emotional encounters with Friedgen, including the frequent question, "How's my money doing?" But at the same time, the touching moments like when the coach summoned him to the team house to have his finger sized for an Orange Bowl ring in 2001.

A year ago his youngest daughter, Katie, prepared a slide show to celebrate her sister's 18th birthday, and when Friedgen viewed it he broke down.

Just like that the big man with the ferocious bark turned to mush.

9
MOTIVATION

From invoking the name of General George S. Patton to wearing a "doo-rag," Ralph Friedgen has gone to all ends to motivate his players.

Before a game with West Virginia, with a storm coming that forced the Terps to practice in the morning, Friedgen used Patton as an example when the players grumbled about their wake-up call.

"He won World War II because his guys marched 120 miles without rest. We can do the same thing, and you guys will have a little rest," Friedgen told the players.

As offensive coordinator with the San Diego Chargers, Friedgen showed his resourceful side as a motivator. And the lengths that he would go.

He knew how to get to quarterback Stan Humphries, who he said could be "lazy." He simply called Humphries wife, Connie, when in need.

"She would get after his ass. I'd call her up on maybe a Tuesday and tell her, 'We got to get to Stan. He's got to play better.' "

Humphries never knew about the phone calls.

At Georgia Tech, where male and female athletes ate in the same cafeteria, Friedgen would cozy up to players' girlfriends.

"We got to get him ready to go this week," he'd tell the girls.

At Maryland, Friedgen has done that with several players, including J.P. Humber, Jafar Williams and Mike Whaley. The South Carolina native Whaley tested him like few others.

"I used to call Mike in here and say, 'What do you like in life?' He'd say, 'I like to fish and I like girls.' I told him, 'I don't know if I got a curriculum in that,' " Friedgen said.

Friedgen knows how to push the right buttons, be it with ploys or pre-game speeches, while he's been known to even get in boosters' faces about giving more to the program. He has no inhibition.

Friedgen learned well from his father, who was fire and brimstone in the locker room but was part psychologist, too, knowing when to push and when to pat on the back.

Friedgen's flexible enough to know when to lighten the mood to get a point across. He'll even make fun of himself in the process.

During his first year as head coach, while attempting to get the players to wear uniform skull caps (not the wide variety of colors and styles they used) Friedgen walked into a team meeting sporting a red Terps "doo-rag," which had the players bellowing with laughter. "You think this is funny?" he told them. "It's kinda the way I think when I see you in them." Regardless of setting or circumstance, Friedgen seems to have a way to reach the players.

"One of the traits of highly successful individuals is they have a range of personality. Ability to fit in to any given situation, and the key there is to pick the right way to be at the right place and time," Yow said. "With Ralph you have doggedly determined but you also have charming. That is the type of scope and range of personality many successful people have."

Friedgen's father had many tactics, starting with fear, which Friedgen uses as well. He recalled his father's best pre-game pep talk.

"One day he had us all hitting the walls and beams and everything else. He said, 'Either you are ready to play, or you are the biggest bunch of phonies I have ever seen.'"

Friedgen said he once saw his father break a clipboard over a player's head during a halftime rage. Once he called a player's home to see if he was in bed the night before a game. The player's father answered and said, "I'm not lying anymore. He's not in."

The player got in so late that he came to see Friedgen the next morning, along with his father. The boy was disrespectful to the father in front of coach Friedgen, who grabbed him by the neck and slammed him into the wall.

But high school teammate and friend Verille said that Friedgen's father would mostly "make you want to knock down the wall."

Ralph has carried on the tradition.

"I see that in Ralph. It is the same thing," said Verille, who has been in the locker room before and after games.

In the locker room after a Terps-West Virginia game, Verille said his friend called out slot receiver JoJo Walker.

Friedgen told him to stand up. Walker didn't know what was coming. Friedgen choked up but was able to mutter, "This is a guy who is giving his all and is really laying it out 110 percent. If everybody else in this room gave what this guy is giving we wouldn't be 1-2 right now. Guys, go look at yourselves in the mirror."

Friedgen rarely backs down. He's on point and relentless with encouragement, however rough it can be at times.

Unlike many offensive coaches, Friedgen is a "quarterback screamer," not afraid to rip his quarterbacks in practices or in games.

Many coaches coddle or protect their quarterbacks. Not Friedgen. They are his most important players, the ones he invests the most in, and he isn't afraid to express whatever opinion he believes he needs to them.

Like men's basketball coach Gary Williams with his point guards, you need thick skin to play the position at Maryland.

"The man is so intense, so emotional. He is about as intense, emotional and competitive as anyone that I have ever been around. He flat-out hates to lose and he won't accept losing. It is very painful for him so he communicates all his emotions onto his players. There is nothing holding back, ever," Blackney said.

"And it's probably pretty good that he can show emotion and vent because if you are a person that stores it up at this level, as intense as it is, it can be unhealthy."

The early-morning winter workouts and punishment runs at Byrd Stadium – something Friedgen instituted once he arrived – had a dramatic effect on the players.

Each morning, Friedgen would roll up in his Cadillac, drive to the edge of the field at Byrd, and sit in his front seat as he watched the players run the steps and go through drills.

The exercise was for the players that missed class, missed breakfast, or slipped up in other ways. The drills began at 5:45 a.m.

The players ran steps for a half hour and then met on the field for more work. The grass was sometimes frozen. As they finished Friedgen, who cracked his car window about four inches, had comments for each as they came by his car. At times he could "crush the kids," an assistant said, if they got out of line.

There were 15 players at the start, later six, and finally one because most eventually got the message.

"They were scared to death," said Galt, who helped run the workouts.

For some, it was every morning as they kept slipping up. The assistant coaches, if their players were in trouble, also had to be there, which wasn't popular with them, either. But Friedgen didn't care.

It led to some funny moments. Blackney was so upset one morning that he made the players roll 100 yards down the field.

Linebacker Leon Joe, Friedgen said, "could run all day."

And he did.

Friedgen brought him in for study sessions, which bothered Joe even more.

"Running to him was no problem. Bringing him in at 5 a.m. to study he hated," Friedgen said.

He was like "Big Daddy" in the film *The Long, Hot Summer*, the bellicose but beloved character actor Orson Welles played, tooling around in his "Caddy."

It was no sweat for Friedgen, who was always at the office by 5:30 a.m. anyhow. The routine got the players to the team house more, something Friedgen was all for.

"When I came in here everything was 'loosy-goosy.' Half the kids were living off campus. Nobody made any meals, any breakfasts. Kids were complaining they didn't have enough food. One reason they didn't have enough food was they were eating at McDonald's all the time," Friedgen said.

Friedgen said some of the players bought lunch for their girlfriends on their meal cards.

He brought discipline right away. He knew that once the players had their personal lives in order their football lives would follow.

Friedgen insisted that the players move back on campus, go to class, and be at breakfast each morning. Or deal with him and the consequences.

He even ran All-America linebacker D'Qwell Jackson. Cornerback Gerrick McPhearson came to him with a sad story about having to run in the ACC track meet the same day as a punishment run. Friegden, never one to give star treatment, told him, "Well, we'll just loosen you up for it."

Another player, Nassau (N.Y.) Community College transfer James Evans, often missed class. So Friedgen ran him every day.

The first winter, after Evans ran every stadium step, Friedgen approached him. Sweat was pouring off of him and steam was coming off his head.

"He was out of breath and I said to him 'You know, James, you are going to be in great shape when you flunk out of here.' And he was. And he did."

Later, "by an act of God he got eligible," Friedgen said, and Evans returned for spring camp, only to flunk out the following semester.

"Either they change or they don't make it," Friedgen said. "And when I watch tape I see kids breaking down the same way. I told him, 'You have to understand. Everything you do in life you have to be accountable. There's a direct response for every action you have. You don't do something then you are going to fail. That's why I want to recruit goal-oriented kids."

Friedgen, in his first spring camp, wanted to make things ultra competitive in goal-line scrimmaging. So he told the players that the losing unit would run.

The offense won, the defense had to run, but five players refused to run. They jogged.

"So I kept running them," Friedgen said. "I said, 'We're all gonna run until everyone starts running full-speed.' "

Henderson approached the malcontents and soon they were sprinting.

"And that was a peer-group pressure form of motivation. That's another way it can happen," Friedgen said.

Friedgen may have motivated through fear at the outset to get his players' attention, but he was nimble enough to get creative over the years, changing with the times and the kids.

He would reward players for good grades or weight room or practice performance, and recognize them after practice as the team huddled up.

Despite the grind, and the hammer that he would often lower on them, the players realized that they would always be prepared, in top shape, and together under Friedgen.

Wide receiver Jafar Williams, who sometimes resisted his new coach's ways, approached Friedgen during two-a-days in the first year and told him, "Coach, we're prepared for everything. We have never been like this before."

Friedgen recalled another receiver, Guilian Gary, a hero from the N.C. State game in 2001, as a player he was never sure that he "reached." But Gary came to Friedgen at the Orange Bowl, after the coach's Friday night pep talk, and told him how much he would miss him.

"It was pretty easy to speak to that team because every week was an emotional happening," Friedgen said.

Friedgen had built-in forms of motivation during the first year. And it wasn't difficult finding new motivation each week.

When the Terps played cellar-dweller Duke, Friedgen feared a letdown. So he brought his AFC Championship and National Championship rings to the locker room, something he rarely does. He listed all of the reasons why they had to beat Duke, finally flashing the rings to symbolize championships.

"After the sixth win now we have a chance to win the conference championship," he said.

Friedgen took the rings and passed one down each aisle of players.

"Do you want one of these?" he asked them.

Later that season he said some of the players' parents approached him after games or at breakfast and said that was his best motivational ploy.

From the "I Believe" wrist bands to the *Gladiator* highlight film, the best thing about Friedgen's motivational efforts – however gimmicky they may be – is that they worked.

Former coach Duffner, in an attempt to fire up his players before playing Florida State, had a horseman ride onto the practice field brandishing a flaming spear, which he hurled into the ground as they do in pre-game ceremonies at Tallahassee.

The Terps never beat Florida State until Friedgen arrived.

Probably his best tactic was the *Gladiator* highlight film that Jess Atkinson prepared before the Virginia game in 2003. Friedgen said it put the team over the top, and "it made the 2003 season for us."

"I really credit that video for that season," he said.

The Terps were 6-3 heading into the contest. But they were not convincing in getting to that mark, losing on the road at Northern Illinois and badly at FSU, while getting a first-half scare at Eastern Michigan. Quarterback Scott McBrien and the receivers were struggling, among others.

Atkinson brought Friedgen a highlight film that he put together scored to music from the hit film and "I started crying," Friedgen said.

Friedgen immediately wanted to show it to the team, and he couldn't wait until after dinner. He got the players up from the table, took over a meeting room at the hotel, and popped in the tape.

It showed the struggles of the season, with scenes starting from the cornfields of Northern Illinois, and the music made it more dramatic. Friedgen got emotional while discussing it two years later.

"When I finished showing it there was no reaction. Everybody was just quiet," he said.

The players had their meal and resumed their Friday routine with a devotional and position meetings.

But getting off the bus for "Terp Alley" the next morning, Harrison and Wilson asked Friedgen if he would show it again. It was just hours before the game.

Always ready to hit while the motivational fire was hot, Friedgen found Atkinson and the two rigged up a system with Friedgen's Bose radio serving as speakers and showed it in the locker room.

The players burst on the field and later spanked the Cavaliers on Thursday night ESPN television. The Terps rolled to a 10-3 mark, culminated by their rout of West Virginia in the Gator Bowl in Jacksonville, Fla.

"There was an emotional thing in that film. Jess finished it with the rest of the season from there. I showed it later at the banquet and people cried at the banquet. They felt the same way that I did," Friedgen said.

Said Merriman, who was at a high emotional pitch on most days:

"I think that film also brought us closer to coach Friedgen as well because it was so emotional. We were all moved."

It was a classic Friedgen moment.

And he's had a lot to work with since he's been at College Park.

When he took over the program in 2000, he inherited Perry, a speedy but sometimes high-maintenance back and track athlete from Philadelphia's George Washington High School.

Like a fine-tuned race car, Perry needed frequent maintenance. The tweak of a hamstring or an ankle would put him on the sidelines. And sometimes in Friedgen's "dog house."

Friedgen was all about players that fought through injury. Missing practice could mean falling down his depth chart. There's nothing worse than missing practice in Ralph Friedgen's world. He can leave you behind if you do.

One of Friedgen's signature comments in the first year came in an offensive staff meeting shortly after he arrived. Assistant coaches remembered the day he said, "Bruce Perry will never play at Maryland."

That didn't sit well with the coaches, including running backs coach Locksley, who had taken Perry under his wing and had a personal bond dating to his recruitment.

Friedgen considered Perry a "smallish" back and favored bigger, stouter backs for his system. No doubt, Friedgen and Perry developed one of the more contentious relationships he's had since he's been at College Park.

Friedgen saw Perry as he did many high school backs. Having the ability to out-run most everyone to the corner, and arrive at college thinking the same, which isn't always the reality.

Perry would sometimes run east-west, and Friedgen stayed on him about "sticking it in there north-south," Friedgen said.

Friedgen preferred Jason Crawford, a 6-3, 225-pound "big" back. The staff, before Friedgen arrived, redshirted Perry his second year to save a year with LaMont Jordan and

Mookie Sikyala ahead of him. Their special back, at least the one they thought was special, Friedgen arrived proclaiming, "He couldn't play for a good high school team." Kind of deflating for everyone involved. But classic Friedgen the motivator.

Friedgen said Perry ran better as his career went on, but that it often took a motivational ploy or barb from the coach to get him started. Friedgen told Perry, "You're not as good as you think you are," which cast doubt on him.

"Every time Bruce felt good, well coach Friedgen would knock him down," Dennard Wilson said. "And Bruce would come out firing like he had bullets in his gun."

Perry got some satisfaction, hanging 116 yards on North Carolina in Friedgen's debut game. Friedgen admitted after the game he was "splitting defensive backs. Running over and through them. Just blowing them up."

"I said, 'Whoa. Is this Bruce Perry?'" Friedgen said.

"It was kinda 'love-hate,'" Perry said. "He would try to motivate me anyway you could, whether it hurt your feelings or not. Most of the time he hurt your feelings."

Perry had his ups and downs with injuries, especially a nagging groin heading into his senior year. But he went to Wake Forest as a sophomore and put 276 yards on the Demon Deacons, the second best day for a Terp rusher ever, and he went on to be named ACC Offensive Player of the Year, the first sophomore to do so.

But that didn't stop Friedgen.

Even Perry's first rush from scrimmage that day, which went for 80 yards, wasn't enough as Friedgen thought he could give more. Perry thought he was giving everything.

As a senior, heading into his final game versus Virginia, Perry had an ankle injury and Friedgen said to him on the sideline, "Are you going to play today or what?"

"I was pissed when he said that," Perry said. "But I learned if I could take it from him, I could take it from anybody. That made me a better person and a better player."

Perry missed 11 games during his career because of injury. He played with a bruised wrist against Georgia Tech in 2001, rushing for 63 yards but playing through. Still, Friedgen wouldn't let up as he always thought there was more in the tank.

"He came up to me Sunday after the game and said, 'You know. I was disappointed in you.' I said, 'Damn,'" Perry said.

Perry would get back at his coach one day. Make sure that he appreciated him. Perry played a April Fool's Day trick on Friedgen. He went to his office crying one day, telling Friedgen on the eve of camp that he got caught cheating on an exam.

"He said, 'Bruce. Bruce. What happened?' I was like, 'April Fool's, man,'" Perry said.

Perry said that despite his dislike for Friedgen at times, he trusted him and called him a "players" coach. And he said that he trusted him more than his predecessor, Vanderlinden, who he said was more of a "politician."

Friedgen said that if Perry stayed healthy, he could have been one of the best backs ever at Maryland. He added that if he didn't challenge him he may not have done what he did as a Terp. Playing hurt comes with the territory as a running back at the college and pro level, he would tell Perry.

During spring camp in 2007, Friedgen compared freshman running back Da'Rel Scott favorably to Perry when asked what kind of back he was, adding "that's saying a lot."

"But with Ralph it was always, 'What have you done for me lately?' It was that tough love all the way," Perry said. "Always picking and prodding you."

Perry went on to play for the Philadelphia Eagles but injuries slowed his career. He said he got to see a more "human" side of his coach during his senior year while attending the ACC's Operation Football in Georgia, along with Friedgen, in addition to their time spent in Orlando, Fla., at the Doak Walker award ceremony.

Perry said the "love-hate" became a "mutual respect" after he played for Friedgen. But after he put 237 yards on Wake Forest as a senior, Perry said that Friedgen asked him, 'Why can't you play every week?' "

Locksley said Perry was one of his "toughest backs ever" to play at Maryland. He remembered a key fourth-and-long catch Perry made at N.C. State to keep the Terps alive in their comeback in 2001.

"Right now," Perry said five years later, "he pretty much made me the player that I am mentally with preparation and knowledge of the game. I wouldn't be where I am if he didn't coach me."

Perry said Friedgen could pull motivational gems out of his bag, especially when the Terps played Virginia and Florida State, because of his competitive feelings for coaches Groh and Bowden. Then Friedgen would be at his best.

Friedgen had great respect for Bowden but after every loss, at midfield, Bowden would point out what Friedgen did wrong, which was maddening to him. For years Friedgen was waiting for the exchange after he won, which came in 2004, and he was respectful. As for Virginia, he always disliked the school, which he called "elitist."

Looking back over Friedgen's playing and coaching career, there were all forms of motivation.

Against Clemson in the 1980s as an assistant under Ross, Friedgen gave a pre-game talk to his unit at the breakfast table. He used butter patties and large containers of cream cheese as props. He made Clemson the butter and the Terps the bigger cream cheese. He showed them a play and told them, "They [Clemson] are the butter and we should be able to dominate them."

Glover related the story to Rychleski in 2006, more than 20 years later, who used it before the Terps-Florida State game that year. After Maryland's victory Haynos approached Rychleski and said to him, "Hey, we just smashed the butter out of them."

Friedgen never lets up. He can have a 20-point lead "but still be calling for blood," Bryant said.

He rarely backs down in looking for ways to motivate.

Another example came in 2001 when the Terps hosted Duke for Homecoming. During pre-game, Friedgen told the players that if they didn't score on the first five possessions "that you all are running on Monday."

The Terps obliged.

Sollazzo recalled a time as a player at The Citadel under then-assistant Friedgen when the team suffered a lopsided loss at Delaware. The following morning, Sunday at 8 a.m., the team dressed out in full gear. The players had to run thirty eight 100-yard sprints for Delaware's 38-point margin of victory. That was a day and age when coaches could get away with "extracurriculars."

"I remember after we ran. Coach Ross ran everybody up to him and said, 'Now, that wasn't a punishment,' " Sollazzo said.

What Sollazzo remembered best from those years was the exactness, the precision, and how fundamentally strong the unit was under Friedgen, their line coach.

As a junior, Sollazzo's defense ranked nationally in points allowed. Sollazzo said he played for Friedgen when he was "full of his most piss and vinegar," in his first full-time position and just starting out. Sollazzo recalled "erasers and pieces of chalk flying through the air in meetings."

"We weren't very big, but we were technicians. That's what coach Friedgen ingrained in my mind to motivate me. You can win even if you are not as good as the people you are playing against. He drilled the hell out of us. Every day the individual period seemed like forever. But every drill was to perfection."

Sollazzo is about as old school as one can be. He still uses a football on a stick in practice to drill his players on reacting to the ball. Sollazzo said he got the habit from Friedgen, who made one from a golf club and a wooden football glued to it years ago. It's called a "dicker stick," and Friedgen joked that he should have had it patented.

"I can remember him hitting me on the ass with that thing many a time," Sollazzo said. "At the time there was a fear factor. You didn't like him at the time."

Because he's so real, and shoots so straight, the simplest motivational spark from Friedgen can send the players into a frenzy.

Wike saw it in Friedgen's first game against North Carolina in 2001. The players went into the locker room at halftime with a touchdown lead and fired up. But Friedgen put them over the top with something they had never heard from Vanderlinden. It was visceral and so Friedgen.

"He got the whole team around him and told us, 'You got them right where you want 'em. You are doing just what you need to do. They're down, ready to fall out, give up. You got your foot on the throat, now you got to pull the trigger. Take them out. Finish them off.' We just went nuts," Wike said.

Many players and coaches point to the Orange Bowl season when the Terps were down big at N.C. State before Friedgen ignited the locker room at intermission, tossing a chair that barely missed the head of an offensive lineman.

Said Wike of Friedgen's graphic words:

"Friedgen said, 'You guys have worked this hard and you are letting it run down your leg right now.' He threw the chair across the locker room and that really woke us up."

He's been known to stop practices in mid-stream and call for a full scrimmage. Sometimes Friedgen gets so into it that he becomes obsessed by his competitiveness.

Once at practice Hollenbach said Friedgen had the Terps in a third-down scrimmage of 10 plays at the end. Friedgen had been all over the offense for making mental mistakes, and he didn't think they could pull it out. The scrimmage went down to the last play and the offense delivered with a touchdown to win.

"The offense was going nuts. We had done it despite what he thought of us that day. But then all of a sudden he said, 'Alright, one more play.' I was like, 'What? What is he talking about?' And so we had to run one more play, the defense stopped us, and both teams had to run. I said 'Coach, c'mon, what are you doing to us?' "

Bryant said that some of Friedgen's best motivational speeches were his shortest. He would get right to the point if it meant he was more effective conveying his message.

All it took in the locker room before the Clemson game in 2001, with the Terps gunning for an ACC title, were these words from the head coach:

"N.C. State just beat Florida State."

Friedgen said that and walked out.

The players poured onto the field like they had been shot from a cannon and went on to upset the Tigers.

"He didn't always have to be a talker," Bryant said. "Because he knew how to get to us."

After the Terps won Friedgen kept it simple as well, saying, "Job well done. You guys were the only ones who believed, only ones wearing red and white," Bryant recalled Friedgen telling the team.

He went on to say: "Even the conference picked us to be at the bottom, but you guys kept fighting. Now you guys are going to a BCS game."

Josh Wilson recalled an emotional conversation he had with Friedgen before his junior year when he was feeling down over some family matters and other stress in his life. Friedgen brought him into his office and recounted some of the difficult times he had, from the disappointment of his college career to some of his lean years as a coach. And how he persevered. Similar words were probably used decades ago by his father.

"He said, 'This is why we play football. We are the chosen. We make the sacrifices. The few that make it from little league to high school to college, and then the one percent that make it to the NFL. Everyone wants to make it but no one wants to work hard enough for it. We do what everyone wants to do. You can't just go to school or go play football. You have to be good football players and students.' "

Wilson said that was one of the reasons why the 2006 team was able to fight through adversity and win a bowl game, finishing 9-4 after nearly being left for dead at halftime at Virginia in week six.

"That's why this team was able to get back. Because we had players like Sam [Hollenbach] and [Adam] Podlesh and myself, who were not only good football players and leaders on the team, but also in the classroom. We graduated. Josh Allen graduated, walked across the stage. We were getting these awards. That exemplified what coach Friedgen stressed for us."

In 2001 when he had a team that didn't quite know how to win yet, Friedgen pushed the players to the extreme at key times, be it practices or games. Most of them fell in line wanting to be led, wanting to be successful.

"Human nature is when things go bad, people want to go bad. They want to give up. They don't want to fight," Friedgen said. "I think human nature wants to go the course of least resistance. You got to get the masses to change that."

Friedgen said nothing prepared him for that like the NFL "where the minute something went wrong in the first quarter, the opening minute, everyone's pointing fingers. Everyone's packing it in. 'We don't want to do this. The coaches suck.' It's shocking," Friedgen said.

Friedgen recalled the game when head coach Bobby Ross was sick and he was charged with coaching the team against St. Louis. The offense fumbled the snap on the first series and all hell broke loose.

"They came off the field cussin' each other. 'F-this.' I said, 'We have four more quarters. This is the first series. Hang in the boat.' "

"We found a way to win the game. And after the game Leslie O'Neal came up to me and said, 'You do a better job than Ross. Why don't you be the coach?' "

Friedgen had, hours earlier, fined O'Neal $1,500 for showing up late to the pre-game.

"Even a guy like him . . . we're always second-guessing. There's winners and there's losers. It's perseverance. You got to hang in there and keep fighting. You get knocked down and that doesn't mean you can't come back to win.

"And that's what they had to learn to do," he said after taking over at Maryland where expectations had been low. "They should have beat North Carolina the year before. They wouldn't have been 5-6. I bet the Clemson game they could have won.

"So why do they win now that they didn't win then? They should have beaten West Virginia, too. They played four lousy games that year, but two of those six they should have won."

Friedgen said it's about "how players carry themselves. What you are doing for the rest of your team." He uses it as motivation for his players.

O'Leary said the key with Friedgen is that he knows how to reach his players, and knows what their pressure points are. O'Leary said his strength is "getting kids to do things they don't want to, and better. He was always looking for what can you do to get to the next level, get more productive, more effective. That's how I saw that. I think if he jumped you it was probably because you did something really dumb on the field and he had coached you not to do it."

O'Leary said Friedgen spent more time working on mistakes than any coach he has worked with.

"Like every good and tough coach that I know, I don't know many people that like him when they first meet him. It takes a while to get to know the guy. I think a lot of people like Ralph after they graduate," O'Leary said, matter-of-factly.

"But I think, for the most part, kids understand sincerity and truthfulness and trust, which I think are much a part of his makeup."

T he MGN Gala, the football booster organization's spring fund-raising event, has always been its best when Ralph Friedgen serves as auctioneer. He has his unique way of poking and prodding, sometimes even shaming boosters into coughing up big bucks for the cause. He pits boosters against each other to help raise the stakes.

One time the group hired a professional auctioneer. It wasn't the same.

Said Gossett of Friedgen's motivational ways, either with players or supporters like himself:

"People would really warm up to him. He would look at me or someone else and say, 'C'mon, you can do better than that.' What am I going to say, 'No?'

"Or it's like, 'Okay, you want to have dinner with me and my wife, and at my house, so you are really going to have to pay for that.'

"He's really in his element. He's relaxed and he's a jovial guy and he's hard to say no to," Gossett said.

Gossett has been known to drop $5,000-$6,000 each year at the event.

"I have bought everything from him," he admits.

Friedgen motivates and inspires most in his circle.

Longtime booster and supporter Grabenstein, past president of the Terrapin Club and current Executive Director of the MGN, often shares Christmas Eve dinner at the Friedgen home, and he has been with him from the start. He's fallen under Friedgen's spell, too.

An investment advisor and president of Potomac Financial Group in Calverton, Md., Grabenstein and Friedgen hit it off from the start. In one of their first meetings, Friedgen mentioned to Grabenstein that he was $50,000 short on a new Avid video system. And it was two days before his first spring camp was to begin.

Grabenstein pulled Friedgen aside and cut him a check to cover it. Former quarterback Boomer Esiason had already donated $70,000 to the project.

Grabenstein also helped expedite electrical work, which needed to be done at the team house, so Friedgen could get started.

R alph Friedgen is always looking for new forms of motivation. After the Terps beat FSU for the first time in 2004, it also marked the first time they had beaten a Top

10 team during Friedgen's tenure. And it was only the eighth time in school history. And he didn't want his players to forget it.

Friedgen erected a mock graveyard, complete with head stones, by the entrance of the practice field. A bold move, no doubt, with the likes of FSU, Clemson, Miami, on the cement head stones. But inspiring.

The addition cost $6,000. But it was well worth it to Friedgen as each time his players walked past it they saw a reminder.

"One of my things in the five-year plan was to beat a Top 10 team," Friedgen said. "When we had done that at Georgia Tech we kinda had arrived. That's not an easy thing to do. Every time those guys go to practice now they say, 'Hey, we beat a Top 10 team.' So that's nothing new to them. I got something I can point to now. Take pride in it. That game is going to be with you the rest of your life."

R alph Friedgen hangs the names of players, their year of graduation, and how many years it took them to graduate on the walls of the team house. It serves as another form of motivation. He says his former players call to make sure they are on the wall.

"I know they are looking at that," he said. "It's all about, 'Hey, a guy does this and he gets recognized.' It's great motivation."

Some forms of motivation can be more subtle.

In 2004 members of the Council came to Friedgen and asked for a favor. They requested that if they had a good enough GPA, could they skip mandatory breakfast. He thought about it and decided that if they had a 3.0 GPA or better, then they would be allowed 10 misses, while a 2.5 GPA earned five misses and a 2.3 GPA three misses.

Friedgen said that a few players abused the system, part of some of the lethargy that plagued the program that year, and one of his few moves that has backfired.

"Some of those 3.0 kids ended up with 20 misses. I should have run the heck out of them. I was soft on them," Friedgen said.

But there was a silver lining as some of the seniors, led by center Kyle Schmitt, came to Friedgen and told him to scrap the new rule as it created divisions on the team. Friedgen cut it back to three misses, and only if they had a 2.3 GPA or better.

"I didn't screw around with them. I ran the son-of-a-guns," he said.

Friedgen, though gruff, can be a savvy motivator and speaker in his own way. Everything he's got he worked for. He learned that early. And he makes a point that his players do the same.

When former players come back to campus and ask him how to break into coaching, or if they can serve as graduate assistants (like Schmitt and Wilson in 2006), Friedgen tells them to pack their bags. And go to the coaches' convention to see the many "out-of-work, middle-aged men networking trying to get jobs," he says before they took the plunge.

It's easy to project a coaching job from the outside looking in, but Friedgen reminds them of when he was "25 or 30-years old and poor for many years" toiling as an assistant.

Both former players joined his staff in January, 2007 as graduate assistants.

But both went to the convention first.

Always picking and prodding to inspire.

R alph Friedgen likes nothing more than self-starters, kids he doesn't have to motivate.

None compare to Georgia Tech quarterback Joe Hamilton, who he calls his "greatest competitor."

"There was a game he had an injured hand and I said, 'Are you okay? Do you need to come out?' He said, 'You can cut it off and I'll still play,' " Friedgen said.

What Friedgen loved about Hamilton was his competitive nature on and off the field. Hamilton wanted to bet his teammates on everything, from whether he could complete 90 percent of his passes one day in practice to "how many times you can throw a rock and hit that chair,' " Friedgen quipped.

The Yellow Jackets played Florida State during Hamilton's senior year, and he had yet to finish a game against the Seminoles. He always got injured.

Friedgen was coaching Godsey in the pre-game, giving him the game plan, when Hamilton approached him and asked why he was talking to the backup.

"I said, 'Well, you never lasted against these guys. So I figured I'd just get George ready from the start. They probably got some bounty on you. You'll be out by the first quarter. I better get George ready to go.' "

Friedgen said that Hamilton hit more than 20 of his first 25 passes, and hung some 500 yards on the Seminoles.

"He was just that type of guy. I have never come across a guy like that. Ever," Friedgen said.

The closest thing he's had to Hamilton, Friedgen said, is Esiason in terms of a competitor. Esiason had a stronger arm and, as Friedgen said, "Boomer is Boomer. Some people don't like him because he was so confident or conceited or whatever. But he's a New Yorker. Tells you what he feels. Is very confident. I love him because he tells you what he feels. The way it is."

Esiason chose Maryland over a baseball offer from Hofstra, his only other scholarship offer. Esiason was a streaky passer, Friedgen said, and when he was hot he was red hot, when he was cold he was frigid. Friedgen remembered a game in which Esiason started 0-for-7 passing.

"I said, 'What the hell is this?' He said, 'Relax. Relax. We'll get this thing going.' "

"And he hit eight straight," Friedgen said.

Friedgen said Esiason was "very bright" and he knew, even then, that he would get into a career in television.

"That's what he always wanted to do," Friedgen said.

Esiason made the $70,000 donation to the program in Friedgen's first year to help with the video system, while he got the program a price break on its FieldTurf practice field in year two.

The former Terp attends Friedgen's golf events from time to time, and his son, Gunnar, was at Maryland's schoolboy camp in the summer of 2007. From the start, after he signed his first pro contract, Esiason has supported the program, first buying a sound system for the weight room in the 1980s.

R alph Friedgen, despite his legendary bluster, seemingly has a good sense of when to ease up.

One story stands out from year two.

A few assistants went to him to get him to lighten up on the players in practice, and he was not pleased. Soon enough he would relent, but not without a zinger to be sure everyone knew who was boss.

An angry Friedgen called the players in a circle before practice and said, "I even have coaches that aren't tough."

His motivational tactics and ploys can also come at home.

Gloria remembered the days at The Citadel when her husband returned from work and the house wasn't totally clean. He'd joke with her, "You know, Gloria, you are falling out of the top ten this week."

Or, after a dinner that was especially good he'd say, "You know, Gloria, you're back up there at number two now."

"And I do have a charm that says 'Number One Wife,' " she said with a laugh. "He knows just the right buttons to push."

O f his return to Maryland, and what he had to do to get his players' attention immediately if they wanted to get things turned around, Friedgen said the ends justified the means.

"I had some people thinking that Attila the Hun came in here. That I was doing all these things that were not right," he said.

"In time it has proven that I am graduating kids and we're winning football games. If I had listened to those people and not do what I thought was necessary to win . . . "

10
MASTER MIND

R alph Friedgen looks old-school in many ways.
Massive. Gruff. Sometimes spittle hanging from his mouth at practice. Often cursing a storm.

But he is anything but.

Many call him an offensive genius, a "visionary," be it with football, fund-raising, academics, marketing or promoting.

"He's old-school in many ways. The older coaches believe the old way works. Be disciplined. Do the right thing. Be difficult. It's funny sometimes the things that come out of his mouth," Dennard Wilson said. "But then there's his other side."

That's the side that surprises many of those around him.

His need for technology. His need to be ahead of the competition with every new video or computer gadget.

As far back as the early 1990s they called him "Cyber Coach."

Friedgen can analyze on the fly with great precision. But those who work with him say he's at his best in the film room. Film is his friend.

Everything is video-taped and dissected. Each day some 20 minutes is dedicated to fixing things at practice. The Terps do more than most programs in this area. Friedgen knows his offense so well, and sees things so quickly, that if there's a breakdown, he can immediately get to the root of it.

Offensive coordinators take a backseat when he's around, for no one knows his offense, and what every player is supposed to do from quarterback to guard, as he. Friedgen took over as offensive coordinator in 2006, and is now in his element.

Quarterbacks may take up to two years to learn his system, and an indeterminable amount of time to apply it depending on smarts, savvy and reps.

Hill and McBrien probably rate even in terms of quarterbacks that were able to run Friedgen's offense best at Maryland. McBrien was physically more talented, but

Hill was savvier. Mentally, it is a huge challenge to be a quarterback under Friedgen.

Friedgen has personality under his tough veneer, but around football he's "98 percent business," one assistant remarked. The film room and the practice field are his laboratories.

Unlike some older coaches, Friedgen is not intimidated by technology. Friedgen knows history, has tremendous intellect and work ethic, but is always willing to learn. That separates him from many of his peers.

If he isn't on the football field, he's usually busy at work on his laptop.

Most mornings and nights he starts and ends with a computer program he developed to track each player and position.

With roster numbers sometimes changing weekly as players leave the program or move positions, Friedgen has his program to chart its daily flow.

He has columns for four year, three year, two year and one year players, followed by their positions. Next to each position, he lists his quota for each spot with 41 on offense, 41 on defense and a column for specialists for a total of 85. He scans the program often to see where things stand.

In 2007, after spring camp, he had four scholarship quarterbacks, which he said was a good number. Conversely, he wanted 17 offensive linemen, but most years he has been between 13-14 so he has been under. In 2007 he unexpectedly lost four offensive linemen, including starters Donnie Woods and Jared Gaither, which put a hole in his depth.

The roster is in constant flux but Friedgen is on top of it each day to see where he is and what his needs are going forward, for example, in recruiting. It also helps him decide whether to extend a scholarship to a walk-on, or determine whether he can "grayshirt" a player by bringing him in at mid-year.

Friedgen has a color code to highlight the names of players that are not being productive, "guys that you may want to lose," he says.

"I color them. If you are a red guy you are a 'hot' guy and may be gone."

He also has a color for players that may be considering transferring or leaving early for the NFL draft.

Friedgen shares the chart with recruiting coordinator Sollazzo, but said he keeps the color code to himself. It's dynamic, for example when he experiments with players in spring camp at new positions.

He asks his top underclassmen in exit interviews in the spring if they're thinking about going pro, as that will alter the team profile as well.

"That's why it's hard to say, for example, we got 17 scholarships to give this year," he said. "I said 14 last year [2006] and ended up with 20. But I am over five guys right now, but I've got five guys that will 'grayshirt' if I want to use that. So if you can talk a guy into a 'grayshirt,' they give you the flexibility there."

One such player in 2007 was defensive line signee Joe Vellano, a legacy as the son of former Terps standout Paul Vellano.

Joe Vellano was coming off senior year shoulder surgery and had the chance for an extra six months of rehab to get stronger in the weight room if he arrived at mid-year. Others in the category in 2007 were linebacker Ben Pooler and defensive end Carl Russell, who the Terps had the option of bringing in late as they developed more in the weight room.

T hose that work with Ralph Friedgen consider him "engineering smart," one assistant coach said, with the ability to solve problems by breaking them down in an analytical way.

His background and experience in college and pro football brought him to College Park with a detail-oriented agenda that he stored, refined and tweaked for years.

Friedgen is a student of the game, dating back to his days of learning from his father, while his start as a defensive coach provided him with a diverse background.

"His knowledge of the game separates him," Rychleski said. "When he was younger he studied the game thoroughly. His X's and O's knowledge of football, how to use people, is what separates him. Everyone has a niche and that's his niche."

From his first practice at Maryland it was obvious that not only would Friedgen challenge his players physically, but mentally. Every practice was run at a pace and speed faster than games to make the games slow down, just as his father did.

"The thing that defines a Ralph Friedgen practice is they are so mentally challenging because he is going to mentally challenge you whether he's ripping your ass, whether he's stomping around, whether he's saying, 'Go faster, go faster,' " Hollenbach said. "Putting the stress on you, the players in practice, the games came easy."

Said Rychleski:

"The old adage, 'The more you sweat in time of peace the less you bleed in war,' kinda sums up what his practice was."

Legendary are Friedgen's walk-throughs, which are supposed to be low-key events the night before games or the mornings of games. But not Friedgen's.

His are "mental practices," Locksley said.

"He has always been on the cutting edge of teaching, always in tune with how best kids learn and it's always a test with him. Those things were like final exams. You covered everything, and if you didn't do it right you did it again," Locksley added.

Every practice period is scripted and fast-paced, with virtually no down time.

"He's one of the most organized, time-efficient coaches that I have been around," Blackney said. "Nothing is left to happenstance. Nothing. Every detail of the game plan is covered during the week, even the unexpected."

Friedgen will have a 50-play script ready with every imaginable variation and formation. He once tossed a player out of a walk-through the night before a game for not having the right socks on. If the bus is leaving at noon, but Friedgen is on it at 11:50 a.m., he's been known to take off. Tight end Eric James was a few minutes late for the bus ride to the airport for the flight to Miami for the Orange Bowl, so Friedgen left him behind. Everything is exact and precise, on and off the field.

Every day was a challenge. Dennard Wilson remembered some winter conditioning drills under Friedgen as the closest he's come to passing out while training. Friedgen was making a point about how to work, tempo and conditioning. A former three-year captain at DeMatha, Wilson loved it.

"Practices were brutal. I would cramp up, full-body cramps and all after practice and everything. It was a brutal process but come game time the game was too easy. I wasn't breathing hard.

"I mean, we were beating teams we weren't as good as. But we were beating them with an attitude, a toughness. And when they were going down in terms of fatigue, we were feeling good. Look at all those games we won in the fourth quarter during those years. That toughness he instilled in us early on in practice."

Josh Wilson said it well about Friedgen's presence, and how he misses nothing in practice.

"He knows everything," the former cornerback said. "He sees everything."

Offense. Defense. Special teams.

Friedgen knows and sees all.

With his background coaching on both sides of the ball, and his uncanny preparation, Friedgen knows what each player at every position is supposed to do. Friedgen's attention to detail is well-known. He has been known to jump in and coach the offensive line, linebackers, etc., at practice if things aren't going well. He's not a patient man.

"He does every bit of research you can possibly do on a team. He has every bit of computer knowledge, everything you can possibly imagine as far as percentages, angles to find fault, little things that he does to find ways to beat the other team," Sollazzo said.

Friedgen's offense is based, in part, on what the defense is doing, a read and react system designed to take advantage of mismatches and break opponent tendencies.

Friedgen knows as much about defense as offense. It's all about making the opponent one-dimensional.

Friedgen calls offensive balance not just being able to both run and pass 50 times a game, but being able to "do both very well." Balance comes when the opponent forces you to do something and you have to adjust.

His voracious appetite for film gives him great command of what the opponent might do. Friedgen is known for being in offensive meetings, whether he is the offensive coordinator or not. Friedgen also tests his defensive players and sits in on their meetings from time to time. In the last two years he believed that the offense had its best chance for success with him calling the plays, so he plans to stick with it for as long as he can.

"That's why it is so hard to play quarterback at Maryland," Josh Wilson said. "But at the same time, that makes my job easier because we'll all know the offensive formations based on that. He expects the quarterback to know exactly what defense they are in and once you realize that, then you have the play that is going to work no matter what. That's how he calls plays because he knows the defenses first."

Friedgen considers O'Leary to be one of the greatest football minds he has worked for, especially defensively, while Ross was the best "worker" he has been around.

"Ralph's very knowledgeable as far as what he is doing. But what he does a great job with is knowing offense and how to get an extra guy in a blocking scheme or get an advantage in the passing game and how to attack defenses," O'Leary said. "Knowing the weaknesses in the defenses, and then having enough offense in his repertoire as far as scheme-wise to be able to move people to get an advantage. He is an inquisitive guy and he gets after it."

O'Leary said it was natural for him to hire Friedgen as offensive coordinator at Georgia Tech.

He said they had such a good thing going that often they wouldn't let other assistants in on what they were up to at practice, "so we could make our point," O'Leary said.

There are stories of practice battles between the two. O'Leary was in charge of the defense while Friedgen ran the offense. Much was said of the autonomy Friedgen had while he was the coordinator at Tech. O'Leary said he controlled decisions on short yardage, goal line, fourth down and punting. He said Friedgen did the rest.

O'Leary said Friedgen, among the offensive coaches he's worked with, was the "most productive offensive mind" he has encountered. He said Friedgen understood that "statistics are not always the most important thing, but the final score."

"It doesn't matter if you threw for 400 [yards] and lose," O'Leary said. "I think Ralph's real key is he understands it's a team game. He may have to run the ball 10 times in a row to eat the clock up to survive to win. Stats weren't very important. He understood that football is the ultimate team game. Did you win the game, and offensively did you do the things to win the game? He always understood that there were certain plays you had to run that sometimes they didn't want to run. That field position was the most important thing, and he understood that probably better than anyone I have ever been with."

They got after each other.

The two watched film of Virginia quarterback Shawn Moore as they prepared for a game. "We had a little scrimmage the day before." O'Leary said. "We blitzed the corner and Shawn [Jones] supposedly read it and threw to the wide-out for a great read, I heard, in the film room from everybody. I kept saying there's no way he read that.

"The next day I was there on the field scrimmaging again and I hear one of the assistants say, 'Be alert now. Be alert.' And all of a sudden I see that quarterback looking for the corner again on the blitz. So about two plays later, and it was all scripted, the scrimmage, the corners start to come and I cancelled it. I hear 'Be alert now. Be alert.' The quarterback took the ball and threw it to the wide-out, but the only thing there was the corner and he caught it and took it the other way for the touchdown.

"Ralph comes charging and says, 'You're supposed to blitz.' I said, 'Wait a second. You're calling the defense now, too?' I say, 'Great read.' So then every time I heard, 'Be alert now' I knew it was some kind of pressure. But it was funny, Ralph's reaction to things like that."

O'Leary joked about how he and Friedgen pulled tricks on each other, but "it was a give and take thing. And I trusted what he was doing and he trusted what I was doing."

Practices under Friedgen are what separate players. If you can make it through the pace and demands, both physical and mental, then you can play for him. It's a challenge, especially for freshmen getting their first taste.

The games are easy, the players say, compared to the break-neck practices. The players don't leave the practice field until things are run right. One of Friedgen's favorite sayings (which players cringe at) is, "Do it wrong, do it long. Do it right, do it light."

Friedgen brought an NFL philosophy to Maryland as far as game-planning. The Terps are very specific with days dedicated to short yardage and goal line, others to third down and "red zone," others to normal downs.

He runs halftime as he did in the pros. His assistants are amazed with how quickly Friedgen can see something, break it down, and adjust at intermission. He hasn't seen film yet or still photos, but already he's spotted what's worked and what hasn't and is adjusting. He spends about 10-12 minutes at halftime on it. He processes information lightning-fast.

Friedgen can be a bull if the Terps are losing when he comes into the locker room at intermission. His anger takes control and it's not always pretty. He doesn't take time to get his emotions in check. He just fires away. The players may not always like him at these times, but they respect him, and they know he will put them in the best position to succeed as far as a game plan.

At practices he sees everything from his golf cart. He got the cart to help relieve some of the pain in his back and leg, and he lords over sessions, cruising from unit to unit. When he needs to make a point he gets out of the cart and instructs.

Friedgen will see a front and jump in and correct a guard, a receiver, the quarterback, in an instant. Many coaches are good in one area or another, not all like Friedgen. The players hope to get it right on the practice field or they will hear about it later in film. The eye is always in the sky at Friedgen's practices.

Wike, who had a conditioning problem and sweated profusely and his legs swelled, would sometimes lose 10 pounds a day at practice because the pace was so fast. It took a while for the players to get used to the demanding repetition and tempo.

Friedgen would start periods, even practices, over if he didn't like what he saw, or he didn't like the players' "biorhythms," he'd say.

Anyone who has observed Ralph Friedgen at practice has seen the "twitch." The Terps film practice from the end zone. Friedgen stands behind the quarterback some 12 yards off the line of scrimmage.

"He has an uncanny knowledge of seeing the whole picture. He has probably trained his eyes that way and even for an older man . . . to be able to see the whole picture, where the quarterback might not see what the free safety did. After the play he'll ask, 'What did the free safety do?' Or, 'What happened here or there?' " Rychleski said.

Rychleski joked that Friedgen probably lives "vicariously through his quarterbacks," but that he has an uncanny ability to see the entire field and all the positions with just a quick glance. And what is transpiring despite the speed of the play, be it a lineman missing a block, a fullback on a chip block, or the kind of blitz the defense brought.

But back to the "twitch."

As a play begins to develop with the quarterback taking the snap and dropping back, Friedgen's side of his body starts to gyrate as if he was dropping back as the quarterback. His head starts to bob up and down through the play. His right shoulder and arm twitch as he goes through the motion as if he were setting to throw. The coaches are used to it, but they still have to shake their head when they see it on film.

"You see the big man on film right behind the quarterback trying to simulate what the quarterback is trying to do. And he knows exactly where it should go," Rychleski said.

Starting with the quarterback through the blockers and moving to the spot the receiver is expected to be when the ball arrives, Friedgen moves his body through the progression of the play.

"Everybody definitely notices it," Hollenbach said. "It's funny because you have a freshman or somebody new in there and they say, 'Hey, did you see what he just did?' Yeah. He sees everything. You better not mess up because he sees it."

Said Perry: "His head goes like a typewriter when the play is run."

"I really think he sees what every player does on the offensive line on every play. It's amazing to me because I have watched so many reps over the years and I can maybe see what one guy does. But it reminds me of the knowledge, the reason why he is such a football guru," Rychleski said. "It takes him just one full-speed practice rep to realize what the problem is and put it back in order the right away and make the right changes."

Wike saw Friedgen stand behind the offense in practice and watch the play unfold from the left side as he checked each player. He could tell right away if the slot receiver broke his route at eight yards instead of 10, or if the flanker was too wide on his route.

"He would tell three or four people what they did wrong just like that, at once, which was pretty amazing," Wike said.

Perry recalled running a play and breaking his route at 4 1/2 yards instead of the required five. Friedgen made them all run it again.

"He could tell even if his back was to you. It was scary. There has never been a man more meticulous than coach Friedgen," Perry said.

Josh Wilson said Friedgen would arrive some days to practice "trying to beat me." And have some creative plays to try and do so.

He recalled one play, a bootleg, when the receiver would do a comeback route. That was the tendency, at least until one instance. It was always a game of cat-and-mouse, with Friedgen trying to get the upper-hand, Wilson said.

"He would just eat us up. And then one time he would see us jump the comeback and have a receiver do a post and he would be wide open. Man, he had to know that I . . .

"If they do that play and we're in a different defense and the safety is sitting over our top, whereas if he sees me playing man-to-man and they do that play and I expect a comeback and they do a post. He knows the guy is going to be wide open. He was just able to find out things like that and drive our coaches and us crazy."

Wilson said during two-minute drills in practice is when he tested his coach the most.

"To me, that was game day for me," he said. "I would do anything to stop them from winning the two-minute."

The cocky Wilson, while playing nickel back, would blitz and easily sack quarterback Joel Statham. He would get even with his coach.

"I would turn and dance in front of coach Friedgen. I was yelling and talking in his face. He would come back at me and say, 'Hey, play football. Play football.' And then I'd get back in there and say, 'I love playing football. I love playing football.' It's competition. We were both perfectionists."

R alph Friedgen has joked over the years that he "keeps his players' brains in a jar." Like a scientist he gets inside your brain, probes and pushes around, until he strikes a nerve.

No one sees this more than his quarterbacks, who face the toughest job of any. Some make it and some don't.

It takes great mental fortitude to make it through as a Friedgen quarterback.

"It's hard to put it all into perspective," Hollenbach said. "For me, there were a lot of times that I would come back to my room after practice or after a meeting and just think there's nobody on this campus that knows what I am going through.

"It's something where you have to really accept the responsibility of being the quarterback here, and that means accepting all ends of it."

Hollenbach, a mechanical engineering major who carried a 3.5 GPA, found himself taking daily naps and eating extra meals to have the energy to keep up.

There are numerous tales that Hollenbach related of his mentor, who became his offensive coordinator as a senior, and the lengths Friedgen would go to toughen him up and prepare him. It was a daily thing.

"He'd say to me things like, 'You better let me know of any bridge you built because I will not be driving over it,' " Hollenbach said. "Or, 'If you are going to build a car, you better let me know what kind as I'm not going to be buying it.' "

Hollenbach said former coordinator Taaffe was a great teacher but Friedgen had an uncanny ability to enter the room and all of a sudden make it "more instinctual for me."

Taaffe would step down after the 2005 season after two years of offensive struggles and Friedgen took over the play-calling.

The offense is predicated on the quarterback reading the defense pre and post-snap, blitzes, etc., and then reacting.

"Coach Friedgen and coach Taaffe would say to me, 'You can't play like you're Ray Charles out there. You gotta look at the safeties.' If there was one thing he said to me more than anything else it was, 'You gotta read the safeties. Read the safeties.' He said that so many times to me.

"He said, 'You know, they are the answers to the test. It's right there in front of you.' He really got into it."

Friedgen hammers his quarterbacks about reading the free safety and the middle linebacker, as well as their depth and width in relation to the hash. This has led to some funny moments over the years.

Friedgen ran drills "on air," with nothing but a free safety on the field to sharpen his quarterbacks' reaction time.

A play in the 2005 opener against Navy brought home the point to Hollenbach, the point about being extremely precise when reading the defense.

Hollenbach spent his college career covered up in engineering but said he never saw someone as exact as Friedgen.

"We had a play called on third down. It was '333 Over' and we had a protection on and basically the quarterback is setting the protection," he said. "So I was going to set the protection based on where I thought the pressure was going to come. I remember I pointed to the weak-side of the formation and then on the snap of the ball they rolled it strong and they blitzed. And I had to get rid of the ball early and we ended up punting. I remember going over to the sideline and him, in not the most polite manner, saying, 'Why did you point there?' I said, 'Coach, the safety was two yards off the hash.'

"And he said, 'Two yards? What did I tell you? It's got to be three yards.' It was unbelievable. I was like, 'Oh my word. Are you serious?' And then it was the same thing on film on Monday. He was exactly right. That difference is what's going to make you a better quarterback. The small, specific things like this."

Quarterback meetings aren't always fun and you have to be on your toes, Hollenbach said. Friedgen would flash plays on the screen, the worded play and the huddle call, followed by defenses flashing for two seconds. He recalled his first meeting with his position mates.

"Then he has all these questions come up. What was the defense? What was the front? What was the coverage? Who's your read? Where are you going to throw the ball? All that stuff. And none of us in the room said a thing. He was like, 'What, do I need to do it again?' So he puts it up again and finally he said we're going to have to add some time to it. I think it was three seconds. And then we started getting it."

Hollenbach recalled the time he was at his lowest under Friedgen, when he was a redshirt sophomore.

Friedgen called him to his office and gave him the deflating news that after an intra-squad scrimmage "I was not going to really be competing for the job. I was not going to be in the mix," Hollenbach said.

Statham, Mitch and Steffy all moved past him on the depth chart so Hollenbach was left to run the scout team. It was the most disappointed he said he was with Friedgen.

"I remember him specifically saying during the bootleg that I ran in the scrimmage, I was booting off to my right side and I threw a comeback [route] but I threw it high," Hollenbach said. "He mentioned that in that meeting. I was like, 'Damn, that's what he's going to say?' I thought I was in the competition. I didn't see that coming. I thought I had judged myself pretty well. I was just so mad at him. That one play. I didn't think he was right. I didn't think he knew what he was doing. It was one of the moments you didn't know what to think."

Hollenbach, however, stuck with it and got his chance during a Thursday night game at Virginia Tech, when he got the final series, moved the team, and a week later started the season finale against Wake Forest and won.

Hollenbach said Friedgen was always conservative and preferred for him to eat the ball rather than take a chance. He's famous for saying, "Turnovers are like death."

"That made me almost. You're writing all this stuff down, trying to remember this stuff, especially being a young quarterback instead of just . . . he would say, 'If you don't feel like you like it don't worry about it as far as a route is concerned,' " Hollenbach said. "If you don't like the situation, your first and second reads, if you don't like it get off it right away. Take the check-down right away, run the ball right way, instead of going through your third or fourth read. He made it more clear as far as just being more on instincts and not having to read everything."

Friedgen's voluminous offense and its multiplicity can be mind-numbing for a young quarterback. And Friedgen was known to pull things out of his bag that even a fifth-year quarterback hadn't seen. He was always pushing the envelope and challenging his players.

"In his offense he has the ability to mix and match different formations and movements and plays in the order that I would know what they were. But I had never called them before. Even up till my last year here I thought I knew the offense pretty well, real well. But he would call some plays in practice and I would say the play in the huddle, break the huddle, and then I had just had to think, 'Okay, what's happening here. What's the formation? How are we moving?' Those kinds of things where I didn't think that he had anymore plays left in him that I did not know," Hollenbach said.

Friedgen said Hollenbach had the chance to climb the charts to be near his all-time smartest quarterback, George Godsey, of Georgia Tech.

Friedgen has a way of getting the best out of his pupils and Godsey was an eager participant despite not having ideal measureables for an ACC quarterback. But he had intangibles, and those are big with Friedgen.

"He really didn't have great physical skills. Maybe he ran a 5.1 [40-yard dash.],"

Friedgen said of Godsey.

Friedgen wanted Andy Hall to be the quarterback. He had the physical skills that Godsey didn't possess, with good size and a big arm to go with it.

But in summer workouts Godsey beat Hall in every distance run. So Friedgen called him to his office and asked him about it.

Hall then started beating Godsey. In testing to see how many laps the players could run in 12 minutes, the quarterbacks had to run at least seven to pass. The two were neck-and-neck and crossed the finish line at seven laps, each with a minute to go. Hall began to slow down, jog in, but Godsey sprinted and nearly finished with eight.

"That told me something right there," Friedgen said.

The Yellow Jackets started the season with Hall as the starter against Central Florida. But they trailed late. With four minutes to go, down by 14 points and facing a third-and-long, Friedgen pulled Hall for Godsey.

"That's the equivalent of taking a batter out with two strikes," Friedgen said.

But Godsey quickly hit a pass play for a first down. Tech scored twice and added a field goal to win.

Florida State was the next opponent and Godsey, now under center, got hit and split his lip, which required stitches.

"He's getting the crap beat out of him. But he's hanging in there and we're moving the ball," Friedgen said.

Godsey then pulled his hamstring. But Tech scored, went on to win, and Friedgen went with Godsey the rest of the season.

"In the end what Godsey proved to me was his heart. His heart and brain and he kinda worked around his ability. We did things that he could do. He ended up being in two years one of the top total yards guys in the ACC."

R alph Friedgen provides a tremendous learning atmosphere in his program. Mike Locksley and Friedgen did not see eye-to-eye on everything, including when Friedgen brought in former Georgia Tech protégé Billy O'Brien to be the presumed offensive-coordinator in-training, which helped hasten Locksley's departure to Florida. But Locksley said he knows where he learned the most.

"I will say this: it was the best football environment I have ever been around as far as the X's and O's. The coaching and teaching.

"From a social standpoint, it was all business. That's what it's got to be like. If you are going to run a Fortune 500 company you can't always be hanging out at the water cooler. I learned more offensive football from him in two years than I did in my entire 15-year career."

Locksley said that as coordinator at Illinois he has taken some of the things he learned and the "offensive recipe" at Maryland. Friedgen said he can see some of his offense when he watches occasional Illinois games or highlights.

Friedgen draws, to this day, on plays that his father used years ago at Harrison High.

In the 1994 AFC Championship Game in Pittsburgh, as offensive coordinator of the San Diego Chargers, Friedgen went deep to the well, proving he hadn't forgotten who taught him the best.

"He ran an old high school play to the tight end. When I saw it I called it right away," said Stoddard. "I called him the 'Riverboat Gambler' as he pulled it off. He's done that a bunch of times. I have seen him call that old stuff many times before. He's done the homework."

R alph Friedgen doesn't miss much.

After the 2004 season, his first losing campaign at Maryland, he noticed in film review that Georgia Tech had 13 players in the huddle. The tight end and fullback, after the play, went back to the huddle, while the receivers left the huddle. New receivers would come in but the fullback and tight end wouldn't leave until the new players got to the huddle.

The result was the defense wouldn't know the personnel group, so they had to make the call by situation.

Friedgen didn't know if it was by design or not. He pressed former Tech assistant O'Brien, who believed they weren't doing it intentionally.

Still, Friedgen implemented something similar in spring practices the following year, always looking for a competitive advantage.

Said Locksley:

"That's just the nature of the true competitor in him. Most true competitors, which I think he is, aren't satisfied until they are done. It's just how you are taught early as an athlete. That satisfaction.

"Only in the end, when it is all said and done and you can sit back, that's where that insatiable quality comes from in him. He knows in his heart that Maryland can win a national championship and that's his goal. If he wins a national championship tomorrow, I wouldn't doubt that he retires."

Winning 31 games in his first three seasons made the confident Friedgen that much more "invincible" at times, one assistant coach said.

Getting off to such a fast start validated his belief in his ability and system, while the back-to-back 5-6 seasons were a shock to his system and humbling.

That made Friedgen look inside the program, and at himself, and he spent the off-season re-evaluating the program from top to bottom.

He didn't lose confidence but did recognize that there are limits at Maryland. And sometimes other ways to approach things. Friedgen was not afraid to admit his mistakes and, most importantly, change.

11

WORK ETHIC

At Ralph Friedgen's home on the stairs leading to the basement hangs a favorite keepsake.

His mother made him a needlepoint sign that she gave him when he left for college. It had a simple message, one Friedgen would take to heart. He passes it each day, and the message has not been lost.

"It's a sign that says 'You Have To Pay The Price.' And everything you do in life you have to pay the price," Ralph Friedgen said. "How true."

Friedgen has long followed it and, fortunately, found a passion in which he could channel it. Friedgen loves football.

He works 17-hour days because of his love for the game that he learned at such an early age. It defined his life and his family.

Friedgen doesn't like to leave the football team house. Sometimes even in the off-season.

He's been known to disappear in the building for hours and sometimes skip meals. It's difficult to pry him away. His red Toyota Sequoia is always in its reserved parking spot in the front row outside. It's there long after most have left, and before many arrive the next morning.

Some say Friedgen lives vicariously through his players. That he'd love to play the game again. His playing dream was derailed in college during a tumultuous time for him at College Park.

There were days early in Friedgen's coaching career when he would get in practice drills and butt heads with the players. His age and artificial hip won't allow it anymore.

It doesn't matter how late a game or a road trip when the team returns to town. Like clockwork, Friedgen is at the office early the next morning. There are few schedule changes in his book. Work is first, and work is everything for him. He rarely varies his routine, maybe only occasionally in the off-season.

"He loves to work. He really enjoys it because he loves the game so much," said an assistant coach. "A lot of us can't keep up with him. We just don't have the passion that he does for it."

While his players fight the battle on the field, Friedgen is trying to win the strategy battle. The facilities battle. The fund-raising battle.

He fights his own competitive battles every day. No one should be better than Maryland. The Terps have everything in place to be among the elite. He can't slow down. Too much still to be done.

Friedgen loves to win and, as obvious to those around him, is consumed by it. Sometimes in unhealthy ways.

He's remarkably driven, and being unprepared is not an option. He works hard and demands the same of those around him.

Few, if any coaches, out-work Ralph Friedgen. He leaves "no stone unturned," his assistants and players say of their head coach when he's in game preparation mode. That's a positive trait but it can be maddening, too.

In 2001 when the Terps traveled to Clemson where they won for the first time in decades, they didn't get back until 3 a.m. But that didn't change Friedgen's schedule to be at mass at 7 a.m. the next morning and in the office for film review despite the coaches dragging beside him. The schedule for the assistants didn't change, either. They seldom keep pace but he insists.

One assistant called him a "legendary slave driver. He works his staff to the bone."

Duffner, the Terps former coach, also worked his staff hard. But nothing compares to Friedgen.

Its remarkably efficient work, and the assistants that spanned the last two staffs say Friedgen can get done in one day what took the previous staff two.

The results speak for themselves in the win column.

The Terps were probably a quarterback away from avoiding their two losing seasons under Friedgen in 2004 and 2005. Had they had a reliable signal-caller, it could have made for a budding dynasty at College Park.

Days begin for Friedgen at 5:30 a.m. It's no problem for him as he's used to waking at 4:30 a.m. He loves the morning. The staff can be at the office well past 10 p.m. despite the early starts.

There are tales of staff members being holed up in offensive meetings for seven consecutive hours, and Friedgen forgetting to break for lunch.

"I remember the first couple of years, and it was like you're in junior high," Franklin said. "You are a grown man and it's almost like you have to ask to go to the bathroom. It's like, 'Excuse me, can I go to the bathroom?' And he's like, 'Yeah, hurry up.' You sprint down the hallway to go to the bathroom and get back. It's that type of intensity all of the time."

At the start, Friedgen didn't want his assistants to compartmentalize. So the receivers coach had to know what the running backs did, the linebacker coach what the defensive backs did, and so on. They learned it all.

Some joked, at the time, of what was written in Friedgen's coaches' manual that he distributed to his new staff. Among other rules and guidelines it listed Thursday night as the staff's night off.

It didn't happen. The coaches either made recruiting calls or left for recruiting trips, that is if they weren't game-planning. One assistant remembered having one Thursday night off in Friedgen's first year.

But the staff knew one thing, that Friedgen would never ask them to do anything that he wouldn't do, a strength of his management style.

"We worked until the job was done. It's that simple with Ralph," said Blackney. "I have had other head coaches who would leave at 6 or 7 p.m. to go home for dinner and leave the assistants to work. Not Ralph."

Wike remembered the time he saw Friedgen late one night at the team house, only to see him beat him back early the next morning, too. Always with a gleam in his eye about the day's challenges and the work ahead. Wike recalled what Friedgen once told him:

"Todd, I wake up every morning, whatever hour, and can't wait to get back in the office. Look at film. Talk to the guys. Get my coaches going. I love it. It's my passion."

Franklin said that when a player or coach left the program, their new employer didn't have to worry about work ethic.

"Our kids work as hard as any program I have ever been around. It's unbelievable to be honest with you. And what they go through at that age. And because Ralph works that hard, or harder, they believe in him,"

Often a bleary-eyed Hollenbach would arrive at Tuesday media luncheons at the Gossett Football Team House for interviews, which didn't begin until about 1 p.m.

He said his typical day started with an 8 a.m. wake-up followed by mandatory breakfast from 8:30-9, classes from 9-11, and then an hour nap until noon. Back to the football complex to grab a quick lunch to take to the film room and dig in for several hours. From 12:30-8 p.m., Hollenbach said he would be at the football complex, either in meetings or at practice.

There was an hour for opponent film study afterwards, and two days a week Hollenbach worked on the Football Simulator in his "spare time," he said.

Position and unit meetings ran from 2:30-4 p.m., followed by practice until 6:30 p.m., then a half hour spent with the media followed by a shower, dinner, and finally study group at the Physics Building at 8 p.m., when he met with tutors.

All while taking four classes in a demanding major.

"I haven't met anybody that had the work that we did," Hollenbach said. "As far as that NCAA 20-hour limit they have each week, I took that right up to that [maximum] every week.

"I have never met anybody like it. Maybe at the next level you hear about guys like [Tampa Bay Buccaneers coach] Jon Gruden, but they are at the professional level. This guy's at the college level doing the same things as the pro coaches. He coached at the NFL level, but now his guys at Maryland are getting that kind of coaching at the college level."

Friedgen usually burns from 5 a.m. to midnight, often getting by on five hours of sleep, remarkable for a man his age and given his medical history. Friedgen is known to recruit coaches like himself, but those are difficult to find. Ones that aren't at his level quickly fall in line and adjust. Or they are gone.

There are tales of Christmas Eve staff meetings running until 7 p.m., not only the day before Christmas, but when the team is scheduled to leave on bowl trips. Not much time for the holiday or family, and most times Friedgen takes his team on Christmas Day. Celebration time comes later, after the game.

Tales of rare weekends off, regardless of the time of year, are legendary as well. Friedgen is a perfectionist, a grinder, and expects the same from his staff regardless of inconvenience.

"He grinds. He grinds. He's wearing down a little, just a little, but it's still there," said Stoddard, who coached for a year at Columbia University. "He still fires the thing up, though. He is the hardest working person I have met."

In one of the first staff meetings, one of the three holdovers from the former staff (Locksley, Franklin and Tom Deahn) boldly asked, "Are we going to have the same vacation time we had last year?"

Friedgen glared at the coach.

After the 5-6 finish in 2005 the staff probably knew what was coming. Friedgen took their spring break and had the assistants travel the country observing at spring camps to get fresh ideas.

Said one assistant:

"Some of the wives weren't happy. But when you go 5-6 this is what happens. There was some weeping and gnashing of teeth over that one."

It's such a high work/high reward environment that Friedgen was fortunate the Terps won big in his first seasons, especially year one. He quickly changed the culture of Maryland football and the expectations with his "shock to the system' style," one assistant said.

Galt instituted the "Iron Terps" Olympics at the end of the school year as a fun, light event after the grind of the year.

Every spring the players compete for a day in a variety of events led by a bench press competition, tug of war, tire roll and "Ultimate Football," something similar to "Ultimate Frisbee."

Galt rewards his best weight room workers with special honors at a ceremony and cookout afterwards, where the players feast on steaks and barbeque chicken. Friedgen seldom attends. Call it the players' "release" from their head coach. He probably knows they need a day on their own away from pressure.

"It's intended to be a reward because of the hard work they put in because the one thing he did bring is increased expectation, both on and off the field. And the players have had to uphold that expectation. Because they do that, it's tough on them, both emotionally and physically. It's a side benefit that builds teamwork, camaraderie," Galt said.

Friedgen's all-consuming drive for perfection and winning defines him in many ways. He's never known any other way.

"With him it has always been, 'If you are going to be in it, be in it to win it,' " Rychleski said. "That's why he's up at 5 a.m., and in the office studying film. The competition and winning part of it drives him most, more than anything.

"There are a lot of guys passionate about winning. But you have to be willing to do the work that goes along with it. That's where he takes it to the next level. You know, he doesn't really have a lot of hobbies."

Friedgen eased up some on his staff since his first year.

Franklin thought he had a strong work ethic, and he was known to log 18-hour days. But he said Friedgen "ramped me up another notch."

"He is very, very hard on coaches. The kids on the field, there is never an exception to work ethic," Franklin said.

The first year the players and coaches had to determine "what's the status point," Friedgen said.

"The neat thing about that first team is we took a bunch of kids . . . that was the only thing they wanted, to win, they just didn't know how to do it. You just had to show them how to do it. They grew and they played better than they had in the past because they believed in themselves and their work and what was going to happen. They didn't care who got what."

Friedgen said he saw the same thing with the New England Patriots during their Super Bowl runs as they didn't have "I guys," he said. "They got rid of all of them. From that it always develops."

Friedgen said work ethic starts with the staff being selfless and ready to work, sans ego.

He said he called Blackney first "because George O'Leary kept telling me he was the best secondary coach in the country."

Friedgen didn't know Blackney well but offered him a job on the spot. And he offered more than he had been making as head coach at Bowling Green, his former post. Later, impressed with Blackney and his eagerness to work, Friedgen upped him to defensive coordinator within a week.

"I was talking to a few other guys during the process. An NFL guy. A guy from Alabama. And it was all 'I' and 'me,' and 'I did this or that.' Blah, blah, blah," Friedgen said.

"And Charlie was the same way. We're not 'I guys.' We're not finger-pointers. And when you have that it filters down to the players and then you got chaos. So I am a real believer in that, that everybody's in it together and working as hard as he can work.

"I probably get too much credit. It is not all me. It's the people I have around me. It just happens that I am the boss."

No assistant knows his boss better than Sollazzo, who has been with Friedgen on four occasions. He said Friedgen leads by example and brings the best out of people working for him. It's like a hurricane wind you get caught up and taken away in, because his personality is so strong.

"He demands your very, very best. He is not going to take anything less than your best effort. If you play for him, or work for him, he's not going to take an excuse for an answer.

"And you respect him because he deserves respect because he's won at every level. And you want to do your best for him. He can piss you off. He can rip your ass. He has little ways of psychology to motivate you. Whatever it takes he'll use it. That's the bottom line."

Friedgen's players emerge stronger because of it.

Grabenstein was so impressed with the work ethic of Wike, a Friedgen all-ACC performer and standout on consecutive bowl teams, that he hired him in 2006 at his investment firm. He is grooming Wike, who played in the NFL for the Los Angeles Raiders and later coached at Georgetown, to someday lead his business, he said.

Friedgen does whatever it takes to build the program.

He's on the front lines like a carnival barker for the program and, on many levels, for the university.

If he's not at his office working the phones, Friedgen can be found at numerous other places stumping for the program.

Friday mornings he hosts his 7:30 a.m. "Breakfast With The Fridge" on campus, an event for fans that he began when he arrived as head coach. They get breakfast, chalk talks, previews of the coming game and video highlights, all from Friedgen or his assistants. Friedgen works the crowd as marketer, promoter, all of the above for the program.

On game day he's up early and working as well, leading "Terp Alley" at home games. It's something he did at Georgia Tech.

The team, led by their coach and the band, walk through the parking lot and the tailgaters and fans to the team house just hours before kickoff.

Friedgen said he knew he would have to wear many hats at College Park if he wanted things to take off. He had to light the spark and stay with it, otherwise it wouldn't get done. He couldn't just be a head football coach at Maryland. He knew the history too well.

"I knew I would have to do that because I had been here before. I knew where Maryland was at. Bobby Ross never would have done that [market and promote the program]. When I took this job I knew what I had to do," Friedgen said.

No one ever thought – probably even Friedgen – he would take so well to being in the public after working for years in the shadows. Booster functions, public appearances, golf outings. Any event to raise money or heighten awareness of the program, Friedgen was there leading the charge. There's little he turns down if it means a possible donation or boost for the program.

"And we never had to do it anywhere else," he said. "Here you gotta do all that if we are going to make it work."

It's another stigma Friedgen had to shake. That he wasn't friendly. That he didn't relate well enough to people to be out stumping. But since he's been back at Maryland, he's been anything but, embracing the effort most of his waking hours.

"So many people say, 'Well, Friedgen can't do that. He doesn't meet the people well. He doesn't do this.' As long as I'm okay, as long as I feel good about what I've done, then I am okay," he said.

Friedgen auctioned dinners at his home and overnight golf trips to boosters and fans. He spent a weekend golfing with boosters at $1,000 a pop.

His greatest tool, he says, is the MGN, which without "we couldn't do it" Friedgen said.

Friedgen channels much of his non-football time and effort into the organization. The football support group raises nearly $500,000 a year, with Friedgen in the lead doing anything for a buck.

Thanks to his tireless work the Terps have been able to add a new practice field, refurbish the team house to include a top academic support unit, cafeteria and meeting rooms as well as an expanded weight room. Most of it has come thanks to the program's fund-raising efforts.

It's difficult to imagine any of it could have happened without Friedgen. It never did before.

And it came at lighting speed under Friedgen, at least based on Maryland history.

Rewards for supporting the program include invitations to his Georgia lake house for the Friedgen's popular Fourth of July bash. One of his favorites are the dances – at $100 a pop – he auctioned at MGN Galas. And the Friedgens don't shuttle everyone off to local hotels. Some boosters stay at their home.

Despite all those years shuttered in an office as an assistant far from the public eye, few probably expected the personality that would emerge when Friedgen got his head coaching chance. His face lights up when he talks of the dances at the Gala, Friedgen cutting the rug in his tuxedo.

"I felt like a gigolo," he quipped. "Girls were coming up putting $100 bills in my pockets. I told my daughters I wish it was like this when I was in college."

Anything for the cause.

12
RECRUITING

R alph Friedgen rolls his eyes when he's asked to recount some of his favorite recruiting stories and "tales."

There are many folksy, even wild, stories from his days spent as an assistant and a head coach, a far cry from where things have evolved with the Internet and technology in today's recruiting game.

His favorite tales go back to a simpler time when coaches didn't text-message prospects. As an assistant coach at Maryland in the 1980s, Friedgen was in a particularly tough part of Queens, N.Y., at a high school watching recruit tape.

Another assistant came in the office and said that he had locked his keys in his car. The high school coach told him not to worry, that he'd have one of his kids pop the lock after film.

When they went outside the teen, coat hanger in hand, anxiously looked around. Friedgen told him, "Don't worry, I'll vouch for you."

The kid responded: "I'm not worried about you. I would never break into a car this cheap. I got my reputation to keep.'"

"He took that slim-jim and he opened that thing up 'bing, bing,'" Friedgen quipped.

Friedgen and Ross were in Queens again, this time recruiting a top defensive end at Andrew Jackson High School. Ross was driving a Cadillac. Friedgen suggested they park out front because police were frequently stationed there.

"Otherwise, it will be up on the blocks," Friedgen told Ross.

The coaches pulled in front of a group of teens that was mingling in front of school. Ross got out of the car and immediately stepped in dog mess. There was no grass to wipe it off on, and the kids starting laughing.

The coaches went in the school, showed the prospect a Maryland highlight film, and spoke for a few minutes.

Ross forgot his cashmere coat in the car. When they got outside the first thing

Friedgen did was make sure the car wasn't on blocks. It wasn't. But as they opened the car they saw it had been broken into, the expensive coat and both of their briefcases gone.

They had to wait an hour-and-a-half for police to file a report, they were late on the home visit that followed, and they eventually lost the player to Ohio State.

The following year, at the same school, a student ran in bleeding from head to toe. He had been hit in the head with a baseball bat.

Friedgen was in a rental car and when he came out, "20 kids were sitting on my car," he said.

"Anyone wearing a tie they think is a 'narc,' " he said.

Friedgen joked with the kids as he walked the halls hearing "narc." He'd bark back at them, "up against the wall," which would scare the hell out of Ross, he said.

Friedgen told the kids that he was a coach. They asked him who he was recruiting. Then they told him, "we're going to steal everything you have, including your radio."

Friedgen shot back:

"You can steal anything you want. The only thing I'm worried about is a baseball bat."

T here were moments in the early years that made Ralph Friedgen realize how fortunate he was.

While recruiting for The Citadel with assistant coach Art Baker, Friedgen went on a home visit in Florence, S.C.

The prospect's family was so poor that it had one light bulb for the entire house. They moved it from the back room to the front room to start the coaches' visit. They had outdoor plumbing. Friedgen sat at the kitchen table and saw mice run up the walls.

"Art Baker is sitting there selling like a champ. One of these mice runs right over his foot. He does nothing. We get in the car and he says, 'I saw it happen. I was worried about it running up my pants.' "

Things worked out well in the end, though.

"He [the recruit] came to The Citadel and didn't have any problem with the military because his life was a hell of a lot tougher," Friedgen said.

Friedgen recalled a time at Georgia Tech, in the rough Liberty City section of Miami, where he went recruiting running back William Bell. The talented back committed to Tennessee only to see the Vols back off his verbal pledge.

Tech got involved, but Ross didn't like Bell because on his campus visit he "acted like 'Super Fly,' " Friedgen said.

They decided to recruit Bell based on Friedgen's word that he was a quality kid, and that "he would take care of it."

Later, Tech won a National Championship with Bell in the backfield and he made the cover of *Sports Illustrated*. Afterwards, he played professionally for the

Washington Redskins and other teams.

Friedgen recalled telling Bell's mother:

"I am going to take care of him, meaning he'd get an education. She thought she would be getting other benefits, as did a high school coach."

The family was so poor that when the coaches arrived at the home a sheet was hanging in the doorway in place of a door.

Bell's mother, at first, would not sign a Pell Grant, thinking it was a loan document. On financial papers, in the section which asked how much money the family earned, "she wrote '$10,000,'" Friedgen said.

Later, Friedgen helped Bell open a bank account. He never had one before.

Years later, Bell called Friedgen for advice. He was about to sign a free agent contract in the NFL. He couldn't decide on the New York Jets or the Washington Redskins.

He said the 'Skins were going to give him $5,000, the Jets $10,000, in signing bonuses. Friedgen told him that it didn't matter, what mattered was "which team could you make?"

Friedgen studied both team's depth charts and recommended that Bell sign with the Redskins. He was named to the practice squad, and at mid-year Dallas called and wanted to activate him. Bell again asked for Friedgen's advice.

"I said, 'Now you're in the money. And tell Norv [Turner] you want $10,000 more.' And he played years for them."

Nearly a decade later Friedgen helped Bell finish his degree at Tech. Friedgen promised his mother that he would graduate and he did. Friedgen and his wife, Gloria, threw a party in Atlanta for Bell's friends and family. A few years later, when Maryland traveled to Atlanta to play Georgia Tech, Bell called his coach and visited the team hotel. He had a box of cigars for Friedgen.

"He said, 'You know, I am a Tech guy but I am pulling for you tonight,'" Friedgen recalled his former back telling him.

Bell later became a coach.

Also deep in SEC territory, Friedgen recalled pursuing a top recruit from Mississippi while he was coaching at Georgia Tech.

Friedgen sent a National Letter of Intent to the recruit's home on four occasions "because the post office was throwing the mail away. You couldn't get him the letter. We finally had to have a courier bring it," Friedgen said.

At Maryland, Ralph Friedgen believes he has a gold mine of recruits, both locally and regionally. It's another reason he couldn't believe the program hadn't taken off.

Talent-rich Washington, D.C. and Prince George's County are in his backyard. To the south, Northern Virginia and The Tidewater region, where the Terps have had some success despite the stranglehold Virginia Tech and Virginia have on the area.

To the north, the fertile grounds of New York and New Jersey, though Rutgers jumped in as a player in 2006. Also Pennsylvania, where the Terps have won past battles over Penn State for top prospects. The Terps have enjoyed a modicum of success in Florida as well, where they've managed to pull a handful of top players (D'Qwell Jackson), many of whom had local ties the Terps were able to work.

Friedgen rattled off the many built-in advantages the university has, like top job and media markets.

But recruiting is a funny business, one that seemingly gets more sensational each year. And it's not something Friedgen has much patience for.

Friedgen is lauded for not pandering to recruits and their "posses," and always "telling it like it is," while some contend he doesn't get as personally involved in the process as some of his peers, relying too much on his assistants until the final months.

Gary Williams, the Terps' men's basketball coach, has been pigeonholed in a similar way.

R alph Friedgen has "heard it all" in his day, and doesn't have much time or patience for groveling to needy recruits or their crews.

He once had an emissary of a recruit ask him for a job, among other illegal benefits, since he has been at Maryland as head coach.

Another time a recruit's father sat in his office, ear piece and cell phone going the entire time, before Friedgen asked him to put it down. He has to laugh about what his father would do in a similar situation.

Friedgen gets to the point. He doesn't dance with recruits or sugar-coat things with slick presentations or gratuitous praise.

One recruit that verbally committed to Auburn in 2005, Eastern Shore star running back Ben Tate, came to campus and met with Friedgen despite his pledge. Sitting at his desk, Friedgen asked Tate and his father what they were doing there if they had already committed.

The visit ended real fast.

"I'm interested in guys that want to be here," Friedgen said. "The rest, you can take all that stuff. Why waste my time."

Like the Terps marketing campaign in his early years as head coach, Friedgen often asks prospects, "Are you in or are you out?"

Friedgen seldom tells recruits "just what they want to hear just to get their signature," he said. He'd rather talk academics and graduation rates with parents and keep things more genuine.

One prospect in 2005, a quarterback from Virginia, narrowed his finalists to Maryland and two other ACC schools. He asked Friedgen if he could play basketball as well. Friedgen didn't mince words, which can have both a positive and negative effect.

"I told him as a quarterback at Maryland then you're going to be missing a lot of things," Friedgen said.

He went elsewhere.

Same for Suitland High School linebacker Navorro Bowman, who wanted to play basketball at Maryland, too. He played for a local AAU hoops power, D.C. Team Assault. But Friedgen told him he would need to be in the weight room bulking up as he was an undersized middle linebacker at 6-0, 215-pounds.

Bowman chose Penn State.

Friedgen won't tell recruits what they want to hear to close a deal.

Despite how many "stars" a recruit has, Friedgen breaks them down and builds them up in his own way. And he treats them the same regardless of All-America status or not. He tries to prepare them for the awakening some have awaiting them at college, where high school press clippings don't mean much.

He recalled Westlake High School star defensive tackle Randy Starks, who he won a heated battle for against Penn State, "couldn't keep the pace [in a high school game as a senior] just getting in and out of the huddle. And we go a hell of a lot faster than they do. I remember saying Dave Sollazzo is going to be kicking him in the butt when that happens."

Starks was a time-intensive recruit. His recruiter, Locksley, once spent three consecutive hours on the telephone with his mother, who was particular about many things, including academics.

Friedgen said Starks came in and played "tremendous football for us. He got better and better. David Sollazzo really prepared him for the NFL. To go in there and play as a 20-year old kid, and end up starting in the NFL as a defensive lineman."

In a dark twist, Starks's teammate, Lavon Chisley, an up-and-coming defensive end, was verbally committed to Maryland for several months before de-committing and signing with Penn State. Chisely was arrested and charged with murder in 2006, accused of stabbing an acquaintance more than 90 times.

R alph Friedgen has such a sense of loyalty that the ugly side of recruiting can quickly turn him off.

Growing up when he did he knew one thing: "that your word is your bond. That's it," he said.

And he lived by it.

A handshake meant something coming from a family of the Depression and World War II eras. Commitment meant something. Families didn't divorce. You did what you said you would and stuck with it despite adversity along the way.

Friedgen often says that he's not interested in "reservations," only commitments when prospects want to make a pledge to his program. He insists recruits shake his hand at the time of their commitment.

But that hasn't stopped some from reneging as recent examples Antonio Logan-El, Nyan Boateng and Chris Rodgers, among others, Friedgen has endured in recent years.

"The problem I have with most of these kids is the word 'commitment.' For some of them it's not a commitment, it's only a reservation. They want you to hold a spot for them but they want to go around and look at other schools. But if the school pulls out on a kid, then all of a sudden the school is terrible. But the kids do it all the time. So it is a double-edged sword there," he said.

New York star receiver Boateng, after he broke his ankle on the eve of his senior year, called Friedgen to make sure his scholarship offer was still good. He committed in the spring during his junior year but Boateng wanted to keep the pledge 'silent' so he could play in the U.S. Army All-American All-Star Game in Texas, which preferred that it's players committed on national television during breaks in the game. It's another thing that drives Friedgen crazy.

"I told him we shook hands on it," Friedgen said of his reply to Boateng.

But as soon as the Terps struggled and "we weren't throwing the ball 35 times" during the first half of the 2004 season, later finishing 5-6, Boateng became uneasy about his pledge and re-opened his recruitment.

He signed with Florida and flamed out after not playing as much as he expected as a freshman, and later getting stabbed by a female acquaintance. He left school.

"I can understand wanting to look around. But just don't commit then. But that's what the process is all about," Friedgen laments.

Friedgen believes that during the recruiting process "it takes eight kids to get one. And then when you get that one you have to tell the other seven that you are no longer recruiting them. Then you have to scramble to fill the slot if a player reneges. And by then there's not much left."

He says he uses a different strategy after getting burned a few times.

"I just keep recruiting. It will all work its way out in the end. That is the way I found it out to be. You probably never get all the kids you want even if they tell you they are coming."

Boateng attempted twice to transfer to Maryland after his Florida experience. Friedgen said "no thanks" each time. Boateng had his chance but embarrassed Friedgen. And he wouldn't get another.

He transferred to Cal in 2007 and must sit out a year under NCAA transfer rules. Years ago the Terps added Cal to their schedule, which could make for an interesting match-up next year.

Boateng "had an entourage we had to deal with," Friedgen said, "talking about how great they were going to be. All the 'hanger-ons,' you know. That's good while the going is good, but what happens when things go bad?"

Another de-commitment who started to rub Friedgen the wrong way was corner-back Chris Rodgers of Florida, who committed only to back out and sign with Alabama. His best friend, linebacker Chris Clinton, stuck with his Maryland commitment and came to College Park.

"We had Rodgers in an academic meeting," Friedgen recalled. "We were talking about how we graduate kids in four years and he was talking about, 'I'm gonna be on the three-year plan because I am going to be in the league the fourth year.' "

Recruiting can also be uncomfortable for Friedgen.

Literally.

Friedgen has never been comfortable dashing in and out of airports. It's made him push for more private jet time, which the school and the MGN have been able to help fund.

Some schools Maryland's size have private planes. Some even airports.

Friedgen's artificial hip sets off alarms at security gates, while just taking his belt and shoes off at airports can be problematic. He sometimes get tired and impatient on the recruiting road over delays and wasted time.

Recruits can be intimated by Friedgen, at least until they get one-on-one with him.

Friedgen said in 2005, in the spring after recruiting wrapped-up, that concerned boosters approached him at an MGN event.

Friedgen had been recruiting for four straight weeks, most of which was without a private plane. That year he was prepared to buy a share in a NetJet for $500,000, using some of his money. He would go out recruiting and get reimbursed for gas.

Each year the department, or boosters, have been able to provide Friedgen with additional private jet time, which has made things a lot easier.

"They come up to me and say, 'God, you look so much better than at the recruiting thing.' I had the shakes. I couldn't sleep. I was a wreck."

But Friedgen hasn't grumbled too much. And he's been able to raise enough money for private jet time during key recruiting periods.

Friedgen can be so direct during visits that ears can shudder.

One time he was direct with Springbrook High School tight end David Jones, who signed with LSU, telling him: "If you come here, great, we'll win. We'd love to have you. If you don't, well, we'll win without you."

That's a sales-pitch you may not often hear. But it's vintage Friedgen, and the leopard hasn't changed his spots.

"He wasn't into wining and dining them. Loving 'em up. All that stuff," former recruiting coordinator Locksley said.

Florida linebacker Jackson verbally committed to Maryland on three occasions. But when Signing Day came around, he got cold feet.

The Nattiel family, with brothers that played at Florida, were cousins of Jackson, and soon started working him to go to Gainesville. Steve Spurrier and the previous staff had Jackson "on hold," not pulling the trigger on an offer, so Maryland was the benefactor and led throughout.

Jackson's coach was a Gators fan, too. But Friedgen had done it the right way, speaking at the Pinellas County football banquet that year. But the pressure from Florida was intense.

His high school coach was not happy with his choice, and his signed letter of intent did-n't show up over the Fax machine at Maryland. N.C. State was also pushing hard.

Friedgen was in a tizzy and on the phone telling Jackson, "Hey, D'Qwell. Just put it in and push the button. You know it is right. There is no need to wait. You know it is in your heart," Locksley recalled.

It was the most feverishly those close to Friedgen saw him work to land a recruit at crunch-time.

Jackson ended up signing with Maryland, and later he went on to a star-studded career despite some negative recruiting against the Terps.

Friedgen finally told him: "If you don't trust me in the morning, then when I come in your fax isn't here. But if it is here I'll be happy."

The letter arrived the next morning.

Jackson was raised by his grandmother. His mother was in poor health and his father wasn't around. His uncle, also instrumental in raising him, came to several of his Maryland games. Jackson overcame a lot, getting out of a poor neighborhood with little family structure. He is one of Friedgen's favorite players, though he put his coach through the ringer once.

Friedgen has battled many last-minute threats to recruits like Jackson.

Friedgen has been pleasantly surprised at times by recruits as well, including offensive lineman Jared Gaither in 2004, who first attended prep school to qualify.

There was a furor over Gaither taking campus visits that winter. But from the start Gaither told Friedgen not to worry.

"When he came on his visit he said, 'Coach, I got to talk to you about something,' " Friedgen said. 'Look, if I don't make my test score I gotta get out of Hargrave. I can't stay there on the weekends. So I am going to take my visits. But I am telling you right now I am coming to Maryland.' "

Gaither stuck to his word and Friedgen felt a bond with him for the next two years, though Gaither would leave school in the spring of 2007, a big disappointment for Friedgen, who had put so much time into him.

Gaither would end all of his text messages to Friedgen with a reference to God.

"A little bit. A little bit," Friedgen said of having his faith restored in the process when Gaither signed despite the best efforts of Virginia Tech, Penn State and others to pry him loose. "Now, [recruit coordinator] James [Franklin] was nervous over it. I told him I feel good about it. I feel good about it."

Friedgen is more comfortable in his office, on his own turf, talking with recruits. He calls it the "living room" area of his office, where he has a sofa and chairs where he lays out what he has to offer in his program and asks recruits if it fits them.

It also became physically uncomfortable for him to get around, especially after hip surgery.

"He hated Southwest [airlines] because it was like a melee trying to get seats," Franklin said.

R alph Friedgen keeps a chart of his assistant coaches, with who they have recruited and how productive the players have been.

As a former coordinator at Georgia Tech, where he didn't have a territory and would only go out one week a year to close on offensive players, Friedgen knows coordinators don't have as much time for recruiting as other assistants.

At Tech, Friedgen ran the show on campus while O'Leary and staff were on the road recruiting, much like Blackney did under Friedgen.

"My job down there was scoring points," he said of his time in Atlanta as offensive coordinator.

Friedgen has a grading system he uses to determine whether to offer a prospect a scholarship. He says he would rather have unused scholarships than waste them on kids that cannot play and are just "taking up space."

Friedgen and staff have 10 areas which they use to grade players led by a "top three, which are all objective," he said.

It's a system he learned from O'Leary.

The first three criteria are height, weight and speed.

"We shouldn't miss on that because when they come here we test them on that," Friedgen said.

Each category has a 0-5 scale so the top number would be 15. Where there is a "gray" area is a player without great measureables but good intangibles, like Joe Hamilton, who scored a 38.

Thirty eight and above is an offer.

When Friedgen first got to Maryland he saw lack of height in the program with too many "squatty bodies." He said he had to be careful recruiting "that really good high school player that's six-foot."

Friedgen said you cannot fall in the trap of having too many of them, though a few in the program isn't bad. Friedgen would rather have a tall and fast kid with potential to grow than a short, slow one with more high school accolades.

The other seven categories are ones the position coaches deem important to their position. For a quarterback, it could be arm strength, vision and maneuverability. For a defensive back, perhaps hands, back-pedal and flexible hips.

The grades are added up with a maximum of 50 points. Sometimes players just below the cut-off, with a 36 or 37 score, can get offers. Also, prospects can enhance their grade following solid camp performances.

"A guy like Joe Hamilton had a low 'top score' but his 'bottom score' was pretty good. He was a 38 and some other guy was a 41. Potentially, he might be better than Joe Hamilton, but Joe's just one of those guys. So when I see a guy with a 38 with a low 'top score,' well then I know he's a pretty good player."

"It's an objective way for me to make decisions," Friedgen said

Friedgen has increased height and speed since he's been at Maryland, especially on the offensive line and at receiver and tight end. Taking prospects like Haynos, Mack Frost, Omarr Savage, Gaither, Nixon, tall players that could run, fit that mold in recent years.

Friedgen has an academic component as well, which includes four categories: regular admit, admit by review, individual admits (which Friedgen is allowed 12 per year), and, lastly, inadmissible.

Prospects get a green, blue, yellow or red stamp depending on their academic situation. Some with reds, the lowest, if they get a qualifying test score are elevated. It can change for other reasons as well.

"What I do is get 38s and above and then I put them in a pecking order of who I want. And then I want to look at them by where are they academically," Friedgen said. "So you want your pool to be 38s and above that are good students because there's no use recruiting all these guys you can't get into school. So it's all on percentages."

Prospects are graded as many as 4-5 times after camps and combines, including Maryland's schoolboy camp in June.

Recruits must commit to Friedgen before they become official "because I'm the one that's got to keep them all straight," he said.

At times recruits have tried to commit to their recruiter. But it's not a "done deal" until Friedgen signs off on the pledge.

It came up early in his tenure as Friedgen juggled a few running backs, including Lance Ball from New Jersey and in-state standout Barrington Edwards.

Ball went ahead and committed to New Jersey recruiter Sollazzo and the news slipped out. But Friedgen later accepted it "because Lance was a good kid," he said.

Edwards, the more highly-rated recruit, signed with LSU, later transferred to North Carolina, and had a nondescript career before leaving school early. Ball was primed as an all-ACC candidate heading into his senior season in 2007.

There's no better example of taking both prospects than when Morgan Green, the in-state star from Lackey High School, committed in 2005 while the Terps couldn't take a very willing Steve Slaton from Pennsylvania, which would come back to haunt them.

The Terps were only taking one back in the class. Later, when Slaton emerged as a Heisman Trophy candidate as a sophomore, Friedgen said he would take both if he had it to do over again.

Green had to attend prep school before he arrived at College Park. He was hoping to get on the field for the first time in 2007.

R alph Friedgen has always had a good eye for talent starting early in his career. He rattles off the names of some of his prized recruits, from Stump Mitchell at The Citadel to William Bell at Georgia Tech to sadly, Mike Mooney, the former South Carroll High School star who played on the offensive line at Georgia Tech. Mooney died in his sleep in 2007.

"He was 6-9, 300-pounds, and a lot of people don't know he was a mixed doubles [tennis] state champ in high school. He said, 'I had a little girl who could go get them, and I had a hell of a serve,' " Friedgen said.

Friedgen earned his recruiting stripes in some tough areas.

Miami was one area that he said took "three years just to get into the school to even get a kid to visit. If they don't know you, you won't even get in on them," he said.

Friedgen plucked standout Ben Jefferson in the 1980s out of New York. That was a stressful one.

Jefferson, a prized line recruit, didn't want to announce his intentions until after Signing Day. At the time, there weren't as many limitations on recruiting and coaches could be at a player's announcement news conference on National Signing Day.

Friedgen was holed up in New York so long during the recruitment that assistant coach Jeff Mann had to bring him clothes from College Park.

Friedgen went to Jefferson's school at 7 a.m. on Signing Day only to hear the news that he would wait. Friedgen was recruiting another local kid at the time so he had Mann bird-dog him while he babysat Jefferson.

Once Mann, a former military man known for his discipline, followed him into a bathroom at his high school.

"I remember Mark Tressman was recruiting for Miami and we're at a kid's house first thing in the morning. I remember telling Tressman, 'You're a lawyer and you're doing this crap? Why don't you just hang your shingle up and go about doing your business,' " Friedgen said.

Stoddard, who coached at Brewster (Conn.) High School, welcomed Friedgen to his school when Friedgen was recruiting for The Citadel.

Brewster's football team was not very good, winning just one game that season, but Friedgen saw something in undersized offensive lineman John Gamby, who jumped out at him on tape.

"He had no technique. He's got no discipline. He's got no nothing," Stoddard said "But when he gets to the ball, 'bam,' something happens."

Friedgen recruited him hard but told Gamby during the home visit that, "The

Citadel is not for everyone," and other reasons he may not want to come. But Gamby quickly committed. Gamby ended up starting at center for The Citadel.

"The kid was a wise-ass back then. He had a problem. A quirky little thing every time he got nervous or stressed he'd giggle or smile. But you don't do that when you're bracing at The Citadel. But later he would come back to the school I was working at and just rave about life because of what Ralph did for him getting him into The Citadel."

Friedgen helped a boyhood friend in the recruiting process, again showing his eye for talent.

Verille's son, Michael, a junior running back at a private school in Florida – Lake Highland Prep – had an assortment of offers. But his parents didn't know what level their son should aim for.

Verille sent Friedgen highlight film and asked for "his honest opinion." Friedgen called Verille after watching the tape and told him, 'Division I-A because he has a burst,' " Verille recalled.

Friedgen told the Verilles to go to three college camps in a good league that summer. He told them to make them as competitive as possible. He said they would know at the end of the process which division fit him best.

Verille sent tape to Georgia Tech but O'Leary told him to consider I-AA schools, not the ACC, a recommendation Verille said he was comfortable with.

But Michael Verille went to Auburn's camp and was named the top running back among some 300 prospects.

The Verilles drove to Georgia Tech's camp. Perry Verille introduced himself to O'Leary, who reiterated that he thought I-AA was the best fit. A few days later, during the awards ceremony at Tech's camp, O'Leary approached Verille and his wife, Joyce. He said he took back what he previously said about Michael. O'Leary said he wanted to recruit him, but as a defensive back. Michael was named outstanding defensive back at the end of camp.

The third stop was Duke. The coaches asked to see Perry Verille when he came to pick up his son. Fred Goldsmith was the head coach and offered Verille on the spot.

Michael Verille had outstanding grades so it appeared a good fit. Bill Buchalter, who covered Verille in high school as a prep reporter for the *Orlando Sentinel*, met the Verilles over lunch when they returned home. He recommended that Michael sign with Duke.

Friedgen made the right call. (Verille would later transfer to Penn after the coaching staff was fired at Duke). He played for two years, and as a senior helped win an Ivy League title.

J ames Franklin, who served as Ralph Friedgen's second recruiting coordinator at Maryland, said Friedgen is "all about business" on in-home and school visits, and is unusually direct.

"Really, there was not a visit I was with him where he hasn't said, 'Are you coming or not? And if not I need to move onto the next guy. I am going to be honest with you and you need to be honest with me.' Some kids respect that and embrace that. Some don't."

Friedgen sold academics, not just the NFL, which turned some kids on and others off.

"Some of these parents now have kinda turned into they want to live through their kids and be recruited and told how great everybody is. And that's really not Ralph's deal," Franklin added.

But there is another side to Friedgen the recruiter.

O'Leary, who worked alongside Friedgen at San Diego in the NFL and at Georgia Tech, first got to know Friedgen when they recruited the same turf on Long Island in the 1980s.

O'Leary was at Syracuse and Friedgen at Maryland. O'Leary said he helped him from the start. Both were New Yorkers and liked a good time.

"We were both after the same kids all the time so we'd run into each other there. It was professional but it was friendship. I was staying at the Marriott right there by Hofstra and he couldn't get in so I introduced him to the manager to get him in. The price was wrong, but I got the general manager to put him on the same price that I was paying."

Friedgen and O'Leary began a long career together and even built Georgia vacation homes at exclusive Lake Oconee a few coves apart. Beamer also built a home there, and the three reunite for golf outings or Fourth of July parties.

Friedgen and O'Leary were coordinators under Ross at Georgia Tech and lived in the same neighborhood. They drove to work together every day.

Dating back to the days Friedgen was an assistant at Maryland and O'Leary was at Syracuse, and both recruited New York, O'Leary joked about how he would send rookie recruiters to intimidating city turf via roundabout directions.

O'Leary sent the coaches on wild goose chases.

"Why'd you send him that way?" Friedgen asked. "You won't see him for weeks," O'Leary quipped.

One time in Brooklyn, O'Leary sent a Penn State assistant coach by way of Fort Green Place.

"He goes, 'We may never see him again.' Fort Green Place . . . there was a murder a day there,' " Friedgen said.

It wasn't always rosy, though. Recruiting can get contentious even among friends. Like in 2006 when the Terps plucked two Central Florida verbal commitments and O'Leary and Friedgen's longtime relationship was put to the test.

Florida natives Terrell Skinner and Marvin Peoples, players that O'Leary expected to sign in his first recruiting class in his new post, took late official visits to Maryland and committed.

Peoples, a linebacker who later gave fullback a try at Maryland before transferring to South Florida under NCAA hardship rules due to a death in his family, told

O'Leary, unbeknownst to Friedgen, that he was going to visit family one weekend during recruiting time.

O'Leary later learned he was at Maryland on an official visit. Because of the 'dead period,' which began that Monday, O'Leary said he missed finding another player to fill the void when Peoples de-committed.

O'Leary called Friedgen and complained about his poor timing.

"I said, 'Hey Ralph, at least I would have called you.' He said, 'Yeah, I should have done that.' I said, 'You're damn right you should have done that.' I wouldn't have done that."

O'Leary and Friedgen didn't talk for six months, missing their annual reunion at the lake before Friedgen broke the ice with a letter congratulating O'Leary on his first season. Later, O'Leary responded with a phone call.

Friedgen, who can be tough in all areas, said, "That's recruiting."

Tim Banks was the Maryland recruiter and both players contacted Banks about wanting to visit, which set the chain of events in motion.

"We're like brothers," O'Leary said. "I should have got a phone call. And it's not like you're dealing with some head coach you don't know."

Said Friedgen of the incident:

"I look at it as just recruiting. I have recruited against George so many years and I can't believe he's doing that. He said we were negative recruiting. We weren't negative recruiting."

Skinner, still a Terp but a safety after moving positions in 2006, contacted the UCF staff about transferring when he got homesick, O'Leary said. But he stuck it out.

"We're friends again," O'Leary said. "But there is a difference between stubbornness and stupidity."

Friedgen first recommended O'Leary to Ross, who hired him at Georgia Tech as defensive coordinator. They lived in the same development, car-pooled for five years, and often raised a little hell together in the early years.

Friedgen and O'Leary had been through the fire many times including O'Leary's resume snafu, which cost him the head coaching job at Notre Dame. Friedgen's were the only phone calls O'Leary took during a dark period for the longtime coach.

"I said, 'George, this is easy for me to say. But it is going to get better every day after this. You gottta fight your way through it. Screw Notre Dame.'

"I came out strong for George. I really believe if they wanted the fighting Irish then there's no better fighting Irish than George O'Leary."

At the same time, Friedgen was upset with Beamer for trying to recruit Maryland verbal commitment Gaither while he was at a Virginia prep school.

But Beamer "wouldn't let me recruit his guy," Friedgen said of quarterback standout Ike Whitaker of Germantown, Md., who had previously verballed to Tech. They also battled intensely over Virginia quarterback Greg Boone.

"Frank and I are going to be in this league together so we're gonna compete because that's what we do. That's our job. Now what we do after that we're not competing, we're friends," Friedgen said.

"I guess what George wanted me to do was say we're not going to take these kids because they committed to Central Florida. But my job is to win. And if I don't win they are going to fire me. It's a competitive, dog-eat-dog world. When you're recruiting it's just like you are playing."

Friedgen, whose Hargrave players, notably Gaither and Melvin Alaeze, other schools tried to recruit though they were verbally committed to Maryland, said he told coaches at the Virginia military academy that if the Terps lost any players "they would be the last we ever sent there."

Friedgen is no-nonsense with recruits. Not always polished like his smooth predecessor Vanderlinden, who could turn on the charm with the best of them but couldn't win at Maryland.

"Ralph was not a car salesman. Vandy was," said Perry.

There are countless other recruiting tales from the Ralph Friedgen era. Brash and speedy cornerback Josh Wilson, the legacy that hailed from Maryland stock as the son of former running back Tim Wilson, never wanted to go to Maryland.

Florida was his dream school growing up, in love with the speed, cockiness, even the uniforms of the Gators. Wilson rooted for them in the 2001 Orange Bowl against the Terps in Friedgen's rookie year.

"I was pretty happy with that game," Wilson said of the Gators' 56-23 rout in Miami. "Danny Wuerfful and all. When they won the championship, I was a Florida fan from the start."

Wilson was a senior at nearby DeMatha at the time, and was put off by his first Maryland impression.

He came to Maryland for an unofficial visit when Friedgen's offices were housed in temporary buildings in the parking lot of the Gossett Football Team House. It wasn't much to see, with the quarters cramped. The Terps were in the midst of an expansion project.

Defensive coordinator/secondary coach Blackney didn't like Wilson, despite his legacy and the DeMatha connection.

"Coach Blackney said I was too small," Wilson said of the staff's toughest grader. "I was ready to come in with a chip on my shoulder, ready to crack heads right away.

"That was great motivation. I went back to DeMatha and told Coach [Bill] McGregor what had happened. But I said I think I am going to play for this guy."

Despite Blackney's protestations, what caught Wilson's attention most was Friedgen's sincerity. He said his pitch never changed, or went over the top with "phony talk." Friedgen humbled the supremely confident Wilson by telling him that he would have to earn his playing time. And that it would be "hard for me to play early" because of returning starters Foxworth, Cox and Dennard Wilson, all of whom would go on to play professional football.

Wilson ended up not even hosting a home visit with Friedgen and staff, instead committing in the coach's office.

The Terps worked the family angle hard, especially former assistant coach Rod Sharpless, who played with Tim Wilson at College Park. The former Terps running back went on to become the lead blocker for Earl Campbell with the Houston Oilers before a massive heart attack, when Josh was 11, ended his life before he got to see his son suit up for Maryland.

"One thing he says is that he's not going to lie to you," Wilson said of Friedgen. "Whether you appreciate it or not, that takes a lot for a man to say that when they are trying to sell you on their school. Everyone wants to tell you you'll come in and play."

Wilson chose Maryland over North Carolina, N.C. State and Syracuse, and went on to become the team's top secondary player in 2006 and team MVP before being selected in the second round of the NFL draft by the Seattle Seahawks. But he has a secret that had Florida offered . . .

"It would have been close. It would have been hard for me to say no," Wilson said of the Gators. "I have never told Ralph that. I couldn't tell him I was rooting for Florida in that game."

In the end, Wilson said Friedgen was the most effective recruiter because "he told it like it is."

Hollenbach, who finished his career as one of Friedgen's favorites, nearly left school before his junior year.

He was buried on the depth chart and was almost moved to tight end by the staff. Hollenbach would turn into a key player and leader in Maryland's turnaround season in 2006.

His rise to starter and MVP of the Champs Sports Bowl was somewhat remarkable given the fact he was not a natural quarterback despite a good pedigree. And certainly not one in Friedgen's system for the first few years.

Long and gangly and not possessing great foot speed or football savvy, Hollenbach was "book smart" but it didn't always convey to the football field. But Friedgen made him into a college quarterback through sheer will.

Hollenbach played for his father, Jeff, at Pennridge (Pa.) High School, who quarterbacked Illinois in the 1970s. He recalled Friedgen being the only head coach to visit him at his high school. And that his direct approach stood out.

"Coaches were generally really nice and forward and personable and all, but what I remember about coach Friedgen was he came in and he wasn't like that. He came in, shook my hand, and said, 'You know, this is the real deal now.' Not a smile on his face.

Nothing like that. He said, 'You are a good player, but this is the real deal now.' That kind of struck me as funny but straight."

Hollenbach committed that summer on the eve of his senior year after attending Maryland's camp in June and, in the end, liking Friedgen's track record with quarterbacks the most among his finalists.

He was joined in the class by Statham, a starter, who later flamed out and transferred after losing his starting job and having off-the-field issues.

"Other recruiters came in and they were real light, easy going. Coach Friedgen was just direct and to the point, He didn't say much. And I remember coach [James] Franklin kinda filling in the spots when coach Friedgen wasn't talking. I got the sense of how committed he is to the program and only wanting to win and not all the other stuff," Hollenbach said.

Hollenbach met with Friedgen months later, along with his parents, during his official visit at the hotel where recruits stayed. There Friedgen showed another side.

"He talked a lot more about academics when my parents were around, especially my mom," Hollenbach said of his mother, Libby, and Friedgen's 'soft side' for mothers.

Hollenbach's father took a backseat in the process despite his football background, making sure his son made the decision on his own. Hollenbach chose the Terps over Michigan State and Pittsburgh.

"He finally came out and said, 'I really think Maryland is a good fit.' And that coach Friedgen would prepare me as well as anybody, if not better, in the country as far as being a quarterback. To hear him say that made the decision a lot easier."

Three years later, on Christmas Day, Hollenbach called Friedgen at his home to tell him of his decision not to transfer. That he would stick it out. Hollenbach went on to become an all-ACC honorable mention pick as a senior, playing in two all-star games after the season, and giving the pros a shot after many wrote him off. He was in the Washington Redskins' camp in the spring of 2007 trying to earn a spot.

Hollenbach came close to transferring to Lehigh before turning things around and finishing his Maryland career rated among the best statistically all-time.

Friedgen has had many recruiting success stories like Sam Hollenbach.

N o story illustrates Friedgen's disdain for how out of control recruiting has become than the case of Antonio Logan-El.

Logan-El was the Forestville, Md., offensive lineman and "5-star" national recruit in 2005 that verbally committed to Maryland after his sophomore season.

He was so inspired by a speech Friedgen gave to campers in the spring during a recruiting event that he jumped from his chair, raised his hand, and proclaimed for all to hear, "Coach. Where do I sign up?"

From there it was all downhill, though.

As Logan-El became more of a national name in recruiting circles and on the Internet, his ego grew. He got so absorbed in the recruiting process that multiple interviews on various Internet recruiting sites each day were the norm. He soon opened up his recruitment to include other schools but never came out publicly and de-committed to Maryland, indicating he was simply keeping his options open.

Logan-El spoke of a grandiose "10-point" grading system, which he used to rate the colleges. It became such a circus, and his family so taken in by the attention, that phone calls made to his cell phone were sometimes answered by his grandfather, who said, "Antonio Logan-El's office."

His grading system would soon ring hollow.

With so much of his time spent on the phone talking about himself, his football skills tanked. His senior year was a bust as he did little on the field to back up his national ranking. He was dropped from "5" to "4" stars by *Rivals.com*. And four stars may have been generous.

His senior highlight film, which ESPN showed clips of on Signing Day, was woeful. But it was probably the best they could find. It showed Logan-El upright, slow to react, getting little push on smaller linemen, and bailing early on blocks.

The Internet recruiting machine fed his voracious appetite but no one, not even Friedgen, who grew more and more skeptical, could anticipate the Signing Day circus that Logan-El helped play host to at the ESPN Zone restaurant in downtown Baltimore.

Friedgen had given Logan-El space to listen to other schools. But all along, he said, Logan-El told him he had "nothing to worry about."

Logan-El was in constant contact with Friedgen through text messages, sometimes getting in half-hour exchanges with him about everything from family to prize fights.

Penn State was building a huge local class, and Prince George's County defensive tackle Phil Taylor, who at one time was a heavy Maryland "lean," had committed to the Nittany Lions a few weeks prior. Now he was working Logan-El, among other locals like Howard County end Aaron Maybin, another PSU verbal pledge.

The Terps could take solace in the fact Taylor, like Logan-El, had become something of a creature of recruiting hype and was removed from the starting lineup on defense midway through his senior year at Gwynn Park because of his ineffective play.

Maybin, from Mount Hebron High School, was, in part, another creation of the Internet, a raw but athletic prospect that Maryland didn't offer until the summer, something he was miffed about. Maybin never dominated in a low-level county.

As National Signing Day approached, Logan-El called Friedgen to invite him to the function in Baltimore. Coaches are not allowed at recruits' news conferences, so he had to decline.

Friedgen was lucky for that.

But his wife, Gloria, was invited and attended.

Gloria had developed a relationship with Logan-El's grandfather in the year since Logan-El committed. They struck up a conversation about one of her favorite movies, *Remember The Titans*, because Logan-El's grandfather said he was friendly with the former head football coach at T.C. Williams, the Alexandria, Va., school on which the film was based.

Gloria arrived at Baltimore and went to work immediately for the Terps. She was armed with Terps' placards and pom-poms, which she attempted to place at each table.

No sooner had she started did the Logan-El contingent began to sneer. She was approached by restaurant management, which asked her not to distribute material to the area where the group was seated.

Ralph Friedgen wasn't there, so Gloria was calling him on her cell phone with updates. There were some 30 Maryland fans in attendance. Gloria said she had told her husband the night before that she had a "premonition" that Logan-El was not coming to Maryland.

Logan-El, dressed in a black suit and a red tie, went on the air and held up a photo of himself and Penn State coach Joe Paterno, taken during his home visit, and then announced for the Nittany Lions.

Bedlam broke out, not surprising as the event was held in the state's largest city before a pro-Maryland crowd, many of whom knew Friedgen had been invited, not to mention Logan El's red tie.

"I remember someone behind me yelled 'traitor.' There was more noise made and then someone in their family turned around saying 'F-Maryland' in our direction," Gloria said. "I then said to the crowd of Maryland people, 'We will win with him or without him.' "

Gloria said she calmly got up from her chair and walked out, but not before seeing Logan-El's mother jumping on two PSU assistant coaches in the lobby outside the room.

"She was jumping like, putting her legs around him. I was like, 'Okay. Well, I got to get out of here.' I went with Debbie [close friend Debbie Bebee] to [a local Italian restaurant] Da Mimmo, I had a glass of wine and an appetizer and then I went to teach CCD."

The nationally televised news conference, carried on ESPN News, was panned by critics, even some in Happy Valley, wailing on Logan El for his sophomoric stunt. Especially galling was the fact he had invited the Friedgens.

It was recruiting gone amuck, with the process perhaps becoming more important than the end result for the star-crossed Prince George's County lineman.

Logan-El, just weeks before while Ralph Friedgen was at the coaches' convention in Texas, called the coach in his hotel room to reiterate that he would be a Terp.

Logan-El's coach, Charles Harley, embarrassed by the event, said a few months later of Logan-El: "He will either go on to become an All-American or a bum. There's no between with him."

Some say Logan-El was manipulated by the parents and friends of other local players heading to State College. And that he was swept up in the process and all the attention.

It didn't help that Eleanor Roosevelt standout Derrick Williams was a freshman at Penn State, and his father, Dwight Williams, a former University of Maryland employee, was laid off years before during budget cutbacks.

Friedgen warned Logan-El and his grandfather about many things, including the fact that Paterno "was about to turn 80, and after that there were no guarantees."

Logan-El wanted to study criminal justice, and Friedgen told him he could have an internship in any field he wanted in the D.C. area. Maryland had the nation's top criminal justice department.

"I said, 'How are you going to do that in State College? Your law enforcement options are limited. I can get him an internship in any area he wants. He's going to make a name for himself here. He could play pro football and come back and who knows what he could do next,'" Friedgen said.

"He gets up there, and what's he going to do up there? There's really nothing to do up there. He went bowling [on his official campus visit]. You think you bowl down here? If we took someone bowling around here they'd think we were nuts."

Logan-El spent part of his freshman year at PSU ineligible, a casualty of the NCAA Clearinghouse. He never got on the field.

In the winter of the 2006 he became disenchanted, missed winter workouts, and took a leave of absence for personal reasons. Then he got a frosty reception when he returned. Paterno said his scholarship was not guaranteed. He left less than a year into his PSU career, never stepping on the field.

The advice he got throughout the process may have been lacking to say the least.

"It's just really funny," said Gloria, who wears her emotions on her sleeve like her husband. "I don't really care where a kid goes. I want them to go to a place where they want to be. And I want kids that want to be at Maryland. If they decide not to come just say, 'I don't want to come. I am not interested. Don't recruit me anymore.' Whatever. But don't do silliness like this.

"The kid was manipulated. There is no question in my mind. I think he thought it was cute. I think he thought it was going to be a ha-ha high school prank kind of thing. A very, very juvenile action.

"I really wasn't upset. If you remember I went back and wrote on the *TerrapinTimes.com* [Internet message board], in Latin, the phrase, 'Don't let the bastards grind you down.'" [Nolite te bastardes carborundorum.]

Gloria got the line from a favorite book, *The Handmaid's Tale*, by Margaret Atwood, from the central character who was an indentured, surrogate wife. The protagonist saw the words carved in a drawer in the room in which she was locked by a previous handmaid.

Looking back, Gloria can only laugh about her conversations with Logan-El's grandfather. They spoke at length about character, the CCD class she taught, and getting kids interested in faith. And especially some of the parallels the two drew between what the ground-breaking coach at T.C. Williams had done and some of the things Ralph Friedgen was trying to do at Maryland.

"It all became a little too Hollywood for me in the end," Gloria said.

Logan-El transferred to Towson in the spring of 2007 with no better offers.

"Every dog has his day," she added. "That's what I said to Ralph then. But he always says, 'But we have to have players, Gloria.' "

Ralph got in a discussion with Gloria over it again last spring and replied: "But he wasn't a player."

A go-between that knew Logan-El called Friedgen in the spring of 2007 to see if he could visit with Friedgen about Logan-El transferring to College Park.

"I told them, 'Don't bother,' " Friedgen said.

Some contend that it was a concerted effort to make Maryland look bad. Former Terps coach Vanderlinden was on the staff at PSU, and he was outside of the ESPN Zone the day of Logan-El's commitment. NCAA rules prohibited him from being in the building for the event, but the minute it was over he and Larry Johnson celebrated in the doorway.

A.J. Wallace is a star in the making. Taylor, the defensive tackle from Gwynn Park, who at one time was heading to College Park to meet and commit to Ralph Friedgen before suddenly pulling back, is in the two-deep. Logan-El is gone, while Maybin has shown promise.

Also compelling is to look back at Logan-El as a sophomore at the time he committed to Maryland. A bit unsure of himself, he committed early not knowing if he would get another offer. He was on the bubble about becoming a player, and in the end stayed the same, if not regressed.

There were stories of Logan-El, before he had an impressive showing at the Nike Virginia Tech combine, forgetting his cleats and not telling his coaches until halfway there that he could not compete. Or having a sudden injury, which kept him from testing.

Friedgen said that after the Virginia Tech combine Logan-El changed.

"And this is where the Internet . . . he goes to that camp and runs well and does well and gets MVP of the combine. All of a sudden now he's inundated with offers. And he was a kid who probably didn't think he was going to go anywhere.

"We were the first to offer at a very early stage and he even said, 'A bird in the hand is worth two in a bush.' He accepted and they were on the bandwagon, he and his grandfather. What character they had and all this and that.

"And he had to go visit Oklahoma and all these other places. He became so . . . and what I see happening now, when I went down to Georgia, the southern schools, if a guy doesn't play well his senior year they drop the commit. There are more teams now that turn these guys into Internet warriors, they're these great guys. But being at a combine is not like playing football.

"Logan-El, the last year, even his coach [Charles] Harley said 'I had trouble find-ing him [on the field during games].' "

Logan-El also had a habit of committing to each coach that he spoke with, so much so that a few thought he was coming, Maryland included, until his final act at ESPN Zone.

The summer after the Logan-El fallout at Forestville, when promising sophomore receiver Kevin Dorsey wanted to make an early pledge to the Terps, his coach put him through the ringer.

He made Dorsey sit on it for a few months to be sure his commitment would be solid. Harley never hid the fact that he was pro-Maryland and wanted some of his players at College Park.

The Terps got another player from the program when "4-star" tight end Devonte Campbell chose the Terps just before Signing Day in February, 2007. This time there was no elaborate ESPN Zone news conference. No national television. But a modest ceremony at the school that featured the band and refreshments. Just the way Harley liked all of his news conferences.

Gloria Friedgen got more satisfaction a few weeks later when Gwynn Park com-mitment Quinton McCree, who grew up dreaming of becoming a Terp, apologized to her for the Philip Taylor flap.

Perhaps the most troubling recruit for Ralph Friedgen since he's been at Maryland was Melvin Alaeze, the "5-star" All-American defensive end from Randallstown who committed in 2005.

Friedgen took heat for cutting him loose in the summer of 2006. But it proved a good call.

Alaeze, the nation's No. 1 end prospect according to *Rivals.com*, was just what the Terps needed to jump-start their defense, a dominant edge rusher they had lacked for so long.

The Terps missed on the last No. 1 end in the nation, also from Baltimore, three years prior when they had to back out of the Victor Abiamiri sweepstakes for recruit-ing violations committed by assistant coach Rod Sharpless, who was released imme-diately and the Terps put on three years of NCAA probation.

A year later the Terps missed on yet another top defensive end prospect, Derrick Harvey of Eleanor Roosevelt in Greenbelt, Md. who chose Florida and went on to star in the Gators National Championship victory in 2007.

Alaeze had drawn comparisons to Indianapolis Colts' star Dwight Freeney for his combination of size, speed, strength and agility.

But he was also a hot-head that bounced from a handful of private and public schools in the Baltimore area due to off-the-field issues including fights. His parents wanted him at Maryland for the tough love and structure that Friedgen would provide.

Alaeze left Hargrave Military Academy mid-year in 2005 under a cloud, and returned home and enrolled at a community college hoping to get qualified.

He had put the Terps through the ringer the year before when as Signing Day approached he began to let other schools, like Penn State and Virginia Tech, get involved late in the process.

His father called Friedgen from San Antonio, site of the U.S. Army All-American Game, to say his son may be wavering. The Terps finally got him back in the fold but he didn't qualify so he went to Hargrave.

At the time, Friedgen worried whether Alaeze "would be willing to pay the price he's got to pay" to be a college football player, "when everyone's kissing his ass."

This was Friedgen at his best.

"One of his coaches came up to me and told me how I had to handle him, put him in this class or the other. I said, 'Let me get this straight. You're telling me what I need to do with Melvin? That's the problem. You better tell Melvin he's in my world now.' "

Friedgen walked away from the coach.

The Terps had another player from Randallstown that was doing well on the field and in the classroom, so Friedgen was incredulous about why the assistant was pushing him to Virginia Tech. The assistant was even bad-mouthing the parents to Friedgen during the process, he said.

"I don't want to hear that crap. And then I hear later he's pushing him to Virginia Tech. What the hell. I got after him," Friedgen said.

Alaeze's parents were nervous about missing their flight to San Antonio, concerned with the negative influences around their son in Texas.

Friedgen recalled a Sunday afternoon when he spent three hours with Alaeze's parents at his office trying to arrange things for their son. Explaining how he would take Alaeze under his wing and provide the structure that they sought.

Alaeze had already been calling Friedgen about what jersey number he would get (he wanted No. 7), and if he could move positions. Friedgen told him the same thing that he told quarterback Jeremy Ricker from Pennsylvania when he requested jersey number five. That seniority rules.

"That was the problem with Melvin all his life. Everybody giving Melvin the easy way out his whole life. Melvin needed to learn how to be a man and step up and do it the right way," Friedgen said.

Alaeze's mother and Melvin never saw eye-to-eye and she played the role of "heavy" in the household. She was always on his case. But Melvin would tune her out. His mother was hard-working, well educated and traveled overseas to Africa a few times a year working in health care, Friedgen said.

No sooner had Alaeze been back in town then he was picked up on drug and assault charges in Baltimore and later attempted second-degree murder charges in the winter of 2006. He allegedly shot a man three times on a playground. It happened on Christmas Eve and Alaeze, a month later, was indicted and pleaded guilty.

Going back six months to the spring of 2006, Friedgen called a June meeting with Alaeze and his father at his office. Friedgen, after learning of the initial drug charges, wanted to see if Alaeze would be contrite and accept responsibility for his actions.

He didn't. The conversation quickly deteriorated and the Terps pulled their scholarship offer.

Friedgen came into the meeting with trepidation. He had seen shocking images on Alaeze's personal web page. There were photos of money, guns, even drug jargon like "Trapper," the street name for a dealer. Maybe he was just trying to look tough, but it was shocking imagery for Friedgen and staff, nonetheless.

Friedgen wanted an explanation, and in Melvin's words, and wanted to hear a remorseful Alaeze tell him that he would change. He got none of that.

Friedgen had enough concern about negative influences around the program to take a high-risk kid who had run-ins with the law.

"After spending two years of recruiting this kid you know I just . . . I could see more problems for me and an embarrassment for the school and me. So it was best severing things now before it got any further. Whichever way I went I had the backing of the administration. I just had to make that call, but it was a tough call."

Friedgen went over the past with Alaeze, including why he bolted mid-year at Hargrave. Still, he got nothing to show remorse.

He told the family that the scholarship was off the table, news the family did not take very well. Alaeze's parents thought Friedgen and his program would be the perfect place for their son to finally get straight.

"But that's not a good reason to come. I am not a miracle worker," Friedgen said.

Alaeze was too far gone and Friedgen had no choice but to cut him loose.

Alaeze got up from the meeting and told Friedgen, "I didn't want to come here anyway. I'll go somewhere else."

"Just like that," Friedgen said. "I think he felt that anybody would pick him up."

Alaeze lasted a little more than a month at Illinois, where former Terps assistant Locksley brought him in, but he soon was asked to leave for "personal reasons."

Friedgen had players in the past that could not rise above their old neighborhood, like running back Jason Crawford, who left school early.

"Some of these kids don't know how to be successful. We live in a society now where it's self-gratification. If it feels good we are going to do it. If it doesn't we're not going to do it. They don't want to get out of their comfort zone.

"It's tough playing football. Lifting weights. Staying on training. All the things you are supposed to do. And guys can't do it. And that makes it harder on us."

To fans on the outside, those not privy to all of the circumstances, there was hue and cry over the program losing its most promising recruit. And after a two-year wait. But Alaeze was a walking time bomb.

In the end, Friedgen knew he made the right call, despite all the talent Alaeze had. And at a position they recently lost the two former No. 1 ends, and from their backyard.

"Oh man, it hurt. Especially between him and Abiamiri. We screwed up one and had to tell the other one no," Friedgen said. "You put so much time and effort and calls. How many times he came down and visited us. I met with the parents not even in their home but my office.

"But I am to the point right now that I am no longer concerned with how many stars or points they have, but what kind of people they are. In the long run, if they don't make it here academically, it doesn't matter how good they are because you are better off with a guy that's gonna work every day to get better. But when you lose a guy after putting 3-4 years of work in him you can't replace that guy with a freshman right now. So it really becomes a big loss, a hole in the program."

The other heartbreaker, but for decidedly different reasons, was Abiamiri.

Both of his older brothers were already at Maryland. But Victor, the youngest, was clearly the best of the lot.

A budding defensive end prospect at Gilman in Baltimore, it was long expected Abiamiri would be a Terp, following brothers Rob and Paschal, a tight end and receiver, respectively, to College Park.

Many believed that Paschal, who was a fringe player at Maryland, was signed to help secure Victor, who would hopefully follow suit three years later.

Rob, a physically gifted prospect, had a solid career at Maryland and was signed by the Baltimore Ravens and made the team as a free agent.

But Victor was the gem, and he had every top program in the nation in hot pursuit including Notre Dame. Gilman had not sent a player to College Park in decades, and there seemed to be a chill between the schools that Maryland hoped would thaw with his signature.

Victor Abiamiri was set to break the ice and finally give Maryland a dominant rush end in the process. But the recruitment, which Friedgen began when Abiamiri was a sophomore and he never put as much personal time into a recruit, just two months before National Signing Day blew up in his face.

Assistant coach Sharpless, a longtime Terp who both played and coached at College Park, was an old friend of Friedgen's.

Friedgen had coached during Sharpless' days as a receiver at Maryland and later hired him to coach linebackers when he arrived as head coach in 2000.

Sharpless, who recruited Abiamiri's area in Baltimore, was old-school through and through. No matter how hot it was at two-a-days he wore the same khaki slacks to practice each day, the only coach in long pants.

But Sharpless had struggled in recent years to land top recruits. Still, Friedgen was certain the Terps would get Abiamiri, so he let Sharpless stay with him. Maybe it would boost his confidence when he committed.

"I didn't panic. I thought it would be okay," Friedgen said.

Friedgen was in Florida coaching at the Gridiron Classic and recruiting when he got a phone call from Gilman Coach Biff Poggi, who began to explain what happened. Friedgen said, "I really couldn't believe it" and went to sleep.

The next morning Friedgen called Sharpless, who denied it.

Poggi called again and said it did happen. And this time he had Abiamiri's teammate, Ambrose Wooden, verify the story to Friedgen over the phone.

Friedgen then called the Abiamiris, spoke to his mother and later Victor who told him the story.

Sharpless had given Abiamiri $300 to buy an X-Box video game, which he expressed interest in at a recruiting breakfast, a comment Sharpless overheard.

Abiamiri's mother was against it, which further compounded things when Sharpless gave him the gift.

Friedgen called Yow, told her of the situation, and called Sharpless again, this time telling him, "Don't lie to me."

"I told him you're probably done. Then the whole thing started," Friedgen said.

As a backdrop, young, up-and-coming Maryland recruiters Franklin and Locksley were kidding Sharpless at the breakfast table about the X-Box.

Sharpless went to an ATM machine and got the cash. It was a remarkable lapse of judgment, and it cost him his job.

"Locksley and Franklin were kind of the young guys, Rod an older guy, and they would ride him. But he's a fighting son-of-gun. One day I saw him nearly throw James through a wall over something else earlier," Friedgen said.

It was especially painful for Friedgen, who knew Sharpless while he was a graduate assistant at Maryland. There's a story in Maryland football lore about Sharpless and how he got his start as a player fresh out of the military.

He literally slept on the doorstep of Claiborne's office waiting to meet the coach to ask if he could walk on the team.

That he did, later earning a scholarship, followed by a coaching career at Maryland, Virginia Tech and Rutgers before returning to College Park to coach under Friedgen. He rose as high as defensive coordinator at Rutgers.

Beamer had given Sharpless a strong recommendation, and Sharpless coached some great ones at College Park, including Henderson. He didn't have a lot of success recruiting in later years, and may have succumbed to the pressure when it came to Abiamiri.

Friedgen had been on Sharpless to pick it up, but it had never gone to such an extreme. At least no one thought. It was a sad moment in the program on many levels.

"I was the first guy to see him that morning sitting on the steps of Cole with his green Army bag," Friedgen said. "I let him in the building."

The Terps had to back out of Abiamiri's recruitment immediately. There went the highest rated recruit that Friedgen had been involved with at Maryland.

The "5-star" Rivals.com All-American signed with Notre Dame, and finished his career in 2007. Abiamiri was drafted in the second round just after Terps defensive back Josh Wilson.

Friedgen said it was the toughest thing he's gone through at Maryland.

"I don't think there was any question Victor was the biggest loss," Friedgen said when asked to compare some of the losses. "Victor was a character kid, a high draft choice, a three-year starter at Notre Dame. Melvin was a very good player but Melvin played streaky, he never played the whole thing. Victor had better growth potential. Ran better. Was a better student."

The Terps got three years probation from the NCAA. But because they reported it immediately, they didn't receive tougher sanctions. Midway through his career at South Bend, Abiamiri looked into transferring to Maryland.

More recently, in 2006 during recruiting time, Friedgen had to make another judgment call. This time with the nation's No. 1 defensive tackle, also in his backyard, Marvin Austin, of Washington's Ballou High School.

Another "man-child" and seemingly just what the doctor ordered for the Terps along a starless defensive line, Austin didn't get swept up as bad as Logan-El in the recruiting process.

But he came close.

The last thing the Terps wanted in the 2007 class were more high-maintenance recruits after the Logan-El fiasco. But soon that's what Austin became.

The 6-foot-2, 280-pounder, who began his career at Coolidge High School before transferring on the eve of his senior year, early in the process called a national recruiting evaluator and asked him what the record was for scholarship offers.

Because he wanted to break it.

Austin visited campus unofficially dozens of times in the three years leading up to his commitment, from spring practices to games to men's basketball games at the Comcast Center. He would stay long after football games in the locker room, sometimes with his little sister, visiting with players and coaches.

The Terps spent more than two years with Austin as their top target. But when the time came for his official campus visit in December of 2006, he blew it off.

Austin, who became enthralled with National Champion Southern Cal, later the glitz of Florida State, and ultimately the NFL pedigree of former Cleveland Browns coach and new North Carolina head coach Butch Davis, called on the eve of his Maryland official campus. He wanted to postpone, or miss large portions of the weekend, because he hoped to attend Friendly High School's state football playoff game in Baltimore.

Not only would he miss the Friday night segment of the weekend, which included a trip to the ESPN Zone in Washington, D.C., for dinner and games with other recruits, but he wanted to leave early on Saturday to see the other prep games in Baltimore. All told, he would miss the balance of the 48-hour weekend visit, including the academic portion. But he saw no problem with that.

This was a prospect recruit coordinator Sollazzo, local recruiter Bryan Bossard, Friedgen and virtually the entire staff put years of effort into, only at the "11th hour" to get blown off for high school games.

The Terps held their ground, telling Austin that he would need to make his scheduled visit.

Later, in the final month of recruiting, the Terps cooled in their push for Austin and never rescheduled. They never visited his home.

Despite the immediate help that Austin would bring, the coaches were tired of being held hostage by petulant recruits that were just going through the motions.

In the end, the 2007 class, ranked 34th by *Rivals.com*, was loaded with blue-collar types, mostly "3-star" recruits that impressed the coaches in summer camp with their effort and not their "needs."

Austin was a recruit that traveled to spring and summer combines with countless changes of clothes, sunglasses or different hair styles. Not much different than Derrick Williams, who had a different glitzy outfit or pair of shoes for each event, be it a 40-yard dash, vertical jump, or pro shuttle.

More and more Friedgen saw recruits more concerned with style rather than substance. And he wanted no part of it.

"He got enamored with Butch Davis and his success at Miami with Warren Sapp and all that," Friedgen said of Austin. "When I had a relationship with a kid since he was a sophomore and he wouldn't take my calls? It didn't take a lot to see we weren't in there anymore. He just didn't have the common courtesy to call me and tell me. Like a guy like Lane Clelland who did that and Arrelious Benn. They both called me. They did it the right way. I'm not mad if a kid chooses another school. Just do it in a classy way."

The Terps discussed backing out of Austin's recruitment altogether but thought that may not go over well. Friedgen didn't bother watching his announcement, also on ESPN, as he had seen enough of those productions.

Austin, a physical talent with a flair for the dramatic, liked reading his press clippings too much.

"You get to a point where . . . I mean, I will show you film on [2007 nose tackle signee] Dion Armstrong and Marvin Austin and you'll go, 'Whoa.' That doesn't mean Marvin doesn't have the potential. He has all the potential in the world. But as far as a finished player right now?"

Austin never took his Maryland visit, opting for the high school games instead. Friedgen set him up with professors and deans of academic departments for his official visit weekend only to see him cancel at the last moment.

T he Terps took a body shot over the losses the year before of all the local talent, especially the seven that went to Penn State. Logan-El, Bowman, Wallace, Maybin, Bani Gbadyu, Taylor and Evan Royster.

Wallace, the cornerback/athlete from McDonough, clearly hurt the most and played and started as a true freshman.

Others, like Akeem Hebron (Georgia) and Andrew Phillips (Stanford), went elsewhere, too. But the pain was felt the most perhaps in Prince George's County, where some said the effect of Derrick Williams was being felt.

It was the perfect storm. Maryland lost ace recruiting coordinator Franklin to the NFL, and he, like his predecessor, Locksley, locked down the local area. Coupled with Penn State's re-emergence, and Larry Johnson's work in the area, not to mention Derrick Williams acting as a pied-piper.

Two losing seasons for Maryland didn't help, either. But never had it hit home so hard. Before, the Terps had their pick of the local litter.

So Friedgen set up a meeting that spring with Prince George's County high school coaches at his office to clear the air of any problems, real or perceived. Some complained that Maryland wasn't offering enough local kids or offering early enough. While some had heard of the Williams' whispers and wanted to know what it was about.

"It was kind of a bitch session," Friedgen said. "But the fact that I met with them was good. They got a chance to air some of the problems. One of the concerns was we weren't getting in their high school every year regardless of whether they had a player or not. Locksley had done that they said."

New assistant coach Bossard was ramping up, getting to know the local turf after arriving from I-AA Delaware that spring.

Friedgen heard it all, including one coach that asked, "Why don't you recruit Prince George's County for scout team players," something which would not happen. There were other misconceptions that got cleared up as well.

Friedgen said that some of the best feedback he got from the community, both in D.C. and Baltimore, was following the Alaeze ordeal, with coaches commending him for drawing the line.

"They said, 'You got our respect now. You made a stand about who you are and what you stand for.' "

Friedgen said Danny Hayes, head coach at Gwynn Park, among others, told him not to worry, that he was behind him and the program.

"It's better just to go out and meet the problem head-on," Friedgen said.

Since then the Terps have taken their clinics to the community in Prince George's County, at schools and hotels, where the coaches meet. The Terps have done it a few times a year, and get approximately 100 coaches at each event, Friedgen said.

Friedgen went out of his way to interview local high school coaches when he had staff openings. The closest one came to getting hired was Suitland coach Nick Lynch, who Friedgen said impressed him during the interview process.

O f late, the Terps have seen a shift back in their favor. In late 2006 and early 2007 they landed four junior commitments – one each from Prince George's County, Howard County, Baltimore City and Washington, D.C. – to start their 2008 recruiting class with a bang.

All are talents with Forestville receiver Kevin Dorsey and Milford Mill defensive tackle Teddy Dargan "4-star" recruits according to *Rivals.com*.

Friedgen has never groveled for 18-year olds. More and more you hear him say, "We want guys that want to be here, not guys that we have to beg to be here."

All four early pledges came without much pomp and circumstance. The players committed quietly to the staff without news conferences and drawn-out recruitments.

T here have also been misadventures and light-hearted moments for Ralph Friedgen on the recruiting trail. Like the time he suffered a flight delay on a tiny commuter plane to New Jersey in 2006 to see linebacker Alex Wujciak and others in the New York/New Jersey area.

Friedgen sat next to someone similar in size on the cramped flight, Sollazzo recalled, and as he got off the plane he barked at the top of his lungs, for all to hear, "that flight sucked."

Friedgen immediately called the football office and booked a train for his return trip.

More significantly, Friedgen says recruiting has spun out of control because of the "adulation" kids are getting now, thanks in part to the proliferation of media focusing on recruiting, as well as Internet sites and all-star games.

And that "respect," in general, has eroded, he said.

Friedgen recalled a time in 2004 when he traveled to see Jacksonville, Fla., "5-star" running back Maurice Wells for a home visit. He used valuable private jet time, but had a tie-in with a former coach at The Citadel that was coaching Wells, not to mention Wells spent part of his childhood in Maryland.

During the visit Wells wouldn't turn off the television set, which was blaring while Friedgen was trying to give his presentation. Friedgen had to ask him to turn it off. Wells finally did, grudgingly, and Friedgen turned to him and said, "You already know where you are going, right?' Wells said, 'Yeah. Ohio State.' "

Friedgen and recruiter Al Seamonson got up and left.

It hasn't worked out yet for Wells in Columbus, who was buried on the depth chart. As a sophomore Wells considered transferring, and Maryland was on his initial list.

"They are so blown out of proportion now, everyone telling them how great they are and this and that. Then you are rating them now. Who's to say what's a "3" or "4-star" kid. [National recruit analyst] Tom Lemmings is a former mailman. He doesn't know that. He doesn't know if a football is pumped up or stuffed but he's making a hell of a lot of money."

Friedgen sees prospects come into the program with higher expectations for immediate returns, "5-star" kids who if they don't excel right away "feel that they have failed," he said.

Friedgen recalled a simpler time when he was a freshman at Maryland. The varsity came to August camp followed by the freshman, which today is reversed. The ceremonial rite of passage came when the freshmen ran though the gate and onto the practice field and their names and "credentials" were announced to the team, Friedgen said.

"It was, 'Ralph Friedgen. All-county. All-met. Westchester County MVP.' And all those varsity guys sitting on the hill were like, 'Oh, we're going to kick your ass tomorrow, big boy.' "

Friedgen says recruits are so wise to the process that they "have fun telling you guys all kinds of lies." Not to mention they don't know who could be at the other end of the telephone during their nightly flood of calls.

"They don't know if you're really Keith Cavanaugh or really Jimmy Cavanaugh [the assistant coach at Virginia Tech]. And don't think a lot of guys don't really do that," Friedgen said.

Friedgen takes the Internet with a grain of salt and believes that some recruit highlight video is "doctored" to make prospects look better than they are.

"A guy may throw a pass but somebody else caught it than the guy saying he was," he says in all seriousness.

Friedgen said parents are sometimes worse than kids trying to pump up their sons, as well as their own egos.

It never was like that under his father's rule. In fact, just the opposite when his father tried to downplay his son to local media. But how times have changed.

In the end, Friedgen said it's "best to be yourself." And to get to know the kids personally as best you can and not through the Internet and other forms of media.

Friedgen skims opponent's web site message boards for information and links to relevant stories. He e-mails and text-messages prospects frequently, but sees a day that the NCAA will curtail it all, which they began in August, 2007, by abolishing text-messaging.

"The song, you know it goes 'I Gotta Be Me,' Well, I'm just going to be myself and I am just gonna try to tell these kids the truth, whether they want to believe it or not," Friedgen said.

I n the end, players with entitlement and a belief that things should be handed to them because of their star power don't always fit in Ralph Friedgen's system.

"I don't want that in my program. Because they are '5-stars' or played in an all-star game in San Antonio or whatever. When they get on the field here none of that matters. What matters is can they get it done on the field," he said.

One prospect that Friedgen took a pledge from – a "4-star" player from the South who later de-committed – well, his high school coach approached Friedgen one day at the school. He told him it wouldn't be a bad thing if he lost him. The kid had substance abuse problems and soon transferred from the college he spurned Maryland to sign with.

Friedgen can turn on the recruiting charm and add a personal touch.

In 2003, he hosted a "Champions Weekend" for his biggest recruit event of the year at his home. It was headlined by the likes of prep All-Americans Vernon Davis and Wesley Jefferson.

Once, during such a visit, Gloria Friedgen, who gives the blessing before dinner, helped the Terps get a verbal commitment. Virginia defensive end Patrick Powell was so moved by her words that he committed on the spot.

"I think that is when I am at my strongest, when I have them one-on-one," Ralph Friedgen said. "I am not a used car salesman. I tell them this is the way it is. This is what we do. I sell education.

"It's not that I don't want pro football. But to me the goal is beyond pro football. The goal is to be set up for life. If I were a parent I'd tell them what I would want to hear as a parent. If the coach came to me and I had a son and he said he's going to be in the NFL in three years, I wouldn't be interested in them."

R alph Freidgen would like to see changes in recruiting, notably the "Internet taken out of it," which he admits will never happen.

An early signing period should be added like in basketball. He said that may not happen, either, as schools in remote areas have more difficulty getting unofficial visitors to campus than urban schools.

Friedgen said there should be more contacts and evaluations in the spring, which he said would cut down on illegal "bumps" later on. And that more of the process should be put back in the hands of the high school coaches.

He'd also like to see the proposed five years of eligibility rule go in effect, as then coaches wouldn't have to recruit as many kids. He's been pushing for that for years but it appears a long shot.

Friedgen complains that some of the all-star games "blackmail kids" to play in their games in order to get higher recruiting grades if they wait, while the practices and hotels at the game sites are full of "runners" representing everything from colleges to agents. He said such a group got ahold of Alaeze and tried to get him to open up his recruitment.

Street agents are a group that Friedgen dislikes just as much. He had a former team manager try to burrow his way into the program and befriend recruits and players, attempting to funnel them to agents. He was banished from the program.

Friedgen requires that recruits sign waivers when they arrive that they will not visit adult clubs or drink alcohol while on their official campus visit. He said it helps kids overcome peer pressure by not having to go out or off campus, which he said is ideal. He does not let his host players drive recruits during their weekend visit, either.

R alph Friedgen always keeps his sense of humor even in the sometimes seamy world of recruiting.

He once was at a league meeting and was asked, along with other coaches, to share a favorite recruiting tactic, which he thought was absurd to share with his rivals. When they got to N.C. State's coach Chuck Amato, the former Wolfpack coach got the crowd roaring when he replied, "All the good things I thought we did they just outlawed."

Among the all time recruiting tales Friedgen tells is one that involved a player during the Randy White era at Maryland, a player Friedgen called "the greatest rags-to-riches story to ever play at College Park, without a doubt."

Flushing (N.Y.) athlete David Vissaggio's tale touched Friedgen like few others. Vissaggio never played high school football, only at the club level.

Friedgen was a graduate assistant at the time and recruiting had just ended. The coaches found an 8-mm film that had fallen behind the radiator in their offices at Cole Field House. Vissaggio paid to have a highlight film prepared and sent it to coaches across the country, Friedgen said.

"The [town] butcher was the coach of the team. And it was like *Conan the Barbarian*. I mean, he was like just killing people," Friedgen recalled of the highlight film. "This was his shot."

The coaches were so intrigued with what they saw on the tape that, with one scholarship left, they brought the defensive lineman to campus for a face-to-face meeting.

"He was like 6-1, 245-pounds. They offered him a scholarship and he broke down crying. Well, he was the most intense individual that I ever met," Friedgen said.

Later, while on the staff at The Citadel, Friedgen watched the Maryland-Clemson game on tape and saw Vissaggio get his knee "torn up, yet still play three more plays before they took him out with nothing left in his knee. You ask Randy White. You ask anybody on that team who was the toughest individual they ever met and they will tell you him."

"Talk about a rags-to-riches story. He was an important guy, a starter on coach Claiborne's teams that won. He was a wild man."

R alph Friedgen has had countless "feel-good" recruiting stories at Maryland, including one player that is busy blossoming into a star.

Receiver Darrius Heyward-Bey, who broke out in 2006 as a redshirt freshman and was named Freshman All-America by *Rivals.com*, was a highly-touted recruit and track star coming out of high school. But he had confidence issues as a true freshman in 2005 and was on the ropes about sticking with a college football career.

A year later, after countless one-on-one sessions with Friedgen and his wife, the 6-foot-3 talent with 4.3 track speed developed into Maryland's top offensive threat. His two dramatic touchdown catches and runs against Miami highlighted his break-out season, while just months before he wasn't sure if he would stick it out.

The Friedgens became close to his mother, Vivian, who sang Ralph's favorite song, "My Way," with Gloria during her son's official campus visit.

Heyward-Bey entered the 2007 season on several All-America watch lists.

Maybe no recruit's home visit fit Ralph Friedgen's 'MO' better, and summed up the man's style, than the one he had with quarterback Jordan Steffy in 2003 at his Lancaster, Pa., home.

Straight-forward and to the point. Classic Ralph Friedgen.

"That was one of the shortest home visits I ever had. Twenty five minutes. Because it all had been said," Friedgen said.

"I said to Jordan and his mom, 'We've been through this 1,000 times. I am going to tell you one more time. These are the reasons you should come to Maryland. 'Bang, bang, bang.' I'm not going to bother you anymore. Let's go.' "

A few weeks later the "3-star" signal-caller, Friedgen's projected starter in 2007, chose the Terps.

"And you know, I think sometimes you are better off doing that," Friedgen said.

13

WAR STORIES

R alph Friedgen loves a good story.
His life is full of rich and colorful ones, some that grow larger with each year.

And he loves telling them, sometimes to players to make a point, others to boosters and fans while entertaining a crowd.

Friedgen is candid, fun-loving, and has long had a mischievous side even to this day. That set the stage for a lifetime of tales, some fantastic, which have followed in his wake. Many are hard to visualize considering the man that he is today.

One of the favorites from his childhood involved a summer job.

His cousin, Stoddard, got Friedgen a gig replacing the roof at the General Motors plant in Tarrytown, N.Y. The work day was scheduled to run 5 a.m. to 2 p.m., and they would be "out before it got too hot and we'd be able to go out at night," Friedgen thought.

It paid $7 an hour, a good wage in the 1960s. Stoddard served as tin smith.

The "macho" Friedgen, as his cousin called him, "came out like a house on fire" ripping the old tiles up. Meanwhile, the other workers paced themselves.

Soon the sun came up, hit Friedgen in the face, and he was done. Friedgen lasted three days after the rude awakening on the new job. He said it probably helped get him into coaching, and away from hard labor.

"I was going to get a college degree because I wasn't going to do that crap my whole life," Friedgen said. "When that sun came out I was done. That damn black stuff got on your legs, your pants, onto your skin. Man, it was awful."

Friedgen quickly moved to bartending later that summer.

Stoddard is tied to Friedgen and the 1983 season when Friedgen was an assistant at Maryland. The Terps faced Tennessee in the Citrus Bowl, a time Friedgen showed his great attention to detail.

Esiason was the quarterback and Stoddard said that he attended practices and stood with NFL scouts, including one from the Cincinnati Bengals, while they watched the lefty work in drills.

Tennessee completed a pass and the Maryland coaches exploded on the sideline. The Volunteers' receiver got open easily and caught the pass that set up the go-ahead touchdown. After the game, Friedgen said he rushed to his hotel room to see the replay. Moments later he screamed to Stoddard, "I knew it. Son-of-a-guns had 12 men on the field."

A year later, when Maryland met Tennessee again, this time in the 1984 Sun Bowl, the Vols' coaches joked with Friedgen, asking him, "Are you ready for our 12th man?"

Friedgen fired back, "Are you ready for mine?"

"But he was so fit to be tied. He was so mad," Stoddard said.

One of Friedgen's favorite tales from the early years at Maryland also came on the Sun Bowl trip in El Paso, Texas.

During practice week both teams were invited to a dude ranch for a Western style show and barbeque. They should have known something was odd about the trip when on one of the first nights bowl officials took the players to a strip club.

The Terps loaded the bus and soon found themselves in a desolate area. The bus stopped abruptly and suddenly there appeared a handful of "banditos."

Friedgen was in a car behind the bus, which assistant coach Greg Williams drove. Assistant Dick Portee was in the front seat and Jimmy Cavanaugh was next to Friedgen in the back.

"It's getting dark. Tumble-weed is blowing by," Friedgen said. "And suddenly the buses stopped."

In an instant, graduate assistant Sollazzo and assistant coach Gib Romaine were yanked off the bus and put in handcuffs. They were put in the back of a pickup truck, which had also suddenly appeared. The "banditos," as Friedgen called them, had bandanas covering their faces and guns in their hands. Soon they were grabbing players and taking them off the bus.

No one knew that it was a gag put on by the bowl organizers.

Glover, the standout offensive lineman, had hopped out of his seat thinking the team had arrived at dinner. One of the banditos put a .32 pistol under his nose, and Glover jumped back in his seat and cut his eye, which later required stitches.

Sollazzo heard one coach, Romaine, shout, "I got a wife and kid at home. Don't take me."

"And there were players going under the seats of the bus and all," Sollazzo recalled. "I was scared at first."

The banditos told the players that they were looking for Donald 'Turkey' Brown, who played for Oklahoma the year before in the Sun Bowl before transferring to Maryland. They wanted him because "he knocked up my sister, and we want him," they told the team.

"So they took Turkey. Everybody pointed, 'He's right there,' " Friedgen said. "So they had Turkey, David and Gib Romaine."

The pickup truck took off and bolted across the desert with the Terps in the back bouncing around. A police car soon appeared, and right on the pickup's tail. The truck fishtailed around and the banditos jumped out and began firing their guns, one in the direction of Friedgen's car.

"I'm thinking Greg Williams is dead," Friedgen said. "The other guys didn't duck. For me, I'm from New York. If someone points a gun at me, I'm ducking."

As it turned out, they were off-duty policemen with blanks in the guns. And it was part of an over-the-top gag. Not something seen at bowl games anymore.

"Actually, an article in *Sports Illustrated* was called 'No Fun In The Sun,' and it told how stupid it was," Sollazzo said. "But I just remember coach Friedgen laughing his ass off. He always tells that story because I was one of the guys torn off the bus. But nobody, not even coach Ross, knew it wasn't real."

The high-jinks didn't end there.

Later that night was a talent show between the Terps and the Volunteers. Wildman linebacker Chuck Faucette was the first to perform, and he did a rendition of Chuck Berry's song "Johnny B. Goode."

Little did the Terps know that Tennessee star running back Johnny Jones' theme song was "Johnny B. Goode." Faucette was dancing and singing, he knew all the words. But the Vols' were incensed.

One of the Tennessee players did an imitation of coach Johnny Majors, while Terps lineman Ben Jefferson did one of Ross, which didn't go over well with the head man.

Finally, things got heated when a Tennessee player slapped the faces of a few Terps players as part of his skit.

"Bobby finally just had it with this whole thing. He got on the bus and said, 'I am on the bus,' " Friedgen said. "Shortly after that the thing broke up but it almost broke up into a fight. Later, Ben went to Bobby and apologized."

That night, Terps assistant coach George Foussekis, who knew a DEA agent that lived in the area, told his friend of the incident.

"This DEA agent said, 'Shoot, if I had gone on that trip and been in the bus, I would have blown those guys away as soon as they got on the bus.' Then it could have been really ugly," Friedgen said.

Friedgen laughed when he looked back on the zany day.

"But the thing is, Bobby Ross didn't like it because he never knew any of this was going to happen."

Friedgen recalled a dinner party that week, at a ranch, for the coaches and the official travel party. They were served "warm Mexican beer" and margaritas followed by a meal.

"Let's just say it was a fairly lengthy cocktail hour," Friedgen said.

The guests were taken in the back afterwards where the host had a bull ring.

Things got more interesting.

"Oh, this was a great bowl game. One of the best you have ever been to because of all this stuff," Friedgen said.

They saw a mangy-looking bull with one horn down and one horn up.

Soon, bowl officials were in the ring fighting the bull from behind a cage.

The participants had to sign a waiver if they wanted to enter the ring and many did. Several coaches jumped in and urged Friedgen to join them.

Todd Goodman, the Terps equipment manager, was, as Friedgen described, "short and with thick, thick glasses. Maybe the worst athlete I have ever met in my life. Todd was going to go fight the bull. It was the funniest thing I have ever seen in my life," Friedgen said.

Friedgen said the bull had fought three people already "but as soon as Todd walked in the bull thought he could win. He turned and started looking at Todd, stomped his feet a couple times, and he tore ass off for Todd. But Todd hadn't even got set yet. He panicked, threw his cape up in the air and hit the dirt, and the bull runs right over his back. I was crying laughing. The sponsors went in, got the bull's attention, and Todd had a bull's footprint right on his back. We were just crying."

A Tennessee graduate assistant was the next to go in, Friedgen said, and got drilled by the bull. Friedgen said he "slithered off the wall."

"I said, 'This place is sick, man,' " Friedgen recalled.

Ron Zook, at the time an assistant at Tennessee, later saw Friedgen. He asked him how the GA made out and Zook replied that "he peed blood for six weeks."

It was Sollazzo's – Friedgen's graduate assistant – first bowl trip. He went out every night with the players in Juarez.

"They don't make bowl trips like that anymore. No they don't," Sollazzo said.

On another bowl trip, this time to Hawaii for the 1982 Aloha Bowl, came another memorable tale that went down in Terps' lore.

The night before the team left, while at a party where the players hosted recruits, Bobby Gunderman reportedly slipped on the ice and cut his hand. Because the team was leaving on Sunday he had to wait until Monday to get stitched up, so Gunderman had to take a separate flight.

Gunderman had a connecting flight in New York but got on a flight to Venezuela instead. In flight, when he noticed no one was speaking English, Gunderman realized he was on the wrong flight. And with no passport. It took him two days to get out, Friedgen said, and he finally showed up on Wednesday of the practice week in Hawaii.

"The kids were going nuts. 'Wrong way Bobby Gunderman' is what they called him after that," Friedgen said.

Sollazzo said that in those days Friedgen would mess with him.

Sollazzo prepared the practice scripts each day. If one player was lined up an inch off "Friedgen would jump me," he said.

" 'David. David. David. Get that guy lined up right, would you?' " Sollazzo recalled him barking.

One day in camp at the Sun Bowl, Sollazzo, single at the time, admitted he stayed out past curfew the night before. At practice the next day, three times his scout team lined up incorrectly.

"Well, to be honest with you, I don't think I went to bed that night," Sollazzo said. "I came right from the street to practice and he comes running over to me, rips the script out of my hand, looks at the script, and threw it at me. I had the script from the day before. That's why every time he broke the huddle I was lined up in the wrong defense, a completely different split. I learned my lesson then."

Sollazzo recalled a time in 1986, during a scrimmage, when the coaches pitted the offense against the defense in the final practice of two-a-days. They called it the "Christians against the Lions."

The scout team was the Christians while the first team, the Lions, was led by quarterback Neil O'Donnell. The Lions, naturally, expected to dominate. True to Friedgen's competitiveness, he bet Sollazzo a case of beer that the scout team couldn't hold them to two touchdowns.

"That night, for whatever reason, the scout team played out of their ass," Sollazzo said. "I remember coach Ross was fired up. We held them to one touchdown. We had a goal-line stand and another time they had a fourth and one and we stopped them. They had a tough time scoring.

"The next morning I was sitting in the GA's office but who comes walking in but Ralph, who says 'Here's your case of beer.' I wasn't even going to say anything because he was pissed off. But that was a very rewarding day.

"That next morning he showed his brighter side, no doubt. He said, 'It was a bad showing for the offense last night.' "

Sollazzo is tied to another of Friedgen's favorite recruiting stories.

A 6-3, 225-pound defensive lineman out of Harrison High School, Sollazzo remembered the day, in December, 1972, when he arrived home from high school. His mother had the news that "Coach Friedgen had called from The Citadel and they liked my tape and they really liked you."

Friedgen spotted Sollazzo on film after scouting another Harrison player.

"That kind of brings tears to my eyes," Sollazzo said years later when discussing his late mother and the day of his big offer. "Talk about going down memory lane. That was a hell of a memory to be honest with you. She was so excited."

The Citadel, Bridgeport and Delaware were involved. But when Friedgen called it was over as far as Sollazzo was concerned. Friedgen's father was the athletic director at Harrison when Sollazzo played there.

Friedgen's recruiting style was the same as it was now, the coach always "telling it like it was." But he showed his softer side, too. Friedgen and wife Gloria took

Sollazzo out for a lobster dinner in Charleston. It was Sollazzo's first lobster. He was thoroughly impressed.

Sollazzo went home with plenty to think about, especially a military college experience. But Friedgen was a step ahead of him, bringing Sollazzo in for his official visit over Christmas break, thus no cadets, and no one in uniform, was around.

"That was a good tactic he used on me, one I used later when I was an assistant at The Citadel," Sollazzo said.

The two have had a strong relationship ever since.

"It's the best thing that ever happened to me, that I went there, because now I am here working for him after developing that relationship," said the 50-year old Sollazzo.

Nothing compared to the time Sollazzo, after committing to Friedgen, set off to Charleston to watch a spring scrimmage. It helped create their bond.

Sollazzo, traveling with a high school teammate, missed his connecting flight in Charlotte, N.C.

Friedgen was waiting for Sollazzo at the airport in Charleston. The airline asked Sollazzo if they could take him, by limousine, the three hours to Charleston. Sollazzo never thought to call Friedgen, who he figured would get word that the flight was delayed.

Not the case.

Six hours after the flight was expected to arrive, Sollazzo pulled up and found Friedgen waiting by his car at the curb. And with a nasty look on his face.

"He just turned and started walking towards the car. Not one word," Sollazzo said. "Not a word was said from the airport to the campus at The Citadel."

Another recruiting tale came during Friedgen's first year at College Park as head coach, when on an official visit Randy Starks's mother couldn't eat her steak without her favorite sauce, "Heinz 57."

So graduate assistant John Donovan slipped out of the Inn & Conference Center and ran to Shoppers Food Warehouse, grabbed a bottle, and was back in time for the dinner and, later, the commitment followed.

One of the wackiest things that happened to Friedgen on the football field was the day Randy White punched him in the face.

It happened when Friedgen was the defensive coordinator of the freshman team while serving as a graduate assistant. The Terps were playing heated in-state rival Navy. The team would send seven players onto the NFL led by White and quarterback Bob Avellini.

The game was in Annapolis and Friedgen knew something was up when five Terrapin touchdowns were called back on penalties. On the last one, Avellini threw a touchdown pass to Mike Modzelewski, who got hit after the play. He popped up from the cheap shot and hit the culprit but got tossed from the game. The Terps punted on the next play and after the returner ran out of bounds, several Terps jumped him on the sideline.

"They got him over there and they are beating him over the head with his own helmet. And I ran over there to stop them and Randy [White] punches me right in the face. No, it wasn't an accident. That was the only game they lost all year," Friedgen said.

Friedgen told freshman coach Buddy Beardmore after the game that they "needed to get the hell out of here." Beardmore called the game and when the Navy players stood at attention, the Maryland players got in their faces and taunted them.

"That's how intense that rivalry was," Friedgen said.

The Terps and Middies played again, the freshmen teams that is, but the varsity ended their series not long after.

"I remember I went home that night and had a date with Gloria that I didn't show up for. She comes over to the apartment at about 1 in the morning and I opened the door. My eye is shut and she says, 'What happened?' I said, 'Randy White hit me in the eye. I didn't feel like going out.' "

Friedgen is a quote machine ready to pop off at anytime even with the media present. And sometimes before he thinks about what he is saying.

After '9/11,' when asked a day later if he would practice for the coming game against West Virginia, which was eventually postponed, Friedgen responded, "Well, they're practicing up in Morgantown."

Said Dennard Wilson of Friedgen's tunnel vision that week, when the nation was on edge but he, more or less, dismissed it:

"We thought he was crazy."

"I am just a very focused guy," Friedgen said. "When I make a statement like on '9/11' and call it a distraction, in my mind it was. I wasn't trying to be an asshole. I was there to beat West Virginia. If they are practicing, I'm practicing. If you tell me you are going to drop the A-bomb tomorrow, I would probably be thinking the same way. It's just the way I am and people can't relate to that sometimes.

"Now that I look back on it, it was pretty insensitive. But it's just the way I am," Friedgen added. "You just get in your own little world. I was just trying to get a game-plan together. Let's go. People just don't understand our world. It's such a different world."

Some of the players had family members in New York and New Jersey, some they could not contact immediately in the aftermath. Like Fowler, who had a brother in New York City. No incident better illustrated Friedgen's incredible focus, and it quickly went down in Friedgen lore.

On '9/11' the coaches were in a staff meeting game-planning for West Virginia. After the first plane went into the tower, one of the administrative assistants entered the room to tell the coaches that a plane crashed in New York. Friedgen kept going.

A few minutes later she came in to tell the coaches that a plane just crashed into the Pentagon. He kept going.

Not until after 1 p.m., when the players with family in New York came to express concern, notably Fowler and Sal Aragona, did it start to sink in for the head coach.

It was a big prep day during game week, and Friedgen was intent on playing the game. "Afterwards I saw what he was doing. You can't stop being what you are," Dennard Wilson said.

Said one assistant:

"I think the entire nation took a step back after '9/11' but he didn't. Now, I think afterwards he did, as he is very patriotic and it affected him. But I also think his tunnel vision was just pure and so intense right there that he didn't take the time to let it happen."

The coaches said they were "barely functioning" that day, but "he didn't even miss a beat." Some were unnerved. Some said there should have been more reflection on the event as it unfolded.

R alph Friedgen seemingly never knows what's going to come out of his mouth, which has led to some edgy moments.

After the D.C. sniper episode, which gripped the metropolitan area in 2002 leaving 10 dead, Friedgen said, in the wake of a rash of football injuries, "I got more guys going down than the D.C. sniper."

He practiced through the shooting spree. Players such as Wike said: "We were kinda looking at the top of buildings, between plays, for a white van all the time."

Players spoke of keeping their helmets on their heads on the sidelines. They were making jokes but inside some were scared to go to College Park gas stations to fill their tanks.

Former assistant Franklin said there was not a lot of time to be "sitting around thinking" under Friedgen.

"At the time it was a little edgy," he said of practicing during the drama. "But people have short memories. If you take a few days off and go lose the next two games, well there is a very small window. And opportunity opens and closes real quick and Ralph knows that. I learned that going through the first fire with Ron Vanderlinden."

Friedgen said he asked one of the state troopers that guard him, Butch Rhoderick, for bullet-proof vests for everyone to wear on the practice field, telling him, "I'm a pretty easy target now."

The tornado that hit campus in 2001, which killed two people and packed winds of between 175-200 miles an hour, hit as the players were about to practice.

Tackling sleds were thrown from one side of the field to another. Friedgen watched the funnel coming toward the team house, seemingly right at his office, hoping it would pass. Blackney got Friedgen moving first.

"I was in his office and I saw it come right up over the stadium, from Route 193, and I said to Ralph, 'Get out of here. Run.' And I know he ran a 4.7 (40-yard dash) because I know I was a 4.6 [laugh] and he was right on my heels."

They all shoved into the coaches' locker room in the basement of the team house, "with Friedgen sprinting the fastest we've ever seen him move," Wike said.

Newscasts reported the storm might not be over. But Friedgen was back in his office checking the Doppler radar on his computer with plans of going back though nightfall had arrived.

"Finally a bunch of the seniors that were on the [Terrapin] Council went up to his office and said, 'Coach, you know a bunch of people died on campus. The place is a mess. We don't think it is a good idea to go out and practice tonight.' He [Friedgen] was, 'No, wait. The radar . . . everything is fine. It's blowing right past us.' "

Friedgen relented and the players drew a sigh of relief. It was rare when he cancelled practice.

The tennis bubble at the golf course, where the Terps practiced during inclement weather, was destroyed. The new Fine Arts center on campus lost more than 150 windows, while some temporary buildings were destroyed. Amazingly, though 50 were injured, more didn't perish as it made a direct hit on campus.

"It was a little surprising," Blackney said of Friedgen trying to keep practice scheduled so soon after the tornado. "But he's so single-minded when it comes to that. There's not heat, not sun . . . we're going to push through, get the mail there no matter what. It's always business as usual."

Rychleski said Friedgen's focus is second to none. He compared it to one of the all-time coaching greats.

"There are stories about Vince Lombardi driving down the road, parking his car, walking in his house but a half hour later he realizes he was in the wrong house. That happens. That's his whole focus."

Rychleski said that there are things Friedgen takes a little more time to digest before he comes to reason and does the appropriate thing.

Rychleski cited an example at the Champs Sports Bowl when Friedgen called a Christmas morning team meeting for 7 a.m., after telling the team it would have the day off.

Rychleski was sitting with his boss on the bus returning from practice when he slipped in a suggestion. To hold the meeting on Christmas Eve. The coaches and their families, some with young children, were hoping to spend the day together, many at Disney World.

"I asked him if we could do the meeting right after practice, right after we got back, you know, get it out of the way," Rychleski said. "And he jumped me, snapped at me. But it was about a 30-minute bus ride so by the time I told him about it till we got back, he realized, 'Hey, we can get this thing done right after we got off the bus.' Everything worked out great.

"But being a head football coach now, as Frank Beamer found out this year [after the Virginia Tech campus shooting], there are outside things. You got other things in the community you have to deal with. You have to be careful."

Friedgen pulls one-liners from his collection that few but he could get away with.

Friedgen would go on bar sweeps in downtown College Park to make sure his players weren't out past curfew. Later, he would tell reporters "how provocative the co-eds dress these days."

Friedgen is legendary for his over-the-top comments and even putting his foot in his mouth.

In the spring of 2006, at a Terrapin Club event when the topic of trying to add Navy as an annual series came up, and why the Academy couldn't decide, he quipped: "No wonder we can't win over in Iraq. We can't even vote on this game, for goodness sakes."

"That's what people love about him," Blackney said. "His candidness. He's not a slick-talking, smooth dressing, thousand-dollar suit, $800 dollar alligator shoes, silver-tongued used car salesman that can charm you out of anything. Ralph is refreshing because on the other side are so many angling, smooth-talking kinds of guys.

"With Ralph, you are going to get directness, and you are going to get substance. And you always know exactly where you stand."

The Council went to see Friedgen after the three tragic events occurred on campus in his first two years. They said it proved that the Council could have a say in things, which was a key early as they got comfortable with their new coach.

Sollazzo said it is part of Friedgen's fabric and working for him.

"You have to know everything that is ingrained in me as a coach I got from coach Friedgen," Sollazzo said. "I felt the same exact way as he did. When I walked out on the practice field it didn't faze me. I didn't even think twice about the sniper. Maybe I should have, maybe that is stupidity on my part, but that was ingrained in me."

It's all about the game for Friedgen, and the singular goal of preparing to win.

"Football is everything. He brainwashed me in a good way for a focus like that. When it was time to walk out on the practice field you had to put everything else aside," Sollazzo said.

Friedgen rarely heaps lavish praise on his assistants. He uses one word instead of 10. As with most everything, he says exactly what's on his mind at the time.

His harshest comments came after the embarrassing Thursday night loss at Virginia Tech in 2004. Some of it was directed at himself. But he's got more humorous ones than dark ones.

Friedgen lets loose at his Georgia lake house, especially at his Fourth of July party. When a booster once asked him, in mixed company, about local topless clubs he responded to the crowd, "I don't want just that. I want all-nude."

Friedgen can be disarming and funny. He has no problem poking fun at himself, be it his waistline or hairline. Nothing is sacred. He is such a large man that when things happen out of the ordinary they get magnified.

One day at practice Bryant saw Friedgen get stung by a bee. Friedgen dropped immediately to the ground and rolled around thinking he was getting swarmed. It was the first spring with Friedgen, and everyone was intimidated by their new coach. But to see him dancing around, and on the ground pulling his shoe off after he got stung on the foot, it was a new experience, and something which helped ease the tension.

After the tornado hit College Park, players and coaches joked for months about the reaction of their coach, who ran down the hallways "yelling and screaming for everyone to hit the deck." They had never seen him move like that.

Friedgen even has a favorite "fish story." And it's true. The proof hangs on the wall of his basement at his lake home, above the bar.

A 48-pound citation Jack Crevalle, which he caught off the coast of Florida with his uncle in the 1980s. Even this event led to a story.

"They were kidding me because it was hotter than hell. I had this blister on my hand from catching that fish, sweating. Of course by the time I got him in I was miserable and they were all laughing," he said.

His uncle told him to get it measured as it could be a record. His uncle urged him to get it stuffed but it "set me back like $400 or $500, which was a lot of money in those days."

Friedgen fought the fish for 40 minutes.

Now he kicks back in a more relaxed way on Lake Oconee, angling for hybrid stripers from his boat. It's become one of his favorite pastimes after hip surgery slowed his golf game. In the spring of 2007 he went bone-fishing in Great Exuma.

The players love the light-hearted moments with their coach, some at his expense since he's often riding them. They like a little payback.

At Peach Bowl practices in Atlanta, fullback Ricardo Dickerson ran a drill out of the backfield and plowed into Friedgen, knocking him over. After he got up and collected himself, Friedgen was fired up. The players loved it.

From a coaches' standpoint, there were few light-hearted moments like the one at the Orange Bowl, in his suite on New Year's Eve, just days before the game. Friedgen danced, to the delight of unsuspecting assistants and boosters, who had never seen that side of him.

Friedgen has had many favorite players over the years, few as adored as quarterback Esiason, who has remained involved with the program and donated both time and money since Friedgen took over.

Friedgen recalled a game against Miami in the early 1980's when Esiason came to the sideline and over-ruled his play call.

"Bobby Ross asked what's the play and I said, 'Hell if I know,'" Friedgen said.

"Boomer just drew one up in the dirt. Next thing you know, he throws the touchdown. It was just like that."

Some of his greatest years were spent coaching the offensive line in the early 1980s. Ralph and Gloria hosted the line for dinners at their home in the summertime. One of his linemen, former walk-on transfer Doug Miller from Montgomery

College, suited up for the opener against Penn State. Not an exceptional athlete, Miller was a competitor. Miller was the No. 2 center and the Terps were trailing. He came up to Friedgen and tugged at his shirt.

"He said, 'Are you gonna let me in this thing or what?' " Friedgen said.

Friedgen put the second team line in the game and the Terps went down the field and scored. After that he rotated Miller in every few series. And that's when he had standouts Edwards, Solt, Glover, Lenny Lynch and Maarleveld. They all starred, but Friedgen had a fondness for Miller, who later became a coach. It may have gone back to Friedgen's belief in playing kids that may not be as talented, but that wanted it the most. Back to his own playing experience at Maryland.

The offensive line would crack him up.

Some of the players didn't always make it to class, later telling Friedgen "Don't worry. We're here all year and we'll make it up in the summer," Friedgen recalled.

During the season (this was a different time), the players hunted in the morning, returned to campus to lift weights, watched tape, practiced, and then lifted more weights "because they had to get their 'guns' looking good for Saturday. Then they'd work an extra hour after Thursday's practice so their arms would look good for game day," Friedgen said. "But they loved to play football. But, then again, Maryland was a different place back then. Kevin [Glover] went to class but the rest were 'different.' "

When asked about those days Edwards, who coaches at Damascus High School, confirmed the story of hunting in the morning on school days. They woke early, shot ducks, geese, squirrels and other small game at Edward's uncle's farm in Beltsville, and returned to campus in time for their favorite cook at the dining hall to prepare their game.

Once, when Friedgen was riding them especially hard, the linemen had personalized hats made with a special greeting for their coach. They entered their position meeting wearing the hats, which had the image of a hand "flipping the bird," and lowered their heads in Friedgen's direction. After the initial shock, their coach had to chuckle.

Going back to his Murray State days, Friedgen had a funny story there as well.

He had a player that stole a steak from a grocery store. Friedgen had to take him to jail.

Fellow assistant Beamer had it set up with the judge that the player would get off. Or so Friedgen thought.

Friedgen took him downtown but the judge gave him five days in jail. He served his sentence over Thanksgiving break. The player's nickname was 'Earthquake.'

"We went to the prison and there were dogs, German Shepherds barking all over the place. He was a big-old tight end, 6-5, 230-pounds, and I remember taking him in there and the guy let me walk back there past the cells, showed him his cell, and the next thing it closes shut, 'clink.' I tell him, 'Quake,' I'll pick you up Sunday.' He spent Thanksgiving in the clink."

Another story stands out for Friedgen and O'Leary from their Georgia Tech days.

They were on their way to see a recruit in Matawan, N.J., during the winter in a basketball game.

Not long into their flight to Newark they received word that the landing gear was not functioning. A crew member came out of the cabin and lifted a section of the floorboard near them.

"George says, 'Crap, the landing gear ain't going down,' " Friedgen recalled.

"We started shaking hands. He said, 'Good luck,' " O'Leary said.

"All of a sudden I see the captain leaving the cockpit to go to the back. I said, 'Ralph, we got problems.' The landing gear wasn't locked in so we had to bank over Westchester and Bridgeport, and all these areas, to check the landing gear out. So they were giving us emergency landing instructions."

Friedgen had grudgingly gone on the trip at O'Leary's insistence. They were in the air an extra hour-and-a-half "burning off fuel in case we crash-land," Friedgen said.

"Right before the plane was going down we started to say good luck and he goes, 'Screw you and your good luck. I shouldn't even be on this damn trip,' " O'Leary said.

The plane was to make an emergency landing at Newark. The coaches were in the second row. The crew told them to bend down.

"Then the flight attendant says to us, 'Now, when we hit the land everybody stay calm. Stay in your seats.' I said, 'Lady, when we hit land I am out of here,' " Friedgen said.

Friedgen was at a window seat and could see fire trucks on the runway. They managed to land without crashing but the passenger in front of him "peed his pants," Friedgen said. The flight attendant told Friedgen that in her 22 years of flying it was only her second landing without gear.

The Terps ended up getting their man (the recruit), but two years later he quit the team. Friedgen still shakes his head about the trip he shouldn't have been on in the first place.

O'Leary's favorite tale from their recruiting days came after trips to Miami for jamborees. O'Leary dropped Friedgen off at his home and told Gloria, with the kids in the driveway, the same thing every time: 'Hey, Gloria. Ralph's one heck of a dancer.' "

And he'd leave on that note.

"A half-hour later I'd get a call from Ralph and he'd say, 'Will you tell her that I wasn't dancing?' " O'Leary said.

Friedgen recalled the times O'Leary, at recruiting stops, bought a few cases of beer and loaded his hotel bathtub with cans. He invited other coaches over for free "cold ones." While they were indulging O'Leary hit prospects' homes by night. He would do it every trip, Nassau and Suffolk counties followed by New York City, making hay while the competition drank.

The two trekked to Florida for jamborees where they'd recruit and play golf by day and hit Miami by night, sometimes country and western dance spots. These were the trips after which O'Leary would kid Gloria about Ralph's "dance moves."

R alph Friedgen had a favorite play as well, the 'bumarooskie,' which he used under Jerry Claiborne.

It called for a quick break from the huddle and for the players to simulate a quick kick. The center would yell "quick kick" but he would snap the ball to the up-back. The up-back would bend over, put the ball between his legs, and hand it to the player behind him. He hung tight at the line before running in one direction while the line went the other way.

Friedgen had the play at The Citadel under Ross, and they called it once but it failed. The next day in film study Friedgen was in a particularly bad mood and his players started laughing. He began to tear into them before one of the players told the coach that a guard, "not the smartest guys in the world," said that when he heard the center yell "quick kick," he responded, "No, this is 'bumarooskie.'"

"So the play broke down right there. The dumb son-of-a-gun didn't even know it was a fake play," Friedgen said.

Because of Friedgen's fatherly persona, wanting to give kids second chances, its led to incidents that are also part of his lore. Some good, some not so good.

But many contain a lesson, nonetheless.

When the Terps went to the Peach Bowl in Atlanta and dominated SEC power Tennessee, their road trip to Atlanta was not without incident.

Senior defensive tackle William Shime, a transfer student from Cameroon, Africa, who played at nearby Bishop McNamara High School, took a fancy to an older woman he met on the team's first night in Atlanta.

Harrison, an Atlanta native whose father owned some adult night clubs, served as unofficial "tour guide" for the team. That had its pros and cons.

On one of the first days, at a bowl luncheon recognizing the seniors, Shime's name was called but he never came to the stage. In fact, no one saw Shime for the next 24 hours.

Shime had been caught the night before breaking curfew. He said he had been calling his family in Cameroon.

"Then at the banquet, when he didn't come up, I accepted his bowl watch when they tell me he's in the bathroom," Friedgen said.

Shime bolted with the woman and, when Friedgen found out and Shime finally turned up, he was suspended for the game. Friedgen put him on a one-way bus back to College Park. Shime was so smitten that at the first stop he jumped off the bus and returned to his friend.

Defensive end Durand Roundtree, a team leader, approached Friedgen and told him, "Shime's bulling you."

Some of the others players knew it, and that was the last straw as Friedgen soon learned the full story.

This left the Terps in a tight spot as already they were down starting nose tackle C.J. Feldheim, who suffered a knee injury at Duke and was lost for the season. Now his replacement, from an already thin line, was gone. Adding to their woes, Dennard Wilson was battling a stomach virus.

From a teaching standpoint, Grabenstein, who once taught at Good Counsel High School in Wheaton, Md., said Friedgen shined, even though he put his team in a tough spot in its biggest game of the season.

"Ralph is consistent whether you are black or white, star or reserve," Grabenstein said. "He is going to be consistent and fair, and he has that reputation that he will look you in the eye and that is what he had to do with Shime. Because Shime kinda thought he was above the law in that situation."

Shime was one of Grabenstein's summer workers at his investment firm, and Grabenstein was the only person Shime would talk to while he was having his episode in Atlanta.

To this day, Shime, who works for another investment firm in the area, has not received a Peach Bowl ring. Friedgen refused to give him one because he did not participate in the game.

"He did screw his team," Grabenstein said. "Ultimately, I think he did learn a lesson. You have responsibilities to other people. Ralph helped him learn that."

Said Wike, who was worried about going into the game with walk-ons up front: "He told us if you mess up he would send you home on a bus from the bowl game no matter who it was. Shime did that and he was gone. The attitude on the team was we don't need him. He thought it was more important to do what he did rather than help the team out. Coach Friedgen did the right thing."

Friedgen and his staff pulled a coup in the game with Shime AWOL, while they also lost star defensive tackle Randy Starks on the first series to a groin pull.

Friedgen and defensive line coach Sollazzo juggled the line at the last minute, going with undersized walk-ons Justin Duffie, a former lacrosse player who overcame Crohn's Disease to play for the Terps at nose guard, and fellow walk-on Tosin Abari. Looking back, they were the most unlikely of heroes.

They shut down Tennessee's vaunted run game from the start to help set the tone for the underdog Terps' rout. Sollazzo asked Friedgen that morning in a unit meeting what he wanted to do. Sollazzo said that Duffie and Abari "couldn't have played anywhere else in the country. They weren't recruited by a soul. But he was loyal to them because they were loyal to him."

Friedgen said he was rubbing his pocket rosary extra hard that day, especially after Starks went down. He said coming into the contest that it was the kind of game that could establish the Terps as a national program after the letdown with Florida in the Orange Bowl.

At the meeting that morning, after learning that Friedgen put Shime on a bus, Sollazzo recalled asking his boss:

"I asked him, 'What do you want me to do? Who do you want me to play there?' He said, 'Find somebody.' That was the end of the conversation."

"The right decision was made regardless of what happened in the game. You knew it was going to be one of those life lessons he [Shime] would say 'Thank you' later on when he was 30, 32-years old. He certainly wasn't going to be happy about it when he was 22-years old," Grabenstein said.

Adding to the turmoil, Sollazzo's mother had a stroke the day of the game. There was little time to celebrate for the defensive line coach, who helped coach one of the more memorable bowl performances in school history.

As an aside, Gloria spent time helping Shime through a difficult period the year before when his younger sister drowned in Cameroon.

A final postscript came two years later when Friedgen helped Shime get a job.

But Friedgen still remembered the episode like it was yesterday.

"I remember Debbie [Yow] was very concerned that I put him on a bus and not a plane. I said I wanted to make him walk," Friedgen recalled.

"Meanwhile, my rear-end is tighter than a drum because I got to play Justin Duffie, who had never played the game before at nose guard, and the second play of the game Starks goes down and we're playing Tosin Abari. Those were our two nose guards.

"And [linebacker] E.J. Henderson didn't even know his [Duffie's] name. In the press conference after the game he said he's a baseball player or something. He didn't even know what he was."

Duffie would come out of the game and vomit at Friedgen's feet when he reached the sideline. His stomach was acting up, not to mention his nerves.

Later, Shime came to Friedgen and told his coach that he deserved a ring. He said, "The Council wanted me to have a ring."

"I told him the Council has 10 votes. I got 11. Hell is going to freeze over before you get a ring, William," Friedgen said.

Friedgen said Shime began staring at him "like he was going to kick my ass."

"You are not going to get that ring. I'll melt it down before you get that ring. You did not deserve that ring. If you look at the ring it says 'Peach Bowl Champions.' The ring was for the bowl team, which you decided to not be a part of. I would cheapen that ring for all the other guys if I gave it to you," Friedgen said.

Perhaps nothing was going to stop that team. The Terps had been embarrassed the year before against Florida, something they had to live with, not to mention the whispers that they were "one-hit" wonders. Theirs was the only game on television that night, New Year's Eve, for the nation to see.

"I didn't care who was coming up to the line. We had another opportunity, against another powerhouse team, Tennessee, and this was our chance. All the other distractions . . . shoot, you got to get rid of those. We are going to go get the job done. I didn't care who had to play," Friedgen said.

Another funny incident during the trip came when Barnard asked Friedgen to let Latrez Harrison and Jafar Williams out of their 10 p.m. curfew Friedgen had imposed on the players for being late to the team's first meeting in Atlanta. Barnard said "they didn't feel safe without them" while on the town, especially their unofficial tour guide Harrison, the Atlanta native.

"About 10 minutes later E.J. Henderson calls me up. 'Coach, will you let Jafar and Latrez out tonight.' I said, 'What are you guys doing?' Then at about a quarter to nine I get a knock on my door and its Bruce Perry and 10 players. 'Coach, can't you let Jafar and Latrez out.' I said, 'What part of 'no' do you not understand? They are not going out. I don't give a damn. That's just the way it's going to be.'

"And then Latrez comes to me after the game and says, 'That's the best thing you could have done for me. I played so good.' " They wanted to go back to the night club but not without Latrez being there. That was another sideshow that went on during that trip."

The best one-liner of the week may have been when Friedgen came to members of the Council about Shime, Dennard Wilson in particular. After the players got off the bus at practice one morning, Friedgen asked him his thoughts on sending Shime home. Friedgen asked Wilson if he agreed.

"He said later at a team meeting, 'F-Shime. We're going to beat these guys with or without Shime,' " Friedgen recalled.

Said Wilson:

"We had that game. You know the feeling you have when you are so well prepared for something and you have practiced, right? Well, I said, 'I don't give a hell who it is or what's his name. We're gonna win this game.' "

As a testament to his sometime over-the-top competitiveness, no story stands out like the coaches' trip to the Dominican Republic after the Gator Bowl win.

It was a long-weekend reward for the staff, on Friedgen's dime, in appreciation for the great season, including the rout of West Virginia in Jacksonville.

Little did anyone know what they were getting into, that Friedgen would take his competitiveness to the 5-star resort for what they thought was a rare opportunity to decompress in the company of their boss.

It was an idea Friedgen first got from Beamer, who did it as a reward for his staff after bowl seasons at Virginia Tech.

A fun, relaxing time? Well, maybe.

While unwinding pool-side the coaches got involved with what started as a fun game of water polo with locals. That didn't last long.

Friedgen was in the pool with assistants Sollazzo, Donovan, even wife Gloria, among others, tearing into them verbally to "win the damn game."

Tourists around the pool started taking notice when the game got physical with the score tied late.

Sollazzo had seen the streak in Friedgen before when they played their infamous player-coach pickup basketball games years ago. There were no-holds-barred.

Back in the pool the coaches, including Friedgen, were jumped as both sides clamored for the ball.

Franklin had returned from a day trip with his girlfriend and they came upon the scene.

"I come walking in. I am trying to figure out what is going on as guys are being thrown around, men are trying to grab the ball, and guys are smashing them all over the place. Ralph is screaming out orders to people and he's got the ball and is plowing over anyone who would get in his way. It was like a melee, a competitive, competitive melee."

Franklin saw a player picked up, ball in hand, and thrown into the net. Gloria was first acting as ball girl, chasing errant balls that flew out of the pool. Then her husband demanded she get in and play. Gloria recalled seeing her husband dunking an opponent momentarily trying to get the ball.

Said Sollazzo: "People off the street challenged us to a game and he wasn't about to lose. He was throwing people off his back and soon we all were. That was their sport, water polo. They came in like they were loaded, like they did it for a living. They didn't realize we were going to whup them.

"But he's like that no matter what. It could be checkers with his daughter."

The coaches won, Franklin said, by the score of 11-10, and "celebrated like they had just won the Super Bowl."

It's Friedgen through and through, never letting up even in paradise.

Beamer recalled a golf tournament a few years ago when Friedgen, trailing his buddy, hit a shot that hit him in the leg. A few shots later one zinged past his head. Beamer joked that he didn't think it was by accident.

The two spent their early years attending LeMaze classes as their wives prepared to give birth, "taking shots of whiskey," Beamer joked, "to help us make it through.'

They even went in on real estate together at Lake Oconee.

But just don't put Friedgen in a competitive situation, where he never allows an advantage, sometimes even with his family.

"He's very, very competitive. We all are as a family," Gloria said. "Heck, we play a game at home, 'Scene It?' when you put in a video of movie scenes and stuff like that. And we're like cut-throat."

14
THE FUTURE

While Ralph Friedgen may be rooted in the past he clearly has his eye on the future. Friedgen is on the cutting edge of technology, a slave to the computer. Be it creating programs, amassing data, or pouring over statistical minutiae, he is at it night and day, in-season or off-season.

And he plans to stay that way, ahead of the curve on many of his coaching peers.

"Ralph is kinda a paradox because he is a throw back. And we've been accused by some people of being throw backs to the '60s [laugh]. Yet he is incredibly adept technologically to the game and everything around it," said Blackney.

Most everything has its roots in the 1950s and '60s when Friedgen was growing up, when he aligned formations on checkers boards as a child.

Friedgen is cerebral, overlaying innovation on top of his traditional roots.

"He is like a kid in the candy store with his computers," said Gossett. "I think back when I was a kid playing football and it was just throw the football around. He has shown me a few things on the computer, and how he can analyze all these plays and come up with how many permutations and variations. How scientific and sophisticated the game has become, and how Ralph has really adapted to how the game has changed. Now his quarterbacks sit down and play video games with the plays."

Wherever Friedgen is you're likely to find a computer nearby.

Hollenbach recalled tales of his coach taking his laptop on his boat at Lake Oconee in Georgia while on vacation. He'd load plays as they came to him. Hollenbach said he always had it with him in position meetings, and most everywhere else.

"I just remember asking myself how long must he have spent putting it all together," Hollenbach said. "He would go on his boat in Georgia and put them in in the mornings. I said, 'How is that vacation?' "

Friedgen rolled up his sleeves with software developers to assist with his latest gadget, the virtual reality Football Simulator. His players began using it in 2006. Friedgen asked Hollenbach to draw up a list of improvements he'd like to see, like how to align the safety, which was soon implemented.

Friedgen's players use practice, film study, and now the Football Simulator to learn his complex offense.

"It's helped me a lot, but it's just starting off so it will help future quarterbacks that much more," Hollenbach said.

I n keeping with the times and looking ahead, Friedgen has always been flexible enough to adapt to his players, a group that seemingly changes every year as technology advances and societal mores change seemingly overnight.

"I never thought in a million years that coach Friedgen would play music during stretching at practice. His father probably turned over in his grave the first time he heard that," Sollazzo said of Friedgen's warm-up music that he pipes in over speakers at practices. "He's old school in many ways but he's innovative enough to do the little things like that."

Friedgen didn't have music at practice during his first year. But after the players requested it, he changed his policy in year two.

Friedgen sometimes surfs the 'Net, checking out websites, message boards. He's been known to surprise players with e-mails of plays, especially his quarterbacks, and quiz them.

Technology has changed the game so much, even since Friedgen arrived, with tools like text-messaging for recruits, as well as the explosion of the Internet in general and how players are covered by the new media.

Friedgen is mindful of what is reported or passed on via the 'Net, from practice injuries to schemes or formations to 40-yard dash times at his summer camp. He's barked at a few reporters for divulging such information.

Friedgen got his assistant coaches started text-messaging recruits in 2005, while he assigned staff to every school's web site in the league as well as other opponents' pages.

In-season, Friedgen doesn't allow injury information to be reported by the media unless he releases it. In 2006, he closed practice when a reporter violated the rule after observing a player being carted off the field.

Friedgen has seen the downside of technology. He said the Internet has "created monsters" among recruits. The non-stop news cycle – as well as the competition between traditional print media and new media – has led to a barrage of attention for the players, some of it starting when they are sophomores in high school. Athletes are savvy to the media nowadays with such early starts.

Friedgen said he sees more high school prospects "heads blown up" with the constant coverage, and sometimes gratuitous praise, of the Internet, only to see them get to camp in August "in store for a big surprise," he said.

Friedgen likes many of the advantages technology has brought to his world, and he has most gadgets on the market. But he's wary of some of the new forms of media cropping up.

Some schools, like Virginia, limit their players' and coaches' contact with the media. They won't permit them to interact beyond game day or special occasions. Friedgen welcomes the media and he has one of the more open programs.

"It is a double-edge sword there," Friedgen said. "Some coaches, like Al [Groh], he won't let any of his players talk to the press. It's that 'one voice.'

"[Bill] Parcells does that, and there's a lot to be said for that. Who controls what comes out, you know."

Friedgen believes that dealing with the media, however, is "part of your education" for the players, while he respects the job the media has to do and the competition that exists to get the story.

"For the most part, I think the press has been very fair to us," he said.

Friedgen said part of that is because he has been accessible and open "and I have dealt with them honestly."

"I am usually myself . . . most of the time spontaneous," he said for the media, and usually chock-full of colorful comments. Friedgen said that way is better than "being guarded," like other coaches he has been around, and not giving reporters much to report.

Friedgen relies on the media, especially beat reporters that know him and his penchant for racy comments, to filter and clean up some of his comments in their daily sessions with him.

Each year Friedgen has training sessions for his players to go over rules of engagement with the media. Like never criticize coaches or teammates in the press or give fuel to the opposition with controversial comments.

Only once did Friedgen need to muzzle a player, running back Jason Crawford, who on the eve of a game against Eastern Michigan said of the opponent, "They don't even deserve to be on our schedule," Friedgen remembered.

"That was it for him talking to the press. And in that game they read that and they were cheap-shotting us, hitting us low, trying to hurt us. All because of those things Jason was saying," Friedgen said.

Friedgen is smart enough to know that a good rapport with the media can be a boon to all. He credits ESPN, in part, for helping him land a head coaching job.

"For whatever reason they took a liking to me and really promoted me. I don't think I would have got a head job if ESPN had not promoted me," he said.

For his players located in a rich job market, it can be a windfall, too, with the numerous forms of media relating their personal stories.

"It's kinda also an advertisement for them, for their name to get out. And you never know what door that can open. D.C. is a big job market, and especially with TV," Friedgen said.

While granting access, Friedgen is also cognizant of always protecting his program.

Threats can come in many forms.

Nothing stirs him up more than the presence of pro agents or "runners" around his program. The runners, sometimes college students, work for agents and try to shadow the players. Friedgen has chased them off campus, away from dorms, and even banned a student from the program after discovering him bird-dogging players at College Park night spots.

They hang around stadiums, sometimes practices, hoping for a chance encounter with players or their parents. The problem seems to grow each year, as contracts get bigger and the demand for top players mount.

"All that has to happen is one of them buying a kid a soda and they could be ineligible," Friedgen said of NCAA rules prohibiting gifts.

They get to players earlier and earlier, identifying even the top seventh and eight graders, while trying to make their pitch.

Friedgen said many problems, across the board, could be solved by an early signing period.

He said if prospects can sign in August "then I know it is done," he said. It would eliminate time for things to get out of control in the process, or other outside influences to get control. Friedgen would also know how many players he had before he went out recruiting, which would make his time and money better spent.

Some coaches don't want an early signing period. They contend it would make summer a recruiting period and they would never get vacation. Also, city schools would be at an advantage. The schools, which are more accessible, could bring prospects to campus many times for unofficial visits, while rural schools would find it more difficult.

R alph Friedgen is focused mostly on preparing a winning football team. To that end he has become more reflective in recent years.

He admits when he slips up. And there have been a few times. After all, he's in his first head coaching post, and learning and evolving more each year.

After his three winning seasons and bowl appearances, Friedgen said that complacency set in the program. And he wasn't focused on the future enough.

Friedgen typically goes back at season's end and looks at everything, analyzing every game and every play, "making sure we're doing what we are saying we are doing," he said.

However, he didn't do that after the Gator Bowl rout of West Virginia in 2003 because the staff was intact and things were rolling along. He was feeling great, and didn't believe anything needed changing.

He got a contract extension and salary bump and treated the staff to the trip to the Dominican Republic after the season.

"I'll never do that again," he said of becoming content with the "status quo."

Opponents, he said, got more in-tune to what the Terps were doing. Maybe they knew their schemes and tendencies better after three seasons while the Terps didn't counter.

For example, Friedgen said he noticed in film review that opponents were getting an extra man to the "play" side. He said he had used some of the same schemes for decades, but he wasn't afraid to change.

Friedgen sent his staff on the road to observe college and pro camps, and when they returned they met for 10 straight days.

"We got that all cleared up, trust me. Sometimes you got to coach the coaches. And that's on me," he said.

That season, when the Terps suffered their first losing campaign under Friedgen, Statham was at the helm before losing his job at Virginia Tech in the Thursday night meltdown on ESPN.

Friedgen said Statham refused to "do what we asked of him."

In both losing seasons much of the woes could be traced to poor quarterback play, Statham struggling in 2004 and Hollenbach in 2005.

Not to get too deep in the X's and O's,' Friedgen said that in his system the quarterback must either read the progressions and routes, which takes time, or read the flat defender. Friedgen said he learned it in the pros, and that the second method is faster.

Former quarterbacks Hill and McBrien had trouble with it initially, but later it clicked. But Statham, he said, never looked at the first progression so never moved the flat defender. It contributed to his inconsistent play and, ultimately, his inability to run Friedgen's offense.

"That flat was always wide-open. But he would try to force it into the curl or something," Friedgen said.

The Terps bounced back with a 9-4 bowl season in 2006 after Hollenbach improved his ability to manage the offense and got hot at mid-season. The Terps were within striking distance of another ACC title before faltering in the final two games. Still, the program was back and had a quarterback in control after two years of disappointment.

Friedgen told Hollenbach:

"You're a smart guy and it's time you take the bull by the horns."

Friedgen said another contributing factor that brought the 2004 and '05 teams down was that he became lackadaisical with a few "negative players, who I shoulda gotten rid of. I should have got rid of them the year before. But they were popular with the fans. But I'm not going to worry about that now. I know what I should have done and I am going to do it," he said.

The players, which included both a senior and a popular receiver, were "cancers" and brought other players down.

There were only a few but "they influenced like eight or 10 kids," Friedgen said.

"It would have been messy. But next time I will do it based on what I know now. It probably would have gone over well with the team with what I know now. I think if I had done it, it might have changed the whole thing around."

Friedgen has become more mindful of team chemistry and has put more control in the hands of the Council as a self-regulating internal mechanism.

S am Hollenbach said that in his travels on the senior all-star circuit in the winter of
2006, in conversations with players from other schools, he never met one that
faced the demands like those of Ralph Friedgen players.

From morning workouts in the off-season to e-mails from their coach, none experienced
what Hollenbach did at College Park. He said he met a player from Michigan who told him
the team practiced once a week in pads. The Terps typically go three days in pads.

"You need a lot of mental toughness just to make it through, to go through what you
do every day and every practice, at every meeting, to always strive for excellence. Talking
with guys from all kinds of other teams I am getting more of an appreciation for how
coach Friedgen ran the team. His discipline and his schedule for us. I haven't heard from
anybody that was tougher. He pushes us to be the best in every area," Hollenbach said.

Hollenbach, who had a star-crossed career riding the Friedgen roller-coaster for
five years, hugged his coach after the Champs Sports Bowl in December of 2006.

Friedgen told him after the post-game media conference "this is just the start. You
are just beginning in your career."

Hollenbach said the void in his life when he left the program was great. And
despite the demands of his coach, his in-your-face style to always strive for more, he
couldn't have asked for more.

Hollenbach is one of Friedgen's greatest turnaround stories as he molded an average
quarterback into a player capable of winning nine games, including a solid bowl game.

"To me, I know that I will miss the game of football at Maryland," Hollenbach
said. "It's so demanding, there's so much time going into it. I can remember my last
practice feeling real bad. I'm not going to be able to do this anymore. Suit up. Be in
this setting with the coaches and players.

"I think I will miss him, but just don't let anyone else in the program know
[laugh]. He runs such a tight ship but I think that's something that for an 18-20-year
old athlete, that's something you need in your life. And I think he realizes that.

"How I feel after it all is how you kinda feel after you just worked out real hard.
You feel that was tough but you feel so much better now. You feel like you did yourself right after doing that."

R alph Friedgen is at a critical stage in his career at Maryland, coming off his sixth
season, getting back in bowl contention, and looking ahead to Byrd Stadium
expansion, which could define his final years as a head coach.

He said Byrd Stadium expansion "had to happen," or else the program would start
losing ground in recruiting.

As he looks to the future he knows the MGN will remain vital to his program-building,
something that is constantly going on around him. Not always at the pace that he'd like,

but it's happening thanks to a supportive boss in Yow and president in Mote.

"The MGN is bringing this program into the 21st century. I mean, we won't be able to recruit anybody, we wouldn't have any of the facilities we got, the class room things we do, without the MGN," Friedgen said.

Friedgen believes the Terps are still underachieving as far as fund-raising, especially with the "great numbers of people around here." He believes there is a deep well still to tap. He also knows Yow has done everything she can do and now it's just winning over more of the masses.

He'd like to get MGN membership over 2,500, which he said is "very doable, because we got 150,000 alumni within an hour radius of here."

Friedgen said that when Maryland re-seats Byrd Stadium it will be the time "this whole thing turns around."

He admits, though, he must keep winning for that to happen.

L ooking to the future, it's difficult to avoid the topic of Ralph Friedgen's weight and health. In addition to his wife Gloria, boosters and others have urged him to diet and exercise.

Said Gossett, the program's top donor:

"I talked to him about his weight and his size a few times. And we had the little contest [to lose weight]. My counseling to Ralph a lot of times was, 'Ralph, you are so driven and consumed with this winning and so forth. But you got to take time for Ralph. Because if you do not take time for Ralph, well Ralph is not going to be here.'

"He and I talk about exercise. I try to have a fairly regimented exercise routine for myself. I tell him, 'Ralph, it took me a long time. It took me 60 years to learn that it's okay to do something for Barry. And you got to learn it's okay to do something for Ralph. That's important because if you don't do that, it's like your hip. You're going to be in a position you can't do what you want to do.' "

Gossett said that's the only lesson Friedgen still has to learn.

"I'll keep after him on it. But you have to know when to pick your points. Sometimes I'll say it and he'll get that look where I'm, 'Okay, he's gonna make me run laps if I say anything else.' "

As far as historical perspective, Gossett said Friedgen was the right man at the right time for Maryland.

And Gossett should know.

Gossett goes back to the words of Wilson Elkins, Maryland's president from 1954-78, who said Maryland would not be a "football factory," but a university, after its national championship in 1951.

But everything was in place for Friedgen as far as the administration and leadership on campus to help make it happen, finally, for football.

"To some degree Elkins was right," Gossett said. "But I think when you go through a lot of things, like [Jerry] Claiborne, and they felt they were getting the support. The whole dynamic there.

"But I think with the current president, Dr. Mote, who I love dearly. His academics and arts and athletics all working together to make everything well. I think Ralph fits that very well. I think other coaches look at Ralph and say, 'I can do that, too.' "

Friedgen knows his clock is ticking, especially after he got a late start as head coach. But he's never shown much bitterness over it, when friends like Beamer had a huge jump.

Friedgen admits that he has "mellowed" more each year. He's become more tolerant and flexible with his staff and players, a far cry from the way his father ran things, or even he seven years ago when he arrived.

His players still experience his explosions and bluster, though 30 years ago a Terrapin Council wouldn't have existed in his world.

"That's also a sign of a good coach. That you can change the way you do things," Grabenstein said. "Before that it was always a dictatorship.

"Ralph has raised the expectations, he has demanded excellence and he's gotten it," Grabenstein added. "He's also got the attention of the athletic department."

At the end of the day, how Friedgen stood by his players, be it a star like Josh Wilson or a walk-on like Henry Scott, not just wins and losses, is what also mattered to him.

"When he thinks about where he made the difference, and if it hadn't been for him the kid would have been up you-know-what creek without a paddle. When all is said and done, the measure of his success, in his mind, will be where he made that, as opposed to the wins column," Grabenstein said.

When his coaching days are over Ralph Friedgen plans to retire to his Georgia lake home.

In 2006 the Friedgens remodeled their South Carolina beach house. In keeping with some of his better investments, he bought the house on the water for $37,000 nearly 20 years ago while he was at The Citadel. Now he says its worth over $2 million. It was the first home he bought, and it's proven a great investment.

Gloria's brother, who lives in Charleston, looks after Friedgen's home and boat. The two often fish when Ralph's in town.

The lake house in Georgia he bought on his second tour at Georgia Tech. Friedgen built it after he purchased one of the prime lots for $155,000 in 1997. The house is worth well over $1 million. He got a deal on it as part of his package to return to Tech.

At the time he thought he would finish his career in Atlanta, so he went ahead with building in 1999. He said he "knew it would happen like that," when he got the call from Maryland once he started the home. It was completed a year later, but the Friedgens had already moved north.

"My father always told me, 'God only made so much land next to the water,' " he said of his investments.

Among Friedgen's favorite things to do at the lake is get up early, take his boat to a country breakfast spot, read the morning paper, and fish before hitting the links in the afternoon. Sometimes he takes his wife Gloria and daughters fishing. He likes bringing home the catch for dinner.

Friedgen's favorite room is his custom walk-out basement, which has a bar and a big-screen television. The bar looks out on the lake. The stuffed Jack Crevalle hangs at the bar, as does a vintage Susan Anton Terps football "Passion" poster from the 1980s when the actress was part of a marketing campaign touting the high-octane offense. Friedgen does his best relaxing – anywhere – in this room.

"It's all right there for me. I don't have to go anywhere," he said.

B ut everything seems to go back to his roots and his father.
Ralph Friedgen bears a striking resemblance to his father. He has morphed into him in many ways, those that know him say.

Not only physically, as both were large men, but even down to the mannerisms.

Like his father, Ralph puts his hands on his hips on the sidelines, with the back of his hand on his hip, palm facing out. Just like his father.

His father would never be without his clipboard, Ralph without his laminated play card.

The way he talks to his players, pre and post-game and much of the time in between, is the same.

"I have been in the locker room after games, both at Maryland and of course when we played for his father," Verille said. "Just when you think he is going to slam you he puts his arm around you. Just like his father."

With Ralph its family, faith and football, just like his pops.

Ralph has carried another tradition to College Park, frequenting a favorite diner on Sundays after mass. It's Plato's at Maryland, back home while growing up it was the Mamaroneck Diner, which was noted for its rice pudding.

Gloria said Ralph's father would sit at the dinner table just like Ralph today with the feeling of "great respect, love, and admiration from those around him."

"He'd command attention just like Ralph. I see it and it is so much like that. And he has the soft side of his mother. What he really has is the best of both of his parents," Gloria said.

While he got his father's toughness, many close to him believe the soft side of his mother comes through just as much.

"What I saw was his mother was very giving, very compassionate. I think she put up with a lot," Gloria said.

Gloria regrets that because Ralph's mother was ill for much of their daughters' formative years, the girls didn't get to see that side.

"My mom was like a lot of moms. She was never going to tell me bad news. She was always on the brighter side of things. My dad was, 'Hey, suck it up. You're not tough,' " Ralph Friedgen said.

Friedgen joked that for years his father didn't believe his shoulder would dislocate in games. Once it did while father and son were in the swimming pool years later.

"Finally it came out in the pool one day. There was a hole right in my shoulder. I went over and showed him and popped it back in myself in front of him. He said, 'What in the hell is that?' That's my damn shoulder,' " Friedgen said.

Friedgen seems to strike a balance between his disciplinary side and his nurturing side.

He said he sees an erosion of youth and families more and more so he has to be on-point dealing with student-athletes and their many issues. It's nothing like the black-and-white world he knew growing up.

"Kids today are not tough. I think we're so afraid of lawsuits and everything else that we cover our butts with the little things. Half of these injuries we get we can play through them," he said.

Gloria recalled the time she visited with Georgia coach Richt at the Atlanta Touchdown Club awards banquet, where Ralph was honored as coach of the year. Richt asked her to describe her husband.

"I told him, 'family, faith and football. But probably not always in that order [laugh].' That's how he is.

"I describe him to people that he loves hard. That's probably why he is so candid. Why waste time and energy beating around the bush?"

When his daughters came home from school with good grades they always wanted to see Ralph first, Gloria said, "Because they wanted to please him so much."

Thier youngest daughter, Katie, worried at first about attending Maryland because she might not equal her sisters' academic successes. Katie, like her father, had to work and grind for long hours, unlike her sisters who got good grades more easily.

Friedgen would take time with his daughter that his father probably never did.

"She would say, 'I don't know if I will be as successful.' I said, 'Why not?' Ralph Friedgen said.

" 'Why would you think that?' She'd say, 'I'm not as smart as them.' I'd come back at her with, 'What grades did you get? Well, I get good grades,' she said.

"I say, 'So, what's the difference? No one's counting how you get them.'

"I told her I'm more proud of you than I am with Kristina and Kelley. She said, 'Why would you say that? Because you are like me, you got to work for what you get. You study three hours a night to get 'A's', and they don't have to do that. But the results are the same. That's all that matters.' "

Friedgen tells his players much of the same when he applies life lessons.

"I tell the players, 'God has blessed you in some ways and hasn't in others. It's a matter of how hard you work. What's inside you is going to determine the difference.' "

"I say people forget that. They are never satisfied. Don't ever look away from whether you won or lost the game, that's what counts. It doesn't matter how you did it. It's not a beauty contest."

Ralph Friedgen wants to continue coaching until "I'm not enjoying it," he said. His wife, he jokes, "never wants me to retire."

"But I like to relax. I love being at my lake house. I just love it. I'll just see where I am at. But I do know this: I am probably a guy that has worked so hard for so long, it's probably not going to be easy for me [to stop]," he said.

Friedgen cut back in areas in recent years. He's adjusted his schedule to be more involved with coaching, especially running the offense.

He hosts the MGN Gala every other year instead of every year. He also cut back his Friday morning breakfasts to three or four a year instead of before every home game. And he's cut back on personal appearances as well.

After two losing seasons, Friedgen said he had to get back to the task at hand, coaching, while he was driving himself into the ground as offensive coordinator.

He spoke at his daughter's graduation ceremony but "got 50 invitations after that to speak. I can't do that anymore," he said of where his focus is.

The last two years, he admits, he has gotten up later, at 6 a.m. instead of 5 a.m., if you consider that late. He still keeps remarkable hours.

Friedgen said that he is recruiting harder than ever, and in 2004 he got a cell phone which allowed him to text message recruits.

"Now I am a text messaging fool. I text message 4-5 kids every night. I never did that before."

Ralph Friedgen is outspoken. Just ask him anything and you'll likely get a candid response.

And the subject of the Byzantine world of the NCAA gets him started very easily.

Friedgen wants to see major changes in recruiting with the process going back to the high schools.

He said college coaches have to stop attending combines and endorsing shoe companies and take it back to the grass-roots level.

The senior all-star games, he said, the same. They drag out recruiting and sometimes interject shady individuals into the process.

"If we don't go to the combines the kids wouldn't be going to the combines. They are going because we go. We got to stop helping these guys make money off them," he said.

In the spring of 2006 the ACC coaches, because of a rule change, were not permitted at combines. But that changed at the last minute so they all had to go just to keep up.

"Right now what's happening is we're losing it. We're going down the same road as basketball. The street agents are getting involved. The Internet guys are getting involved. The shoe companies are getting involved. They are even talking about having AAU football."

Friedgen said most AAU basketball players that he recruits for football have outside influences trying to shape their decisions.

"If that ever happens," he says of AAU football, "I'm out. I'm too old to deal with that stuff. We got to correct that. And we want to correct that. But at times the NCAA doesn't know the difference between a camp, a clinic and a combine. Hey, group them all the same."

Friedgen said that typically whatever the coaches agree on at their annual meetings and convention it never gets done. He complains that football, the greatest revenue producer, "is the most legislated sport there is."

The silliest rule, he said, was when the NCAA voted to take testing away from the college schoolboy camps in 2007, which would have defeated the main purpose of camp. Fortunately, it was overturned.

Friedgen complains that there are "no coaches on the committee, and that they know I am so vocal" that they don't want him there. He has threatened to skip conventions because nothing gets done.

The early signing period is another hot topic each year, as well as a playoff system and five years of eligibility, but "nothing ever happens," he said.

Friedgen would like to spend more time in the off-season with his players, something the NCAA severely limits but in men's basketball allows.

Football graduation rates across the country, and at Maryland, are higher than the male student population in some places, so Friedgen would like to see changes to football's APR minimums.

Friedgen's program peaked with a 79 percent graduation rate in 2006. The senior class that's expected to graduate in 2008 will likely have 20 of a possible 21 players walk at ceremonies. Only Matt Deese, who transferred as a sophomore, will count against the total. Few things Friedgen takes as much pride in as his graduation rate.

"Eric Lenz and Dennis Marsh both transferred in good standing. If Scott Burley and Keon Lattimore graduate then we're 20 of 21," he said. "And you know what? They're all pretty good players. They are all pretty good kids. Almost all of them are competing. And I don't think it was the greatest year in recruiting, but it was a solid year because they all stuck around."

In the spring of 2006, Friedgen told a few players, including J.J. Justice and Jason Goode, seniors with pro potential, that if they leave to train elsewhere in the spring and don't graduate, that he won't let them work out at the Terps' pro day. Graduation rates have been hit in some sports, like football and men's basketball, with players bolting early for the pros, many after being on pace to graduate. With the threat of losing scholarships under the APR, Friedgen has to be mindful.

"As much as we've accomplished here, there's so much more to do. I see that, I really do, in every way," Friedgen said of the balancing act between football and academics.

R alph Friedgen envisions Byrd Stadium bowled in all the way around. He wants the field lowered for better sight-lines and to create more desirable seating areas. He sees more potential and growth and has often pushed when it's not popular.

His vision for the program continues, and everyone at Maryland has to share it and keep up or get run over by him.

"People thought I was nuts when I said we're going to put another deck on this place. That's closer to reality than when I got here. Or, that we'd fill this place and that's happening now. If you don't think that way it's never going to happen," Friedgen said. "I think we have a heck of a product to see."

Yow and staff unveiled renderings of the multi-phase renovation project at Byrd Stadium in the spring of 2007.

The project, which got a boost when Maryland and Chevy Chase Bank entered into a $20 million agreement for the naming rights to the field at Byrd Stadium, will break ground at the end of the 2007 home schedule (Nov. 10 vs. Boston College).

Maryland and Heery International, the project architect, worked to develop plans for the new five-story Tyser Tower for six months.

The focus, first, will be on the sale of the 64 luxury suites, 10 of which sold immediately.

Phase I of the project, which will cost $50.8 million, could be completed as soon as August 2009, and will include a dramatic expansion of Tyser Tower on the south sideline; the addition of 64 luxury suites that will feature indoor and outdoor seating; a university suite with seating for 200; a new team store; and the installation of a new state-of-the-art LED scoreboard by the start of the 2007 season.

The luxury suites in the new Tyser Tower will seat between 16 and 24 people and will cost between $40,000 and $50,000.

The renovations will cause "minor inconveniences" during the 2008 season, according to Maryland officials, and the loss of a small number of temporary seats. Ultimately, phase I will add 94,000 square feet to Tyser Tower and 842 new seats.

The cost of the project will be covered entirely by private funds.

"There is no state funding and there is no expectation in any way that this campus will participate in any funding of the improvements," Yow said. "All of the dollars - 100 percent - will need to be raised privately."

The Terps will pay for Phase I with a $35.8 million loan from the state system and $15.8 million from the sale of the naming rights and the luxury suites. The Maryland athletic department, which was $54 million in debt when Yow took over in 1994, was expected to reduce its debt to $8.7 million by July of 2007. The sale of luxury suites will also help cover the cost of future expansion.

Phase II will include the installation of railings in the north and south lower bowls to enhance fan safety; chair back seating in the 200 level on the north side; new restrooms and concessions; lowering the playing field to improve the sight lines for seats on the first 10 rows, making 3,000 seats that are currently obstructed view into the some of the stadium's best; and painting all the roofs that are currently blue.

The most dramatic renderings unveiled were those that included the project's future expansion. Eventually Byrd Stadium will grow by nearly 8,000 seats in the west end zone, bringing its capacity to approximately 60,000. The Gossett Team House will also be enlarged to upgrade training areas and locker rooms.

"I'm really excited about the unveiling of our plans and the realization of Dr. Yow and my vision for the football program," Friedgen said. "It's amazing how much we've accomplished in six years and now we are taking it one step further . . . We've made more improvements in the last six years than maybe we have in the history of the program."

The Terps hope to lower the field for better sight lines and premium seats sooner than expected. The varsity team house will be razed and re-built, while the locker room may be expanded to include a players' lounge. Also, the weight room and training room are expected to expand.

Friedgen said it will be determined by how well the suites sell. He said he hopes that once the suites are up, the Terps can put in chair-backs in the mezzanine level "and make that eventually a club level, which is pretty easy to do," he said.

The final stage will be to bowl it all in, he said.

R alph Friedgen is always pushing the envelope to get his message out. In the spring of 2007 he helped get a weekly television program — "Terrapin Rising" — on the Comcast network. It ran on Monday nights in prime time and was sponsored by Under Armour.

The series offered an inside look at the program, much like "Fridge TV," but in a broader, public forum. And it came at a perfect time for recruiting, season ticket sales, and Byrd Stadium expansion. Yet another feather in Friedgen's cap.

"To me it comes at a great time for all of us," he said.

Atkinson and crew spent the spring accumulating footage and stories for the show.

Friedgen has had to pay for most things in the football program with cash, with the exception of the practice fields, which Yow went to bat for on campus.

Though sometimes it's a struggle, Friedgen sees things coming together nicely, though he knows some of the limitations at Maryland.

He said it doesn't have to be that way, and he looks forward to the day it changes. The day he no longer has to be out stumping for the program and he can just be the coach.

"It's nice," Friedgen said of the team house and football facilities. "I don't know if anybody has the location on campus, everything that we have right there. There may be some bigger and better, but I don't know if anyone is any more efficient. It has really helped us."

Friedgen sees the day that once Maryland sells all of its season tickets, like the men's basketball program did, there will be such demand that they will have to re-seat Byrd Stadium.

"Then the Terrapin Club will jump from 8,000 to 20,000," he said, "because people are going to have to join the Terrapin Club to get into Byrd Stadium. That's when we are going to start making a major move. That's when we are going to start hitting the big time."

Friedgen said he knows of few coaches that had to work as hard at fund-raising as he, while he said if it were not for the MGN "we would be as stagnant as we have been here for the last 18 years."

Friedgen understands the dynamic at Maryland and knows how to approach it, unlike some of his predecessors.

He said it's the reason he didn't call plays early in his tenure, not having the time for that "and to sell Maryland football. And get the fans involved. And be a promoter. You couldn't do both. It's an impossible job."

Friedgen credited Taaffe for the job he did while in his post, and recalled many Thursday nights when he left to go fund-raising and Taaffe stayed at the office working on the game plan.

Friedgen said that while he was away from Maryland he "got more motivated to succeed here, given how little everyone else before had done here." He said he knew he could not be "just a football coach" to get things done. He had to take on other responsibilities.

In 2006 he began calling plays after Taaffe's departure, something that takes up more of his time. So he has cut back on non-football duties more.

Friedgen's goal is a national championship, and he has proven he can coach at the highest level. He has to keep up in recruiting by signing the elite prospects to make it happen.

The facilities are getting better with Byrd Stadium expansion scheduled to begin.

Friedgen recalled his first week on the job, eagerly telling Yow of his plans to bowl in the stadium.

"It's a special thing. It's a vision that I have had and I think Debbie has had, really since we have been here," he said.

Friedgen sees the revised expansion project as enough. And he can be a hard man to please. It's a modified version of an initial plan, which was priced over $100 million, which Maryland couldn't afford.

"I am hoping everyone embraces it. Right now we have to be careful because Debbie [Yow] keeps talking about an "arms race." But we're a Third World country because the arms some of these other guys are getting. Everybody is expanding their stadium, doing renovations to their stadium. To me, this is a necessity."

Friedgen points to Maryland's top-notch facilities and how the campus has been upgraded, especially the Comcast Center. He says the Terps are "very efficient" in other areas despite some of the financial limitations.

"The pressure is you got to keep winning. I mean, money is so tight around here," he said.

Friedgen continues to push and no one is safe. Not even boosters who he's constantly riding to give more.

He bemoans the fact that fans approach him at booster functions complaining about losing their seats "after 40 years." This type person is not in the Terrapin Club, he said, which is only $125 to join, while nearly 1,000 football season ticket holders are not in the Terrapin Club, which pays Maryland's scholarship bill.

Friedgen told the fan bluntly, "You are the reason we are being held back."

"I told him, 'Boy, you are the last of the big-time spenders. Do you realize a place like Georgia sells 90,000 season tickets and you got to pay $800 [seat charge] to get the worst seat in the house. To get a good seat you got to pay $10,000.'

"That's what we're dealing with. And you know what? We got more people here than at Georgia."

Maryland's attendance average was only 22,000 when Friedgen arrived but was over 50,000 in recent years, including the temporary seats the Terps installed early in his tenure to meet rising needs.

At first it was suggested the Terps build 10 suites in expanded Byrd, which Friedgen was against and helped change. At Georgia Tech, for instance, he said there are some 75 suites and the school makes between $35,000-$85,000 per suite. And there is a waiting list.

H ad Ralph Friedgen got his coaching start earlier he could have been "up there with the Bobby Bowdens and Joe Paternos of the college world," one friend said.

Said Verille:

"I think you would have seen a coach who had been rolling along with . . . one of the best programs in the country. Bowls every year. Winning program for 15-20 years. You would have seen a Beamer.

"For the years that I have followed his career he was the man. You always knew that he had the chance to pull it out. And he did."

Said another admirer that has followed his career closely:

"It may have taken him 30 years to be a head coach," said Stoddard, "but he was primed and ready. He's got the whole package. He is past all that, getting his first head job late. He wants to win a national title at Maryland. That's the goal that will make him happy. The rest doesn't matter."

Said one of his top players at Maryland:

"He's going to be a coach that's going to be hard to forget," Merriman said.

Yow has hung on and enjoyed the ride though it's been bumpy at times. Twice she extended Friedgen's contract, which will max out at $1.8 million during its term.

"This is how I look at it," she said when asked if anyone could have pulled off what Friedgen did in his first years at Maryland and have the program poised for the future. "There's nobody anywhere who's irreplaceable but there are people who are special. And he's special. I am willing to do [extra things] because he is willing to do the extra things to do the special things for this program."

Friedgen said that he's not looking to go anywhere else, and that he wants to "finish this thing right."

He said he is pleased that he runs a "good, clean program," and there have not been many major off-the-field incidents with players getting in trouble. He said that with the media and Internet today "everything is an over-reaction."

R alph Friedgen keeps plugging, up before dawn and to bed well after most. He looks back to his father during times of reflection.

"I really owe a lot to him. A lot of things he taught me I use every day. Be resilient, keep fighting for things. He always used to tell me when I was in college, as frustrating as that was, moving positions ... 'You got to be patient. You got to work. You'll get your day. This is what life is about.' It took a long time but it finally happened. I am proud of what I have done here."

Maryland hadn't won in so long that, by winning 31 games in his first three years, many didn't understand what a feat Friedgen accomplished at College Park.

In 39 years of coaching Friedgen had experienced just seven 10-win seasons. Maryland hadn't been to a bowl game in a decade before he arrived. The Terps were within an eyelash of another great season in 2006, finishing 9-4, but with a chance to advance to the ACC title game and compete for another BCS bowl.

Best of all, after two down years fun returned to the program.

"One kid [Haynos] told me last year that it was the greatest time he had ever had," Friedgen said. "They want to do that again. Now this group has tasted it. Now there is some confidence."

Like his first team at Maryland, which once it tasted victory the mind-set changed.

As he enters the final years of his contract, and given his age and work schedule, many hope his health keeps up. He said he felt great coming off a productive 2006 season and a more relaxed off-season as he headed into the summer of 2007.

"I am doing well. I am feeling better," he said.

Since his 60th birthday party in March, Friedgen has gotten his weight down 20 pounds thanks to eating smaller meals and eating slowly. He played more golf, and he hoped to start walking regularly.

Friedgen was walking many of the holes at spring golf outings, and was aiming to get his weight below 300 pounds.

"It's not that I feel bad. But you are carrying around a lot of weight. My ankles swell, that kind of stuff. Plus, I got to do it because I am getting older," he said.

President George W. Bush even asked him about his publicized diet when he visited the White House a few years ago.

"I'm a little bit like Gloria. You can only tell him so many times before you give up," Rychleski said. "It's his life, and he's got to decide that for himself.

"Watch, he'll go and out-live us all. I have said that since I have been here. But he should be about his health the way he is about football."

By that same token, Friedgen helped break the mold for heavyset coaches. Mark Mangino, another large man, credited Friedgen with helping him get the Kansas head job a year later. He, too, won the assistant coach of the year award, like Friedgen, before getting his first head job, helping bring home the point of substance over style.

"He has become the loveable Santa Claus type. He made heavy an 'in' thing," Rychleski joked.

R alph Friedgen's break-neck schedule continues. Gloria is trying to get her husband to slow down and appreciate things, enjoy more away from football, and take a longer break each year.

For years he turned down invitations to off-season coaches' outings and junkets. This year, Gloria and Ralph accepted many of them for the first time.

In the spring of 2007 it was golf at the ACC Meetings in Amelia Island, Fla. There was also a trip west to play famed Pebble Beach in California. In June he hosted the Ralph Friedgen Invitational at Lowes Island in Virginia, where he hung out with members of the band "Hootie and The Blowfish," among former players and other notables. That was followed by the Orange Bowl coaches' junket to Great Exuma for more golf and fishing. He had never been on those trips before.

Friedgen is enjoying the finer things more. And the summer of 2007 got off to a momentous start when the family convened in Washington, D.C., for the 'Father of the Year' awards ceremony.

It was a time for reflection for his loving family, his legacy at College Park, which with Byrd Stadium expansion takes another step. And how, simply, he always knew he had it in him.

Said Gloria Friedgen, his wife, confidant, and consummate partner, filling a role few could have so graciously:

"He's not going to rust out. He is going to drive and drive to finish what he started here. He has said for years that Maryland is a sleeping giant and somebody's got to wake it up."

ABOUT THE AUTHORS

Keith Cavanaugh has covered the Terps since 1988 and Ralph Friedgen's football program since the coach's arrival at College Park in 2000. Cavanaugh is Editor & Publisher of Terrapin Times Magazine, an independent publication covering University of Maryland athletics.

Cavanaugh resides in Bel Air, Md. with his wife, Kelley, son Jack and daughter Madie.

Ralph Friedgen, national coach of the year in 2001, has led the Maryland football program's turnaround since being named head coach in 2000. Friedgen has taken the Terps to four bowl games in six years, including the BCS Orange Bowl during his first season. He is a former Maryland football player and assistant coach.